Frank Lloyd Wright and the Art of Japan

Frank Lloyd Wright and the Art of Japan

THE ARCHITECT'S OTHER PASSION

Julia Meech

Japan Society and Harry N. Abrams, Inc., Publishers

PROJECT MANAGER: Diana Murphy

EDITOR: Julia Gaviria

DESIGNER: Miko McGinty

LIBRARY OF CONGRESS CATALOGING-IN-PUBLICATION DATA

Meech, Julia.
Frank Lloyd Wright and the art of Japan : the architect's other
passion / Julia Meech.
                p. cm.
Includes bibliographical references and index.
ISBN 0-8109-4563-0
 1. Wright, Frank Lloyd, 1867–1959. 2. Art dealers—United States—
Biography. 3. Art, Asian—Collectors and collecting—United States.
4. Wright, Frank Lloyd, 1867–1959—Art collections. 5. Prints, Japanese—
Collectors and collecting—United States. 6. Prints—Private collections—
United States. I. Title.

N8660.W75 M43 2000
720'.92—dc21
                                          00-063982

Printed and bound in Japan

Japan Society Gallery
333 East 47th Street
New York, N.Y. 10017
www.japansociety.org

Harry N. Abrams, Inc.
100 Fifth Avenue
New York, N.Y. 10011
www.abramsbooks.com

NOTE TO THE READER:

Japanese personal names are printed according to the Japanese
system, surname first, except in the case of individuals who
have chosen to adopt the Western system. In discussion,
Japanese artists are referred to in the form most commonly
cited, usually by the given name. Katsushika Hokusai, for
example, is known as Hokusai.

Dimensions: height precedes width. For paintings, including
screens, measurements are for image exclusive of mounting.
Dimensions for Japanese prints are given in the glossary.

CONTENTS

FOREWORD

Frank Lloyd Wright and the Art of Japan: The Architect's Other Passion is published to coincide with an exhibition of the same title held at Japan Society Gallery, New York, in spring 2001. Both tell the remarkable story of Wright's self-described "obsession" with Japanese art, and explore the architect's interaction with Japanese culture and aesthetics—an encounter that is recognized as profoundly influential in the history of American modernism. Japan Society is honored to present Julia Meech's groundbreaking research in this exhibition and book, and to celebrate her original contribution to the expansion of Frank Lloyd Wright scholarship.

This publication is supported by a generous grant from the Mary Livingston Griggs and Mary Griggs Burke Foundation. Japan Society Gallery programs are supported in part by the Lila Wallace–Reader's Digest Endowment Fund and the Friends of Japan Society Gallery.

The Japan Society exhibition is organized in cooperation with The Frank Lloyd Wright Foundation, Scottsdale, Arizona. We thank H. Nicholas Muller III, president and chief executive officer, for his support. At the Frank Lloyd Wright Archives, housed at Taliesin West in Scottsdale, director Bruce Brooks Pfeiffer, Penny Fowler, administrator of the Fine and Decorative Arts Collection, and registrar Margo Stipe lent expertise and assistance at every stage of the project. The Frank Lloyd Wright Foundation is the principal lender to the exhibition and we are grateful for its generosity.

Other institutional lenders whom we thank are: The Metropolitan Museum of Art, New York; The Art Institute of Chicago; Rare Book and Manuscript Library, Columbia University, New York; Frank Lloyd Wright Preservation Trust, Oak Park, Illinois; Honolulu Academy of Arts; Kyoto University School of Architecture; The New York Public Library, Print Department; State Historical Society of Wisconsin, Madison; Library of Congress, Washington, D.C.; The Grunwald Center for the Graphic Arts, UCLA Hammer Museum; State University of New York at Buffalo, University Archives; University of Illinois at Chicago, College of Architecture and the Arts; Elvehjem Museum of Art, University of Wisconsin-Madison. To these institutions and the curators and archivists who facilitated our loans, we offer our appreciation. We also extend our gratitude to the individuals who generously lent works to the exhibition: Karen Johnson Boyd, Racine, Wisconsin; the Gillham family; Geoffrey Oliver, Pittsford, New York; Max Palevsky, Los Angeles; Mrs. William Palmer, Ann Arbor, Michigan; Seymour Persky, Chicago; Dr. John C. Weber, New York; Mr. and Mrs. Erving Wolf, New York; and those who wish to remain anonymous.

At Harry N. Abrams, publisher Paul Gottlieb supported this project from its inception. We thank senior editor Diana Murphy, who oversaw the book's production. We also appreciate Julia Gaviria's work on the manuscript and Miko McGinty's splendid design. At Japan Society, we are grateful to Ambassador William Clark, Jr., president, for his enthusiasm for this project and his belief in its importance within the society's programming. John K. Wheeler, vice president, and Carl E. Schellhorn, vice president and treasurer, have also provided support throughout. The following individuals contributed to the exhibition's realization: Elizabeth Costa, director, and Diana Worth Foster, assistant director, Development; Jane A. Rubin, former assistant director of Japan Society Gallery, and Annie Van Assche, curator of education. The gallery benefits from its Art Advisory Committee, chaired by Samuel Sachs II, and the Friends of Japan Society Gallery. I am grateful for their encouragement of new directions in the field of Japanese art.

Frank Lloyd Wright and the Art of Japan: The Architect's Other Passion broadens our understanding and appreciation of Wright's unique relationship with Japan. We are still catching up with all that he saw and translated into his own unmistakable idiom.

Alexandra Munroe, Director
Japan Society Gallery

PREFACE AND ACKNOWLEDGMENTS

In 1980 I began a study of the history of the Japanese print collection at the Metropolitan Museum of Art, New York, for an article that would be published in the museum journal. The museum acquired its first Japanese woodblock prints in 1894 and I was curious to learn the identities of the early donors and vendors. I scrutinized the many catalogue cards and was surprised to come across some four hundred examples sold to the museum in 1918 and 1922 by "F. L. Wright." Was it possible that *the* Frank Lloyd Wright had been a vendor of prints? Certainly his interest in Japan was well known, and I myself had admired the Imperial Hotel in Tokyo prior to its demolition in 1968, but the countless books and articles about the greatest genius of American architecture made no mention of this side of his career. I immediately turned to the museum archives, where, to my amazement and delight, I discovered copious correspondence between Wright and S. C. Bosch Reitz, the Metropolitan's first curator of Far Eastern art, concerning these very transactions. I believe I was the first person to read these letters since 1922, and I was soon caught up in the task of piecing together the story of Wright and Japanese prints, a story that has never been fully disclosed. As I traveled from one archive to another learning more about Wright and his collection, I have been awed by his talent and connoisseurship. My research expanded to frightening proportions and it is now clear to me that I have but touched the tip of the iceberg.

Many friends and colleagues have assisted me with this complex but fascinating project. My work was made possible first and foremost by the patience, good humor, and experienced research skills of Penny Fowler, administrator, Fine and Decorative Art Collections, and Margo Stipe, registrar, Frank Lloyd Wright Archives at Taliesin West, Scottsdale, Arizona. My sincere thanks also go to Bruce Brooks Pfeiffer, director of the Frank Lloyd Wright Archives, Oskar Muñoz, assistant director, and Sara Hammond, administrative assistant. It is impossible to overstate the magnitude of their contribution to this book.

The director, James K. Ballinger, and staff of the Phoenix Art Museum, especially Dr. Claudia Brown, curator of Asian art, gave me their full support over the course of several years,

encouraging me to write this book and to organize the exhibition *Frank Lloyd Wright and Japan* for the Phoenix Art Museum in 1995, funded by the Flinn Foundation. The book has finally seen the light of day thanks to an exhibition in the spring of 2001 at Japan Society, New York. Ambassador William Clark, Jr., president of Japan Society, and Alexandra Munroe, director of the Japan Society Gallery, both gave their enthusiastic support to this project. My work was made easy by the talented and hard-working gallery staff, notably Jane A. Rubin and Annie van Assche. The funding provided by the Mary Livingston Griggs and Mary Griggs Burke Foundation is especially meaningful to me.

I am deeply indebted to those who took the time to read and comment on portions of the manuscript in various stages of completion, notably Melinda Takeuchi (the one and only), Jane Oliver, Mary Laing, Leighton R. Longhi, Kathryn Smith, Donald Hoffmann, and Irwin Weinberg. Their contributions were invaluable. To Irwin, my secret weapon, I owe a further debt of gratitude for meticulous and time-consuming detective work in various midwestern libraries. Heather de Savoye and Keiko Takahashi were excellent research assistants. Kathryn Smith was generous in sharing many unpublished letters and setting me straight on complicated details of the Barnsdall-Wright interaction. My thanks go to Diana Murphy at Harry N. Abrams, and to Julia Gaviria for a really fine job of copyediting. Miko McGinty created the marvelous book design.

The staff at Christie's, New York, indulged and supported me for many years, for which I am certainly grateful. I extend special thanks to Sebastian Izzard for lending his wide-ranging expertise in Japanese prints, and to David A. Silverman, Jeffrey Olson, Toshi Hara, Valery Hoyt, Shira Nichaman, Katsura Yamaguchi, and interns Mie Iwatsuki and Susan Young, who assisted with preparation of the manuscript. Toshihiko Hatanaka, Christie's, Japan, and David Erskine-Hill, Christie's, London, shared their expertise as well.

Scott Elliott, Kelmscott Gallery, Chicago, offered welcome insights and documentation over many years. Angela Howard, Rutgers University, gave guidance on Buddhist sculpture in

Wright's collection, and Suzanne G. Valenstein at the Metropolitan Museum of Art, New York, reviewed the Chinese ceramics for me. William Green answered countless tedious questions about collectors and collecting. Others who were unfailingly hospitable and helpful include Andrew Stevens, Elvehjem Museum of Art, University of Wisconsin-Madison; Christine I. Schelshorn and Andy Kraushaar, State Historical Society of Wisconsin, Madison; Mary Jane Hamilton, Cross Plaines, Wisconsin; William Stuart Morton-Smith, Santa Barbara, California; Gail Kohl, Frank Lloyd Wright Heritage Tour Program, Madison; Narciso Menocal and Julia Murray, department of art history, University of Wisconsin-Madison; Kathy Waddell, Sauk County Historical Society, Baraboo, Wisconsin; Louise Virgin, Maureen Melton, and Money Hickman, Museum of Fine Arts, Boston; Anne Rose Kitagawa, Harvard University Art Museums, Cambridge; Ross Edman, University of Illinois, Chicago; Morton W. Johnson, Chandler's, Highland Park, Illinois; Elinor Pearlstein, Betty Y. Siffert, Mary R. Albert, Noriko Horie, Jamyn C. Flynn, James Ulak, Christina Aube, and Bart H. Ryckbosch, Art Institute of Chicago; Eileen Flannigan and Keshia Whitehead, Chicago Historical Society; Diana Haskell, Newberry Library, Chicago; the staff of the Frank Lloyd Wright Preservation Trust, Oak Park, Illinois; Kathleen Ferris and Luci King, Grand Rapids Art Museum, Michigan; Matthew Welch and Robert D. Jacobsen, Minneapolis Institute of Arts, Minnesota; Cheryl Pence, Illinois State Historical Library, Springfield; Mrs. Joseph Clifford, Scottsdale, Arizona; Florri Dalrymple McMillan, Chicago; Robert H. Ellsworth, New York; Barbara Elsner, Milwaukee, Wisconsin; Jonathan Reynolds, University of Michigan, Ann Arbor; Anne Clapp, Wellesley College, Massachusetts; Shonnie Finnegan and Christopher Densmore, University Archives, State University of New York, Buffalo; Annegret H. Richards and Jack Quinan, State University of New York, Buffalo; B. T. Meech, Buffalo; Douglas Schultz and Janice Lurie, Albright-Knox Art Gallery, Buffalo; Brenda G. Jordan and Sandy Kita, University of Pittsburgh; Edna Hajnal, Thomas Fisher Rare Book Library, University of Toronto; Thomas Lawton and Colleen Hennessey, Freer Gallery of Art, Arthur M. Sackler Gallery, Smithsonian Institution, Washington, D.C.; Howard W. Ellington, Allen-Lambe House Museum and Study Center, Wichita, Kansas; Charles Verbeck, Washington, D.C.; Mrs. Celia Crawford, Washington, D.C.; O. P. Reed, Malibu, California; Ralph Chait and Joseph Seo, New York; Mary Diamond Stein, Palm Springs, California; Joan B. Mirviss, New York; Helen C. Evans, Jeanie M. James, Barbara File, Hwai-ling Yeh-Lewis, Joyce Sitzer, Martin Fleischer, Jennifer Perry, Sara Patterson, Katherine Daniels, Joyce Denney, and Barbara Ford, The Metropolitan Museum of Art; Mary W. Baskett, Cincinnati, Ohio; Kristin Spangenberg and Bernice Weisman, Cincinnati Art Museum; Nicholas and Carol Gillham, Durham, North Carolina; Karen Johnson Boyd, Racine, Wisconsin; Timothy Rodgers, Wriston Art Center, Lawrence University, Appleton, Wisconsin; Phil Feddersen, Clinton, Iowa; Mrs. Tiny Tipps, Denver, Colorado; Brent Svordloff and Kirsten A. Hammer, Special Collections, The Getty Research Institute, Los Angeles, California; Layna White, Grunwald Center for the Graphic Arts, University of California, Los Angeles; Virginia Kazor, Cultural Affairs Department, City of Los Angeles; Carolyn Chinn Lewis and Midori Oka, Spencer Museum of Art, University of Kansas, Lawrence; Christine Mack, Allen Memorial Art Museum, Oberlin, Ohio; Pamela Veerhusen, New York; Thomas Getz, Moline, Illinois; Hiroko T. McDermott, Cambridge, England; Jack Hillier, Surrey, England; Tim Clark, The British Museum, London; Shugio Ippei, Tokyo; Roger Keyes, Cranston, Rhode Island; Robert O. Muller, Newtown, Connecticut; Yonekura Michio, Tokyo National Research Institute of Cultural Properties; Yamaguchi Keizaburō, Risshō University, Tokyo; Watanabe Tadasu, S. Watanabe Color Print Co., Tokyo; Tanigawa Masami and his wife, Yoshiko, at Nihon University, Tokyo; Yamaguchi Chiyo, Tokyo; Joseph Seubert, Geibundō, Kawasaki City; Edgar Tafel, New York; Geoffrey Oliver, Pittsford, New York; and John C. Weber, New York.

The John Simon Guggenheim Foundation supported my work with a fellowship in 1989 and the Asahi Foundation Endowment for the department of Asian art at the Art Institute of Chicago facilitated my research in Chicago.

For his insights into Japanese art and his approach to art history as a discipline, I owe a long-standing debt to my mentor at Harvard University, John M. Rosenfield. This book is dedicated to him.

Finally, I am grateful to all those who have worked with me in opening this new window onto the private world of Frank Lloyd Wright, eliciting the story of his life as a collector and connoisseur of Japanese art.

ABBREVIATED CHRONOLOGY OF THE LIFE OF FRANK LLOYD WRIGHT (1867–1959)

1867
Born in Richland Center, Wisconsin, 8 June

1886
Spends two semesters as a non-degree student in the College of Engineering at the University of Wisconsin-Madison

1887
Leaves Madison for Chicago and works first for architect Joseph Lyman Silsbee and, within a year, for the firm of Adler and Sullivan; builds the Hillside Home School for his aunts in the Wisconsin valley near Spring Green that had been settled by his grandparents, immigrants from Wales (enlarged 1901–3; closed 1915)

1889
Marries Catherine Lee Tobin and begins building their residence in the Chicago suburb of Oak Park

1893
Opens his own architectural practice in Chicago (a loft in Steinway Hall) and Oak Park; sees Japanese architecture at World's Columbian Exposition, Chicago

1903–5
Builds Darwin D. Martin residence, Buffalo, New York

1905
Wright and his wife make their first trip to Japan, where they buy Japanese prints

1906
Exhibits his collection of Hiroshige prints at the Art Institute of Chicago

1908
Designs a Japanese print exhibition for the Art Institute of Chicago and is himself a lender

1909
Leaves his family and his fifteen-year practice for Europe accompanied by Mamah Borthwick Cheney, a former client in Oak Park

1910
In Berlin and Fiesole prepares drawings for the Wasmuth publication of a lavish portfolio of his own designs; returns to Oak Park

1911
Takes second trip to Berlin in the spring; opens an office in Orchestra Hall, Chicago; builds a new home and studio for himself and Mamah Borthwick (who resumes her maiden name after her divorce that summer) called Taliesin (Welsh for "shining brow") near Spring Green; Gookin recommends Wright for the Imperial Hotel job; Wright sells prints to the Chicago collector Clarence Buckingham

1912
Publishes *The Japanese Print: An Interpretation*; sells prints to Clarence Buckingham and the Boston collectors William and John Spaulding

1913
Returns to Japan with Mamah Borthwick to pursue the Imperial Hotel commission and to purchase prints for the Spauldings

1914
Sells prints to the Spauldings and mentions designs for a Spaulding print gallery; exhibits his preliminary plans for the Imperial Hotel at annual Chicago Architectural Club exhibition in April; Mamah Borthwick, her two children, and four employees are murdered and Taliesin is burned by a deranged servant on 15 August; meets Miriam Noel, who becomes his constant companion and eventually his wife

1915
Wright rebuilds his home as Taliesin II, with the addition of a loggia

1916

Signs a contract memorandum for the Imperial Hotel commission on 17 March; convinces Francis Little in Minneapolis to accept prints in exchange for two mortgage notes on the Oak Park property; sells prints to the Spauldings; leaves for Japan with Miriam and his son John on 28 December to begin work on the Imperial Hotel (construction begins August 1919); makes many long trips between the U.S. and Japan through 1922; Antonin Raymond begins working for Wright at Taliesin

1917

Sells prints to the Spauldings; stages a Japanese print exhibition at the Arts Club in the Fine Arts Building, Chicago; is featured in November issue of *Kenchiku gahō*

1918

Sells Japanese prints to the Metropolitan Museum of Art and to the Spauldings

1919

Buys several big print collections in Japan; is a lender to the Harunobu exhibition in Tokyo in May; sells prints in New York to Howard Mansfield and others, which are later found to have been revamped

1920

Builds new annex, which includes his own rooms, for "old" or "first" Imperial Hotel; agrees to exchange revamped prints in October at Taliesin

1921

Completes Hollyhock House for Aline Barnsdall in Los Angeles; designs poster for Hashiguchi Goyō memorial print exhibition in Tokyo

1922

North wing of the Imperial Hotel opens 2 July; leaves Japan for the last time 27 July; sells Japanese prints to the Metropolitan Museum of Art, his last major transaction as a print dealer; has final exchange of revamped prints with Mansfield; divorces Catherine

1923

Opens an office in Los Angeles hoping to re-establish his professional identity; Imperial Hotel opens and survives the Great Kanto earthquake on 1 September; returns to the Midwest in October; marries Miriam Noel in November

1924

Returns permanently to Taliesin; is abandoned by Miriam; meets Olga (Olgivanna) Lazovich Hinzenberg

1925

Olgivanna moves in with Wright, divorces Vlademar Hinzenberg, and assumes mother's maiden name, Milanoff; she obtains custody of her daughter; fire caused by faulty wiring destroys residential wing at Taliesin II, providing the opportunity to enlarge the house once more; Wright and Olgivanna have a child out of wedlock; Wright completes four textile block houses in Los Angeles by 1925, but this is a period of many unbuilt commissions

1926

Is deeply in debt owing to legal fees and the cost of rebuilding Taliesin III; gives William McFetridge prints as security for a loan; flees to Minnesota with Olgivanna and children but is arrested there on Mann Act; Bank of Wisconsin forecloses on mortgage and takes possession of prints from Wright's vault as security

1927

Bank of Wisconsin forces sale of 346 of Wright's Japanese prints at the Anderson Galleries, New York, in January; another fire at Taliesin; Wright divorces Miriam

1928

Vacates Taliesin on order of Bank of Wisconsin in January and moves with family to Phoenix to consult on the Arizona Biltmore Hotel; Taliesin is sold to Bank of Wisconsin for $25,000; Wright marries Olgivanna Lazovich in California in August; Miriam Noel sells her prints in Chicago; Bank of Wisconsin sells five thousand of Wright's Japanese prints to E. B. Van Vleck, a professor at the University of Wisconsin; Wright, Inc. (a group of Wright's supporters founded in August 1927), buys back his property (minus the Van Vleck prints) from the bank at the end of September; Wright returns to Taliesin and tries to sell prints

1929
Wright and family are in Arizona from January to May

1932
Founds the Taliesin Fellowship, a resident group of student-apprentices, and publishes *An Autobiography*

1936
Construction begins on both the Johnson Wax Building, Racine, Wisconsin, and Fallingwater, the Edgar J. Kaufmann, Sr., residence, Mill Run, Pennsylvania

1937
Builds Herbert F. Johnson residence, Wingspread, Windy Point, Wisconsin

1938
Begins work on Taliesin West, Scottsdale, Arizona, his winter residence and studio; a migratory pattern begins between Wisconsin and Arizona

1940
Establishes the Frank Lloyd Wright Foundation; *Two Great Americans: Frank Lloyd Wright, American Architect, and D. W. Griffith, American Film Master* opens at the Museum of Modern Art, New York

1943–59
Works on the Solomon R. Guggenheim Museum, New York

1951
With apprentices designs an exhibition of his work entitled *Sixty Years of Living Architecture*, which opens at Gimbel's in Philadelphia, then travels to Palazzo Strozzi in Florence, Italy, and to New York in 1953

1954
Opens office in the Plaza Hotel, New York; continues to purchase Asian art, much of it in New York

1959
Dies in Phoenix on 9 April; Olgivanna now presides over the school and architectural practice

1962
Olgivanna lends Wright's Japanese prints to *Frank Lloyd Wright: Japanese Prints Exhibition,* at the Municipal Art Gallery, Barnsdall Park, Los Angeles

1965–66
Frank Lloyd Wright Foundation begins to sell many Japanese prints and illustrated printed books from Wright's collection

1967
Frank Lloyd Wright Foundation sells a large portion of Wright's collection of Asian art at auction at Parke-Bernet Galleries, New York, in December

1985
Olgivanna dies on 1 March

1986
Box of *surimono* prints and trunk with Japanese textiles rediscovered at Taliesin West

1989–90
Frank Lloyd Wright Foundation commissions conservation of Wright's remaining collection of textiles

1992
Frank Lloyd Wright and Hiroshige opens at the Alpha Cubic Gallery, Tokyo, to commemorate the reprinting of Hiroshige's 1857 series *A Collection of Assembled Pictures of Famous Places in Edo* from an almost complete set of woodblocks rediscovered in the archives of the Frank Lloyd Wright Foundation in Scottsdale; Frank Lloyd Wright Foundation commissions conservation of Wright's remaining collection of Japanese screens

1995–96
Frank Lloyd Wright and Japanese Art, an exhibition drawn from the Frank Lloyd Wright Foundation and from public and private collections throughout the United States, is organized by the Phoenix Art Museum and the Los Angeles County Museum of Art, and is accompanied by a publication of *surimono* prints from Wright's collection, discovered in the archives at Taliesin West

1997
Frank Lloyd Wright and Japan, an exhibition drawn from the holdings of the Frank Lloyd Wright Foundation, circulates in Japan

2001
Frank Lloyd Wright and the Art of Japan: The Architect's Other Passion, an exhibition drawn from the Frank Lloyd Wright Foundation and from public and private collections, opens at Japan Society Gallery, New York

The print is more autobiographical than you may imagine.
If Japanese prints were to be deducted from my education,
I don't know what direction the whole might have taken.

—Frank Lloyd Wright, *An Autobiography*, 1932

INTRODUCTION

This is the untold story of the role played by Frank Lloyd Wright (1867–1959) in the world of Asian art connoisseurs. It is the story of Wright's other passion and of his other clients as well. One of Wright's biographers, Brendan Gill, evoked the kaleidoscope of "many masks" worn by the architect. Among them was certainly the mask of Japanese art expert. In his role as connoisseur and dealer, Wright connected with a far-flung group of rich collectors, most of whom never considered commissioning a building from him. Surprisingly, Wright's career as a dealer at one time rivaled that as an architect in terms of both the attention he devoted to it and the financial gain.

When Wright died at the age of almost ninety-two, he owed money to several Asian art dealers in New York, and there were six thousand Japanese color woodblock prints in his personal collection, not to mention some three hundred Chinese and Japanese ceramics, bronzes, sculptures, textiles, stencils, and carpets, and about twenty Japanese and Chinese folding screens. Today there is still Asian art in the archives of the Frank Lloyd Wright Foundation at Taliesin West in Scottsdale, Arizona, but much of the collection was discreetly sold off in the 1960s and '70s by his widow, Olgivanna Wright (1898–1985). We will never know her precise motives for liquidating Wright's collection, but it was probably a natural desire to improve her situation after thirty years of living in the shadow of the master. She came into his life in the mid-1920s, after his years of travel to and from Japan were finished, and there is no reason to think she appreciated his spending so much of their income on Asian art. More important, there was an unexpected bill for about $1 million in back taxes: the U.S. government had ruled that the Frank Lloyd Wright Foundation, established in 1940, did not have non-profit status.

Parts of the collection have survived by accident more than by design: an unpretentious wood box, for example, was moved from Taliesin, Wright's home in Spring Green, Wisconsin, to an off-site storage facility in Phoenix in 1966 together with the rest of the contents of his vault. Twenty years later, after Olgivanna's death, and after the box had been transferred to the refurbished archival storage at Taliesin West, a visiting conservator opened it and identified the contents as *surimono* (literally "printed things"). These are small Japanese color woodcuts privately commissioned by connoisseurs and amateur poetry clubs in limited editions with luxurious printing techniques, often for New Year celebrations (ill. 1). Considered the jewels of the Japanese printmaking tradition, *surimono* are made with the finest and most costly pigments. At Taliesin West, no one had imagined that the box contained anything exceptional. Once the roughly seven hundred small *surimono* were discovered, their value was immediately apparent to the staff at Taliesin. These prints have now been carefully catalogued, studied, published, and exhibited.[1]

Also found after Olgivanna's death was a long-forgotten oversize suitcase marked "Mrs. Wright's Brocades." It was assumed that these were table runners, but when an unsuspecting intern at Taliesin West unpacked them in 1986, the contents proved to be marvelous eighteenth- and nineteenth-century Japanese textiles (ill. 2). They were found wadded together like dishrags, crumpled and soiled. Wright acquired many of these fabrics in Japan during his years in Tokyo building the Imperial Hotel (1916–22), and they were in constant use as decoration in his apartment in Tokyo and in his home in Wisconsin. Now, thanks to the finest of modern conservation skills, a great number have been restored to their original beauty and are being cared for in a way they probably never were during Wright's lifetime. Today the Frank Lloyd Wright Foundation has museum-quality archival storage and is proud to publicize and exhibit what remains of Wright's Asian collection.

This book traces Wright's career in Asian art in the form of a chronological biography. It begins with the early years of Japonisme in Oak Park and continues with his rapid evolution as a vendor of prints in Chicago. In the 1910s he emerged as a major dealer thanks to the patronage of the wealthy Spaulding brothers in Boston, whose money he spent freely in Tokyo. His clients included all of the big names in the print world in the United States: in addition to William and John Spaulding there

Opposite

1.
Totoya Hokkei (1780–1850). *Raikō Attacks a Demon Kite*. c. 1825. Color woodcut with metallic powders, *shikishiban*. The Frank Lloyd Wright Foundation (3017.012)

Raikō was an eleventh-century warrior celebrated as a slayer of demons. An auspicious poem at the upper right alludes to the custom of banishing demons on the last day of the lunar year.

were Howard Mansfield and Louis V. Ledoux in New York, Charles H. Chandler in Evanston and Mary Ainsworth in Moline, Illinois, Arthur Davison Ficke in Davenport, Iowa, and the Metropolitan Museum of Art in New York, to name a few. Should we be troubled by Wright's dealing and the discovery that self-interest played a part in his pursuit of the print? It would be naive to ignore the close link between creativity and salesmanship in the world of art. These become parallel paths; artists often need to rely on a commercial enterprise for support. Wright himself was justly proud of the collections he helped form and boasted of them whenever possible. Around 1920, however, a scandal involving revamped prints (faded prints brightened with new color blocks) seriously damaged his reputation as a dealer. In the lean years that followed he faced bankruptcy, and thousands of his prints were sold off by the Bank of Wisconsin under the most unfavorable circumstances. Later, during the years of the Taliesin Fellowship, he used prints as a teaching aid for apprentices and gave them to clients to commemorate special events. Taken as a whole, this is an amazing saga of greed, rivalry, double-cross, devious dealings, arson, murder, infidelity, and acquisition fever.

We have a vivid picture of Wright as a collector thanks to his own prolific writing (his autobiography and his letters, in particular), the photographs he used to document and promote his long career, and a legacy of prints he sold to the Metropolitan Museum of Art and to wealthy private collectors, or traded with his architectural clients during hard times. Just as an example, there are still several thousand prints in the Elvehjem Museum of Art, University of Wisconsin-Madison, that came with an original group of five thousand purchased

from Wright's collection in the late 1920s by a local professor, Edward Burr Van Vleck. In addition to those in the Elvehjem and, of course, the Frank Lloyd Wright Foundation, prints with a Wright provenance can be found in more than a dozen public institutions.[2] Other collections will no doubt come to light in the future. If we add them together with thousands more that passed through his hands as a dealer, the numbers, perhaps as high as 20,000, are impressive.

Architectural historians have difficulty putting Wright into a meaningful context within the evolution of modern architecture. They treat him as an isolated genius, a fantastic eccentric, which tends to marginalize him. The architect himself reveled in his role as an outsider. In the field of Asian art, however, and especially in the world of Japanese prints, he was very much in the mainstream, a man of his times. He was limited only by his pocketbook, and sometimes not even by that; he liked to buy on credit. Wright interacted with Asian art on many levels: as a successful art dealer; as a modernist inspired by Japanese graphic design; as a teacher lecturing to apprentices at "print parties" and staging print exhibitions in the Midwest; and as the typically compulsive collector, unable to restrain himself, always obsessively acquisitive.

To illustrate this self-indulgent passion for Asian art, there is the anecdote told by the architect's cousin Richard Lloyd Jones (1873–1963) about the time Wright appeared at his office at *Collier's* in New York in 1905 asking for train fare back to Chicago. Richard helped him out and, "an hour later, Frank was back again. He was carrying a beautiful Japanese print that he had just bought, and he still needed his rail fare back to Chicago."[3] Wright's second-eldest son, John Lloyd Wright

3.

"The Han." Wine vessel (*hu*). China, Han dynasty, second century B.C.–A.D. first century. Bronze, 18¼ in. high

The Frank Lloyd Wright Foundation sold this vessel in 1967 at Parke-Bernet Galleries, New York (sale 2636, lot 170), for $2,000.

(1892–1972), an architect who worked with his father on the Imperial Hotel, tells an amusing story about a Chinese Han-dynasty (206 B.C.–A.D. 220) bronze (ill. 3). After the family had left the Oak Park home and realtors had been instructed to sell or rent it, John returned one day to rummage about in the pony stable. He recalls,

> There I found the Han. It was on a rubbish heap, covered with dust and grime. It had been deposited there by the cleaning woman after Dad moved.
>
> I had always loved that bronze—the lines, proportion, the patina, the butterfly handles, the quiet beauty of it. I was with Dad in the Orient the day he bought it from a Chinese dealer…. Some time later Dad saw it in my home.
>
> "Oh ho, so here it is!" said he. "I'm glad you cared for it. I'll take it home with me."
>
> "Oh, no, let go! It's mine!" said I….
>
> The following Christmas, Dad sent each one of his children an oriental screen. That is, each one but me. He sent me a note: "Since you already have the Han, let it be your merry Christmas present this year from Dad."
>
> A cunning gleam crept into his eye each time he caught sight of it. He would stroke it tenderly, all the while glancing furtively in my direction. He wanted to clutch it and run. But, fortunately for me, the bronze was too heavy. He would shove, drag and shift its position, always working it toward the door. Then he stood back a little distance to see if it appeared to better advantage. The closer its position became in relation to the door, the better he liked it.[4]

Wright surrounded himself with Asian art, which he tirelessly arranged and rearranged in artful combinations. There was inevitably a certain amount of accidental breakage, not to mention general wear and tear—the large Ming jar that rolled down a hill, or the precious ceramic knocked over and broken into smithereens by a vacuum cleaner. "Well, that's life among the amateurs," he would say. His homes (with his first wife, Catherine, in Oak Park, Illinois, between 1893 and 1909; at Taliesin in Spring Green, Wisconsin, designed for himself and his lover, Mamah Borthwick, in 1911; and at Taliesin West in Scottsdale, built in the late 1930s) were embellished with Chinese, Japanese, Korean, and even Indian art, including tex-

Opposite

2.

Six fragments of a robe (*kosode*) with scattered chrysanthemums and fences. Edo period, early eighteenth century. Figured silk damask (*rinzu*) with silk embroidery, couched gold-wrapped threads, and stitch-resist tie-dye, 36 x 82 in. The Frank Lloyd Wright Foundation (1097.089)

There is almost enough fabric to reconstruct a complete robe. The two end pieces have been identified as sleeves and the remaining four as body sections.

4.
Frank Lloyd Wright at
Taliesin, Spring Green,
Wisconsin. 1924

White chrysanthemums
on a Japanese folding
screen frame Wright's
head like a halo. Two
antique Japanese tex-
tiles are draped over
his desk.

5.
Time magazine cover
for 17 January 1938, of
Wright with a perspec-
tive rendering of the
Edgar J. Kaufmann, Sr.,
residence, Fallingwater
(Mill Run, Pennsylvania,
completed in late 1937),
and an eighth-century
Tang-dynasty Chinese
tomb figure from
Wright's collection. The
Frank Lloyd Wright
Foundation (1019.540)

The Frank Lloyd Wright
Foundation sold the
figurine in 1967 at
Parke-Bernet Galleries,
New York (sale 2636,
lot 399), for $425.

tiles, paintings, prints, sculptures, lacquers, ceramics, and bronzes. As just one classy example, he kept his pencils in a thirteenth-century B.C. Chinese Shang-dynasty ritual bronze tripod cup for heating fragrant wine.[5] His own home was his best advertisement, the self-portrait of a man of taste and prestige. The Asian collection set him apart as someone with access to arcane icons of distant cultures that were still little known in the West. At Taliesin there were garden terraces dotted with picturesque Chinese Buddhist sculptures and Ming jardinieres; a cast-iron bell from a Chinese Daoist temple was sounded to announce dinner. The nature of his décor was so well known that when his Wisconsin home burned in 1925, the *Chicago Daily Tribune*, in an article entitled "Blaze destroys love cottage of Frank L. Wright," described it as "a rambling bungalow filled with exotic art, largely Japanese."[6] Not everything he owned was a masterpiece, by any means. The pieces he used for interior decoration were a mixed bag ranging from marvelous to spurious, with a great deal of just plain mediocre. Some things he obviously purchased for their design, rather than for their rarity or high quality, and it is doubtful that he ever paid top dollar.

When he spoke of his "Collection" he generally meant his large print inventory, and he always kept an easel with a few Japanese prints on display. Carefully stored in the massive stone vault in his drafting studio in Wisconsin, the collection was available for special occasions, a constant source of vital energy. He shared the prints with the initiates of his inner circle and graciously bestowed them as gifts, often accompanied by a personal inscription. The size of the collection waxed and waned according to the fortunes of its owner.

A man with a keen sense of his own self-importance, he documented his life and career with a succession of portraits, and it is remarkable how often a piece of Asian art is carefully positioned beside or just behind the great man, taking equal billing with an architectural model or a drawing (ills. 4–7). A cover of *Time* magazine in 1938 featured Wright with his new masterpiece, the residence of Edgar J. Kaufmann, Sr., known as Fallingwater. As if this superb structure were not enough to establish his legitimacy after several decades without much work, the architect casts a significant glance over his shoulder at a lovely eighth-century Chinese clay tomb figurine from his own collection; it gives inspiration but also functions as a talisman, seeming to empower him.

In his autobiography he wrote glowingly of Japanese domestic architecture: "Becoming more closely acquainted with things Japanese, I saw the native home in Japan as a supreme study in elimination…. So the Japanese house naturally fascinated me and I would spend hours taking it all to pieces and putting it together again."[7] Clay Lancaster, who chronicled Japonisme, or the taste for things Japanese, in America, thought it "evident that Wright grasped some of the significance of East Asian architecture at first glance," long before his first trip to Japan.[8] Ever defensive, however, Wright denied the influence of Japanese architecture on his own work, calling it a matter of "resemblance." "You are all wrong," he once said of his debt to the Japanese. "I'm not indebted to the Japanese—the Japanese are indebted to me."[9] He always made much of the fact that his was an indigenous American architecture. There are many instances of overt Japonisme in American architecture around the turn of the century (the glamorous Greene and Greene bungalows in southern California, for example), but Wright steered clear of this kind of derivative and eclectic adoption of Japanese design elements. Japanese houses simply reinforced his own

6.
Wright in his study-bedroom at Taliesin on his eighty-sixth birthday in 1953 with Hiroshige prints from the Kisokaidō series. On the table are the tools of his trade, a T-square and pencils

way of thinking, he said. It is true that his Prairie School style was fully developed before he made his first trip to Japan, in 1905, but his protests must be taken with a grain of salt—he was never one to give credit to others. Scholars have long grappled with apparent resemblances; some mention Wright's emphasis on the continuity of interior and exterior, or the correlation between the large display alcove in a Japanese home and the fireplace integral to the early Prairie House. Others suggest that the hulking form of the Imperial Hotel echoes the pyramidal shape of Mount Fuji, or that the pagoda form inspired the 1936 Johnson Wax Research Laboratory tower.[10] Certainly cross-cultural sources have proved useful to great artists at moments of stagnation or repetition. Borrowing can reinvigorate and effect a real transformation.

Be that as it may, there is no doubt that a serious study of Wright and Japan must focus on the central role of wood-block prints, which, as he admitted himself, contributed in so many ways to his life and art for more than sixty years. He once explained to his apprentices how he was swept away by the collector's passion to see more and more of these masterpieces, and by the artist's curiosity to learn from their mysterious secrets of design.[11] The early decades of the twentieth century, before the Japanese themselves had entered the market as competitive bidders, were the golden years of print collecting in the United States, and prints played a pivotal role in introducing Japanese art to the West. Artists were among the first to collect and appreciate them. For some, prints reinforced romantic ideals, for others they acted as a catalyst in the exploration of modernist aesthetics. As Wright put it, "intrinsically the print lies at the bottom of all this so-called *modernism*."[12]

Wright understood the educational value of prints. "The print is more autobiographical than you may imagine," he wrote. "If Japanese prints were to be deducted from my education, I don't know what direction the whole might have taken."[13] He tacked prints on the walls of the playroom in his Oak Park home for his children at the turn of the century, and in the last decade of his life he installed them in the corridor of the educational wing of the Meeting House he built for the First Unitarian Society in Madison. From the 1930s on prints served as a kind of library at Taliesin, where Wright genuinely hoped they would be a source of inspiration for his apprentices, as they had been for him. He thoroughly enjoyed hosting "print parties," at which he explained the history and beauty of Japanese prints. At one such gathering in September 1957, speaking to his "boys," as he called the apprentices, he summarized his views:

> I remember when I first met the Japanese prints. That art had a great influence on my feeling and thinking. Japanese architecture—nothing at all. But when I saw that print and I saw the elimination of the insignificant and simplicity of vision, together with the sense of rhythm and the importance of design, I began to see nature in a totally different way.[14]

Wright was deeply affected by the expressive properties of Japanese art but he also took advantage of an opportunity for easy profits. Trading on his reputation as a famous architect, he was conspicuous as an aggressive dealer in ukiyo-e prints from about the time of his first voyage to Japan in 1905 until around 1922, immediately following the completion of his work on the Imperial Hotel in Tokyo. He formed his collection at a time when prints were still relatively inexpensive and when it was possible to buy in bulk at wholesale prices. It was common then for American collectors to have thousands, even tens of thousands, of prints, something quite unimaginable today. Wright had a good eye for design, enlisted several top-notch advisers, and found clients among all of the great private collectors from the Midwest to the East Coast. Around 1918, at the height of his career as an art dealer, he was selling prints privately to both the treasurer and the president of the board of trustees of the Metropolitan Museum of Art.[15] He had run-ins with some collectors, but others were forever in his debt, their lives changed for the better by knowing him. Although he was too arrogant to befriend the Japanese dealers (and they disliked him in return), he did come to acknowledge that in the matter of selling prints he was himself a merchant. Wright liked to picture himself as standing alone against a united front of Japanese dealers, but the record shows that he often purchased directly from them. In the end, the income from print sales allowed him to remain a visionary as an architect.

Of course, it is well known that Wright was a man of expensive tastes who always lived beyond his means. His wives would only encourage him, saying "If you have it, spend it." He wore elegant clothing; his hats were custom made at the Ritz in Paris and his shirts at Brooks Brothers (the collars had to be just so).

Opposite

7.
Wright at his drafting table in the studio at Taliesin III. 1947

On the ledge behind Wright are a Chinese Han-dynasty ceramic wine vessel similar to the bronze *hu* in ill. 3 and a model for the twenty-two-story *San Francisco Call* Building, a 1913 project. A Chinese carpet decorates the floor. Wright stored his Japanese print collection in a fireproof stone vault visible directly behind his drafting table.

But he could never pay his bills. It is not hard to understand why he took as his motto the immortal words of Oscar Wilde: "Let me have the luxuries and the necessities will take care of themselves."[16] Even at the end of his life, when work was finally coming from big building commissions, he remained short on funds because "the backdrag is too great, the hole is too deep, and an architect's reward in any final outcome is too small."[17] Wright normally charged a flat 10-percent commission for his work, but most projects stopped at the design stage and the fee was accordingly less than expected. On top of this there were always cost overruns, thanks to his willful tendency to change plans as they evolved; he also kept bad records. Because of his high overhead—big homes in both Scottsdale and Spring Green, staff salaries, engineering fees, and so on—Wright never made as much as his colleagues who worked out of large, well-organized, highly professional architectural firms. Despite his modest practice, however, he always lived as though he were rich.

Wright was very reluctant to part with money for goods and salaries. Ultimately, he felt, the bills would somehow all be paid. It has been said that he adopted the credit card system long before it came to be sponsored by bankers as the American way of life, and certainly Japanese woodcuts were his primary source of credit for many years when he used them as collateral for loans (in which case he overvalued them). Antique dealers around Baraboo and the Wisconsin Dells still turn up the occasional bit of Asian art with a Frank Lloyd Wright provenance—things he sacrificed in exchange for food during lean years at Taliesin. Like the Chinese emperor Wanli (r. 1573–1615), who sometimes used the imperial collection as currency, giving his court officials works of art instead of their salaries, Wright at times handed out prints to his staff in lieu of payment. Wright left the architect Walter Burley Griffin (1876–1937) in charge of the Oak Park studio staff when he went to Japan in 1905. Displeased with Griffin's performance, he eventually discharged him, paying him off with Japanese prints for his overdue salary. The two men apparently never spoke to each other again, but the incident must have rankled Griffin because as late as 1910 he received a letter from a mildly penitent Wright, purportedly stung by petty innuendos and rumors, offering to take back the prints and pay up.[18]

But prints were much more than a business investment for Wright. They were windows through which he looked at his own work. "The pursuit of the Japanese print became my constant recreation while in Tokio," he remembered. "A never failing avocation in fact. The adventures and excursions would take place at night or sometimes call for a journey by day to distant

HOUSE FOR MR. AND MRS. V. C. MORRIS
SAN FRANCISCO, CALIFORNIA
FRANK LLOYD WRIGHT ARCHITECT.
SEACLIFF

places, in search of them. Endless the fascination of this quest. Some said obsession."[19] Fond of romantic hyperbole, he said he was "enslaved" by prints "because it is no secret that the prints choose whom they love and there is then no salvation but surrender."[20] A passionate collector, Wright hated to part with his fine prints. He often wrote about them in philosophical terms, and appreciated them as designs. He collected images of enormous graphic power, whose color, composition, and linear rhythms seemed to him inherently modern. He was surely justified in his oft-repeated assertion about prints that "these documents have been of fundamental value in the development of what we call modern art."[21] In his perspective renderings, which tend to be quite colorful, he (and his studio draftsmen) often adopted the devices of Japanese printmakers: the eccentric format of the narrow, vertical pillar print or the unexpected breaking of conventional bounding lines by foliage or buildings. Utagawa Hiroshige (1797–1858), for example, strikes a humorous note when he lets a kite or the cone of Mount Fuji soar beyond the rectangular "frame" enclosing the image (ill. 9). Wright often aimed for this effect himself (ill. 8).

Because Japanese prints were a popular medium, an inexpensive substitute for paintings, they fit Wright's supposed ideal of a "democratic" art form. Hiroshige proved that it was pos-sible to give quality in production for the masses. Wright recognized ukiyo-e as a "humble" art form, more "democratic" than anything else. The art of Hiroshige, he wrote in 1906, was "that of the artisan class, the common people, in the strict sense of the term, and attests the infinite delight, the inherent poetic grace not of the Japanese nobleman but of the hard-worked, humble son of Nippon of seventy-five years ago. His face was deeply furrowed with pleasant lines and tanned the texture and color of brown leather; he wore out patiently and soon…."[22] Wright wants us to see the print not just for its aesthetic appeal but as a democratic expression of *vox populi*, a trope for his own philosophy of architecture. Whether he ever held genuine sympathy for the masses is another question: Brendan Gill describes Wright as a charlatan who in actual practice was contemptuous of humble folk. The color print was, in fact, a commercial art aimed at the plebeian middle classes, fairly inexpensive in its day (a Hiroshige print cost little more than a bowl of noodles), not valued as "high art" by Japanese collectors, and often discarded or mishandled as a result. In Edo-period (1615–1868) Japan a wealthy collector acquired an original painting of a kabuki actor or a beautiful courtesan, but most people made do with a woodcut.

9.
Utagawa Hiroshige. *Hara, Mount Fuji in the Morning* (*Hara, Asa no Fuji*), from the series *Fifty-three Stations of the Tōkaidō* (*Tōkaidō gojūsan tsugi no uchi*). 1833–34. Color woodcut, *ōban*. Elvehjem Museum of Art, University of Wisconsin-Madison, Bequest of John H. Van Vleck, 1980 (1980.0796). Ex coll. Frank Lloyd Wright; E. B. Van Vleck

Opposite

8.
Frank Lloyd Wright. V. C. Morris House, Seacliff, Scheme #2 (project), San Francisco, California. 1955. Delineator, John H. Howe; waves, rocks, seabirds, and foliage added by Wright. Perspective; graphite and colored pencil on tracing paper, 21 x 35 in. The Frank Lloyd Wright Foundation (5412.001)

CHAPTER ONE

JAPONISME IN OAK PARK

SUPPLY AND DEMAND

Japanese art began to fascinate the Western world in the late nineteenth century in part because it was "new." Closed to the outside world for two and a half centuries, Japan retained a mysterious allure, and for many artists it remained a place of refuge and escape from the decadence and disillusionment spawned by the Industrial Revolution. Whistler's *The Golden Screen*, painted in London in 1864, testifies to his early infatuation with Japan as a source of both erotic and exotic forbidden pleasures (ill. 10). He drapes a European woman (his mistress, Jo) in not one but two seductively loose kimono and surrounds her with Asian art: a set of Hiroshige landscape prints, a gold-leaf folding screen painted with scenes from the *Tale of Genji*, a lacquer box, and a blue-and-white Chinese porcelain vase. Hiroshige's images of happy peasants in idyllic settings reinforced the romantic perception of Japan as a primitive country, inhabited by naive and childlike people who were accordingly morally superior to the educated and the mature. Because this was the near-mythical Japan Americans longed for, even Japanese photographs exported for the Western armchair traveler as late as the 1890s show peasants in evocative, idealized landscapes. Wright adopted the same nineteenth-century bias. The Japanese, he said after his first visit to that country, were very poor, very simple, and childhearted.[1] The American encounter with Japan occurred at a moment when there was a great longing both in Japan and the West for the "other," the distant shore. Japan was mysterious in part because of the language barrier. Few foreigners were aware of the rich inner life and intellectual heritage of the Japanese.

Almost all forms of Japanese art were available in America by the turn of the century, but it was color woodcuts that had the biggest impact. Prints were in demand as superb designs and because they were inexpensive, plentiful, portable, and easily stored. The technical challenge of the medium itself was important to graphic artists in an age that promoted handmade arts and crafts. Prints were also a window opening onto the cornu-

copia of a newly discovered culture. Because most Japanese purchased woodblock prints for their topical, documentary interest rather than as works of art, there was no show of concern when first Europeans and then Americans began to purchase them in ever-increasing quantities, instigating a vogue for all things Japanese, or Japonisme. Ironically, today the largest and finest collections of ukiyo-e are found in the West, including some designs no longer seen in Japan. The word "ukiyo-e" means pictures of the floating world, or brothel district. These pictures represent a kind of "low taste": they take as their subject matter prostitutes and kabuki actors, popular, sexy figures from the entertainment business.

Japanese prints were circulating in Paris as early as the 1830s and '40s. By the end of the century Western artists responded to their dazzling colors, flattened shapes, asymmetrical compositions, abrupt cropping, high angle of vision, general stylization and abstraction, and genre themes. Prints encapsulated and made vivid the time-honored conventions of classical Japanese painting traditions and as such they were excellent missionaries of Japanese art.

While many American artists and collectors began to include Japan in their world tours, most could not. Where did they find Japanese art? The Japanese government took the lead in disseminating knowledge of Japanese arts and crafts. Promoting itself as a major player in the modern world, Japan contributed lavish displays to the world's fairs, including Vienna in 1873, Philadelphia in 1876, Chicago in 1893, Paris in 1900, St. Louis in 1904, and London in 1910. Much of the material was export ware.

Even more than the fairs, it was art dealers who made it all happen, beginning with Siegfried Bing (1838–1905) and Hayashi Tadamasa (1853–1906), both of whom began selling Japanese decorative arts and prints in Paris in the 1880s. Bing, a German who became a naturalized French citizen, staged public exhibitions of ukiyo-e, and the thousands of prints heaped in the attic rooms of his shop attracted Monet, Degas, Toulouse-Lautrec, Cassatt, van Gogh, and Emile Bernard. Bing began building his business during the 1870s with the help of his acquisi-

10.
James McNeill Whistler
(1834–1903). *Caprice
in Purple and Gold: The
Golden Screen.* 1864.
Oil on panel, 19¾ x 27⅛
in. Freer Gallery of Art,
Smithsonian Institution,
Washington, D.C.

tive brother-in-law, the German consul in Tokyo, and he himself spent a year in Japan around 1881. He reminisced about that trip: "Once arrived in Japan I beat the drum in order to procure from one end of this remarkable Island Kingdom to the other all the artifacts that money could possibly buy. I…let it be known everywhere that a wild man had come ashore to buy up everything."[2] Bing also published the influential illustrated journal *Le Japon artistique*, which ran for three years from 1888. Translated into English as *Artistic Japan*, it was a source of exciting new imagery for artists and industrial designers.

Bing's chief competitor was the aggressive entrepreneur Hayashi Tadamasa, regarded as one of the most knowledgeable connoisseurs of his day. Prints with Hayashi provenance are still prized today. From about 1889, when he established himself in sole proprietorship as a merchant of prints, until 1900, when he ceased his commercial activities, he imported 160,000 prints and nearly 10,000 illustrated printed books.[3] Thanks to Hayashi, Paris was the center of the print market at the turn of the century: there were at least thirty-six print auctions in Paris between about 1891 and 1912 as great private collections were formed and then dispersed. Eventually, demand drove up prices in Europe

to a level that few could afford, and many artists, including Degas, bartered their own paintings in exchange for prints. Hayashi has been criticized as a plunderer of treasures, but at the time prints were still perceived as embarrassingly vulgar by his fellow Japanese. When he represented his country in 1900 as commissioner general of the Japanese section of the Paris Exposition Universelle, he took the high road and excluded prints from the display.

In America one of the first resident Japanese art dealers was Matsuki Bunkio (1867–1934), whose family were art appraisers. He arrived in Salem, Massachusetts, at the age of twenty, learned English at Salem High School, took an American wife, and opened a gallery on Boylston Street in Boston. By 1898 he was sponsoring annual auctions of Japanese art in Boston, New York, and Philadelphia, but he fell into irreversible financial difficulties by 1909.

Perhaps no one was more successful as an advocate for Asian art than Yamanaka Sadajirō (1866–1936), who opened a shop in New York on Broadway in 1895 (soon moving to Fifth Avenue) with a staff of five, including a print specialist. Unassuming and astute, Yamanaka sold everything from the finest early Chinese bronzes to cut-velvet framed pictures of tigers for the tourist trade. Yamanaka and Company, an international firm with headquarters in Osaka, became a Mecca for collectors and eventually opened additional branches in Paris, London, Boston, the Boardwalk in Atlantic City, and, by the late 1920s, Chicago.[4] Wright was doing business with Yamanaka in the 1930s if not earlier.

Bing, who knew everyone, encouraged the growing market for ukiyo-e in America with several exhibitions. His March 1894 sale of 290 prints and illustrated books at the American Art Galleries on Madison Square caused something of a sensation; it was the finest selection that had ever appeared on the market there and the first time that ukiyo-e prints of real quality were available for purchase in the United States.[5] The following month he held a sale exhibition of prints at the Museum of Fine Arts in Boston with the encouragement of Japanese art curator Ernest Francisco Fenollosa (1853–1908).

Fenollosa is a complex figure whose story has yet to be told in full (ill. 11). He is considered one of the first serious Western interpreters of Japanese culture; many American collectors, even Wright, were touched by his lectures, publications, and exhibitions and looked to him as an authority.[6] Fenollosa graduated from Harvard, studied oil painting for a year, and in 1878 was hired to teach philosophy at Tokyo Imperial University (now Tokyo University). He stayed on in Japan for twelve years as a voracious collector, a student of Japanese art, an advisor to the Japanese government on preservation of the nation's ancient arts, and cofounder of a national art school in Tokyo. Joining Fenollosa on trips into the countryside to forage for art were Bostonians Edward Sylvester Morse (1838–1925), a Harvard-trained zoologist who had taught Darwinism at Tokyo Imperial University in the 1870s and who returned in 1882 to collect pottery, and William Sturgis Bigelow (1850–1926), who spent seven years in Japan in the 1880s as a student of Japanese culture and a disciple of esoteric Buddhism. Bigelow's family fortune allowed him to collect in overwhelming quantities, and he did so with an enlightened breadth of vision that encompassed all fields ranging from Buddhist paintings to sword guards. In 1911, when his collection was donated to the Museum of Fine Arts, of which he was a trustee, the prints alone numbered a staggering 40,000. (The figure is approximate—no one has undertaken an exact count.)

Fenollosa was one of many foreign specialists hired to "modernize" Japan during the Meiji period (1868–1912). Inevitably

11.
Ernest Fenollosa and a nineteenth-century Utagawa-school Japanese print. c. 1900

there came the moment when his hosts felt they had absorbed all he had to say; the art school let him go in 1890. He returned to Boston and was hired that same year by the Museum of Fine Arts as its first curator of Japanese art. (Most of that collection was Fenollosa's own: he had sold it in 1886 to a wealthy Boston Japanophile, Charles G. Weld [1857–1911], with the understanding that Weld would give everything to the museum in their joint names.) Five years later, when he fell in love with his assistant at the museum, his career changed course quite suddenly. His divorce and remarriage in 1895 were perceived as a sex scandal in conservative Boston and the museum fired him. Fortuitously, at the end of 1895, Frederick Pratt invited Fenollosa and his protégé, the artist Arthur Wesley Dow (1857–1922), to teach at the Pratt Institute in Brooklyn, but the scandal had re-

verberated and in March 1896, after only a few lectures, Pratt fired him. Fenollosa went back to Japan for several years, supporting himself by teaching English.

Fenollosa proceeded to reinvent himself. Thanks to his prestigious career in Japan and Boston, the breadth of his first-hand knowledge, and his outgoing personal style, he was already perceived as one of the foremost Western authorities on Japanese art. Now, funded by a series of partnerships with Japanese print dealers (including Yamanaka in New York), he was active as a virtuoso lecturer and a consultant to rich collectors of Asian art. His zealous promotion of ukiyo-e is quite remarkable considering that even at the end of his life he believed that nineteenth-century prints, with the exception of those by Katsushika Hokusai (1760–1849) (everyone's favorite), were hideous, degen-

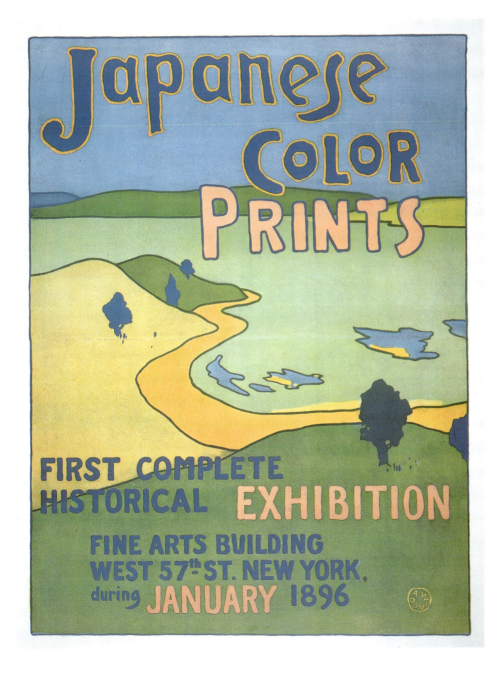

12.
Arthur Wesley Dow.
Poster for the exhibition
Japanese Color Prints.
January 1896. Lithograph, 25½ x 19½ in.
Solton and Julia Engel
Collection, Rare Book
and Manuscript Library,
Columbia University,
New York

erate, decadent, and vulgar.[7] Evidently he took a hard look at the art market in America in the 1890s and realized that prints were commercially viable.

Fenollosa masterminded a major exhibition and sale of 440 ukiyo-e paintings and prints in the Fine Arts Building in New York in January 1896 and produced a well-researched catalogue that proved very influential.[8] Dow created a stunning poster in the simplified style of Hiroshige with an overlay of curvilinear American Art Nouveau and Arts and Crafts (ill. 12). It seems to confirm a belief propagated by both Dow and Fenollosa that prints transformed the decorative arts and were "the grammar, so to speak, of pictorial composition."[9] Dow shared his own collection of ukiyo-e with his students at Pratt and probably did more than anyone to enlist Japanese art in the cause of good design.

It is likely that Fenollosa's Tokyo partner Kobayashi Bunshichi (1864–1923), who was backed by W. E. Ketcham, a local framer and print dealer who provided the business front, supplied many of the goods for the exhibition. (He would later supply Wright as well.) The show attracted some high-profile collectors from around the country. Two of the lenders, Howard Mansfield, a New York lawyer, and Clarence Buckingham, a Chicago businessman, became Wright's print clients some years later. Other lenders were Charles J. Morse (1852–1911), a civil engineer from Evanston, Illinois, and two New Yorkers, Samuel Colman (1832–1920), an artist-decorator who collaborated with Tiffany, and George W. Vanderbilt (1862–1914). The scholar Frederick W. Gookin, who wrote the catalogue preface, was to become a guiding force in Wright's career as a print dealer. Charles Lang Freer (1854–1919), a Detroit businessman and self-made millionaire who later gave his collection to the Smithsonian, purchased most of the ukiyo-e paintings in the show.[10] Freer was converted to Asian art when he purchased five ukiyo-e prints at Boussod-Valladon in New York in 1894. As for so many of his contemporaries (including Wright), prints were his introduction to Japanese art. He made his first trip to Japan in 1895 and soon assembled a substantial group of four hundred prints, primarily works by Hokusai and Hiroshige. Because he sold the lot in 1905, Freer's interest in woodcuts has gone unnoticed. Good prints by eighteenth-century masters were costly even in those days: Freer paid $80 for an Utamaro design he purchased in New York in 1894.

In 1917, long after Fenollosa's death, Wright seemed to pinpoint this exhibition as having had special significance for him. "When I first saw a fine print about twenty-five years ago, it was an intoxicating thing. At that time Ernest Fenollosa was doing his best to persuade the Japanese people not to wantonly destroy their works of art…. On one of his journeys home, he brought many beautiful prints. Those I made mine were the narrow tall decorative forms—*hashirakake* [pillar prints]—that I appreciate today even more than I did then."[11] Fenollosa was often in and out of Chicago in the 1890s, and Wright may have heard him lecture at the Art Institute in 1894 (sponsored by Gookin) or at the University of Chicago in 1904. On at least one of these occasions Fenollosa stayed with his cousin, the architect Joseph Lyman Silsbee (1848–1913), an early Japanophile and Wright's first employer in Chicago.[12]

JAPANESE ART COMES TO CHICAGO: THE 1893 WORLD'S FAIR

Wright came to Chicago in 1887 directly from engineering school at the University of Wisconsin at Madison. He apprenticed briefly with Silsbee, an architect of the Shingle Style who had a taste for Asian art: Silsbee displayed a Japanese hanging scroll in his dining room and decorated the hall mantel with a large gilded statue of a Lamaist Bodhisattva as well as a pair of porcelain vases.[13] The Japanese vogue fostered by the centennial exposition in Philadelphia in 1876 had left its imprint on the interior decoration of "artistic" homes throughout America. After about five months Wright, at age twenty, joined the office of Adler and Sullivan as a draftsman, and remained with them until 1893. Here, too, Japan was in the air. In 1892, when Louis H. Sullivan (1856–1924) moved to Lake Park Avenue, he had a number of books on Japan and Japanese art and was eagerly enlarging his art collection. He sent Wright off to poke around the salesrooms and bid at auction for him, acquiring Chinese ceramics, Persian carpets, and Indian sculptures.[14]

Japanese architectural elements were beginning to appear in American homes during the last quarter of the nineteenth century, and the country was more than ready to appreciate the buildings erected by Japanese carpenters at the World's Columbian Exposition in Chicago in 1893. As if to counteract Chicago's image as a frontier town, a conservative, Neo-classical style was chosen for the fair buildings. The Japanese structures, located on a small wooded island on the lagoon in Jackson Park, were very modest when compared to the pretentious exhibition

13.
Hōōden, World's
Columbian Exposition,
Chicago. 1893

14.
Hōōden, interior. 1893

halls looming around them (ills. 13, 14). Some critics found the smaller buildings quaint; others were simply disappointed: the scale seemed small, the materials insubstantial.

The architect Kuru Masamichi designed the buildings in Japan; the materials were shipped to Chicago and assembled there by Japanese carpenters. A symmetrical configuration with a large central hall and two smaller flanking structures connected by covered passageways, the Hōōden, or Phoenix Hall, as it was called, was said to be loosely based on the plan of an eleventh-century Buddhist chapel near Kyoto known as the Hōōdō (Phoenix Hall) of the Byōdō-in. (The Hōōdō was actually built in Chinese style, and painted a bright red; it also had a long axial protrusion behind the center hall that resembled the tail or body of a bird, the side extensions, which were nonfunctional, being the wings.) The three buildings making up the Phoenix Hall in Chicago were a curious medley of styles, each representing a different period of Japanese history. Japanese officials were evidently intent on perpetuating the exotic image of Old Japan, however awkward the result. The left or north

15.
Frank Lloyd Wright.
Warren Hickox House,
Kankakee, Illinois.
c. 1900

wing reflected the classical style of eleventh-century temple and court architecture; the south wing reproduced a portion of the fifteenth-century Silver Pavilion in Kyoto, with tea room and study alcove indicating the tenor of the times; and the central hall was in the grand style of Edo Castle, home of the Tokugawa shoguns during the Edo period. Walls, sliding doors, ceilings, and hanging scrolls were painted by the leading establishment artists on the faculty of the Tokyo School of Fine Arts (Fenollosa's project), and rooms were furnished with lavish sets of lacquered cabinets and tables, tea implements, musical instruments, and the like.

The buildings were a great novelty, and the local press described and illustrated the methods of construction, tools, and the structures themselves during the period of preparation in 1892. Wright's hometown newspaper, the *Oak Park Reporter*, carried an extensively illustrated story on 16 December 1892, and articles on Japanese culture and Buddhist temples soon followed. There was even a full-page article describing tatami mats for functional use as floor covering and as modular measurement (six by three feet) in the *Oak Park Reporter* of 14 April 1893. As for the pavilions themselves, they were available for study long after the fair had closed, having been presented to the city of Chicago and maintained there as a museum and teahouse until their destruction by fire in 1946. There were other, unofficial Japanese pavilions as well, including a Japanese village on Midway Plaisance.

The Japanese section in the Fine Arts building contained some four hundred pieces commissioned from Japan's leading artists and craftsmen, including enormous tapestries, paintings in traditional style (there were only three oil paintings in European styles), large metal sculptures (twelve bronze falcons specially commissioned by Hayashi Tadamasa), realistic carvings in ivory and wood, cloisonné, ceramics (several hundred porcelains were also offered by Hayashi), photographs, and architectural models. The printmaking process was fully explicated for the benefit of graphic artists: the official guide to the fair lists prints (possibly modern), engraved blocks, and cutting tools provided by Kokka, the art publishers.[15]

An insatiable reader, Wright was certainly familiar with the one book in English from this period that featured illustrations and detailed firsthand accounts of Japanese domestic architecture. *Japanese Homes and Their Surroundings*, originally published in Boston in 1886, went into a second printing in 1887 and was reviewed in the 2 January 1886 issue of *American Architect*. It was full of wonderful illustrations by the author, Edward Sylvester Morse. (Morse lectured at the Art Institute of Chicago in 1900.)

Wright never acknowledged his sources, needing to keep alive in himself "the romantic myth of the artist as isolated creator and superman."[16] It seems clear, however, that Japanese architecture, with its sensitive human scale and simple, everyday materials was one of many "starters" for him once he broke away from Sullivanism and started to cast around for his own mode of self-expression. Wright's Prairie Houses of 1900–2 have sculptural roof lines with multiple deep gables and walls articulated by slender, dark, wood strips to set off light-colored, vertical, stucco panels that are so reminiscent of the seventeenth-century Katsura Detached Palace in Kyoto, probably the most famous example of secular architecture in Japan (ill. 15). The Japanese modular system may also have impressed him. His own unit system of design, with plans composed of units grouped in a systematic way, was considered a major innovation in American architecture at the time.[17]

Of course, his love of natural materials, of warm, earthy colors and low, horizontal profiles had everything to do with his roots in the flat plains of the midwestern prairies. It is often asserted that Wright's early houses are to be seen as an extension of the prairie, echoing the landscape, but this is probably an overly romantic interpretation of these suburban residences. Likewise, one should not make too much of the similarities with Japanese architecture. Certainly no one would mistake one of Wright's Prairie School houses, massive and heavy structures of stone, brick, and stained glass, for a Japanese house constructed of rather flimsy wood and paper, open and susceptible to the elements, leaving its occupants keenly sensitive to the climate of the passing seasons, especially the intense heat and humidity of summer, and the biting cold of winter. In his Prairie School houses Wright espoused the principles of simplicity, geometric abstraction, and utility that point the way to the modernism of the 1920s. Over the years his buildings became increasingly informal, open, and immediate in their association with their natural surroundings.[18]

In 1889 Wright married Catherine Tobin (1871–1959), the tall, redheaded daughter of a prosperous Chicago businessman, and they built a two-story shingled house on Forest Avenue in Oak Park, described as a "pious, self-righteous village nine miles west of the Chicago Loop."[19] (Wright would go on to build more than twenty houses there.)

In his 1932 autobiography Wright confessed that "during the years at the Oak Park workshop, Japanese prints intrigued me and taught me much."[20] It is apparent from early interior views that even at this date he was forming a collection of Japanese art. He tacked Japanese prints on the walls of both the children's playroom and the master bedroom. A Christmas present for his twelve-year-old son John in 1904 was a new book, Edward F. Strange's *Japanese Illustration: A History of Woodcuts and Colour Printing in Japan*.[21] In the living room he hung a late-eighteenth-century Japanese painting of a hanging flower basket from a curtain rod beside the piano.

Wright enlarged his home in the late 1890s with a studio complex facing Chicago Avenue. There were four rooms: a re-

16.
Frank Lloyd Wright.
Frank Lloyd Wright
House, Oak Park,
Illinois. Drafting studio.
c. 1898

Wright hung a Japanese Buddhist painting from the second-floor balcony. In other photographs, the same painting is shown hanging from a curtain rod in the inglenook off the living room. This photograph was published in *The Architectural Review*, June 1900.

17.
Wright House, Oak
Park. Octagonal library.
c. 1906–8

The left-hand panel
of a diptych by Torii
Kiyonaga is propped
against the slanted
easel of one of Wright's
gate-legged oak print
stands at the right.
Wright used the small
clerestoried octagonal
library as a conference
room for clients. This
photograph was pub-
lished in *Architectural
Record*, March 1908.

ception hall, a small clerestoried octagon used as a library and conference room for clients, a private office, and a two-story drafting room accommodating half a dozen desks. A Buddhist hanging scroll was sometimes the focal point of the drafting room, suspended like an icon from the second-floor balcony (ill. 16). A photograph Wright used to publicize his work in the Chicago Architectural Club's 1902 exhibition at the Art Institute of Chicago shows two Japanese scroll paintings rolled up on the architect's library desk. A strip of Japanese brocade with paulownia-leaf motif creates a handsome backdrop for several of Wright's bronze flower containers. Around 1906–8 Wright hired the master photographer Clarence Fuermann to document the interior of his home. Fuermann worked in a Chicago firm with his father, Henry, who was business manager, and a broth-er, the technician. Fuermann's photo of the small conference room for clients shows the left-hand panel of an eighteenth-cen-tury diptych by Torii Kiyonaga (1752–1815) propped up in the place of honor against the adjustable slanted easel of a gate-leg oak table (ill. 17). This handsome piece of furniture, useful for display of portfolios, prints, and drawings, was designed by Wright, as were all of the furnishings. (The table folds up into a slim but stable container for storage of valuable large prints.) He installed similar print tables, a sign of status, in the homes of several of his collector-clients in the early days.

JAPONISME AND PHOTOGRAPHY

Around 1896–97 we can point to a concrete example of the in-fluence of Japanese prints on Wright's work. In keeping with the spirit of the newly founded Chicago Society of Arts and Crafts, Wright and his good friend and former client William H. Winslow (1857–1934) collaborated on publishing a lavish, large-format book, *The House Beautiful*. Winslow was the publisher, the text was written by William Channing Gannett (1840–1923), a Unitarian minister, and Wright designed the graphics. Winslow was a manufacturer of ornamental ironwork, a musi-cian, and an inventor, and he had a printing shop, the Auvergne Press, in the stable at the rear of his house in River Forest, two miles east of Oak Park.

Gannett stressed the Arts and Crafts philosophy of simplici-ty, truthfulness, and the influence of nature in ornament, and Wright found one source for his stylized ornaments in the seed pods of weeds. He photographed wildflowers and weeds—icons of the prairie—in carefully arranged still lifes. These were printed on thin Japanese paper as a fourteen-page folio that was sewn into the front endpaper of the book (ill. 18). Each of the twelve modest but elegant little images is outlined with a thin red line in a vertical format that imitates a Japanese hanging scroll. These simple compositions have their parallel in the narrow vertical woodcuts of wildflowers by Hiroshige that Wright collected (ill. 19). The photographs echo the flat, two-dimensional effect of prints. The red seal in the lower right corner of each set (a cross inside a circle enclosed by a square) has been identified as a Celtic cross, an allusion to Wright's Welsh origins, but it also resembles the personal crest used by actors of the Ōtani

family, and appears on many of the actor prints Wright owned. From about 1906, Wright switched to a square red seal, a more obvious homage to Japanese artists.

The architect was a talented amateur photographer in those early years; according to his son John he owned an 8 x 10-inch plate camera and built a darkroom off the balcony of his studio.[22] Wright spoke of the weed photos to Pedro Guerrero (b. 1917), a photographer who worked for him in the 1940s and '50s. According to Guerrero, Wright "knew enough to be technically conversant, although not entirely in modern terms. He once showed me a few 'bromides' of leaves and weeds he had photographed around his first home in Oak Park, Illinois. They were quite good, and he seemed very pleased that I told him so."[23]

18.
Frank Lloyd Wright.
"Weeds and Wildflowers," insert in William C. Gannett, *The House Beautiful*, 1896–97. Photographs, collotype (or photogravure) prints on thin Japanese paper, 7¼ x 2⅝ in. (image); 12 x 5 in. (page). The Frank Lloyd Wright Foundation (1028.021)

Opposite

19.
Utagawa Hiroshige.
Nadeshiko (Pink), Butterfly and Poem. c. 1840. Color woodcut, small *tanzaku*. The Art Institute of Chicago, Clarence Buckingham Collection, 1925 (1925.3652). Ex coll. Frank Lloyd Wright

Wright experimented a few years later with Japonesque photographs of the scenery around the Hillside Home School that he designed in 1887 for his aunts Ellen (1845–1919) and Jane Lloyd Jones (1848–1947) in a farming valley near Spring Green, Wisconsin. (Wright later built his own home on adjacent property.) These miniature landscapes were published in the brochure advertising the school for the year 1902–3; his daughter Catherine was then a third-grader at the school (ill. 20). The horizontal format and spare, poetic composition are reminiscent of Japanese ink paintings in the form of handscrolls.[24] Wright described these images in a note to Mrs. Felix Morris, whose daughters had been pupils at the school: "In mounting these almost forgotten little views of Hillside for a small Arts and Crafts exhibit I have enjoyed them so much—if I did take them myself—that it occurs to me they might give you pleasure too. If so kindly accept them."[25]

THE FIRST TRIP TO JAPAN

By the turn of the century a trip to Japan, whether a honeymoon, business trip, or just plain adventure, was increasingly popular among Americans. Japan had proved itself a modern nation in 1894 by going to war against China on the Korean Peninsula and winning easily. In 1904, taking on Russia, a Western nation, it was again victorious on the battlefront, and cemented its credibility as an impressive world power in the eyes of all Americans.

20.
Frank Lloyd Wright. Jones Valley, looking northwest, with Taliesin Hill at center. c. 1902. Collotype, 2¾ x 9¼ in.

On 21 February 1905 Wright sailed to Japan for three months with his wife, Catherine, and Mr. and Mrs. Ward Willits from Highland Park, Illinois, clients for whom the architect had designed one of the first Prairie Houses in 1902. The little group embarked at Vancouver aboard the Canadian Pacific steamship *Empress of China*. Wright claimed that the trip was made in pursuit of prints, but an album of carefully composed snapshots with which he documented the journey makes clear his paramount concern with Japanese landscape gardens and architecture, particularly temple and shrine roofs (ills. 21, 22).[26] He was uncharacteristically silent about this trip, saying only that he had gone off to rest after the tiring experience of constructing two major buildings in Buffalo, New York: the Darwin D. Martin residence and the Larkin Administration Building.[27]

A conscientious architectural historian, Tanigawa Masami, scoured hotel registers to retrace Wright's path through the Japanese countryside.[28] On 23 April Wright and his wife registered at the Kanaya Hotel in Nikkō (he was to visit the hotel again in 1918 with Miriam Noel). Nikkō, a good half-day trip by train and rickshaw due north of Tokyo, is the site of the ornate mausoleum of the first Tokugawa shogun. The extravagance of its baroque carvings and the great natural beauty of the site have always made it Japan's premier tourist stopover. On 25 April Wright's name appears on the register of the Fujiya Hotel

in Miyanoshita, Hakone. A beautiful summer resort area high in the mountains southeast of Tokyo, Hakone was one of the fifty-three stations celebrated in Hiroshige's views of the Tōkaidō, the old highway between Tokyo (Edo, in former times) and Kyoto. This early Western-style hotel, incidentally, is still standing. Wright continued on to Nagoya where he photographed the magnificent double roof of the nineteenth-century worship hall of the Higashi Honganji temple.

In Kyoto, Wright documented another monumental temple complex, the seventeenth-century Chion-in. He visited the Sambōin, an elaborate late-sixteenth-century garden associated with the general Toyotomi Hideyoshi (1537–1598), four miles southeast of Kyoto proper. Later (perhaps remembering another trip) he said that he was also impressed by the Shugakuin, a vast seventeenth-century imperial stroll garden on the northern outskirts of town. Wright thought it was the greatest work of art in the world. The garden climbs the side of a hill and incorporates the surrounding mountains and forest in a seemingly natural way. "All that was like an open book to me," he remembered, "and I knew how to read it. I could read every word in it…. It was a great educational experience."[29]

Then, continuing southwest along the Inland Sea to Okayama, he stopped to visit the Kōrakuen, a stroll garden designed around 1700 for a local daimyo, and considered one of

21.
Frank Lloyd Wright.
Kōrakuen park with
En'yōtei teahouse,
Okayama. From an
album of photographs
of Wright's first trip to
Japan. 1905. Silver
gelatin print, 3½ x 4 in.
Frank Lloyd Wright
Preservation Trust,
Oak Park, Gift of David
and Gladys Wright
(1981.1.50)

the three most famous gardens in Japan. His party crossed the Inland Sea by boat to Shikoku, the smallest of the four main islands of Japan, where Wright photographed the architecture of the Shinto shrine at Yashima and yet another garden in Takamatsu. He also visited an art school in Takamatsu where he was impressed that students drew wildflowers as an inspiration for their craft designs: "Marvelous little art school," he recalled many decades later.

> And I brought back all sort of things they were doing,
> along the same lines that had been taught to me when
> I was a youngster. They were going out in the field
> and bringing in a dandelion, see. And I used to have
> those drawings around the office—I guess they've all
> disappeared now.[30]

In America, manual training in art schools, instigated by the Arts and Crafts movement, was still relatively new and controversial. There was heated debate over the dialectics of fine arts versus technical instruction. In newly founded industrial art schools, like the Pratt Institute, drawing was a utilitarian skill deemed necessary for good design (and social reform).

Wright's 1905 trip included a comprehensive tour of large garden estates characterized by a combination of small hills,

22.
Frank Lloyd Wright. Japanese gentleman and Buddhist ascetic on a mountain path. From an album of photographs of Wright's first trip to Japan. 1905. Silver gelatin print, 3½ x 4 in. Frank Lloyd Wright Preservation Trust, Oak Park, Gift of David and Gladys Wright (1981.1.50)

23.
Child's kimono with wisteria and fence design. Late Meiji period, early twentieth century. Stencil dyeing (*katazome*) on silk, 35½ x 33½ in. John C. Weber Collection

Wright gave this robe to his three-year-old son Llewellyn (see ill. 44) after his 1905 trip to Japan. Until recently it remained in the collection of Llewellyn's widow.

rivers, ponds, and bridges, with carefully constructed scenic "views." These principles may have aided him later when he landscaped Taliesin, his own estate in southern Wisconsin.[31]

WRIGHT'S FIRST EXHIBITION OF JAPANESE PRINTS

Wright was already a fledgling contender in the Chicago print world before he left for Japan: he contributed one pillar print to Gookin's pioneering exhibition of sixty works by Suzuki Harunobu (1724–1770) held at the Caxton Club (a men's club for bibliophiles) in the Fine Arts Building on 4 February 1905. Rubbing elbows there with wealthy collectors like Buckingham may have encouraged him.[32]

In Japan the Wrights invested heavily in prints, stencils, textiles, and a fascinating array of contemporary pattern books, some intended to decorate their home and educate their children (ills. 23, 24).[33] Later that year, when the architect complained to his client Darwin Martin that he was carrying a debt of $3,000, Martin countered by chiding Wright on his "expensive vacation trip and large investment in art incident thereto" following closely on the heels of "investments at Saint Louis."[34] The latter may have been purchases made at the 1904 Saint Louis World's Fair.

In any case, Wright returned with several hundred Hiroshige woodcuts, which he catalogued and displayed in March 1906 at the Art Institute of Chicago (ill. 25). These were the first ukiyo-e to be shown at that museum and, more remarkably, the world's first Hiroshige retrospective. Fenollosa's wife, Mary, had already generated enthusiasm for Hiroshige with her 1901 book *Hiroshige: The Artist of Mist, Snow and Rain.* The historian Henry Smith credits Mary Fenollosa with positioning Hiroshige as quintessentially "Japanese" and skilled as an artist of "Nature," concepts that became entrenched in the minds of connoisseurs.[35]

There is no record of who interceded on Wright's behalf to expedite the exhibit—perhaps Gookin or Buckingham, a trustee. The prints were on view from 29 March until 18 April, exactly the same dates as the museum's nineteenth annual exhibition of the Chicago Architectural Club—no coincidence.

Wright's display was uncomfortably crowded; no wall surface was left uncovered. His first published essay on prints, a checklist titled *Hiroshige: An Exhibition of Colour Prints from the Collection of Frank Lloyd Wright,* was available for perusal in the gallery area. Inordinately proud of his accomplishment, he pencilled this inscription on the back of a copy of the brochure now in the Art Institute of Chicago archives: "This exhibition was the first solo Hiroshige exhibit held—I initially introduced Hiroshige to America—The paper on which this catalogue was p[rinted] I brought from Japan." He began his introduction for this brochure with an odd disclaimer that seems designed to get himself out of thorny connoisseurship problems: "So obscure is the origin of the mass of work bearing the name of Hiroshige; so conflicting and useless is most so-called expert testimony concerning the chronology of proper assignation of the color prints here represented…that attributions of this nature can be little better than speculation." The show was ostensibly devoted to Hiroshige, but photos of the installation show that Wright added pillar prints by earlier artists (late-eighteenth-century images of actors and courtesans) on the projecting wings of the table cases as a framing device. Pillar prints (*hashira-e*, literally "pillar pictures," also known as *hashirakake*, "pillar hangings") were a particular passion for the architect. Named for their presumed placement in Japanese homes, pillar prints have a novel, eccentric, and uniquely Japanese shape (extremely long and narrow) that originated in the 1740s.[36]

At least one Chicago artist may have been galvanized by Wright's exhibition. B. J. O. Nordfeldt (1875–1955) produced a memorable "Hiroshige Suite" of ten color woodcuts in the Japanese manner that year. Japanese models helped modernize and simplify his imagery. Other artists who began to see nature through the eyes of Hiroshige were the American Impressionist painter J. Alden Weir (1852–1919), whose *Red Bridge* of 1895 draws on Hiroshige's composition *Twilight Moon at Ryōgoku Bridge*, a print in Weir's own collection, and the New York photographer Arnold Genthe (1869–1942), whose 1908 bird's-eye view of Japan's Inland Sea adopts the perspective of Hiroshige's *Whirlpools at Awa*.[37]

From about this time Japanese prints and Japanese art begin to figure quite prominently in Wright's life. In March, just as he was preparing working drawings for Unity Temple in Oak Park, a local paper reported that he hosted a Japanese social for the Unity Club, the group that financed the publicity brochure for Unity Temple. Wright used lantern slides to illustrate his Japan trip. The next month his wife, Catherine, gave a lecture to the local Nineteenth Century Club on the architecture of Asia, and especially Japan. A month earlier the Wrights had hosted a

24.
Furuya Kōrin (active c. 1900). *Ocean of New Art (Shinbijutsukai)*, vols. 29–30. Kyoto: Unsōdō, 1905. Color woodcut, illustrated books, 8½ x 6½ in.; 9⅝ x 6½ in. each. Frank Lloyd Wright Preservation Trust, Oak Park, Gift of David and Gladys Wright (1990.34.16–17)

25.
Exhibition of Japanese
prints from the collec-
tion of Frank Lloyd
Wright at the Art Insti-
tute of Chicago. 1906

function for the Unity Club at their home: a stereopticon lecture on Japan given by Mr. and Mrs. Booth (perhaps Sherman Booth, Wright's lawyer and future client). Tea was served by young ladies in Japanese costume. The week before, on 24 February 1906, it was reported in the *Oak Park Reporter-Argus* that Mrs. William H. Winslow, one of Wright's clients, gave a talk on Japanese art at her home in River Forest and had an exhibition at the clubhouse of her collection of Japanese bronzes, ceramics, and prints.[38] One wonders whether some of these prints might not have been purchased from Wright; a pattern of promoting Japanese art to clients was already beginning to develop.

Wright was often short of money during these years, in part because he and Catherine were raising six children. After sons Lloyd (1890) and John (1892), their third child, Catherine, was born in 1894, quickly followed by David in 1895, Frances in 1898, and Llewellyn in 1903. Then there was the expense of constant renovations to his house. The Oak Park architect Charles E. White, Jr. (1876–1936), who trained for a year with Wright, described the scene in a 1904 letter from the studio, saying: "The studio is again torn up by the annual repairs and alterations. Twice a year, Mr. W. rearranges and changes the different rooms. He says he has gotten more education in experimenting on his own premises, than in any other way."[39] In addition, the Wrights were developing expensive tastes. There were dinners at fashionable Chicago restaurants, the best finery for dressing the children, season tickets for the symphony, horses to be entered in the annual Chicago Horse Show (the black horse Wright rode on the prairies north of Oak Park was named Kano, after the Kano family of Japanese painters), and a constant round of luncheons, musicales, and fancy dinner parties at their home. Said Wright,

> This love for beautiful things—rugs, books, prints or anything else made by art or craft or building—especially building—kept the butcher, the baker and the landlord always waiting. Sometimes waiting an incredibly long time…. It was my misfortune, too, that everybody was willing to trust me…. Only the banks would "N.S.F." us. So we came to distrust and despise banks.[40]

Another letter written by White, dated 4 March 1906, alludes to Wright's ongoing financial difficulties; the architect had spent too much money in Japan: "It cannot be said that his affairs have

26.
Frank Lloyd Wright.
Thomas P. Hardy House,
Racine, Wisconsin. 1905.
Perspective; watercolor
and ink on paper, 18¾ x
5⅜ in. The Frank Lloyd
Wright Foundation
(0506.003)

27.
Frank Lloyd Wright. K. C. DeRhodes House, South
Bend, Indiana. 1906. Delineator, Marion Lucy Mahony.
Perspective; ink and watercolor on paper, 18¾ x 25¾
in. Inscribed by Wright in 1950: "Drawn by Mahony
after FLLW and Hiroshige." The Frank Lloyd Wright
Foundation (0602.001)

Opposite

28.
Utagawa Hiroshige. *Maple Trees at Mama, Tekona
Shrine and Linked Bridge* (*Mama no momiji Tekona
no yashiro Tsugihashi*), from the series *One Hundred
Views of Famous Places in Edo* (*Meisho Edo hyakkei*).
1857. Color woodcut, *ōban*. The Metropolitan
Museum of Art, New York, Purchase, Joseph Pulitzer
Bequest, 1918 (JP 646)

Wright sold this print to the Metropolitan Museum of
Art in 1918 for $62.50.

44

been particularly prosperous lately. If it hadn't been for the Buffalo building [the Larkin Company], he would have been in straits long ago. He made a great mistake in going abroad just when he did."[41]

The influence of prints is often apparent in presentation drawings by Wright and his staff architects, especially in the work of Marion Lucy Mahony (1871–1962). Born in Chicago and only the second woman to graduate with a degree in architecture from MIT, Mahony worked in Wright's studio off and on for about eleven years. Although described as homely and gaunt, she was vivacious and talkative, and there was a real sparkle when she and Wright interacted. She is renowned for the perspective drawings she made for Wright's clients or created expressly for exhibition and publication. (Beautiful renderings of projects or completed buildings were major promotional tools of the late-nineteenth-century architect.) It is surely no coincidence that some of Mahony's finest renderings, filled with the spirit of Japonisme, date from between 1905 and 1907, in the wake of Wright's Japan trip and his Hiroshige exhibition.[42] Wright later penciled a notation on her 1906 drawing for the K. C. DeRhodes house in South Bend, Indiana: "Drawn by Mahony after FLLW and Hiroshige" (ill. 27). The remark was obviously occasioned by her arbitrary insertion of an enlarged detail of a bird on a flowering branch in the lower left corner, in the manner of Hiroshige,

but Wright must also have been conscious of her use of the flattened tree trunks cropped at the sides and rising out of the composition in the immediate foreground with a canopy of foliage overhead, framing a sort of window opening through which the viewer looks into deep space. Hiroshige used this device in *Maple Trees at Mama* from his last and one of his most commercially and artistically successful series, the *One Hundred Views of Famous Places in Edo* (ill. 28). The small figure of a woman emerging from the doorway in Mahony's rendering enlivens the composition and gives a sense of scale just as do the tiny anonymous figures in Hiroshige's print.

An unusual watercolor perspective of the 1905 Hardy house in Racine, Wisconsin, imitates the distinctive shape of a narrow, vertical Japanese pillar print (ill. 26). The house itself is perched dramatically high on a hill, seen from below, with most of the area given over to empty space, very similar to Hiroshige's 1834 composition of a daimyo cortege climbing toward a castle on Mount Kameyama (ill. 29). Wright later reworked the original drawing and included it in the portfolio of lithographs published by Wasmuth in 1910 (ill. 30). The result is streamlined and spare, a strong statement of formalism and a step well beyond the era of Arts and Crafts. The branch protruding into the empty center is again an allusion to the work of the artist Wright favored throughout his life, Hiroshige.

29.
Utagawa Hiroshige. *Kameyama, Clearing Weather after the Snow* (*Kameyama, Yukibare*), from the series *Fifty-three Stations of the Tōkaidō* (*Tōkaidō gojūsan tsugi no uchi*). 1833–34. Color woodcut, *ōban*. The Dallas Museum of Art, Gift of Mr. and Mrs. Stanley Marcus, 1984 (1984.202.47). Ex coll. Frank Lloyd Wright

30.
Frank Lloyd Wright.
Thomas P. Hardy
House. 1910. Detail of
a plate from Wright,
*Ausgeführte Bauten
und Entwürfe von Frank
Lloyd Wright*, 1910.
Perspective; lithograph,
25 x 15¾ in.

CHAPTER TWO

WRIGHT BECOMES AN ART DEALER

THE MOST LOYAL PATRON: DARWIN D. MARTIN

One masterpiece of Wright's Oak Park years is the Martin house in Buffalo, New York, constructed during 1904 and 1905. Standing at the beginning of his career, it serves as a kind of microcosm of the architect's earliest involvement with the arts of Japan.

Darwin Denice Martin (1865–1935), philanthropist and business leader, was identified for almost half a century with the civic and industrial life of Buffalo (ill. 31). Typical of many Wright clients, he was a self-taught, self-made millionaire, described as a workaholic and a diamond in the rough. By the age of twelve Martin had left home and was selling soap door to door in New York City for the Larkin Company, a soap manufacturer and mail-order business with new, incentive-based marketing techniques. At fourteen, in 1879, he was sent to the company's Buffalo headquarters. Seven years later, by age twenty-one, he was made general manager. He became a director in 1892 and the following year was made secretary, or merchandise manager, a position he held until his retirement in 1925. Throughout his life he was committed to improving the cultural, artistic, and educational institutions of the city. His interest in education no doubt stemmed from his own scanty formal studies.[1] A successful, energetic businessman, with a keen interest in modern technology, he was open-minded and willing to be an innovator.

Martin was co-owner of Martin and Martin, makers of E-Z stove and shoe polish in Chicago, with his brother William E. Martin, who had commissioned Wright to build a house in Oak Park in 1902. W. E. Martin enthusiastically recommended the architect to his younger brother as "one of nature's *noblemen*… highly educated and polished, but *no dude*—a straightforward businesslike man with high ideals…. You will fall in love with him in 10 min. conversation—he will build you the finest most sensible house in Buffalo—you will be the *envy* of every rich man in Buffalo…it will be talked about all over the east."[2] He was absolutely right. Darwin Martin immediately invited Wright to Buffalo to discuss designs for a new office building for Martin's employer, John D. Larkin (1845–1926), and to inspect

the large, flat property on Jewett Parkway where he proposed to erect a complex of buildings, including two houses, one for the George Bartons, his sister Dorothy and his brother-in-law, and one for himself and his wife, Isabelle ("Belle"). The Barton residence was begun in the fall of 1903, and Martin's a year later, on the eve of Wright's trip to Japan, and concurrently with Wright's new administration building for the Larkin Company.[3] Martin was intoxicated by his contact with Wright (his daughter later said that he was hypnotized by Wright), and was persuaded from the outset that money was too gross a subject to take into account when working with a true artist. He gave his architect carte blanche.

Working for Martin with an unlimited budget, Wright could "indulge his most extravagant ideas about the fittings and furnishings of a Prairie House."[4] The house was accordingly large and lavish in its details. Everything was designed or supervised by Wright—lamps and lighting fixtures, all of the furniture, including a grand piano, the art-glass windows, rugs, hangings, even the garden—creating a total unity in keeping with the ideals of the Arts and Crafts movement. As noted by Grant Manson, a Wright historian, "apart from some good Japanese decorative objects, always harmonious with Wright's style, there was almost nothing in the Martin house that was not a product of his own fertile mind."[5] In Wright's philosophy of architecture "the very chairs and tables, cabinets, and even musical instruments, where practicable, are of the building itself, never fixtures upon it."[6]

A stunning glass mosaic of wisteria, a popular Japanese design motif, wrapped around four faces of the double-sided chimney between the living room and entrance hall (ill. 32). Just as the gold or silver leaf on a Japanese screen reflects light from the garden by day or candlelight at night, bringing a warm glow to the dark interiors of Japanese castles and temples, so, too, the Martins' mosaic must have sparkled inside the dark, cavernous space of the squat living room, where the only source of daylight was blocked by the overhanging roof of the large porch.

On a luxury commission such as the Martin residence, Wright worked with a number of gifted craftsmen and independent designers. The fireplace design, which would have

31.
Darwin D. Martin and
his son in one of
Wright's barrel chairs.
c. 1908–12

32. Frank Lloyd Wright.
Darwin D. Martin
House, Buffalo, New
York. Living room
fireplace with wisteria
mosaic. c. 1908

Hanging on a brick pier
to the left is a late-
eighteenth-century pillar
print (*hashira-e*) by
Isoda Koryūsai.

been closely supervised by the architect, has been attributed to the Chicago artist Blanche Ostertag, and the glassmaker was Orlando Giannini (1861–1928) of Giannini and Hilgart, an art-glass company in Chicago.[7] The mosaic deteriorated and was destroyed after the house was abandoned in the 1920s. Only a few pieces of the original survive: some dull gold background tiles, some green leaves, and a taupe fragment that may have come from a spray of cascading wisteria blossoms. For the interior Wright chose the warm, autumnal colors that he always favored: brown, golden yellow, orange, and green.

It was about the time of the Martin commission that Wright started opening up interior spaces to create a low, horizontal flow of space that is also characteristic of Japanese residential architecture. He began to dissolve walls, a revolutionary concept. Walls were associated with the boxy houses and boxy rooms that he so despised. The dining room, living room, and library in the Martin house are separated only by clusters of free-standing, square brick piers; the central fireplace is also free-standing. The architect used russet Roman brick both inside and out, a bold attempt to break down the distinction between the exterior and interior of a house.

Although Wright did not go to Japan until the spring of 1905, when the Martin house was already under construction, "an obviously derivative element appears prominently in the design. The low band of molding running throughout the house just above head level is the equivalent of the *nageshi* band in Japanese domestic architecture, used to define spaces within larger spaces, as it does in the Martin house."[8] In Japan, sliding doors (*fusuma*) run in channels in the bottom of the *nageshi* to create separate rooms, as seen in ill. 33. There is a stylized chan-

nel in the bottom of the Martin house moldings (a vestigial *nageshi*), and the rooms are separated by heavy curtains (*portières*) running on brass rods directly beneath the bands.

By 1906 the Martins were finally settled in their new home and adding the finishing touches to the interior decoration. They began purchasing prints as soon as they moved in. In February, Martin reminded Wright that the immediate necessities still pending for the house included—in addition to the specifications for such things as dining room chairs—a collection of Japanese prints. By early March, Wright, who would open his Hiroshige exhibition later that month at the Art Institute, had sent off a package to Buffalo: "A word about the prints," he wrote Martin, adopting the self-confident tone typical of a dealer. "I have selected remarkable specimens in perfect condition. Then, they are rare at any price. I have marked them at what seems to me a low figure as the market prices go. I am not pretending to sell them to you at cost. I hope you will like them."[9] Wright visited Buffalo on 16 March and may have helped Mrs. Martin hang the prints at that time. Later that year, in a letter to Isabelle, he gave detailed instructions on dimensions and colors for mats for their prints. These included some vertical diptychs by Hiroshige (Wright called them "panels") to be hung as "a good sized decoration—just the thing needed" on the brick piers in the living room.[10] Entering the Martins' front hallway, for example, visitors faced Hiroshige's goshawk on a pine bough of about 1852, displayed on a pier between the hall and the living room (ill. 34). It was visible from many vantage points.

Large vertical prints were ideally suited for the regularly spaced brick piers that are a special feature of the Martin house.

33.
Utagawa Toyoharu (1735–1814). *Perspective Picture: Snow-viewing Banquet (Uki-e yukimi shuen no zu)*. c. 1771. Color woodcut, *ōban*. The Art Institute of Chicago, Clarence Buckingham Collection, 1925 (1925.3184)

Wright sold this print to Buckingham in June 1911.

Opposite

34.
Martin House, Buffalo. Entrance hall and view down the pergola toward the conservatory. c. 1908

A Hiroshige *kakemono-e* purchased from Wright hangs on a brick pier.

Color woodcuts with strong, simple patterns could hold their own against the aggressive surface of Wright's brick with its deeply raked joints. Most of the Martin prints have survived and some are in the original muted gold mats designed by Wright to pick up on the matte gold effect of bronze powder mixed with varnish that is painted on the mortar joints between bricks. The prints are toned and faded from exposure to light (the vegetable pigments are fugitive) but were probably in that condition when Wright sold them: the warm colors—brown, gray, and pinks—harmonize nicely with the russet brick walls. (It is very rare to find pillar prints in fine condition. They seem to have suffered more than others from exposure and mishandling by their original Japanese owners.)

The South Room was a comfortable reception space used by the family as a living room and for entertaining (it is relatively sunny). For this room Wright selected Hiroshige bird-and-flower images and landscapes from the Tōkaidō series, as well as prints by Katsukawa Shunshō (1726–1792):

> I have wrenched my heart strings and have put in two of my set by the peerless Shunsho, which you may have for the spaces each side of the South Room fireplace if you will let me have them some day when I might want to sell the set intact to keep me from going "over the hill." They will be fine, the rose color will be fine with the green wall.[11]

The "green" wall color was a combination of gold and green known as Dutch metal. Recent color analysis indicates that the ceiling of the South Room was also a light bronze (bottle green

covered with gold wash). In the Martin house collection there are still two rose-colored (but badly faded) figure prints by the "peerless" Shunshō, probably the very ones Wright recommended for the spaces on either side of the reception room fireplace; he actually included a measured drawing of their mat dimensions. They were originally in a three-volume illustrated book, *Mirror of Beautiful Women of the Green Houses* (*Seiro bijin awase sugata kagami*), published in 1776. Wright must have cannibalized the book and removed the pages to sell them separately—a common practice for dealers. The book is, indeed, regarded as a masterpiece.

In Clarence Fuermann's 1908 view of the South Room the Shunshō prints are not in evidence, but we see a Hiroshige landscape (obscured by flowers) to the right of the fireplace (another hung to the left) and a pillar print by Isoda Koryūsai (active 1764–88) on the brick pier close to the front door, at the right (ills. 35, 36). Perhaps it was Wright himself who positioned Isabelle in her reception room arranging flowers beside this pillar print of young lovers rescuing a kite that has been caught in a flowering tree; the close-spaced vertical slats of the fence contrast effectively with the horizontal striation of the Martin house brick wall. Mrs. Martin's graceful pose and the lines of her gown deliberately echo those of the figures in the print, creating a sort of body art.[12]

What Wright liked to see hanging on the walls of his clients' homes were Japanese prints, and, in the manner of the great dealer Joseph Duveen, he encouraged his clients to purchase these from his own stock. The Japanese print resonated with the quest for simplicity that was fundamental to the American Arts and Crafts movement. In a 1916 issue of *The Craftsman*, an influential magazine published by the furniture manufacturer Gustave Stickley (1858–1942), the Japanese print was enlisted as a "reformer" with "power to influence home decoration": putting up one good print would lead a homemaker to gradually remove all of the crude bric-à-brac crowding her walls.[13] Those who worked with Wright followed his lead: his Oak Park office manager and close friend Isabel Roberts (1871–1955) hung a pillar print on either side of the brick fireplace in the living room of the home Wright designed for her in 1908. Architect William E. Drummond (1876–1946), Wright's chief draftsman in Oak Park, also used a pillar print as the sole decoration in his own living room.[14]

36.
Mrs. Darwin D. (Isabelle R.) Martin arranging flowers in the South Room of the Martin House. 1912

A pillar print (*hashira-e*) by Isoda Koryūsai purchased from Wright creates a strong accent on a brick pier (see also ill. 35). It shows a young man beside a fence holding the string of a kite supported by a girl above him.

Opposite

35.
Martin House, Buffalo. South Room with prints

This photograph was published in *Architectural Record*, March 1908.

Frederick William Gookin (1853–1936) and Clarence Buckingham (1854–1913) were two early stars of the Japanese art world in Chicago. Born in Vermont, Gookin grew up in Joliet, Illinois, and began his career as a manager at Northwestern National Bank in Chicago (ill. 37). Buckingham's father was president of the bank and the two collectors may have met in this context. After serving as assistant city treasurer from 1901 to 1902, Gookin left the world of banking to become a full-time consultant on Japanese prints. His own collection, begun in the 1880s, was one of the earliest of its kind in this country. (Three years after his death in 1936 his daughter, Nathalie, presented the Art Institute with 1,502 ukiyo-e prints, more than 300 illustrated books, and several paintings, the bulk of her father's estate.) Gookin was closely associated with the Chicago Literary Club, a club for professional men with an interest in literature, located on the third floor of the old building of the Art Institute. He served as secretary-treasurer for forty years and as president in 1921. He gave his first lecture on Japanese art at the club in 1888 in conjunction with the club's exhibition of early Japanese ink paintings on loan from the dynamic Paris-based Japanese art dealer Hayashi Tadamasa.[15] A stickler for detail and a rather talented self-taught graphic designer, Gookin was a scholarly man with a conservative manner and a prim, professorial appearance. (One contemporary also characterized him as a social climber and a name dropper.)[16] Although his only trip to Japan came toward the end of his career, in 1925, he soon gained recognition as an authority in his new field and was responsible for the serious and well-informed cataloguing of numerous collections includ-

ing those of Buckingham, Charles Freer in Detroit, the Spaulding brothers in Boston, the New York Public Library, the Metropolitan Museum of Art, and the Worcester Art Museum. Gookin had considerable influence through his many exhibitions and publications, and through his consulting work, which included appraisals and conservation.[17] Occasionally he also sold his own prints. His lectures drew enviably large crowds: 350 people came to hear him speak at the Japan Society in New York in 1911, among them the Japanese ambassador.[18] Like most of his contemporaries, Gookin was unable to read Japanese and relied on the assistance of Japanese friends.

Buckingham was a gregarious business tycoon who sat on the board of directors of several banks and at one time served as president of the Northwestern Elevated Railroad Company (ill. 38). He bought his first Japanese woodcuts in 1894 from Boussod-Valadon and Company in New York and never looked back. One of his most significant purchases was the group of six hundred prints he acquired in 1909–10 from the widow of renowned Japanophile Ernest Fenollosa for $34,000. These included a substantial portion of the early-eighteenth-century figure prints (the so-called "primitives") for which his collection is best known. Another of his many sources was Yamanaka and Company in New York, the largest and most experienced Asian art firm in America. By the time of his premature death from heart failure in August 1913 (he died at the relatively young age of fifty-eight, a year after his father), Buckingham had accumu-

38.
Clarence Buckingham

37.
Frederick Gookin.
c. 1915.

lated an outstanding group of almost 1,500 ukiyo-e. They remain the centerpiece of the department of Asian art at the Art Institute, where he was a trustee for thirty years.

Buckingham was generous in sharing his collection with others and enjoyed hosting day-long print study meetings at his home, with Gookin presiding as master of ceremonies. Among his guests at such events were his sisters, Lucy Maud (?–1920) and Kate Sturges Buckingham (1858–1937); the artist Helen Hyde (1868–1919), who lived in Tokyo for fifteen years producing popular woodcut images of exotic Japan; Howard Mansfield, a New York lawyer; Judson D. Metzgar (1869–1956), an attorney from Moline, Illinois; Arthur Davison Ficke, an attorney, poet, and print connoisseur from Davenport, Iowa, just across the river from Moline; Charles H. Chandler, a businessman from Evanston; and the young Helen C. Gunsaulus (1886–1954), a graduate of the University of Chicago who became assistant curator of Japanese ethnology at the Field Museum and later worked at the Art Institute.[19]

Buckingham, who never married, left his collection to his sisters and they wisely put it on loan to the Art Institute for safekeeping. Because Gookin had been mentor and de facto cu-rator to Buckingham, the museum appointed him keeper of the Buckingham Print Collection in 1914 and he cared for and exhibited the prints for the next twenty years.[20] Kate Buckingham donated them to the museum in her brother's name in 1925 (ill. 39). Kate, with Gookin as agent and advisor, added another two thousand prints to her brother's collection by the time of her death, including a few from Wright; she acquired the entire Alexander Moslé collection in 1928 and bought forty-five Sharaku from Chandler in 1934.

THE 1908 PRINT EXHIBITION

It is clear that Wright used museum exhibitions throughout his life to publicize his work as an architect, disseminate his views on aesthetics, and promote his other passion, Japanese art. The architecture historian Edgar Kaufmann, Jr. (1910–1989), has shown that during the seven decades of Wright's working life there was scarcely a year when his own work was not being exhibited, except the period of 1917–28, when he was working in Japan and California. He was a regular contributor of anywhere

from one to more than thirty items in the annual show sponsored by the Chicago Architectural Club at the Art Institute. This show was an important cultural event in the city and Wright, while not a member of the organization, was featured in 1902, 1907, and 1913.

In March 1908 Wright contributed 218 of his Japanese prints to a huge exhibition of ukiyo-e at the Art Institute. Thought to be the largest such display ever mounted in America (prints were double and triple hung), it included a total of 655 examples drawn from a handful of local collections. (There were only about fifty prints in the museum's permanent collection at the time.)[21] Wright was the major lender. The others, all from Chicago, were Buckingham with 162 prints, Gookin with 130

examples, Dr. J. Clarence Webster (1863–1950) with 115, and John H. Wrenn (1841–1911) with twenty-four.

Gookin's 132-page illustrated catalogue quickly sold out. As the acknowledged scholar in the group, he served as a kind of acting curator with responsibility for the proper chronological ordering of prints in six temporary exhibition galleries (ill. 40). He hung the so-called "primitives," early black-and-white and hand-colored works, in the first gallery; Harunobu and Kiyonaga dominated two rooms; actor prints by Shunshō, a favorite of both Gookin and Wright, had a room of their own; Utamaro, Sharaku, Toyokuni, and Shumman hung together; and the finale was an extravagant selection of landscapes by Hokusai and Hiroshige. (The Hiroshige were mainly from Wright's collection.) Not mentioned

Opposite

40.
Exhibition of Japanese
prints at the Art Insti-
tute of Chicago. 1908.
Installation designed
by Wright

in the catalogue were several rooms hung with *surimono*, a special type of privately published Japanese print that Wright adored (ill. 41). There was didactic material as well. Wright loaned a wood keyblock (the cherry wood block used for printing the black outlines) for a theatrical design by Utagawa Kunisada II (1823–1880) dating from 1862. (The block is still in the collection of the Frank Lloyd Wright Foundation.) A Japanese brush, nine woodcut engraving tools, and a baren for printing were borrowed from the artist Arthur Wesley Dow, who was now an influential teacher at Columbia University Teachers College in New York. Dow had toured Japan in 1903 and was the first American artist to attempt his own color woodcuts in the Japanese manner.[22]

Wright designed the installation, which attracted much attention and favorable comment. The *Bulletin of the Art Institute*

41.
Surimono galleries with
print stands in the 1908
exhibition of Japanese
prints at the Art Insti-
tute of Chicago. Installation and print stands
designed by Wright

for April 1908 noted that the prints were in neutral color mats just as they came from the collectors' portfolios. They had narrow frames of unfinished chestnut and were suspended from green cords that made a charming arrangement of vertical lines against walls covered with grayish-pink paper. The works were separated by artist but carefully grouped for decorative effect. The stark simplicity of the design is surprisingly modern. By alternating the length of the cords, Wright created a rhythm of vertical and horizontal lines that suggests the abstract geometry of Piet Mondrian.

Additional hanging space was secured in the larger galleries by using free-standing screens covered with the same gray paper used on the walls. These were flanked by posts bearing pots of Japanese dwarf trees and azaleas in bloom, and hung below with pillar prints. The subdivision of space with "floating" screens as well as pillars for showing off long vertical prints recreates many of the display concepts the architect had used to show his own work in the annual exhibition sponsored by the Chicago Architectural Club in these same galleries the year before. The bonsai and flower arrangements were probably supervised by the Chicago Horticultural Society, but plants were always an important element in Wright's approach to interior decoration. Continuously circulating space and extended vistas are somewhat reminiscent of the interiors of his Prairie Houses. Kaufmann noted that in the early decades of Wright's career "his exhibition designs were demonstrations of his architectural style."[23] (Later he used another, more casual approach.) By this time, as we know, Wright was using pillar prints on posts and piers in the homes of some of his clients.

The 1908 exhibition marks the first appearance of special print stands designed by Wright and used later to good effect in his own home (ill. 42). Shown in the *surimono* galleries (see ill. 41), they provide an architectural frame for prints and resemble nothing so much as miniature versions of the austere, high-backed dining chairs he favored during the Oak Park years. Only one such stand is known to have survived and close inspection shows it to be more decorative than practical; the prints are secured by a strip of wood trim that must be nailed in place, an awkward system that precludes easy rotation. Once a print is "installed" in one of these stands, it is probably there for the duration.

Wright's work as an architect had its first major critical reception a few months after the Art Institute display. The *Architectural Record* of May 1908 featured illustrations of his drawings and buildings, including the Martin residence, as well as his own essay "In the Cause of Architecture."

42.
Frank Lloyd Wright.
Print stand. c. 1908–14.
Stained oak, 35½ x
6⅛ x 5¾ in. Seymour
H. Persky Collection

MRS. SALLIE CASEY THAYER FROM KANSAS

As Wright raised the visibility of his collection and became a full-fledged dealer, he increased his client base, adding Sallie Casey Thayer (1856–1925) to his list of conquests. Mrs. Thayer, a Southern belle from Kentucky, was the widow of a Kansas City department store owner, William Bridges Thayer, who died prematurely in 1907. She was the doyenne of Kansas City art lovers, helping to found the Fine Arts Institute (now the Kansas City Art Institute) in 1907 with the hope that it would be the first museum and art school in Kansas City. When she returned to Kansas City in 1911 she was elected a trustee. Thayer moved to Chicago in the summer of 1908 to spend three years studying its art schools and museums, thus launching a decade of travel and collecting during which time she assembled a wide variety of European and Asian art. She purchased her first ukiyo-e prints in the summer of 1908 in Chicago. By the end of the year she was buying compulsively and in quantity—$5,000 for hundreds of prints at a time—from Earl Deakin's gallery on the second floor of the Fine Arts Building. Deakin and his father had been art dealers in Yokohama for many years and their Chicago gallery reportedly had the largest inventory of Asian art in the country.

People often ask, "Where did Frank Lloyd Wright buy Japanese art?" There isn't much of a paper trail in the early years but Thayer's invoices, preserved with her collection, certainly indicate that there were ample sources right in Chicago. Aside from Deakin, she made purchases from Maruyama of the Toyo Company, an importer of Japanese art on the corner of Michigan and Monroe; from Robert Bensabott on Wabash Avenue; and from Ito Tokumatsu on Clark Street. Ito advertised "especially old prints by famous artists." Thayer's Asian purchases include Buddhist shrines, Japanese armor, embroidered textiles, hair ornaments, and stone lanterns, not to mention screens, hanging scrolls, sculpture, jade bowls, snuff bottles, and netsuke. The Art Institute gave her its seal of approval when it exhibited her Chinese, Japanese, and Korean art in the spring of 1909.[24] Perhaps this exhibition brought her to the attention of Frank Lloyd Wright.

As far as can be documented, Thayer's first purchase of prints from the architect was in September 1909 when she paid $2,750 for thirty single-sheet images of Hokusai's *The Thirty-six Views of Mount Fuji*. A few months later she bought sixty-two prints by various artists for $2,000 at the New Gallery, a sales gallery of the Chicago Academy of Fine Arts, an art school at 6 East Madison Street. These were items Wright had placed on consignment (he was in Europe that winter) and the gallery took a 10-percent commission. The curator of the gallery, Mrs. Herman J. Hall, was one of the local Asian art experts; she lectured frequently on Japanese prints and East Asian culture.[25] Wright continued to do business with Thayer: in January 1911 they concluded another deal for a whopping $10,075 worth of prints.[26] Thayer donated her wide-ranging collection, including over one thousand Japanese prints (of which hundreds are Hiroshige and Hokusai landscapes) to the University of Kansas in Lawrence in 1917 as a memorial to her husband; it is now housed in the university's Spencer Museum of Art. Wright later often referred with pride to the "collection in Kansas" that he had helped to form.

In 1933 Thayer's daughter-in-law wrote to Wright hoping to sell back a few remaining prints.[27] Wright's finances were at an all-time low then, and he had to forego the opportunity.

NEGOTIATING WITH THE SOCIETY OF FINE ARTS IN MINNEAPOLIS

In the summer of 1908, after visiting Minneapolis to consult with Francis W. Little (1859–1923) about plans for a new house, Wright opened negotiations with Edwin H. Hewitt (1874–1939) for a loan exhibition of two hundred Japanese prints at the Minneapolis Society of Fine Arts (later the Minneapolis Institute of Arts) (ill. 43). Hewitt was an ambitious young Minneapolis architect with a degree from MIT and the École des Beaux-Arts in Paris. He had been elected to the society's board of directors in 1905 and served as president from 1910 through 1912.[28] Japonisme was flourishing in Minneapolis in those years. One founding member of the society's board of directors was a serious student of Japanese design. John Scott Bradstreet

43.
Edwin Hewitt

(1845–1914) took the first of many trips to Asia in 1886, and by 1905, as the city's most fashionable interior designer, he was employing Japanese craftsmen in Minneapolis in his art-and-crafts studio, the Bradstreet Craftshouse. Here he sold Asian antiques, designed furniture inspired by Japanese motifs, and even aspired to remodel an island in downtown Lake of the Isles with a pagoda and *torii* shrine gate as a re-creation of Miyajima, a shrine island in the Inland Sea.[29]

The society's plan to borrow prints from Wright fell through in the end, in part because of the architect's high insurance valuations ($20,000, or $100 for each print), but also because new interests took him to Europe in 1909. Correspondence with Hewitt, however, indicates that Wright was taken seriously as a print collector, and that his collection was already a substantial one. Hewitt wrote the architect on 20 June 1908:

> Apropos of our conversation at the time you called upon me I wish to take up again the question of obtaining your Japanese prints for exhibition in Minneapolis next fall. This exhibition, I am sure, would be properly hung, displayed and advertised well. The Society of Fine Arts would naturally assume all the charges of collecting, boxing, insuring, transportation, etc., and would take the most extreme care of your prints.
>
> Do you think that it would be possible to obtain the consent of other private owners in Chicago to send a selection of prints at the same time with yours?
>
> We would appreciate very much your courtesy in permitting us to see your prints in Minneapolis; personally I am more than anxious since I believe it would be most educational and something entirely out of our experience.[30]

Wright readily agreed to the idea:

> The transportation charges would be small—four or five dollars, I suppose—and the cost of installation depends entirely on the manner in which you chose to do it. The prints would probably be worth eighteen or twenty thousand dollars and a considerable wall space would be necessary, in fact the size of the exhibit would be determined only by the wall surface at your disposal. The prints ought to be exhibited under

glass, and the cost of framing them we found here to be—borrowing the glass—about fifty cents each; you would probably have two hundred prints.[31]

By October 1909 the matter was still up in the air and Hewitt was trying to arrange a joint exhibition for the coming winter with the Saint Paul Institute of Arts and Letters, which had a large, well-equipped gallery. Hewitt was unaware that Wright had left for Europe the previous month in the company of Mamah Borthwick Cheney (1869–1914), an Oak Park neighbor and client. (He built a house for Mr. and Mrs. Cheney in 1903.) After burying himself in his work for twenty years while his wife raised their six children, Wright had fallen in love with another woman. His departure and the ensuing scandal it provoked brought an end to the Oak Park era; without his leadership the remaining staff soon disbanded and went their separate ways. On 16 September Wright had written to his friend D. D. Martin: "I am leaving the office to its own devices, deserting my wife and the children for one year, in search of a spiritual adventure, hoping it will be no worse."[32] Wright, his eldest son, the architect Lloyd Wright (1890–1978), and Oak Park draftsman Taylor A. Woolley spent most of the next year in Italy preparing drawings of Wright's work for the lavish folio of drawings of the architect's buildings published in Berlin in 1910 by Ernst Wasmuth A.G., the great art publishing house (see ill. 30). This monograph and its companion volume of photographs, *Frank Lloyd Wright: Ausgeführte Bauten* (also referred to as the *Sonderheft*), published in 1911, are known as the Wasmuth portfolios.

Left behind in Oak Park, Catherine dutifully took over her husband's correspondence with Hewitt: "Mr. Wright is in Europe and is not to return for some time. His prints are here in a vault and cannot be taken away without a sufficient insurance" (ill. 44).[33] Shortly thereafter she followed up with a second note to Hewitt: "It might not be possible to hear from Mr. Wright within the next month as he may not remain in the one place and I am willing that the prints be exhibited by you under the proper protection of insurance and glass and packing.... They are our treasures, still I would rather have them giving pleasure than shut up in the vault."[34]

Hewitt had by this time found a better solution. The Chicago Academy of Fine Arts (which Wright used himself as a venue for print sales) had agreed to lend prints for exhibition without any fee for insurance and framing—the prints would simply be matted and mounted with thumb tacks and they would also be for sale. It is not clear whether Catherine agreed to participate on these terms.

44.
Catherine Wright
and her son Llewellyn.
c. 1907

In October 1910, when the prodigal architect returned from Europe (Mrs. Cheney stayed behind for some months in Berlin), he was a social outcast, shunned by former friends. His conduct shook Oak Park from top to bottom. In order to sort out his affairs Wright temporarily moved back in with his family, who put up a brave front of being happily reunited. He wrote Martin as follows:

> At least I will know who my friends are now—anyway. They are surprisingly few. Never in any sense popular, always an affront to the intelligence of the plain man, I have finally kicked the props from under what tolerance he ever had for me, and nothing but some extraordinary virtue can save me for my work.... Now I am hanging to you all who have encouraged me to rise.[35]

Around this time Wright began the practice of using prints as collateral for loans: Martin in Buffalo and Little in Minneapolis both loaned him money, accepting in exchange boxes of prints they did not want and of which they did not know the value. Wright's print sales during these years represent impressive sums, to be sure, but the profits were never enough. To be fair, the impecunious artist is, if anything, a stereotype of modern society, fondly romanticized in opera and literature. Martin, like any patron of the arts, probably hoped a little of the glamor and glory of America's greatest architect would rub off on him. The architect's financial problems were aggravated by the expense of supporting two households after he left his wife and family. There was the cost of remodeling his Oak Park home and studio in order to create a rental facility that would provide income for Catherine and the six children, two of whom were now in college—yet another expense. Then there was the $6,000 mortgage to be paid off on the Oak Park property. Last but not least, in 1911, the year Wright first sold prints to Buckingham, he built an expensive new home called Taliesin (Welsh for "shining brow") on two hundred acres of ancestral land near Spring Green in southern Wisconsin, forty miles west of Madison. Here he would live with Mamah Borthwick, who was now divorced and using her maiden name.

Martin continued to support Wright through good times and bad. Conservative by most standards—he expressed his strong disapproval of Wright's new liaison—he nonetheless endorsed the controversial architect during this time of trial. Reaching out to save a drowning man, he took over the bulk of the mortgage on Wright's Oak Park home, lent him money, helped underwrite publication of the Wasmuth portfolios, and even offered to serve as his intermediary in the sale of prints, with the following proviso: "I hope that the possession and pursuit of this hobby is not to be allowed to interfere seriously with the main question which is the practice of your profession. I hope you will keep that first in view at all times."[36] In November 1910 Martin generously urged Wright to send along a few dozen Japanese prints and some Oriental "fancy-work": "Every piece sent should be marked with the price at which you will sell it. We will, if you send enough, hold a bazaar for a few of your friends here."[37]

In the meantime Wright had sent off a panicky proposal to Larkin, president of the Larkin Company in Buffalo, asking for a loan of $20,000 and assuring him that this could be repaid quickly through sales of his Berlin books and his Japanese prints. Valuing his collection at $45,000, he claimed that he could easily make $10,000 by selling some prints. (A few months later he actually made more than twice that amount on a sale to Buckingham.) Larkin does not seem to have responded.[38] (The value of Wright's prints was often inflated: in the fall of 1911 one newspaper account referred to Wright's "marvelous and much-envied $200,000 collection of Japanese prints.")[39]

Martin began to act as middleman and confidant in the complex financial arrangements that had developed between the architect and another of his early patrons, Francis Little. The Littles were prosperous, energetic midwesterners keenly interested in the arts. They were active founding members of the Art Institute of Chicago; Mary Trimble Little (1868–1941), originally from Iowa, had studied music in Cologne for several years before her marriage. Francis Little, born in Illinois, trained as a lawyer in South Dakota but eventually owned a public utilities company in Peoria, Illinois, and later became vice president of a bank in Minneapolis. They commissioned Wright to build their home in Peoria in 1902, and when they moved to Minnesota to be near Mrs. Little's parents five years later, he was again their choice of architect for a country house overlooking Lake Minnetonka in

45.
The Littles showing off their new Frank Lloyd Wright house in Wayzata, Minnesota. c. 1915. Stereopticon photograph taken shortly after the house was built

Wayzata, near Minneapolis (ill. 45). As Edgar Kaufmann observed, "when the Littles turned to Wright the second time, they became involved with his rapidly changing personal and professional life.... They also were willing to postpone their building plans while Wright found his way through the entanglements of marital separation and a new relationship.... It was four years before the permanent structure was begun, and two more before it was habitable."[40] Known as one of the last great statements of Wright's Prairie School style, the house, completed in 1915, was dismantled in 1972. The living room, one of the largest Wright had built (Mrs. Little intended it as a recital hall), was installed in the American Wing of the Metropolitan Museum of Art in 1984, furnished much as it was when the Littles used it. Three of the Little's landscape prints by Hiroshige form the sole wall decoration (ill. 46).[41]

The Littles were not print collectors as such, but over the years they accumulated more than three hundred of Wright's prints as well as quite a few Chinese and Turkoman carpets, a legacy of the architect's ongoing financial insolvency and poor bookkeeping (ill. 47).[42] Little (like Martin) advanced funds for both the Oak Park mortgage and for the handsome Wasmuth portfolios. By 1909 Wright was in debt to Little for almost $11,000, of which $2,500 was secured by a mortgage on the Oak Park property in the form of Illinois trust deed notes and about $8,500 by a block of prints stored in the vaults of the Chicago Safe Deposit Company.[43]

Shortly before his first big print sale to Buckingham in January 1911 ("Buckingham is coming out with Gookin...and the game commences"), Wright tried desperately to retrieve some of his better (museum quality) prints from Little in partial exchange for six pillar prints. He then rashly offered Little $7,000 to release the prints; Little agreed but only if Wright would send him the full $8,000.[44] This was an embarrassing situation, as Wright did not have $7,000, let alone $8,000. Their complex financial negotiations continued. The architect's state of mind is vividly conveyed in a letter to Martin excoriating Little as a "commercial minded coward":

> After deducting my natural desire to throw the money at Mr. Little...I wrote him a letter yesterday—asking him to release those prints needed in the deal with Buckingham—if I would substitute a package of unwanted prints [pillar prints "unwanted" by Buck-

46.
Frank Lloyd Wright.
Francis W. Little House,
Wayzata, Minnesota.
Living room with Japanese print on the wall.
Photographed around
1960. The room is now
installed in the Metropolitan Museum of Art,
New York

ingham] which I have been holding for a rise and which at the same basis of estimate I consider worth $10,000.

The prints I want are valued in his list at $6800.... He knows well I am not going to abscond—I think he feels perhaps that he must put the pressure on hard and *sting* me to redouble my efforts to pay him out.[45]

Two days later a hasty note followed: "I offered [Little] $10,000 worth of prints to release $6000 worth so I could make a deal. He has—but does this look good to you—when a man is down? I want to admit the best possible construction."[46]

Little sent a letter the next day, 6 December 1910, estimating Wright's indebtedness to him at about $11,000.

> If Mr. Martin will sign a note with you for one half of this due in 90 days at 6% I will when it is received release the prints mentioned in your letter...and at that time will accept the six pillar prints at $1000 and apply this amount on the remainder of your indebtedness to me.[47]

Little's attempt to be businesslike (he was, after all, a banker) annoyed Wright, who fired off a petulant letter to Martin the

47.
Utagawa Hiroshige. *Shōno, White Rain* (*Shōno, Hakuu*), from the series *Fifty-three Stations of the Tōkaidō* (*Tōkaidō gojūsan tsugi no uchi*). 1833–34. Color woodcut, *ōban*. The Minneapolis Institute of Arts, Gift of Francis Little, 1917. Ex coll. Frank Lloyd Wright

The Tōkaidō was the main roadway linking Edo (modern Tokyo) and Kyoto, which are nearly three hundred miles apart. There were fifty-three checkpoints along this route, including Shōno. See also ills. 9, 29, 197.

next day: "Let us in heavens name get rid of Little. Does he suspect I am trying to get money to liquidate a financial obligation to a woman or what does he think?…He is going to get all he can, evidently…. His attitude is doing me absolute harm, inside."[48] Martin figured that Wright's debt to Little had now been reduced to $7,500: $2,500 was secured by Little's mortgage on the Oak Park property and now $1,000 was accounted for by pillar prints. He then offered to take on responsibility for half of the unsecured portion of the loan, making this request of Wright: "Whatever you realize from the sale of Prints, of which amount I can form no estimate, knowing nothing of the business, is to be first applied to the payment due to Mr. Little in full of all his claims and next to me."[49] Martin refused to loan outright the thousands of dollars Wright needed to buy back Little's prints.

On 30 December 1910 Wright reported to Martin that he had proved the value of his collection by selling one-sixth of his prints to Buckingham for $15,000, and, possibly, as much as $20,000, a figure that would make his entire collection worth about $120,000. The final meeting with Buckingham was set for the following week: "I told him he could take his own time for payment in order to give him every encouragement to blow himself—I know even rich men don't have ready money always." As a postscript he added:

> Buckingham is assisted in his buying by Frederick W. Gookin of Chicago, an acknowledged expert and collector of 15 years standing…. Gookin and I do not agree always on price for he is a "Hiroshige" bear—He let them go by until it was too late—but I am going to have him go through my collection and appraise it from his point of view. This relieves me of the embarrassment of price making. Would you then care to have a couple thousand dollars worth of fine things the intrinsic value of which would never be less but be a good investment at the same time that you derive joy from it. Let me know now and I will lay aside those that would grace your establishment from my viewpoint—Faithfully, Wright.[50]

Wright's prints during these early years (his "priceless treasures," as he called them) were often faded, dirty, and torn. Their margins were trimmed and they were from late printings. This did not trouble the Martins because they were not serious collectors. Martin responded on 4 January 1911:

> Replying to your letter dated Dec. 30th (hooray!). I note with pleasure the sale of at least $15,000 of Prints, which I suppose will, when settlement is obtained, enable you to straighten up financially with everybody….
>
> You will remember that Mrs. Martin asked you for two Prints for the dining-room north window walls, to be possibly somewhat larger than those on the corresponding walls of the library. These, we think, are the only ones we shall want, and these need not be expensive. If beautiful we do not care how unrare they are. Sell the rare ones to Buckingham.[51]

On 13 January Wright confirmed that he had indeed just sold Buckingham about $21,000 worth of prints, not to mention the big sale ($10,075) to Thayer, and $3,000 worth to "another man," a cool $34,000 in total, but he could not restrain himself from adding,

> You make a mistake not to take some of my fine things when you can. They would never be worth less than you would pay for them and would cultivate your taste meantime more than anything else in the world. I hate to see you let them go when you could so well afford to hold a couple of thousand dollars worth of them. I will pick out two anyway, but I have no very 'cheap' ones.[52]

Wright made a second trip to Europe in January 1911 to meet with his German publisher, but also to pick up more prints at a Sotheby's auction in London. The collection of an anonymous importer of Japanese products was being offered on 24–27 January and Wright was hoping to "make his way" at this sale, although he solemnly promised Martin he would be "conservative" and cautious in his purchases.[53] It is entirely possible that Wright bought prints when he was in Europe the year before, as well. Sotheby's, London (then known as Sotheby, Wilkinson and Hodge), was now a leader in the Japanese print market, with two to four sales a year. Even Gookin used this venue when he sold a part of his collection in May 1910.

After returning from Europe Wright sent Martin a hopeful note asking him to take some more prints: "You *need* some of my good ones and I have it in mind to send you a selection to choose from…Mr. and Mrs. [Avery] Coonley have manifested an interest and will probably take some."[54] (There is no immediate follow-up on this tantalizing reference to the Coonleys, for whom Wright had completed a magnificent home in Riverside, Illinois, in 1909.) Martin eventually took a packet of prints with the idea that his wife might be able to sell them to her friends at a tea she planned in early November while her chrysanthemums were in bloom.[55] Some probably ended up on the walls of Martin's home, however. Eleven prints, most still in the Martin house, are itemized on a priced list from Wright to Martin dated 20 December 1911. Martin paid $200 for a rather nice pillar print by Koryūsai dating from the mid-1770s, a parody of the letter-reading scene in act 7 of the kabuki drama *Kanadehon Chūshingura*. The other ten prints were horizontal landscapes by Hiroshige from various series. None of the Hiroshiges are very special (the impressions are poor and the designs are considered modest), but they cost Martin up to $150 each, for a grand total of $990. For purposes of comparison, a complete set of the *Fifty-three Stations* sold for $195 at auction in New York in 1920, when the market was quite strong.[56] Martin was paying a celebrity premium.

By 1912 Wright was again desperate for cash to support his obligations to his family in Oak Park and Martin was simultaneously pressing him for interest payments. Wright urged patience, confirming that he would be able to sell prints, was even then getting them in order for that purpose, but "must look elsewhere for a market and patiently—it is no snapshot affair. They are good security and good property handled intelligently. I need the money from the prints to pay you back and defend the children—and my work."[57]

In April Wright agreed to secure a loan of $4,000 from Martin with 110 Hiroshige landscape prints valued (by Wright) at $8,020. He selected from various series including thirty-nine from the *One Hundred Views of Famous Places in Edo*, a vertical series published by Uoya Eikichi in 1857–58 (see ill. 28). Some of the *Hundred Views* were priced as high as $150 each.[58] Rather than storing the prints in a bank vault, as had been done for Little, Wright put them in a box and sent them directly to Martin for his "study and entertainment," since the Buffalo

house was practically fireproof. "That box of Prints? It's such a little box! (I haven't opened it yet)," his patron moaned. "Could you borrow much at the Hottentot Providence Loan Co. on a box of printed paper that size? 'I am that Hottentot.'"[59] A year later Martin was still grousing about the box of prints, "which may be worth a lot to a connoisseur, but which could not find a market in this sordid community."[60] He had so little interest in Wright's treasures that he never even opened the box, which he still had in his possession as late as 1922.[61]

SUPPORT FROM BUCKINGHAM

Wright sold about three hundred prints to Buckingham between January 1911 and May 1912; Gookin conscientiously recorded the vendor and date of purchase on each Buckingham catalogue card.[62] The group includes some wonderful eighteenth-century figure prints, including examples by Kitagawa Utamaro (c. 1754–1806) (ill. 48). However, 244 of these prints are by Hiroshige, many of them late impressions and in poor condition, toned from mat burn and faded. On some examples the rounded corners of the black keyblock lines framing the image have been squared off with colored pencil, probably by Wright. Is it possible that Buckingham made some purchases simply as a gesture of support for a great architect?

Gookin, who was a loyal friend to Wright, was always the intermediary in transactions with Buckingham, acting as agent. (He may have taken a commission from both men.) On 20 May 1912 he wrote to the architect:

> Mr. Buckingham decided to go on to Buffalo with me last Wednesday so I had a good opportunity to talk to him about your prints. I urged the wisdom of not letting the opportunity slip to take more if he wanted them, and so, on our return we again looked through the Hiroshiges together, and he laid out seven concerning which he has written you. None of the others seem to attract him, so he is willing, as I understand it, to release them and hold the Shunshos as security for the loan.[63]

Buckingham had loaned Wright close to $7,000 and took as security eighty-four actor prints by Shunshō. Gookin (perhaps goaded by Buckingham) worked feverishly to help liquidate this

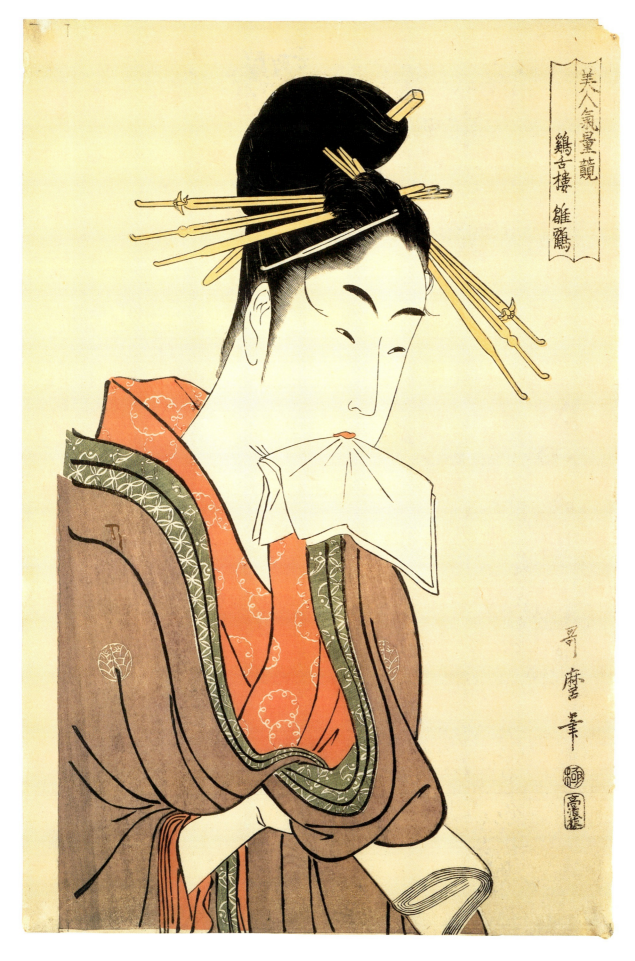

48.
Kitagawa Utamaro.
The Courtesan Hinazuru of the House Called Keizetsurō (*Keizetsurō Hinazuru*), from the series *Comparing the Charms of Beautiful Women* (*Bijin kiryō kurabe*). c. 1794–95. Color woodcut with white mica ground, *ōban*. The Art Institute of Chicago, Clarence Buckingham Collection, 1925 (1925.3047)

Wright sold this print to Clarence Buckingham in 1911.

debt, offering the prints first to the Metropolitan Museum of Art and then to a new client in Boston (probably William Spaulding, of whom more later), who did come through with a big purchase.[64]

Buckingham had already bought some fine Katsukawa-school kabuki actor prints from Wright in January 1911. Shunshō injected a new degree of "realism" in actor portraiture from the late 1760s and was the best of the Katsukawa artists. He had about twenty pupils, the most important being Shunkō (1743–1812), Shun'ei (1762–1819), Shunchō (active 1780s–'90s), and Hokusai. In the 1908 Art Institute exhibition Gookin had given an entire gallery to Shunshō.[65] It is recognized that Wright was a great theater buff; some form of stage, playhouse, or cabaret was integral to his homes over the years. He favored Katsukawa-school prints, a taste he may well have picked up from Gookin, and later boasted that almost all of the actor prints in any of the collections of the world were once his. At one time, so he claimed, he owned 1,100 Katsukawa *hosoban*, woodcuts of small size in narrow, vertical format.[66] What did they mean to him?

AN INTERPRETATION

There was a handful of scholars, like Gookin, who aspired to date each kabuki performance and identify every actor. This was definitely not an issue for most collectors, who, like Wright, were attracted by the purely aesthetic appeal of the Japanese print. It is clear, as Rafael Fernandez points out, that "much of the fascination of Japanese prints rested on the fact that few of their dedicated Western admirers could tell what they were about…. However, lack of knowledge of what information was encoded in a print allowed and encouraged a purely visual experience."[67]

In 1912, drawing on a lecture he had given for the Chicago Woman's Club at the Art Institute at the time of the big 1908 print exhibition, Wright published a booklet entitled *The Japanese Print: An Interpretation* (ill. 49). In it he described the cultural use of prints for Westerners, in particular the mathematics of structure, the "spell-power" or psychic qualities of geometric forms. "Japanese art," he said,

> is a thoroughly structural Art…. And at the beginning of structure lies always and everywhere geometry…. The word structure is here used to describe an organic form—an organization in a very definite manner of parts or elements into a larger unity,—a vital whole…. So, these prints are designs, patterns, in themselves beautiful as such; and, what other meanings they may have are merely incidental, interesting or curious by-products. Broadly stated, then, the first and supreme principle of Japanese aesthetics consists in a stringent simplification by elimination of the insignificant.

This could equally well be a statement of Wright's own philosophy of architecture. He concluded that the mystery of the "spell-

49.
Frank Lloyd Wright. Cover of *The Japanese Print: An Interpretation*. 1912. Book inscribed in pencil "To my dear Frederick W. Gookin from Frank Lloyd Wright June 20, 1912." The Art Institute of Chicago

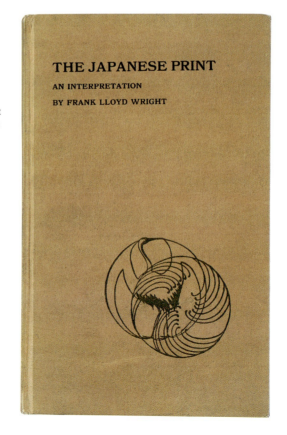

THE JAPANESE PRINT

AN INTERPRETATION

BY FRANK LLOYD WRIGHT

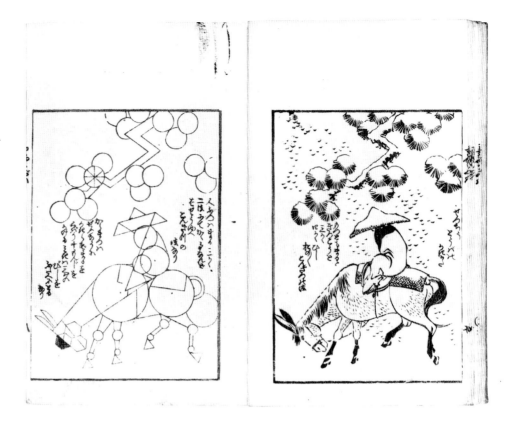

50.
Katsushika Hokusai. *Quick Lessons in Simplified Drawing* (*Ryakuga haya oshie*), vol. 1 (Edo: Kadomaruya Jinsuke, 1812). Woodcut, illustrated book, 8¾ x 6⅟₁₆ in. The Art Institute of Chicago, Martin Ryerson Collection (29732). Ex coll. Louise Norton Brown

Hokusai analyzes the geometrical structure of one of his own drawings of a traditional subject, the eleventh-century Chinese poet and scholar-official Su Dongpo riding under snow-covered pines.

power" of geometry is "reduced by Japanese masters to its scientific elements, as exemplified by certain textbooks by Hokusai, wherein the structural diagrams are clearly given and transformation to material objects shown progressively step by step."[68] Wright is making reference here to an illustrated book of 1812–14 by Hokusai called *Quick Lessons in Simplified Drawing* (*Ryakuga haya oshie*) (ill. 50). As he later explained: "I took with me, when I first read this paper to a women's club in Chicago, a little volume of diagrammatic studies of various plants, animals, nearly everything on earth, by Hokusai. And I separated the plates and took the book apart. It was almost invaluable because I have never seen a copy before or seen one since."[69] This fascinating volume, a didactic manual for the novice artist, focuses on the essence of design, and sets out to prove that everything can be broken down into circles, squares, rhombuses, and triangles. Richard Lane, an ukiyo-e scholar, points out that while Hokusai may actually have taken his idea from seventeenth-century Dutch painting manuals, he made the concept his own and the result is astonishingly modern. Hokusai "somehow managed to foresee significant artistic movements that we tend to think of as belonging to our own times."[70]

As late as 1952, still advocating the Japanese "process of elimination of the insignificant," Wright counseled his apprentices that,

> you can all practice it when you draw, [or] whatever you do…. This process of simplification…—and this is important—is a dramatization of the subject…. To dramatize a thing is to do precisely what a Japanese does with these prints when he draws…. Well, now, buildings can be like that, too…. And what I am saying of the print is apropos of your office as an architect and as a designer of buildings. All these things apply.[71]

By way of analogy he then brought up Mies Van der Rohe's dictum "less is more" and alluded to his own design for the Guggenheim Museum.

HOWARD MANSFIELD: SHUNSHŌ DECLINED

On 30 June 1912 Gookin wrote again with the disappointing news that the Metropolitan Museum of Art in New York, represented by Mansfield (1849–1938), who was acting as de facto curator of Asian art (there was no curator until 1915), had turned down Wright's collection of Shunshō (ill. 51). Gookin had already broached the subject of this sale while he was in New York the previous winter cataloguing the collections at the Metropolitan Museum of Art and the New York Public Library. Wright would have been shocked to know that the straitlaced Gookin secretly wanted him to be tarred and feathered by the philistines in Spring Green for his adulterous behavior with Borthwick, who was now living at Taliesin. "It would be about the best thing that could happen to him," Gookin had assured his wife, Marie, somewhat smugly. "I am done with him, though I should like to sell his Shunsho prints to the Metropolitan Museum if I could make a little by so doing. They are about all he has left."[72] As it turned out, Gookin's Shunshō mission was a failure: "Mr. Mansfield writes me that the conclusion reached was that in view of the very limited extent of the present collection of Japanese prints owned by the museum it would not be advisable to buy so many examples of one school."[73]

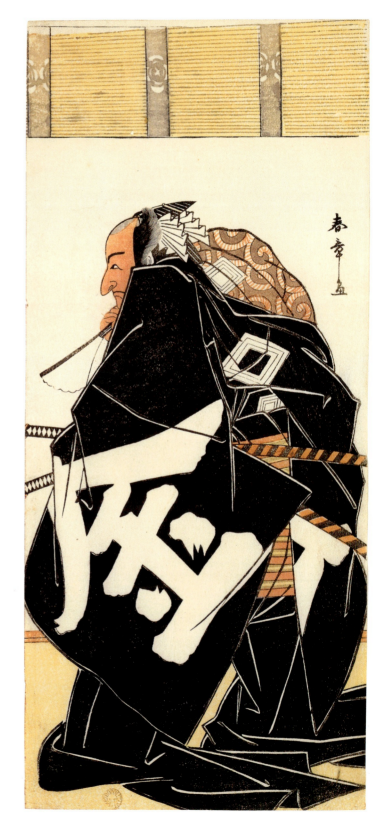

Over the next decade Mansfield would facilitate many print sales for Wright. He was a graduate of Yale and of Columbia Law School and worked for the law firm of Lord, Day, and Taylor until his death at age eighty-nine (ill. 52). A man of charm and discriminating taste, he was prominent in the cultural life of New York City for fifty years. In 1891 he was elected a fellow for life of the Metropolitan Museum of Art, became a trustee in 1909, and served as treasurer until 1921. Mansfield may have come to Japanese art through his first love, Whistler. In fact, he had one of only two comprehensive collections of Whistler etchings and lithographs. The other belonged to Freer, whom he had introduced to Whistler's work. Mansfield's remarks in 1896 on the occasion of his Ladies' Day lecture at New York's Grolier Club, of which he was a member and later president, make clear his own strong bias: "Taken as a whole, the art of Ukiyoe…prints is, in my judgment, not only one of the most remarkable phases of art expression in Japan, but deserves to rank as one of the most notable forms of pure art which the world has seen."[74] As the price of Japanese prints went up, Mansfield began to sell off other parts of his collection. In 1909 the trustees of the Art Institute of Chicago voted to pay him $33,000 for the complete works of French etcher Charles Meryon (1821–1868). Mansfield was a thorough and knowledgeable print collector; the Meryons include great rarities and different impressions of the same image. Perhaps his friend Buckingham, who helped finance the purchase, persuaded him to place these prints in Chicago. In those days Chicago was a city of Francophiles and also of rather adventurous big money.

Mansfield's collection of more than three hundred outstanding ukiyo-e prints (many purchased from Wright), as well as hundreds of Japanese lacquers, paintings, pottery, sword fittings, and textiles, was acquired by the Metropolitan Museum of Art in 1936 as a combined gift and sale.

52.
Howard Mansfield.
c. 1909

Opposite

51.
Katsukawa Shunshō.
The Actor Ichikawa Danjūrō V as Sakata Hyōgonosuke Kintoki in "Shitennō tonoi no kisewata" (*Raikō's Four Intrepid Retainers in the Costume of the Night Watch*). 1781. Color woodcut, *hosoban*. The Metropolitan Museum of Art, New York, Purchase, Joseph Pulitzer Bequest, 1918 (JP 344)

Wright sold this print to the Metropolitan Museum of Art in 1918 for $60.

CHAPTER THREE

THE SPAULDING BROTHERS:
OPPORTUNITY OF A LIFETIME

A GOOD CATCH

In the summer of 1912, when the Spaulding brothers first came in contact with Frank Lloyd Wright, they were already serious collectors of Japanese prints. The 6,495 prints that they later left to the Museum of Fine Arts, Boston, are still ranked among the best in the world on the basis of an unbeatable combination of quality, quantity, rarity, and representation. As the Spauldings often acknowledged, much of the credit for their collection goes to Wright, who acted as their agent during the years he was building the Imperial Hotel in Tokyo. At least one-third and possibly as much as half the collection was acquired from Wright. For the architect, in turn, the Spaulding money was the opportunity of a lifetime. The profits he made from the print business at this time (he bought cheaply in Tokyo, and sold at notoriously high prices back home) exceeded his revenue from his own work during this lean period of his career.

William Stuart ("Billie" or "Will" to his intimates) and John Taylor Spaulding were wealthy, socially prominent Bostonians, both of them Harvard graduates. After college, William (1865–1937) worked for the Revere Sugar Refinery, which was owned principally by his family, and then served as director of the United Fruits Company when it bought the refinery (ill. 53). He was a partner in the firm of Nash, Spaulding and Company until it was dissolved in 1905. He was also a director of the Otis Elevator Company, the Massachusetts Gas Company, and several Boston banks, to name but a few of his positions.[1] His younger brother John (1870–1948), who did not marry until late in life, spent a few years in his father's business, became a lawyer, and

then, according to an article in *Life* magazine the year he died, "proceeded to enjoy what his wealth could give him" (ill. 54).[2] They shared a huge granite mansion called Sunset Rock set on fifteen acres in the woods high above the rocky North Shore coastline at Prides Crossing in Beverley, about twenty miles north of Boston (ills. 55, 56). This was the home William Spaulding had built for his mother, who died in 1908. The brothers spent most of the year at Prides, but in the winter they would move to their house at 99 Beacon Street, overlooking the Charles River. July was spent at their fishing camp in Canada. At Prides they had a staff of ninety servants, and a large formal garden with carefully planned vistas, long stretches of rose and grape arbors, a pergola, mirror lakes, a temple, and a greenhouse for raising orchids.[3] On their steel schooner yacht, *Isis*, they steamed back and forth to the city or just as easily cruised the Adriatic (ill. 57).

William's wife, Katrina Fairlee Spaulding (1883–1950), took credit for starting the print collection. Raised by an aunt and uncle in the then fashionable neighborhood of Highland Park on Michigan Avenue in Chicago, she was a student at the School of the Art Institute of Chicago in 1902. She met the Spaulding brothers in the spring of 1909, when they all happened to be circumnavigating the globe on the same steamer. It was a romantic story of love at first sight (ill. 58). William married Katrina, eighteen years his junior, in Kenilworth, an exclusive Chicago suburb, on 14 September 1909. They honeymooned in Egypt and Europe that winter.

The Spauldings disembarked in Japan in 1909 with letters of introduction to William L. Keane, a collector and dealer from Evanston, Illinois, who had been living in Yokohama since the

53.
William Spaulding. 1913

Far right

54.
John Spaulding. c. 1913

early 1880s, and there they saw their first prints. Katrina, being already somewhat knowledgeable on the subject, was able to talk about them. As she was a painter, and it was the era of Whistler, she already had a few prints of her own. She was thrilled when William asked her if she would like some. "He left $1000 with Mr. Keane," she recalled years later, "and that was the beginning of our $700,000 collection!"[4]

Keane's correspondence with William Spaulding has just come to light and it indicates that between 1909 and 1913 he sent the Spauldings a continuous stream of prints totaling ¥81,675.50, or $40,837.75. (Japan adopted the gold standard from 1897 until 14 December 1931, so exchange fluctuations during this period, unlike the situation today, were minimal. Japanese currency had a fixed value: the exchange rate was one United States dollar for two Japanese yen.) The Spauldings entertained the Keanes at Prides Crossing in 1910; and in 1912, when the Spauldings made their second tour of Asia, Keane squired them around Kyoto. Keane had social pretensions; he favored references to tiffin at the embassy and golf games in Tokyo. Still, he deserves full credit for his role in educating the Spauldings to the quality, rarity, and condition of Japanese prints. He performed a valuable service for them, and knew it. "I am ambitious to have your collection rank with the best in

55.
Main gallery of the Spaulding summer home at Prides Crossing, Beverley, Massachusetts. From *American Homes and Gardens*, October 1910

56.
Spaulding rose garden, pergola, and greenhouse at Prides Crossing. From *American Homes and Gardens*, October 1910

57.
Spaulding yacht, *Isis*,
anchored off Prides
Crossing. From *Life*
magazine, 1 November
1948

58.
William and Katrina
Spaulding and their
three-month-old daugh-
ter Katrina. June 1913

the world," he wrote in 1911 around the time he bought them their first Sharaku for ¥600, their most expensive purchase to date.[5] In her history of the Museum of Fine Arts, written in 1910, Julia de Wolfe Addison points out that there were already 2,500 prints in the museum's collection (1,800 came from Denman Ross in 1905). The Spauldings must have known that they would have to do something extraordinary to stand out in this hotbed of serious, highly competitive print collectors. In the end they had fifty-one portraits by the enigmatic Tōshūsai Sharaku, whose career spanned a brief ten months in 1794–95. The only holdings that were larger were those of Clarence Buckingham in Chicago and Matsukata in Tokyo.

The last invoice from Keane, ¥1,406 ($703) for an extra-large print by Okumura Masanobu (1686–1764), is dated 1 August 1914. In fact, it was their only purchase from him that year. Keane was probably not a good businessman and he had been badly hurt by the inflation that followed the economic boom in Japan after the Russo-Japanese War. His final letters to Spaulding are rather plaintive and indicate dire financial hardship ("Dear Billie, It seems many moons since I last heard from you…. This has been a bad year for me & things have gone 'agin me.'…I rarely see any prints now").[6] With inflation, prices of prints had doubled and tripled, but Keane never had a chance in competition with the charismatic Wright, who was not just a dealer but a world-famous architect as well. When the Spauldings no longer needed Keane, the spigot was turned off and they gave him a quick goodbye. To put in perspective this purchase of a single eighteenth-century print for $703, the annual wage of a Ford Motor Company employee in 1913 was $702 for 2,700 hours (a six-day, fifty-four-hour work week). The minimum wage for an adult male worker at the motorcar factory was $2.34 per day.

It was in a letter of 30 June 1912 that Wright's loyal friend in Chicago, Frederick Gookin, first brought up the name of William Spaulding. "I had a call from a Boston gentleman who is interested in prints and wants to see some of [your] Chicago collection," he informed Wright.

> He has quite a number himself, but I have no idea of their quality, except that he says the Buckingham collection and mine were "revelations" to him…. While he was here I took him to see your prints. He says he has most of the Hiroshiges, but laid out about 25 that he would like to compare with his copies, and if agree-

able to you I think would like to have me take them with me when I visit the "Hub."... I am quite sure he will not pay anything like the prices marked upon the prints. They may be all right intrinsically, but the difference between them and the usual dealer's prices are [sic] too wide.

Gookin goes on to say that Spaulding also liked the Katsukawa prints, the very ones that neither Buckingham nor the Metropolitan Museum of Art had been willing to purchase.

> I told him you would take $10,000 for the collection— 84 Shunsho, 15 Shunko, 6 Shunyei, 3 Buncho, 1 Shunsen, 1 Kiyonaga, 1 Kiyomitsu and 1 Toyomasu. The price, however, seemed to him pretty high. He is pretty familiar with prices both in Japan and Europe, I find, and I imagine is rather a close buyer. I have an idea that perhaps I might work him up to $7,000 or $7,500 for the lot, but I don't think he would go beyond that and I am not at all sure that he would pay you that sum. Still as that would clean up your loan from Buckingham and leave you a little over you might let me know how you feel about it and I will see what I can do when I am with Mr. Spaulding for that is his name.[7]

William, in Chicago to see his in-laws, had apparently visited the office at Orchestra Hall where Wright kept his prints, with Gookin acting as Wright's agent. (Gookin was empowered to show Wright's prints when the architect was not in town.) The Spauldings were quick to take advantage of the talents of both men (ill. 59). Gookin became consultant to the Spauldings: within two weeks he had gone East to begin cataloguing and matting their prints (including touch-ups and cleaning where necessary) and to advise them on future purchases.[8] They did buy Wright's portfolio of one hundred Katsukawa actor prints and twenty-five Hiroshige landscape prints. Later they credited Wright with arousing their enthusiasm for Hiroshige and systematically acquired about one thousand fine prints by this artist, almost all from Wright.[9] Gookin's estimate of a possible sale of up to $7,500 for Wright's prints seems to have been conservative. In December, William Spaulding sent Wright a check for $7,500 as final payment on a sale that totaled $22,500.[10]

Wright sent the Spauldings a copy of his newly published booklet, *Japanese Prints: An Interpretation*, for Christmas that

59.
Kitagawa Utamaro. *Okita of the Naniwa Teahouse*, from the series *Pictures of One Hundred Variations of Ikebana Flower Arranging* (*Ikebana hyakuhei no zu*). c. 1793. Color woodcut, *hosoban*. Museum of Fine Arts, Boston, William S. and John T. Spaulding Collection, 1921 (1921.6335)

Wright sold this print to the Spauldings in November 1912.

year. Mrs. Spaulding read it aloud the evening of its arrival, and it reportedly gave them great satisfaction. Hearing that Wright was scheduled to set off for Japan from Seattle on 15 January (as it turned out, he missed the boat), the Spauldings invited him to a conference at their Beacon Street home.[11] It was on this visit that they asked him to find prints for them in Japan, as Wright describes in his autobiography:

> "Would you consent to try to find prints for us in Japan, Mr. Wright? We are both impressed by your experience and your knowledge of the subject and your opportunities in Japan and feel we can trust you completely. We know it is no longer possible for us to find prints unless you will help us." I had expected something like this and had been trying to arrive at something but had nothing definite in mind.
>
> Suddenly I decided. I said, "I will take whatever you want to spend, spend it and divide. I'll keep what I think in the circumstances I should have and you shall have the others." "Well," said John as he laughed, "that's hardly a business proposition, is it, Mr. Wright?" I said, "No, I am not a business man, Mr. Spaulding."
>
> They wanted to know why I would not do it on commission. I said, "Too much bookkeeping." We left it at that and went to bed.
>
> Next morning John and William said they had all thought it all over. "We will be glad to accept your offer. You will find twenty thousand dollars to your credit in the Yokohama Specie Bank when you arrive in Tokio."
>
> There was no scratch of a pen to record the agreement.[12]

This famous conversation, in which Wright implies that the Spauldings gave him large sums of money and let him keep half the prints he purchased, is boastfully recorded in his revised and enlarged life story, *An Autobiography*, of 1943. (The Spauldings are not even mentioned in the original 1932 edition.) Is it possible that Wright was loath to tell this story (his version of the story, that is) while William was still alive to contradict him? There is no doubt that the patrician Spauldings were impressed by the brilliant architect's reputation as a connoisseur and by his potential for enhancing their collection. But they were shrewd Yankee businessmen, able to give as well as they got, and the real story is rather different, if no less compelling.

On 10 January William Spaulding wrote to say how much they had enjoyed Wright's visit and to comment on another group of Hiroshige prints that Gookin had just sent over to them on behalf of the architect. "Many of them are great wonders—and do you not forget the fact that you, my dear Mr. Wright, are fully responsible for getting us so seriously enthused on this artist and we look to you for no end of assistance in assuaging this appetite for other superb copies." William Spaulding expressed concern over Wright's planned visit to Keane, the Yokohama dealer. Fearing a conflict of interest between the two men who were both acting as his agents, Spaulding said he would advise Keane that Wright was visiting Japan "with the idea in view of writing a book on Hiroshige. I shall say nothing as to your purpose of collecting a few prints."[13]

The Spauldings did not buy indiscriminately. Just before setting off for Japan, Wright had his office manager, Harry F. Robinson (1883–1959), send the Spauldings two Hiroshige prints, a vertical *ōban* diptych (a format known as a hanging-scroll picture, or *kakemono-e*) of a goshawk on a snow-laden pine branch and the famous *Eight Views of Kanazawa in Moonlight* (*Buyo Kanazawa hasshō yakei*) of 1857, a triptych that ranks among the last and best of the artist's great designs. They kept the hawk, even though it was torn, but returned the triptych explaining that not only were the margins trimmed but the asking price was beyond its real market value. What's more, they already had an excellent impression of it.[14]

Wright sailed to Japan at the end of January with Mamah Borthwick in search of the commission of consulting architect for a "new" Imperial Hotel in Tokyo. The first Imperial had been built in downtown Tokyo near the imperial palace in 1890 by Watanabe Yuzuru (1855–1930), an architect of the Home Ministry who had recently returned from a period of training in Germany, and who chose an impressive Neo-Renaissance facade (ill. 60).[15] A three-story brick building with sixty guest rooms, it was intended to rival the Ritz in Paris and the Waldorf-Astoria in New York; without question it was the most luxurious hotel in Japan and the social center of Tokyo. The enterprising financiers who founded the hotel were essentially the same men who, less than twenty years later, realized that the steady rise in international tourism required a much larger, up-to-date facility. They included Shibusawa Eiichi (1841–1931), an industrialist with close ties to Mitsui trading company, who was president of the Daiichi Bank, and Ōkura Kihachirō (1837–1928). Ōkura replaced Shibusawa as chairman of the board of the Imperial in 1909, although the latter continued on in an advisory capacity (ill. 61). A self-made man who started as an apprentice in a dried-fish shop, Ōkura went off to study business practices in the West, founded his own company, and rapidly amassed a fortune through arms dealing, construction, and international trade.

In 1906 a two-story wooden annex with additional guest rooms was added to the rear of the main building and negotiations began to lease additional land for a new hotel next to the original building. Owned by the imperial household, this was the most expensive piece of real estate in Tokyo.

In the fall of 1911 Gookin had written to his old friend Hayashi Aisaku (1873–1951), manager of the Imperial, recommending Wright as the man to build the new hotel. Hayashi was agreeable to the suggestion, on the condition that the architect "would not be too radical and would work under reasonable terms."[16] Hayashi had been casting his net wide: by the time he heard from Gookin he already had some nearly completed plans and a scale model for the new hotel. At least one Japanese architect subsequently came forward to say that he had been approached by Hayashi at an early date. The American-trained Shimoda Kikutarō (1866–1931), who had been a licensed architect working in Chicago in the 1890s and was based in Shanghai in 1912, apparently submitted rough designs for a hotel to Hayashi slightly ahead of Wright. He later claimed that Wright had stolen his ideas.[17] By 1911 most Japanese architects were trained in the West and could pick and choose appropriate Western elements for their work. The foreign consultants who were hired to modernize Japan in the early years of the Meiji period had pretty much receded from view. Hayashi himself had succeeded a Swiss as manager of the hotel. So why did the Imperial choose an American as its architect? Perhaps it comes down to something as simple as the "old boy" network coupled with the perception that America was on the cutting edge of modern technology.

Now, in 1913, following a brief delay caused by the death of the emperor Meiji (r. 1867–1912), Wright was off to meet Hayashi, with whom he would develop a close friendship. They

60.
Watanabe Yuzuru.
The first Imperial Hotel, Tokyo. 1890

Wright and Mamah Borthwick stayed here in 1913.

61.
Ōkura Kihachirō.
c. 1897

Ōkura wears the Japanese Order of the Rising Sun Third Class neck badge.

62.
Torii Kiyomasu I (active c. 1696–1716). *Tsutsui Jōmyō and the Priest Ichirai on the Uji Bridge.* c. 1710–16. Hand-colored woodcut, *ōōban*. Museum of Fine Arts, Boston, William S. and John T. Spaulding Collection, 1921 (1921.5423)

Wright sold this print to the Spauldings in July 1913.

63.
Torii Kiyomasu I. *Kabuki
Actor in a Female Role.*
c. 1710–15. Woodcut,
ōōban, sumizuri-e.
Museum of Fine Arts,
Boston, William S.
and John T. Spaulding
Collection, 1921
(1921.5422)

Wright sold this print to
the Spauldings in July
1913. The writing that
shows through from
the back of the print at
the upper right edge
is a Japanese dealer's
inventory number.

had more than a little in common: Hayashi had studied at the University of Wisconsin before going into the art trade. He was well known to many American collectors, including Charles Freer in Detroit, having worked for years at Yamanaka and Company in New York selling Japanese art. In 1909 he returned to Japan intending to spend some time with the Yamanaka firm in Osaka. Thanks to his years with Yamanaka, Hayashi was an experienced world traveler with wide-ranging social contacts and ample business skills when the Imperial lured him to Tokyo that fall to take up his new position as managing director. Two months later he was elected to the board of directors. The directors of the hotel believed that an artistic turn of mind was the most important qualification in a hotel manager. The first thing a guest notices is the décor, they reasoned, and the facilities must stir an aesthetic response.[18] Hayashi had been a close personal friend of the art historian Ernest Fenollosa and had sponsored his series of twelve lectures on Asian art in New York in 1907. It was Hayashi who had Fenollosa's ashes brought over to Japan for burial. Many years later he presented Wright with an ukiyo-e painting of a courtesan that had belonged to Fenollosa.[19] Following Wright's visit in 1913 Hayashi actually offered to help find prints for Wright, and Wright designed Hayashi a handsome little house in Tokyo in 1917.[20] Hayashi remained loyal to the end, even though it cost him his job.

The new Imperial, Wright told Darwin Martin, "is to cost seven million dollars—the finest hotel in the world. Of course I may not get it—then again I may—it would mean forty or fifty thousand dollars and a couple of years employment if I did—so wish me luck." He also assured the good-humored Martin, to whom he now owed money on two big loans and a mortgage, that he would have an opportunity, on his return, to realize on more prints. He never mentioned the Spauldings in his correspondence with Martin.[21] At this point both Martin and Little were still holding prints as security on loans to Wright.

Wright misplaced a decimal point when he calculated the dollar cost of the hotel budget. When he was hired in 1916 the budget was only ¥1.3 million, roughly $700,000, not $7,000,000. By the time it was finished, however, cost overruns had tripled the budget, bringing it close to $3 million.[22]

On 18 January William Spaulding wrote to Wright in care of the Imperial Hotel, where the architect was staying with his traveling companion, Borthwick. Spaulding reminded Wright that they wanted "*supreme* Shunsho and exquisite Hiroshige

more than any other two artists—and for this feeling of ours, we must hold you responsible! Don't forget to return with an exquisite copy of the 'Monkey Bridge'!" The *Monkey Bridge in Kai Province* (*Kōyō saruhashi no zu*; also known as *Saruhashi*), in double vertical ōban format, depicts a famous "beauty spot," the bridge over a deep moonlit gorge in Kai (or Kōshū) province (modern Yamanashi prefecture). It is still coveted by collectors as Hiroshige's most striking design in this format.

Spaulding enclosed a draft for ¥10,000 (approximately $5,000 at that time) "to be invested for us in prints according to our conversation. As soon as we get in possession of further funds we will forward you another check."[23] He was anxious about Wright's expenditures. "I know you will not permit yourself to pay exorbitant or fancy prices for any finds you may make that will interest you. You know, my good Mr. Wright, that many of us feel that your ideas of the value of prints is upon a *pretty* lofty pedestal, and we do not attempt to keep this feeling a second from you."[24]

The original Spaulding money soon ran out. Within only a week or so of Wright's arrival in February he cabled Spaulding: "Opportunity extraordinary wire eighteen thousand dollars tonight." As they had not contemplated making a larger investment than about twenty-five to thirty thousand at the outside, the brothers were understandably nervous, the more so as it was now obvious they would not see their purchases until Wright's return.[25]

Gookin also commissioned Wright to buy some prints for him in Japan, a difficult-to-find Hiroshige landscape and a Shunshō ghost.[26] (Gookin made his one and only trip to Japan in 1925, when he was in his early seventies.) On 3 April he wrote to congratulate Wright on hearing of his success in finding such a wonderful lot of prints for the Spauldings; he hoped that his Chicago client, Buckingham, might get some of the duplicates. The Spauldings meanwhile notified Gookin that they had just cabled yet more "funds needed to acquire the 'crank's' treasures." Gookin was worried by this: "I only hope your eagerness has not led you to pay extravagant prices," he wrote his friend in Japan. "It will work out much better for you and will be much more satisfactory to Mr. Spaulding if you have not. I hear, however, that you are reported to have paid very high prices. Curious, isn't it, how such information travels. It comes to me through two widely different sources."[27] It is difficult to see how Wright had time for Imperial Hotel business.

64.
Kaigetsudō Dohan
(active 1710–16).
*Courtesan Adjusting
Her Comb.* c. 1710–15.
Woodcut, *ōōban,
sumizuri-e.* Museum of
Fine Arts, Boston,
William S. and John T.
Spaulding Collection,
1921 (1921.6645)

Wright purchased this
print from Kobayashi
Bunshichi and sold it
to the Spauldings in
September 1913. It was
first published in 1915
by Arthur Davison Ficke
in his *Chats on Japan-
ese Prints.*

When he returned to Chicago in late April, Wright was too busy to set off directly for Boston. He had first to deal with the annual exhibition of the Chicago Architectural Club held at the Art Institute of Chicago from 6 May to 11 June. To pacify the Spauldings he sent off two packages of the least important of his purchases; Gookin was invited out to Boston to help compare, select, and reject. Gookin was intensely curious to see Wright's things. On the one hand he was Wright's mentor, but on the other hand he was also a competitor. They shared some of the same clients (Buckingham and the Spauldings) and both had reputations as experts. "Among the prints that are here there are many fine things, but by no means all of them are superlative," Gookin confided somewhat cattily to his wife, Marie. "I think I still retain the supremacy so far as Shunsho is concerned, though there are some in this lot I should like to have." Gookin's overall evaluation of Wright's prints was that "on the whole they are more distinguished for their design than for their impeccable condition."[28] Wright paid lip service to condition, but as an artist and architect he recognized that the genius of the Japanese woodcut lies in the element of design, a quality he often praised.

In one of his letters to his wife, Gookin alludes to Tony Straus-Negbaur, of Frankfurt, Germany, who had been building her print collection since the turn of the century with periodic visits to New York, and who prided herself on the flawless condition and perfect color of her acquisitions. Apparently she had questioned Wright's eye for prints. Mrs. Straus-Negbaur "would have no lingering doubts about their genuineness," Gookin says of the 1913 purchase. "The letter from her you forwarded to me was quite amusing."[29]

Wright at once plunged into the business of selling prints again in Chicago, although Gookin had to step in and admonish him on the subject of maintaining professional behavior when one dealer from San Francisco complained that Wright had made off with some prints that were not for sale: "My advice to you as a friend is to settle with her *without a day's delay*…. You have the problem before you of building up your professional business. It has to be done under very considerable disadvantages as you know."[30]

The Spauldings, for their part, went off in June to their fishing camp, Lorne Cottage at Grand Cascapedia in Quebec. Before leaving they were forced to scrape together another $3,500 for Wright, however grudgingly. William admonished the architect,

I am afraid that we, too, are "all in," for we have borrowed and borrowed even beyond the limit of our credit…. This life of an enthusiastic collector is full of vicissitudes—for in consequence of this winter's expenditures, we are now forced to abandon the upkeep of our lovely and cherished Gardens and also our Greenhouses [at Prides].[31]

Like Wright's architectural clients, his print clients often found they had spent a great deal more than intended.

If the Spauldings were feeling pinched for cash, it was not entirely due to their dealings with Wright. Between December 1912 and March 1913 they sent almost $5,000 to Keane in Yokohama. In February 1913 they purchased the entire print collection of Dr. J. Clarence Webster of Chicago, in May they made purchases from the Chicago dealer Ito Tokumatsu, and in June they acquired the print collection of Baron Sumitomo (the "copper king" of Japan) through Yamanaka and Company, New York.

The delivery and study of Wright's prints was set for Wednesday, 9 July, through Sunday, 13 July 1913, at Prides. Gookin and Wright arrived on separate late-afternoon trains on the ninth.[32] Wright recalled in his autobiography,

I was to bring the prints to the Spaulding country home at Prides Crossing…. [They] had Gookin (as consultant connoisseur) present. For three days we laid out prints and prints and more prints and some more prints until neither the Spauldings nor Gookin (he was now leading expert in America) could believe their eyes. Even to me it seemed like some fantastic dream. Sated with riches in the most exquisite graphic art on earth, after three days at a marvelous feast we sat back and rested.

Gratified was hardly the word. William Spaulding especially delighted, said, "Mr. Wright, this goes far beyond any expectations we had. You can't have much of your own after turning this over to us?"

"I have enough," I said. "I've done pretty well by myself, I assure you."[33]

What is the meaning of this last statement? Presumably Wright kept behind a good many prints for himself; he never gave the Spauldings an itemized invoice for this sale. He was not exag-

65. Kitagawa Utamaro. *Reed Blind,* from the series *Model Young Women Woven in Mist* (*Kasumi-ori musume hinagata*). c. 1794–95. Color woodcut, *ōban.* Museum of Fine Arts, Boston, William S. and John T. Spaulding Collection, 1921 (1921.6412)

Wright sold this print to the Spauldings in July 1913.

藝子
きくの
長喜画

住吉屋
中居
ぬい

66.
Eishōsai (Momokawa)
Chōki (active late
eighteenth–early nine-
teenth century). *The
Geisha Tamino of the
Sumiyoshiya and Her
Maid Nui (Sumiyoshiya
nakai Nui geiko Tamino)*.
c. 1795. Color woodcut
with mica ground,
ōban. Museum of Fine
Arts, Boston, William S.
and John T. Spaulding
Collection, 1921
(1921.4781)

Wright sold this print
to the Spauldings in
October 1913.

gerating when he described William Spaulding's state of mind, as can be seen from the letter he would receive from Prides about two weeks later:

My dear Mr. Wright:

The fact that you left us with so many wonderful prints to be made intimate friends of, accounts fully for the reason you have not heard from us. They grow better and better and more precious to us at each and every perusal, and you have given us treasures such as I never dreamed of possessing.

You have more than fulfilled your part of the transaction and now more than ever before it does not seem possible such results could have been accomplished— we never would believe it a possibility from hearsay— but we have the actual evidence before us—and its accomplishment was due to your wonderful power in unearthing things worthwhile, and your discerning appreciation of all that is good.

You have been the means of making our collection as great—or very nearly so—as any in the world— and you should be extremely proud of your child: and I know your pride will always be someday to help in making this Collection without any question of doubt the greatest in existence.[34]

William Spaulding later called Wright the "father of our collection." The Spaulding collection was considered even in its own day to be one of the finest (Gookin called William the "prince of American collectors").[35]

During three heady days Wright, Gookin, and the Spauldings looked through the nearly 1,400 prints the architect had assembled for them (ills. 62–67). Work was broken up by occasional strolls in the garden (which, contrary to William's protestations, seems still to have been flourishing) and listening to Victrola records in the music room.

Gookin was taken aside and consulted privately concerning the details of the final settlement with Wright, which was worked out with no complications. Gookin confided to his wife,

It was made easy by his abandonment of his original stand and his announcement that he would be willing to accept a commission for his services and turn over all of the prints to Mr. Spaulding…. [The] only thing

that remains to be considered is which of the prints— duplicates, that is,—shall be taken by Mr. W for his own capital which he expended in making the purchases. It is rather necessary to go through the entire 1400 prints and several hundred of those acquired elsewhere by Mr. Spaulding in order to tell which are duplicates and which Mr. Spaulding should retain.[36]

In his autobiography Wright reports that Spaulding wrote him a check on the spot for $25,000. This was presumably the commission cited by Gookin. After lunch that day the Spauldings took Wright out for a leisurely drive in their new convertible. As they passed a school playground, one of the boys hit a baseball out over the street. Wright instinctively leaped up from the back seat, caught it, and threw it back into the game. "Well," said William Spaulding in astonishment. "So that is it! Well, Mr. Wright, I know now how you got those prints! It's all clear at last!"[37]

Wright departed on Sunday, 13 July, to visit his younger sister Maginel Enright (1877–1966) on Nantucket. Maginel and her husband were both graphic artists living in New York City.[38] Gookin stayed on for several days to work on the prints; the 1913 purchase was so large that the process of recording the provenance on each catalogue card was expedited by using a stamp reading "F. L. W. Japan. Spring. 1913."[39]

The Spauldings managed to recoup a substantial part of their investment by pruning their collection. Alerted by Gookin, Howard Mansfield went to Prides Crossing in September 1913 to look over the nearly three hundred duplicates with the thought that he would pick out a few for himself. Overwhelmed by the quantity and quality of the pieces they were parting with, he recommended their purchase to the director of the Metropolitan Museum of Art, claiming that "such a chance may never come again. Japan is pretty well drained of prints…."[40] This acquisition, he insisted, would place the museum's collection above that of the New York Public Library. The library had received 1,700 prints as a gift in 1901 from the New York philanthropist Charles Stewart Smith (1832–1909), who bought the lot from the British journalist and collector Frank Brinkley (1841–1912) during his honeymoon in Japan in 1892. The Metropolitan Museum of Art did buy several hundred prints from the Spauldings in 1914, mostly works by Hiroshige, for $17,000, a very substantial sum even by today's standards.

67.
Katsushika Hokusai.
*South Wind, Clear
Weather* (*Gaifu kaisei*),
from the series
*The Thirty-six Views
of Mount Fuji*
(*Fugaku sanjūrokkei*).
c. 1830–31. Color
woodcut, *ōban*.
Museum of Fine Arts,
Boston, William S. and
John T. Spaulding
Collection, 1921
(1921.6756)

Frank Lloyd Wright
sold this print to the
Spauldings in July 1913.

WRIGHT'S BEST FRIEND IN JAPAN: SHUGIO HIROMICHI

Wright's local guide and interpreter in Japan was the cosmopolitan and well-connected Shugio Hiromichi (1853–1927). Shugio stands out as a pioneer in introducing New Yorkers to the fascination of Japanese color woodcuts and illustrated books. He staged the city's first ukiyo-e exhibition in 1889 at the Grolier Club and lectured on the subject well before there were many noteworthy local collections.

Shugio (originally called Shugyō Kenkurō) was born into a samurai family in Saga, the capital of present-day Saga Prefecture in Kyushu, the southernmost of the four main Japanese islands. His family had long been vassals of the Nabeshima clan, who controlled the area during most of the Edo period; his father was once a local governor (*daikan*) and his mother was a blood relative of the Nabeshima clan. After graduating from the clan's secondary school (*kōdōkan*) and spending a year at Nanko University (a precursor of Tokyo University), Shugio and two other young men were singled out for leadership in the new Meiji government; they were sent abroad in 1871 for two years to learn English, probably at Oxford University, and to acquire expertise in foreign trade.[41] In 1875 the Ministry of Foreign Affairs sent Shugio to Amoy, China, as a consulate clerk but he resigned that post in 1877 to join Mitsui and Company, the first and largest international trading company in Japan. The following year he was appointed the first manager of their Hong Kong office. In 1880 he arrived in New York as manager of the quasi-governmental Kiryū Industrial and Commercial Company (Kiryū Kōshō Kaisha), known in New York as the First Japan Manufacturing and Trading Company, importers of high-quality Japanese crafts (parasols and porcelains) on Broadway at Eighteenth Street. (In 1890 Kiryū Kōshō Kaisha transferred its New York business to a local Japanese trader, Fukushima Ototarō [known here as Otto Fukushima], and in 1891 the company itself was liquidated.)[42]

A resident of New York for at least ten years, from 1880 until 1890, Shugio immediately joined the Tile Club, a fraternity of influential New York artists who met weekly for a "tile painting exercise" and other excursions. He probably met such fellow members as Winslow Homer (1836–1910), William Merritt Chase (1846–1916), and the American Impressionists John H. Twachtman (1853–1902) and J. Alden Weir.[43] His nickname at the Tile Club was "Varnish," perhaps because he was trading in lacquer goods. A photograph taken around 1890 and inscribed to collector Freer shows a handsome young man with wire-rimmed glasses and moustache, dressed in formal Japanese attire and sporting two samurai swords, a costume that imparts authority to his image as a connoisseur of Asian art (ill. 68). He must have turned heads on the streets of New York. Shugio joined the Century Club, an organization of gentlemen in the arts and letters, in 1890. The elite membership included the likes of Teddy Roosevelt, Cornelius Vanderbilt, J. Pierpont Morgan, Stanford White, and Albert Bierstadt.

Shugio's social contacts proved useful to his many American friends who visited Japan. He squired Mansfield around Japan in the fall of 1898, for example. The New York painter Robert Blum (1857–1903), who collected Japanese prints, lived in Japan for

68.
Shugio Hiromichi.
c. 1890. Inscribed to
Charles Lang Freer

Shugio and Freer visited
one another in Detroit
and New York during
the 1890s. Freer com-
missioned Shugio to
buy Edo-period paint-
ings for him in Japan.

two years between 1890 and 1892 on assignment for *Scribner's*. He and the New York journalist Henry T. Finck (1854–1926), author of the 1895 *Lotos-Time in Japan*, were often in the company of Shugio (ill. 69). The painter Theodore Robinson (1852–1896), in a diary entry for 1894, describes an evening in New York spent looking at ukiyo-e at the home of Weir together with Twachtman and Shugio, "a Japanese gentleman who explained certain things about prints and [illustrated printed] books."[44] Weir received the following letter from Shugio the next month:

> Your kind note of May 24th came to me today and I am glad to hear that you are enjoying the pure and glorious country air. Yes by all means I would like to have your complete set of etchings if I can have them in trade for Japanese prints or something that I have for I am greatly taken by your etchings. Why can I not send you some Japanese paper for you to print them? I think your etchings will look better on Japan paper.[45]

Shugio became a member of the Grolier Club only two months after this prestigious center for bibliophiles and admirers of fine printing was founded at 64 Madison Avenue in 1884. In an interview in 1911 he said that the founders of the club wanted at least one Japanese member and they encouraged him to join.[46] John La Farge (1853–1910), a fellow member who had been collecting Japanese prints since the 1860s, confided to Shugio that "for forty years I have used Japanese colored prints as a basis of study for my own experiments…in light and color," and had him transcribe the preface to his 1897 *An Artist's Letters from Japan* in Japanese script.[47]

Japanese prints were displayed at the club's inaugural meeting, and for his talk on Japanese books and printing in May 1887 Shugio displayed actual tools and materials used by printers. In 1889 he exhibited two hundred Japanese prints and illus-

trated printed books at the Grolier Club, all drawn from his reportedly superb personal collection. The Japanese print show he arranged and catalogued for the club in April 1896, however, was more ambitious and consisted of loans from Weir and Samuel Colman, as well as from the fledgling Chicago collectors Buckingham, Gookin, and Morse, substantially the same group that lent to the Fenollosa/Ketcham exhibition in the Fine Arts Building earlier that same year. Shugio may have supervised production of the color woodcut posters and the announcement of a lecture by Mansfield, all done in picturesque orientalizing style; perhaps they were actually printed in Japan—he was an active traveler.[48]

Shugio returned to Japan in June 1890 to take up a government position in the Ministry of Agriculture and Commerce. This was the ministry that handled the all-important overseas exhibitions of Japanese arts and crafts that were intended to substantiate Japan's role as a newly minted world power. From about 1891 until 1897 he apparently lived in Washington, D.C. During this period he took part in the selection and judging of Japanese works of art for the 1893 World's Columbian Exposition in Chicago and was a founding member of Chicago's Caxton Club. While living in Georgetown he edited catalogues for the Japanese art collection of the Washington real estate broker and auctioneer Thomas E. Waggaman, printed by the De Vinne Press in 1893 and 1896. Between 1898 and 1901 he edited the *Japanese Art Folio*, a luxurious journal published in Tokyo that featured full-page reproductions of old Japanese paintings, with explanatory text in both English and Japanese. In 1900 he was a member of the Japanese commission at the Paris World's Fair and in October 1904, as one of Japan's commissioners for the Louisiana Purchase Exposition in Saint Louis, he lectured (probably at Gookin's invitation) to the Chicago Literary Club about the Japanese contribution to the fair, praising in particular the work of contemporary painters (ill. 70).[49] Shugio probably visited Chicago again in 1908; Gookin inscribed a copy of his March 1908 Art Institute print exhibition catalogue to Shugio and dated the inscription "Chicago, June 10, 1908."[50] The "Japanese gentleman from Tokyo" described by Judson Metzgar, a print collector in Moline, Illinois, at one of Buckingham's print parties in Chicago must have been the ubiquitous Shugio. When

69.
Henry T. Finck (second from left) and Shugio Hiromichi (far right) in Tokyo. 1890. The young man standing may be Robert Blum

Gookin, acting as "master of ceremonies," exhibited Hiroshige's *Mariko* from the Great Tōkaidō series,

> someone called attention to the inscription on a board which in the print is seen standing against the wayside tea-house, remarking that the love of the poetic had prompted the innkeeper to write a poem for the passerby to read. Thereupon the Japanese gentleman rose, adjusted his eyeglasses with great deliberation, and going to the easel holding the print said, "I beg your pardon, but the writing on the board is not a poem, but says, 'Very nice fish and rice for sale.'"[51]

There is no record of how Wright and Shugio first met—it might have been in Chicago in 1904. Shugio provided several letters of introduction to people in the Kyoto art world for Wright's 1905 trip, and they definitely spent time together in London in September 1910, during the architect's first journey to Europe in connection with the publication of the Wasmuth portfolios in Berlin.[52] Shugio, again representing the Japanese government, probably gave Wright a guided tour of the large-scale Anglo-Japanese Exhibition that took place at the White City in Shepherd's Bush in 1910. His article for the October issue of *The International Studio* promotes contemporary Japanese potters whose work was being shown in London.[53] Japan had sent a retrospective exhibition of "treasures quite beyond price, the finest examples of their greatest masters of all periods, from the eighth to the nineteenth century."[54] The rarest works were changed every fortnight, and included paintings of a quality and antiquity never before seen in the West. There was Buddhist material as well as sixteenth-century Muromachi-period (1392–1573) ink paintings, Edo-period works attributed to Iwasa Matabei (1578–1650) and Ogata Kōrin (1658–1716), and ukiyo-e paintings and prints. Under the circumstances it is ironic that during this stopover in London, Wright had a falling out with the English designer/architect C. R. Ashbee (1863–1942), a leader of the Arts and Crafts movement on the international scene, over the matter of Japanese influence on Wright's work. When asked to write an introduction to the Wasmuth *Sonderheft*, Ashbee pointed out that Wright had adapted Japanese forms in his architecture. Furious, Wright censored these statements, claiming that he had "digested" Japanese architecture, not copied it.[55]

70.
Shugio Hiromichi. 1904

The star Shugio wears on his right is the Chinese Order of the Double Dragon, awarded in 1903 for services rendered to China in the Fifth National Industrial Exhibition in Tokyo; the set of four medals worn on his left comprises the Japanese Sixth Order of the Rising Sun and the French Legion of Honor (both awarded for service on the Japanese commission at the Paris Exposition Universelle in 1900), the Japanese Blue Ribbon Medal, and the Special Red Cross Medal awarded by the Japanese Red Cross Society in 1904.

By 1912 there is evidence that Shugio was acting as agent for Wright in Tokyo. Shugio lived in Azabu-Iigura, which was, and still is, one of the best residential areas in Tokyo, not far from the center of the city. Well qualified to make purchases and negotiate on the architect's behalf, he apparently appreciated the extra income. When Wright sent him a long overdue remittance of ¥440 (worth approximately $220 in those days) in May of that year, Shugio was extremely grateful. He was doing research on Hiroshige, had in fact published a significant study of the artist in *The Japan Magazine* in November 1911, and had tracked down the fourth-generation Hiroshige, hoping to meet him soon. He warned Wright about escalating prices and the scarcity of good prints in the market, citing the high prices being asked by "our friend," the dealer Matsuki Heikichi (?–1931) of the Daikokuya.[56]

The two men worked side by side during Wright's 1913 visit, at which time Matsuki, fifth-generation proprietor of the Daikokuya, located near the Ryōgoku Bridge in Tokyo, was a major source for them. In March, while Wright was on a three-week trip to Kyoto and elsewhere, Shugio wrote to Matsuki: "[Mr. Wright] wishes you would keep the Hokusai *surimono* which I am sending under separate cover, together with the articles he selected the other day, until his return to Tokyo."[57] Shugio continued as Wright's agent until at least 1917. Wright enjoyed dinners of grilled eel on rice at Shugio's home.[58] Their last real correspondence dates from 1921: Shugio had Wright build an annex for his small house but was very disappointed by the shoddy workmanship. The ceiling came down repeatedly.[59]

Sharing credit was not one of Wright's strong points. In his 1932 autobiography Wright mentioned Shugio only in passing as a friend for whose safety he was concerned at the time of the 1923 earthquake, which leveled most of Tokyo but spared the Imperial Hotel (thanks to its architect). Shugio was finally given his due in the revised and expanded 1943 version of the autobiography, when the story of the Spaulding print expedition was added. By then Wright was feeling more secure; he had several important building commissions and was no longer a competitive art dealer. The architect wrote in his distinctive staccato style:

> When I arrived after the usual tedious Pacific crossing… I went directly to Shugio. He who was Mutsushito's [sic] "connoisseur" and my intimate friend. Hiromishe [sic] Shugio had charge of all Japanese fine art exhibits, in the foreign expositions—a friend of

nearly all the great artists of Europe, Whistler especially. He was a lover of London which he liked to compare with Tokio. Shugio was a Japanese aristocrat (there must have been some Chinese blood in him with that name) and highly respected by everyone. He had access to court circles and enjoyed a universal reputation for integrity. I laid the case before him.

> It was my feeling then that, hidden away Japanese-fashion in the *go-downs* of the court beyond the approach of the merchant class, were many as yet untouched collections of the somewhat "risqué" prints.

> Well, it *was* simply amazing. I bought the first collection that turned up on that trial for much less than I ever thought possible. The news (a secret) got around just how and where we hoped it would….

> I was getting excited. Already I had established a considerable buying power and anything available in the ordinary channels came first to me. I picked up some fine things in this way. But aristocratic Japanese people lose face if they sell their belongings, even such taboo things as the prints. But evidently Shugio had found a way. Well, it had begun. The twenty thousand was soon gone and already I had priceless things. Anything unique or superior went to the Spauldings…. I would cable for money from time to time during the five-month [sic] campaign. The money always came, no questions asked. And nothing from me except excited demands for more money until I had spent about one hundred and twenty-five thousand Spaulding dollars for about a million dollars' worth of prints.[60]

Wright mounted and grouped the prints in his workshop at the Imperial, and stored them in Shugio's godown until they were shipped to the United States.[61] It is not likely that Shugio was emptying the cupboards of court nobles, and he was certainly not a confidant of the emperor Meiji (whose personal name was Mutsuhito). However, it is true that many former daimyo and samurai families were selling their collections during these years.

Wright sent off a letter to Shugio immediately after leaving Prides Crossing in July 1913, reimbursing his Japanese partner the hefty sum of ¥27,500 (approximately $13,750). Shugio was obliged to point out that this was in fact considerably short of the actual amount Wright owed him. Wright betrays some residual twinges of guilt in his autobiography: "Shugio got some of the twenty-five thousand but I wish now I had given him all of it. You have here before you a perfect picture of the West looting the Orient. I make no apologies. You may judge for yourself."[62] Shugio was left to clean up after Wright's departure, and spent many days checking on the packing and shipping of some 933 additional prints the architect had purchased from the Tokyo dealer Kobayashi Bunshichi and one of Kobayashi's friends for ¥27,000. (Shugio had known Kobayashi for years. He was a lender to Kobayashi's ukiyo-e exhibition at the Shōgenro in Ueno Park, Tokyo, in 1892.)[63] Kobayashi warned Wright that he had given special terms because they were "good old friends"; all of his prints would be 50 percent higher in the future.

Kobayashi was the premier dealer in ukiyo-e prints and illustrated books in Japan by the turn of the century, but he handled fine paintings as well. He opened a shop in the Asakusa Komagata-chō district of Tokyo around 1887 and had branches in Yokohama and San Francisco, possibly as early as 1898. He is described as handsome, and he spoke English, a big asset in his dealings with foreigners. He also smoked cigars, loved Western food, and drank heavily. His firm, Hōsūkaku, made facsimile prints for the tourist trade but also published scholarly works on ukiyo-e, including an early biography of Hokusai. In the 1890s Kobayashi supplied Hayashi Tadamasa in Paris and worked in close partnership with Fenollosa, publicizing and selling ukiyo-e prints and paintings. According to correspondence between Gookin and Freer in 1900, however, Kobayashi's reputation at the time was none too good, there being a suspicion that copyists in his employ were producing forgeries. By 1902 he was making annual pilgrimages to America. Thomas Lawton, formerly director of the Freer Gallery of Art, observed that Kobayashi "regularly offered Charles Freer objects of exceptionally high quality," including one masterpiece, *Waves at Matsushima*, a pair of screens by Tawaraya Sōtatsu (active 1614–c. 1639).[64] These screens cost Freer $5,000 in 1906.

Kobayashi's private collection, said to have been the largest in Japan, numbered some 100,000 prints and also included 500 paintings by Hokusai and his pupils alone. All were tragically destroyed by fire in the 1923 earthquake a few months after Kobayashi's death from stomach ulcers.

"Now," Shugio wrote in August 1913, just as he was preparing to send yet another batch of prints to Spring Green, "it is impossible even for money to get such a fine collection as you secured…. All the print dealers say Mr. Wright has taken away all the first class old prints and I think they are nearly right."[65]

Buckingham died in August 1913 (on the eve of a visit to Prides Crossing), but this year marked the beginning, for Wright, of the lucrative Spaulding era. The Spauldings were now thoroughly hooked, eagerly awaiting each new shipment from Japan, wanting to be tempted. "We have been hoping to hear from you daily that the prints Shugio was to forward you had been received," William wrote in September. "Whenever an opportunity presents itself, we open up our print case, and are gradually beginning to look upon our newly acquired treasures as old friends…. In the years to come we must plan to have many print feasts together." In October, when the Kobayashi lot—including works by Chōki, Harunobu, Shunshō, Hokusai, and Hiroshige—arrived (having been vetted first by Gookin in Chicago), their expectations were fulfilled. "All that you have claimed for the prints more than holds out—and if only you might have been present when the prints were divulged to our gaze—you would know the 'thrills' we experienced, and how tremendously enthusiastic we were over the lot."[66] They ask for more Hiroshige bird-and-flower prints, and they want to see a group of about twenty Shunshō. Throughout they complain, of course, of their own financial difficulties incurred by mounting print debts (they sent Wright a check for $4,500 in November 1913 and another for $11,500 not long thereafter), by the newly imposed income tax, not to mention higher state and city taxes: "The Garden is gone;…we are dismantling it and trying to sell everything of value in it, mainly to free ourselves of the cost of maintenance which we can no longer afford. We are giving up our horses, and reducing our motor expenditures."[67] They say they can't possibly contemplate acquiring the Hiroshige *harimaze* (literally, "pasted scraps," meaning a print composed of many small pictures) or the collection of 850 Katsukawa-school actor prints that Wright is offering. On the other hand, they still seem to give him carte blanche. "Whenever you receive from Japan any print that you feel deserves a place in our collection," William Spaulding writes, "please do not fail to send it on to us—for we want to be tempted…. It is a terrible fever to be 'blessed' with this longing for the beautiful in Japanese prints. My faith in you is so good that I feel that there will be nothing 'exquisite and desirable' that will escape us from Japan."[68] In early January 1914, skillfully negotiating a 10-percent discount, they parted with another $2,529 for forty-two prints by Hiroshige that they couldn't resist.[69]

THE SPAULDINGS HOST A PRINT PARTY

The following week the Spauldings hosted an exhausting week-long print party, showing off their new purchases to a glamorous Who's Who of midwestern collectors—Mary A. Ainsworth, Charles H. Chandler, Arthur Davison Ficke, and Mr. L. E. Charnley. The guests arrived early every day at the Beacon Street house and did not leave until after dark. "They were crazy about your 'Japan' prints," Spaulding assured Wright. "We did not nearly get through the entire collection, but enough was seen to use up all the adjectives in existence! And with your continued assistance we expect to make it still greater!"[70]

Ainsworth (1867–1950) spent most of her life in Moline, Illinois, where her father was a very successful manufacturer of machinery for farm equipment companies. She purchased her first prints on a trip to Japan in 1906 and continued to collect actively for the next twenty-five years. Ainsworth left 1,500 prints, including many she bought from Wright, to her alma mater, Oberlin College; the collection is now in the Allen Memorial Art Museum, Oberlin.[71]

Ficke (1883–1945), described by those who knew him as tall and handsome, polished and poised, with great personal charm, was a wealthy lawyer and a promising young poet with a passion for Japanese prints (ill. 71). A Harvard graduate, he became a partner in his father's law firm in Davenport, Iowa. Though scarcely remembered as a poet, some of his finest sonnets were inspired by a lifelong infatuation with his friend Edna St. Vincent Millay (1892–1950). Metzgar took credit for sparking Ficke on prints during a visit to his home around 1909.[72] In 1915 Ficke published *Chats on Japanese Prints* (dedicated to Gookin and Mansfield)—a very influential and, for its time, scholarly work on ukiyo-e history and connoisseurship, although today we would have to take exception with his use of the terms "decadence" and "downfall" to characterize the work of everyone from Utamaro through Hiroshige, the last artist whom he

considers worth mention. Ficke and Wright became quite friendly. In 1916, in exchange for a copy of *Chats*, Wright sent Ficke his 1906 *Hiroshige* catalogue. He received this charming note of thanks from Ficke: "I shall preserve it carefully, and doubtless some day posterity will be erecting a monument to you with life-size figures of you and Hiroshige holding hands, he with one foot on the neck of a Philistine, and you with one foot on the neck of a print-dealer. I hope the sculptor will weave me into the decoration of the base, in the form of an admiring cherub." "Dear F," came the reply, "I die now, content, immortality assured by 'the cherub'. The sculptor? But why betray anxiety—again?"[73] (When Ficke traveled to Japan, Korea, and China in the summer of 1917, he visited Shugio and they spent three hours looking at Hiroshige prints together.)[74] In the 1930s Ficke's son was briefly an apprentice in the Taliesin Fellowship.

Wright graciously sent the Spauldings a gift of Hiroshige's set of the *Eight Views of Biwa* and then, having softened them up, paid them a short visit in mid-February 1914 on his way back from Washington. They discussed Hiroshige, and Wright somehow convinced them that he was holding back good examples for Francis Little. William Spaulding, still elated by the recent adulation of his print party guests, rose to the bait and immediately requested right of first refusal on any prints Wright might sell.[75]

TRAGEDY AT TALIESIN

The fire and murders at Taliesin in 1914 were the most devastating blow of Wright's life, "shattering his dreams and all he had worked for."[76] At lunchtime on 15 August, the husband of the recently hired cook, an émigré from Barbados, locked the dining room door, set gasoline fires under the windows, and murdered with a hatchet those who tried to flee from the single exit. Hired only a few months earlier as a handyman, Julian Carleton turned out to be unstable and paranoid, and had evidently alarmed Borthwick enough to give him notice. She was his first victim—he plunged the hatchet deep into the center of her head. (Carleton swallowed muriatic acid, then deliberately starved himself to death in the Dodgeville County jail without explaining his motives.) The living quarters burned to the ground, and Mamah, her two visiting children, three of the Taliesin work crew, and the young son of a fourth were all

71.
Arthur Ficke

killed. This was an unimaginable personal tragedy for Wright, who was in Chicago supervising the Midway Garden site. His son John was with him when he was notified of the fire. "Suddenly all was quiet in the room, a strange unnatural silence, his breathing alone was audible, then a groan. I turned to him startled. He clung to the table for support, his face ashen…. It was difficult for him to speak." John believed that "something in him died with her, a something lovable and gentle that I knew and loved in my father."[77]

Physically and emotionally traumatized by this nightmarish event, Wright now perceived Taliesin as a void, a gaping black hole that mirrored the emptiness of his own life. The tragedy triggered his erratic development over the next two decades, when he turned away from Taliesin and, as Neil Levine observes, "did not even live there on anything like a continual basis."[78]

Print sales continued to be an important source of income for the architect. Gookin presented a big memorial exhibition of Buckingham prints at the Art Institute of Chicago in January and February 1915, and Wright made a sale to Kate Buckingham (ill. 72). Sales to the Spauldings continued unabated, although by May 1915, when they sent Wright a check for $10,000, they admitted to buying some prints, duplicates, for example, as a personal favor since he claimed dire financial need.[79] A year later he continued to bombard them with packages of prints, even though they were by now quite sated (or pretended to be). In trying to dispose of duplicates they had found, to their horror, absolutely no buyers of Japanese prints willing to spend anything near the high prices they had paid Wright. "We have made serious efforts in every direction to dispose of them and we cannot get rid of the blessed things in any way or at any price…. Thus it has been brought home to us how very few buyers there are seriously interested in Japanese prints."[80] The Spauldings were no doubt being deliberately coy about expenses, but the moral here is that art is not a liquid asset, and selling it requires certain skills that do not come naturally to everyone.

72.
Torii Kiyomitsu (1735–1785). *Ono no Komachi Washing the Copybook*. c. 1764. Color woodcut, *hosoban mizu-e*. Seal of Tokyo print dealer Kobayashi Bunshichi on reverse. The Art Institute of Chicago, Clarence Buckingham Collection, 1925 (1925.2003)

Wright sold this print to Kate Buckingham in February 1915.

In October 1915 Hayashi Aisaku, manager of the Imperial Hotel, wrote Gookin from Tokyo to forewarn of his impending arrival in mid-January to begin work with Wright on plans for the hotel; at this point the decision to hire Wright was all but settled.[81] Gookin gave Wright the following, almost fatherly, advice:

> The building of the new hotel gives you I believe your one great opportunity. Do not let your opinions, your wishes, or anything else stand in the way. Modify your plans wherever necessary to conform to Mr. Hayashi's ideas…. If the building is successful, and that means not only an artistic but a practical success, it will be advertised all over the world and cannot fail to bring you renown and further commissions…. Make the building look Japanese as well as like your work…. Hayashi is a clear-headed man. He will have ideas about these things. If he does, do not flout them. Work with him, be adaptable, and go in and score a great success. I shall be glad to do all I can to help. Without my recommendation you could not have got in touch with Hayashi and I know that he will consult me after his arrival before he decides to let you go ahead.[82]

Hayashi, accompanied by his lovely wife, Takako (she impressed Gookin as "a person of rank"), and the Japanese architect Yoshitake Tori (1879–1953), made a study tour of hotels in southern California. They then spent some time in Chicago and Spring Green discussing and fine tuning Wright's plans and drawing up a contract that called for a 5-percent commission for Wright as well as round-trip travel and room and board for him and three assistants (ill. 73). Hayashi returned to Tokyo in late March to recommend Wright to the hotel's board of directors.[83]

In the meantime, Wright was still broke. In April he tried once again to peddle some brocades, pottery, and rare prints to the intractable Martin with the assurance of "a reasonably cheap price for exceptionally fine things." He had the nerve to argue that Martin should exchange some of his stocks and bonds for things of beauty, flowers of the field that would become "blossoms of the human soul."[84]

Financial negotiations between Martin, Little, and Wright heated up in the fall of 1916. Wright sent the bulk of his print

73.
Hayashi Aisaku and his wife, Takako, in the living room at Taliesin II. Spring 1916

A pillar print is mounted in a print stand to the left.

collection, worth $15,000, or so he claimed, to Little in Minneapolis. Little was to make a selection in exchange for the amount still owed him on two mortgage notes on the Oak Park property (Martin urgently needed these notes), although it is reasonable to assume that Little would have greatly preferred a cash settlement. Wright, of course, thought of prints as currency and, in correspondence with Martin, sanctimoniously denounced Little's hesitation as disgusting and grotesque. In November, harassed on all sides, Little finally turned the prints over to his wife, so that she could lay them out and make a choice. Acknowledging Wright's charisma, Martin offered to send the architect himself to Minneapolis, where, with his "line of talk," he would surely convince Mrs. Little to want them all.[85] The next year Little decided to find a proper home for some of these prints: he donated a complete set of Hiroshige's *Fifty-three Stations of the Tōkaidō* to the Minneapolis Society of Fine Arts, where he had been appointed a trustee in 1914 (see ill. 47).[86] This gift represents the beginning of the museum's ukiyo-e collection. The set, known as the Hōeidō Tōkaidō, after its publisher, was produced in 1833–34, the first of more than twenty sets of views of the fifty-three checkpoints on the Tōkaidō Road between Edo and Kyoto that Hiroshige produced during the next two decades.[87] Because the Hōeidō or Great Tōkaidō was a "best seller," many examples have survived, but fine impressions of individual prints are surprisingly rare. The Littles' prints show evidence of backing and have holes at the margin, indications that they were originally in an album, perhaps dismantled by Wright himself. They are of average quality but fine condition and color. Over the years Wright would dispose of many more sets of the *Fifty-three Stations*, each in turn touted as especially rare.

In November 1916, on the eve of his departure for Japan, Wright sold the Spaulding brothers more than $10,000 worth of prints: twenty-six large Katsukawa actor prints at $250 each (the *ōban* size is rare and accordingly more valuable) and thirty-four smaller Katsukawa prints in *hosoban* format at $150 each. Katsukawa prints are not as sought after today as they were in the 1910s, but even so prints that cost the Spauldings several hundred dollars are today worth well into the thousands. They were thrilled to be the new owners of actor prints described as "the finest in existence." "It is needless for me to add," gushed William Spaulding, "that your prints have fallen into hands that appreciate their greatness and loveliness fully as much as you really could have yourself: for it is not possible to prize them to an extent greater than we all do."[88] Two years later, when the market was actually stronger, Wright sold very similar Katsukawa-school prints to the Metropolitan Museum of Art for half the price.

Just before setting off for Japan at the end of December, Wright was up to his old tricks, foisting off some prints on Susan Lawrence Dana (1862–1946), a wealthy socialite for whom he had built a luxurious residence in Springfield, Illinois, in 1902–4. He evidently offered them as a way of discounting her stock in the Hillside Home School corporation in Spring Green, a failed venture. By her accounting, he owed her $3,400. "The prints came tonight," she wrote him on 22 December. "I am going East in three weeks. I will take them to Boston and have Spaulding look them over and give me an estimate on them. We can then talk the matter over when you return." An appraisal of her personal property at the end of her life mentioned a collection of Japanese prints—valued at $2.50.[89]

Before his departure in December, Wright notified the Spauldings that he would be pleased to be their agent again. This time they made it very clear that they would absolutely refuse to make any purchases without seeing the prints first. But once again they were seduced by a cable from Tokyo that arrived in mid-February 1917: "Hundred forty unexcelled unacquired Hiroshige Oban yours five thousand wire Impeho Wright." Due entirely to his use of the word "unexcelled," coupled with the implied urgency of the cable itself, they sent off a draft for $5,000 without a moment's hesitation. What they did not know was that Wright had purchased these prints from the collection of his friend Shugio; the sense of urgency was an artful fabrication. Shugio was a collector, not a dealer, but he did sell to Wright.[90]

Between January 1917, when he arrived in Tokyo to begin the Imperial Hotel project, and July 1922, when he left Japan never to return, Wright made five extended trips to Tokyo in connection with the design and construction of the hotel (ill. 74).[91] He often stayed as long as six months at a time and it seems that every free moment was devoted to prints. "The pursuit of the Japanese print became my constant recreation while in Tokyo," he confessed in his autobiography. Indeed, shortly after arriving in 1917 he received this note from Shugio: "Kobayashi [Bunshichi] sent me words this morning that he is now ready to show you his Hiroshige prints and he wishes me to accompany you to his house either tomorrow afternoon or Sunday afternoon when he will be happy to show them to you. Will you let me know by telephone when it would suit you to go and I'll arrange to go with you."[92]

Wright embarked for the return voyage from Yokohama in mid-April 1917 after spending three and a half months in Japan with his son John (who stayed behind in Tokyo until Wright fired him a year later when he demanded a salary) and Miriam Noel (1869–1930). Noel, an alluring middle-aged divorcée from Kentucky, was a sculptor and had been living in Paris until the outbreak of war in 1914 drove her back to Chicago, where her children were living (ill. 75). She teamed up with Wright within months of the tragedy at Taliesin and was his companion for eight years before their ill-fated marriage in 1923, a year after his wife Catherine finally granted him a divorce. On this trip to Japan she was known as "Mrs. Wright."

Wright was now on the verge of losing the Oak Park home. A creditor had in fact been patiently awaiting his return in order to initiate foreclosure on the mortgage. The architect's only hope of gaining solvency was to reduce his large debt to Martin. This he hoped to do by making another quick sale to the Spauldings. Shugio had been bargaining with Kobayashi over a group of seventy-four pillar prints and 1,987 Hiroshige that Wright had set aside prior to his departure from Japan. Wright (who always had money for prints, if not for his mortgage) offered ¥30,000 (about $15,000) through Shugio, and Kobayashi came back with a counteroffer of ¥35,000. The prints were rushed to Spring Green, then expressed to William Spaulding in Boston, who could only gasp: "I cannot quite make out in my own mind which gave me the greatest shock: the prices quoted by you or the rare beauty of many of the prints…. My!! what prices!!!"[93] He seems to have kept a selection of examples by Hiroshige.

At the same time Wright figured that he could work off his debt to Martin without having to pay cash by trading him some of his newly acquired treasures.[94] Accordingly, on 10 July 1917, he wrote Martin asking whether he would consider purchasing the box of prints he had been holding as security since 1912 as well as an additional $8,000 worth of Chinese pottery and bronzes, Japanese brocades of the Genroku era (1688–1703), Momoyama-period (1573–1615) screens, and some few very rare prints, "all of a quality to delight the Albright museum authorities," in full payment of all debts and all accrued interest. Or perhaps Martin might even get interested enough in these wonderful things (which Wright had hoped to be able to enjoy into his old age) to buy them outright: "I have sacrificed already much in peace of mind and reputation financially to hang on to them as long as I have."[95] The director of the Albright Art Gallery (now the

74.
Chart of Wright's seven visits to Japan, from 1905 to 1922

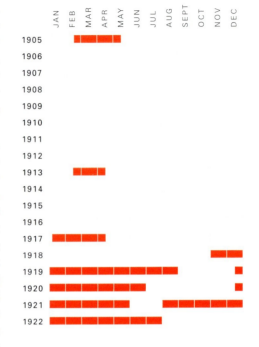

1905
Wright's first visit to Japan, a three-month tourist trip, accompanied by Catherine Wright

1913
Wright, in Japan with Mamah Borthwick, spends two months collecting prints

1917–22
Wright travels to Japan five times while working on the Imperial Hotel in Tokyo. Accompanied by Miriam Noel, Wright spends a total of thirty-four months in Japan

75.
Miriam Noel

Albright-Knox Art Gallery) in Buffalo was Cornelia Bentley Sage Quinton (?–1936), who was known to have a keen interest in Asia, fostered by close friendships with collectors Freer in Detroit and John Ferguson, an old China hand in Boston. (Unfortunately, she never had success raising money for Asian art.) Martin replied:

> In the present state of my finances, it is entirely out of the question for me to consider the purchase of any objets des art, Japanese or otherwise.
>
> But, my dear man, why do you want to part with what you call your heart's treasures, joys of your old age, in exchange for the crumbling pile in Oak Park? Awake instead to the fact that you are well rid of it. Take the $8,000 in cash you can raise and provide Mrs. Wright and the children with a vastly better home (Gee, don't build it; buy it ready-made; then you'll keep within the appropriation)—one that will suit her far better and can actually be heated! and rainproof…. Don't spread your pearls before—me.[96]

Around this same time Wright paid off part of a debt he owed his young friend Alfred MacArthur (1885–1967), an insurance company executive who lived in the architect's Oak Park house between approximately 1911 and 1919, with $2,000 worth of Japanese prints. MacArthur believed the valuation to be outrageously high and was ready to offer them to anyone else for $500.[97]

In the spring of 1918 Wright offered prints that Mr. and Mrs. Little had rejected in 1916 to the Spauldings. John Spaulding wrote to say that despite their determination to get nothing they did not absolutely need, they would nonetheless take twenty-seven from the Minneapolis lot at $3,420 and a group of others at $4,080. These were almost entirely eighteenth-century figure prints. Working from a list priced by Gookin, they negotiated a 20-percent discount.[98]

THE SPAULDING PRINT ROOM

Following the architect's visit to Boston in February 1914, William Spaulding had remarked: "You must tell us of the plans for the Museum print room as they assume shape. Our conversa-tion on the subject has made me so eager to have a room of our own and to know our treasures are in safety that I wish we could start building tomorrow."[99] It seems likely that Wright conceived the plans for a Spaulding print gallery on a speculative basis; it was never built. We know how competitive Wright was; possibly he was goaded by a series of "Japanese" interiors and a Japanese garden court for the Asian galleries in the new Museum of Fine Arts building that opened in Fenway in 1909. The court was designed by the staff of the Japanese department in collaboration with the leading Boston architect Ralph Adams Cram (1863–1942); it was demolished in the 1970s.[100] Cram, like Wright, fancied himself an authority on Japanese architecture; his 1905 *Impressions of Japanese Architecture* was based on a four-month trip to Japan in 1898. Wright, with four years of his childhood spent in the Boston suburb of Weymouth, where his father was the minister of the First Baptist Church, must have longed to build something for one of the grand families of Boston.

By 1917 at Prides Crossing the Spauldings were constructing a fireproof vault for their prints beside the den (on the main floor next to the billiard room), which they used as a "print room"—perhaps a less costly solution. (John Spaulding eventually had an annex for his growing Impressionist collection.) A family used to the monumental doorways, high ceilings, and mottled polished marble of a mansion by the Boston firm of Little and Browne might not have felt comfortable with a Wright interior (see ill. 55). In the summer of 1918 Wright retrieved the drawings from the Spauldings in order to send them to a new client on the East coast: S. C. Bosch Reitz, the curator of Asian art at the Metropolitan Museum of Art. The Metropolitan returned the drawings immediately without comment.[101]

Wright's design for the Spaulding gallery (Douglass Shand-Tucci calls it Boston's first radical modernist work) was suited to the small size and intimate character of Japanese prints. In an early drawing Wright shows the square, high-ceilinged room as having a row of windows across the top, at the mezzanine balcony level (ill. 76). In all later drawings these are eliminated, presumably because prints are light sensitive. The gallery, probably intended for the Spaulding's Back Bay townhouse, is entered from a waiting room with a toilet and coat room at one end and a fireplace at the other. Chest-high storage cabinets with wide, shallow drawers encircle the gallery. On one perspective Wright indicated that the drawers were for prints, hanging scrolls, inro (lacquer medicine containers), netsuke (miniature toggles from which inro are suspended from a man's obi), and sword guards (*tsuba*) (ills. 77, 78). The Spaulding gift to the Museum of Fine Arts years later included nearly five hundred sword guards and small knives (*kozuka*), as well as some Chinese paintings and ceramics.[102] The perspectives reveal Wright's clever and practical solution for print viewing. Pillar prints as well as vertical and horizontal *ōban*, some clearly recognizable as landscapes by Hokusai and Hiroshige, lean against slanted walls above the cabinets. (Sloping walls reappear famously in the Guggenheim Museum.) The room is top-lighted and additional light fixtures hang from the ceiling. Plants, integral to all of Wright's interiors, are set on free-standing plant stands.[103] A row of four low armchairs is arranged in front of an unusually wide, slanted easel, for the enjoyment of individual prints.

Wright's print clients included all of the big collectors from the Midwest and East coast, but the Spauldings were probably the most dependable and certainly the wealthiest. Their last purchases from Wright were made in September 1921.[104] A few months later they announced their intention of giving the entire collection to the Museum of Fine Arts, and with that announce-

ment their Japanese print acquisitions ceased entirely. In searching for an explanation as to why the Spauldings dropped out of the ukiyo-e market, one can point to the fact that William and Katrina were living in the Montecito-Santa Barbara area in California, in part because their son Stuart, born in 1914, was sickly and could not take the harsh New England winters, but also to be near Katrina's invalid mother. In the early 1920s they spent more time in Europe after sending their children to boarding school in Switzerland. John Spaulding, for his part, had cultivated a very serious interest in American as well as French Impressionist and Post-Impressionist paintings and watercolors. In November 1921 the brothers sold off 748 Japanese prints (duplicates and lesser works) at auction through the American Art Association in New York. The catalogue, compiled by Gookin, is impressive. The discarded prints were sufficient in number, quality, and importance to form an exceedingly fine collection in and of themselves, although they brought in a total of only $9,697.[105] By deed of gift dated 2 December 1921 they gave their remaining prints to the Museum of Fine Arts subject to a life estate for the joint lives of the two brothers. They re-

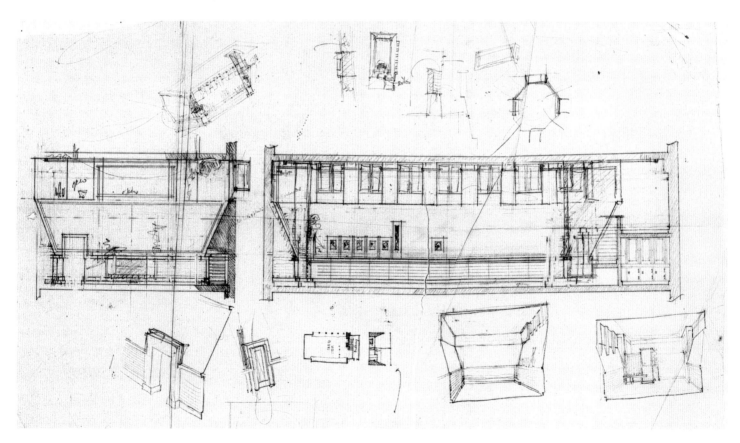

76.
Frank Lloyd Wright. Japanese Print Gallery for William Spaulding, Boston, first version (project). c. 1914. Section with sketches; graphite on tracing paper, 18 x 27 in. The Frank Lloyd Wright Foundation (1902.011)

tained possession of the collection, which could be viewed by appointment. When William died in 1937 custody of the entire collection passed to his brother, who transferred the prints to the museum permanently in 1942.[106] Ironically, the terms of the Spaulding gift prohibit the prints from ever being placed on exhibit, citing the "delicate, fugitive colors." The inability to control light levels in 1921 in the galleries may have provoked this restriction. As a result, sadly, the collection is not well known and is seen only by the occasional scholar.

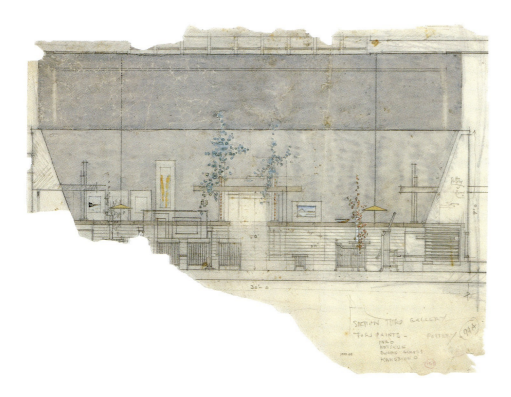

77.
Frank Lloyd Wright.
Japanese Print Gallery
for William Spaulding,
Boston (project).
c. 1914. Section; watercolor, ink, and colored
pencil on tracing paper,
14 x 19½ in. The Frank
Lloyd Wright Foundation (1902.002)

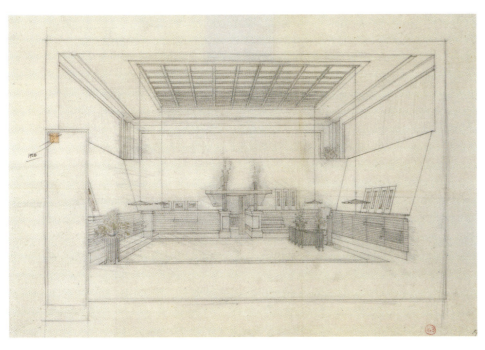

78.
Frank Lloyd Wright.
Japanese Print Gallery
for William Spaulding,
Boston (project).
c. 1914. Interior view;
ink, graphite and colored pencil on tracing
paper, 14½ x 21½ in.
The Frank Lloyd Wright
Foundation (1902.009)

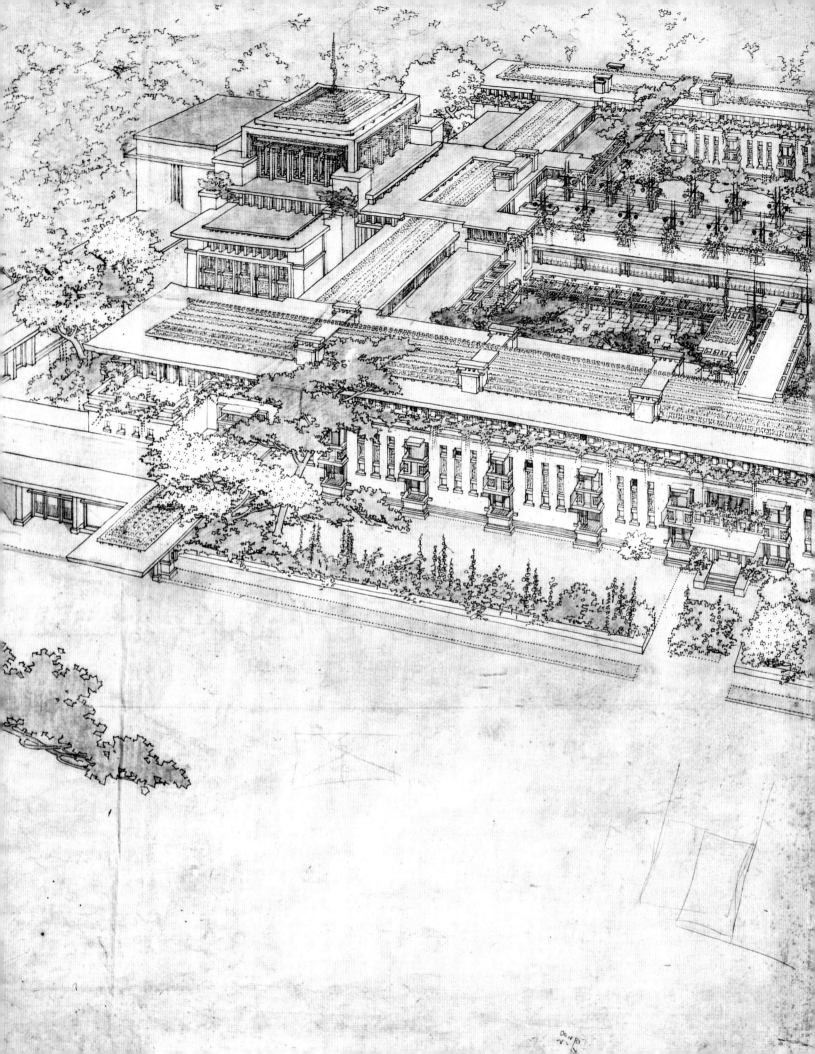

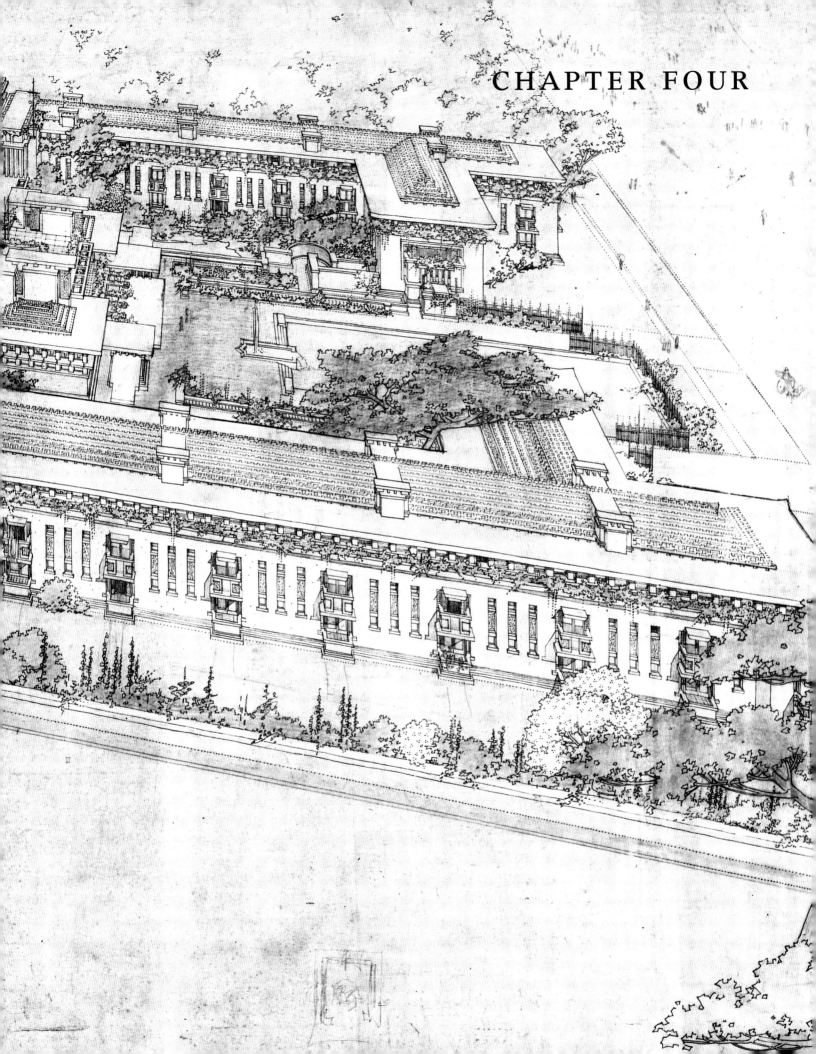

CHAPTER FOUR

AN "ORIENTAL SYMPHONY" IN TOKYO

1914 EXHIBITION AT THE ART INSTITUTE

Wright had a lifelong habit of stocking up on Asian art to embellish his home when it was due to be featured in a publication. By October 1915, when a view of his living room was published in *Architectural Record*, it is evident that he had again filled Taliesin with Japanese prints, screens, and Buddhist sculptures (ills. 81, 82). Stands that Wright had created in 1908 for the Art Institute print exhibition reappear in a tall, slender form suitable for holding pillar prints. A ledge projecting at the bottom serves as a kind of pedestal for a flower basket or, sometimes, for a small, seated wooden Buddha, an unexpected, inventive combination. In a Wright-designed house (including his own) it is often difficult to find wall surfaces suitable for hanging a work of art; a print stand was one solution to this dilemma.

Wright showed stands in three different shapes intended for "interior decoration in the manner of the statuette" in 1914 at the twenty-seventh annual exhibition of the Chicago Architectural Club held at the Art Institute (ill. 80). His approach to display had become quite sophisticated by this time. Edgar Kaufmann noted that "drawings, photographs, and models of his work were rather casually assembled, suggesting a pell-mell of creative activity."[1] The view of the 1914 exhibition shown here includes, in the foreground, a model for Midway Gardens, which opened officially in June 1914, small sculptural models by Alfonso

Iannelli (1888–1965), the Italian-American who worked with Wright on this commission, a child's building blocks for creating architectural forms, and photographs. Toward the back of the room are a ground plan, elevation, and outline perspective of the Imperial Hotel (ill. 79). Wright had not yet secured a formal commitment for the commission but the inclusion of the drawings gave him the cachet of international status. In 1914 he also made a drawing for a United States embassy building in Tokyo, although there is no evidence this design was ever commissioned. Historians have speculated that Wright produced the perspective in order to impress the staff of the Imperial by showing that he could do more than just residential structures.

Of special interest to us are four print stands of various sizes easily visible in the middle distance of the exhibition, with a fifth at the far left partially obscured from view by Iannelli's models. They accommodate every print format. Two on the left hold standard vertical *ōban* prints, both Hiroshige landscapes; the one facing us is *Inside Kameido Tenjin Shrine* from the series *One Hundred Views of Famous Places in Edo*. Elevated at the center is a small stand with a Katsukawa-school actor print in vertical *hosoban* format, its projecting ledge supporting a flower vase. In the center middle ground is a very tall, narrow stand with a pillar print by Koryūsai.

According to the catalogue introduction written by the Chicago architect Alfred S. Alschuler (1876–1940), the 1914 ex-

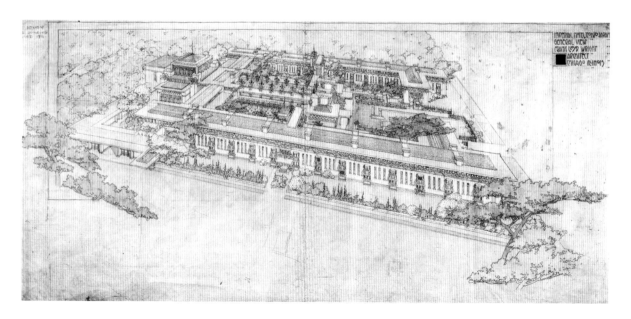

79.
Frank Lloyd Wright. Imperial Hotel, Tokyo. c. 1913–14. Aerial perspective, first scheme; graphite, colored pencil, and India ink on waxed linen, 33½ in. x 6 ft. 2½ in. Erving and Joyce Wolf Collection

80.
Exhibition of Wright's work completed since the spring of 1911, at the Art Institute of Chicago. 1914. Installation designed by Wright

Wright displayed a preliminary drawing for the Imperial Hotel (see also ill. 79) as well as at least five print stands with Japanese prints from his own collection.

81.
Taliesin II. View from the living room to the dining
area. c. 1916–24

There are three tall print stands with pillar prints in this
view—one to the left of the dining table, two at the far
right. A small, six-panel Japanese screen on the wall
behind the dining table has a design of autumn grasses. Japanese Buddhist sculpture—a Buddha (with
damaged halo) flanked by two Bodhisattvas—on the
dining table creates a ritual space. In an earlier view of
the room (*Architectural Record*, October 1915) this
Buddha sits on the ledge projecting from the bottom
of one of the print stands.

82.
Taliesin II. Living room. 1916–24

A Japanese textile with phoenix and paulownia design
is draped over furniture at the right beside the piano.
Two print stands, left and far right, flank the fireplace
alcove and a Chinese eighth-century Tang-dynasty
tomb figure graces a ledge.

Students at work in an
exhibition of Asian bro-
cades from the Nomura
collection at the Art
Institute of Chicago.
1915

84.
Nomura Shōjirō and
family at home in Kyoto,
a robe displayed behind
them

hibition was meant to present a selection of works produced during the preceding year. Wright's portion of the display, however, was boldly labeled "Work of Frank Lloyd Wright: exhibit confined to work done since spring of 1911." The alleged favoritism shown Wright, who had practically an entire room for his work, created a furor among local architects and was reported in the *Record Herald* on the eve of the opening on 9 April under the heading "Wright Exhibit Stirs Chicago Architects." A leading Chicago architect was quoted as saying: "A great deal of unfairness and unethical dealing has marred the exhibition this year. A small group has been able to manipulate things so that wealthy architects have been shown a marked preference over their less fortunate craftsmen. It is not putting it too strongly to say that the Chicago Architectural Club sold out to Wright." A spokesperson for the club denied having received $500 from Wright to make up the club deficit. Although Wright was heavily in debt to several of his clients, he was perceived by his colleagues as wealthy. "Let them talk," said Wright. "Let them say what they will. Let them resurrect all the old scandal of the past three years. What do I care. I have three walls for my work. I'm erecting the Imperial Hotel at Tokio and I'm doing other big work in the world—both the scandal and what I am doing artistically will bring us greater crowds. Let them talk, let them talk."[2]

WRIGHT THE TEXTILE COLLECTOR

Japanese and Chinese textiles (not to mention Chinese, Persian, and Turkoman carpets) were conspicuous in Wright's homes, often draped over furniture (see ill. 82). On his first trip to Japan in 1905, when Wright stopped at the Kanaya Hotel in Nikkō, he visited the Kobayashi Curio shop. Founded in 1873 by Kobayashi Shōichirō (1846–1927), the picturesque shop (still in business today) specialized in old kimonos for the tourist trade. Wright recorded his visit in the Kobayashi guest book. Judging by the roster of famous names, including Fenollosa and Bigelow, Alexander Graham Bell ("I think they have some good things here at reasonable prices"), John S. Pillsbury, and Mary Livingston Griggs, this place was a must for all tourists. In Kyoto, Wright had an introduction from Shugio to Kawashima Jimbei II (1853–1910), "the best weaver in Kyoto," who had a very large collection of old brocades.[3]

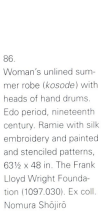

85.
Woman's unlined summer robe (*kosode*) with wisteria and fish nets. Edo period, early eighteenth century. Silk crepe (*chirimen*) with silk embroidery, stenciled dotted patterns, couched gold-wrapped threads, and painting, 62¼ x 48 in. The Frank Lloyd Wright Foundation (1097.028)

Kosode (small sleeves), a reference to the size of the wrist opening, is the old name for the form of dress now known as the kimono.

86.
Woman's unlined summer robe (*kosode*) with heads of hand drums. Edo period, nineteenth century. Ramie with silk embroidery and painted and stenciled patterns, 63½ x 48 in. The Frank Lloyd Wright Foundation (1097.030). Ex coll. Nomura Shōjirō

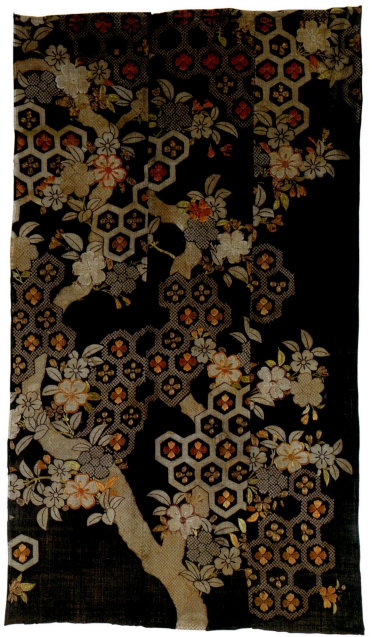

87.
Three joined fragments
of a summer robe
(*kosode*) with a design
of a flowering cherry
tree and a stylized tor-
toise-shell design with
cherry-blossom centers.
Edo period, eighteenth
century. Ramie with
embroidery and sten-
ciled pattern, 54½ x
32¼ in. The Frank Lloyd
Wright Foundation
(1097.010)

88.
Fragment of a robe
(*kosode*) sleeve with
a design of large
chrysanthemums and
waterfalls. Edo period,
late seventeenth–early
eighteenth century. Silk
damask with embroi-
dery and painted and
stenciled tie-dye pat-
terns, 60¼ x 12¾ in.
The Frank Lloyd Wright
Foundation (1097.009).
Ex coll. Nomura Shōjirō

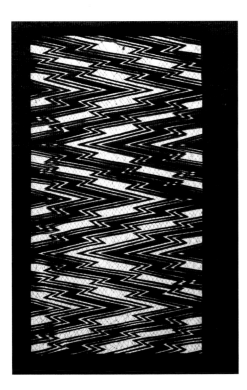

89.
Stencil for textile dyeing with a design of linking pine-bark diamonds. Edo period, nineteenth century. Paper treated with persimmon juice and fortified with silk threads, 12½ x 16½ in. The Frank Lloyd Wright Foundation (3202.024)

Western collectors were especially fond of altar cloths and Buddhist priests' garments (*kesa*), which flooded the market in the late nineteenth century in the wake of Japan's modernization and the persecution of Buddhism. The simple rectangular shapes and lush colors of these gold brocades, shaped like stoles, were ideal for decorative wall hangings, table covers, and the like. Nomura Shōjirō (1879–1943), the legendary Kyoto textile dealer, took his collection of over one hundred such brocades on tour to the United States, beginning with an unsuccessful auction sale estimated (by him) at $17,000 in January 1915 in Boston and culminating in an exhibition at the Art Institute of Chicago in March and April (ill. 83).[4] The Metropolitan Museum of Art bought the lot four years later. Nomura opened a grand shop on Shinmonzen, the antique dealers' street in the heart of Kyoto, in 1908 (ill. 84). He spoke English, having attended high school in Greenville, Illinois, and his business, which included color prints and other antiques, was aimed at rich Western clients, especially Americans, whose company he very much enjoyed. We do not know for certain where Wright purchased his textiles, but "Nomura" is listed as a source in one of his bank books.

Wright owned a number of *kesa*, a noh robe, stencils for textile dyeing, and many antique kimono (*kosode*, "small sleeves"), including a breathtakingly beautiful sheer summer robe with a wisteria design in gold, orange, yellow, green, and lavender (ills. 85–89). The colors that Wright preferred were clearly those he saw in Japanese art, whether textiles or early woodblock prints. Wright also had many fragments that match up with those now located in the Los Angeles County Museum of Art and elsewhere. They all seem to have originated with Nomura, who spent years reassembling robes (*kosode*) from fragments that had been cut and sewn patchwork-style into Buddhist altar cloths; if the robes were incomplete, he pasted them onto two-panel screens. Essentially, he devoted his life to the preservation of one of Japan's greatest artistic traditions, and his collection of several hundred robes and screens is now in the National Museum of Japanese History in Sakura. Wright used his textile fragments to make lampshades and curtains at Taliesin.

As a solution to his ongoing financial dilemma, Wright staged a print exhibition in the Fine Arts Building in Chicago in 1917 (ill. 90). He was now reaching his peak as the preeminent dealer of Japanese prints in America, and there can be no doubt that he hoped the show would promote sales.[5] The red granite Fine Arts Building (originally the Studebaker Building), located near the lakefront at 408 South Michigan Avenue, included within its walls the most important of the artistic, musical, educational, and literary interests of the city. The building was occupied by "sculptors, painters, musicians, actors, writers, illustrators, etchers, gold and silversmiths, carvers, decorators, publishers of special editions; teachers of elocution and expression, the drama and the cognate arts; dealers in the antique and the curious; sellers of pictures, prints, pianos, books, porcelains, fine furniture, laces, linens." It was "Chicago's most important indoor shopping mall."[6] Shops selling Asian art included the Toyo Art Shop, Deakins, and S. H. Mori. The Arts Club, the Chicago Literary Club, and the Caxton Club, not to mention the prestigious Chicago Woman's Club, were headquartered here. Wright, who secured an office in this building in 1908 and again in 1910 after returning from Europe, personally designed Browne's Bookstore in 1907, Thurber Art Galleries in 1909, and the Mori gallery.

Wright's print exhibition had as its venue four rooms of the Arts Club. The Arts Club, composed of both artists and patrons of the arts, was founded by the Artists' Guild in the spring of 1916 to sponsor exhibitions, encourage higher standards of craftsmanship, and foster the mutual acquaintance of art lovers and artists.[7] Wright prepared a handsome little catalogue titled *Antique Colour Prints from the Collection of Frank Lloyd Wright* complete with an annotated checklist and a chatty introductory essay dated Taliesin, 12 October 1917. On the cover the architect repeated the decorative logo of overlapping circular "crests"—a crane and a triple-wave motif—first seen on the cover of his 1912 essay on Japanese prints (see ill. 49). (He later said he had taken this design from the work of the early-eighteenth-century Japanese painter Ogata Kōrin.)[8] The text was printed on a high-quality, heavy yellow paper.

From 12 November to 15 December visitors could study 241 Japanese prints, half of them by Wright's favorite, Hiroshige. There were sixteen prints by Katsukawa Shunshō, fifteen

90.
Part of the Michigan Avenue lakefront, Chicago. c. 1909

The Fine Arts Building is the third from the left, the Art Institute of Chicago is on the extreme right.

Koryūsai (many of them pillar prints), fifteen Utamaro (including many triptychs), eleven Kiyonaga, and a smattering of Wright's other preferred artists. There were also numerous limited-edition *surimono*, privately commissioned prints known for their luxury production, which Wright appreciated greatly.

The architect took pains to arrange the prints in artful groupings disregarding strict historical chronology in favor of what he called "harmonious and instructive contrasts." This allowed him to group the works according to mat size and shape, avoiding monotonous repetition. The middle gallery, however, was entirely given over to Hokusai and Hiroshige, representing "fully developed printing when the craft was at its height." He repeats the perceived wisdom of the day, as promoted most vocally by Fenollosa and Ficke, namely that "the work that came later than their period is worthy of little consideration."

Wright also took the position that toned, or faded, prints had equal value with those in perfect condition: "The most glorious print and eventually the most sought for will be that mas-

91.
Exhibition of Japanese prints at the Arts Club, Fine Arts Building, Chicago, 1917. Installation designed by Wright

terpiece time has mellowed and honored with the development of its inner nature…. Qualities indescribably rich and tender develop in and from the print as verdigris comes to bronze—qualities that as legitimately enhance its value."[9] Presumably he genuinely believed this to be true: apprentices from later years report that he bleached prints in the sun on occasion if he did not like the harshness of the color.[10]

Collectors in Europe at the turn of the century, like American expatriate Mary Cassatt (1844–1926), certainly favored the muted colors of toned prints. Japanese dealers knew this. Hayashi Tadamasa is said to have sometimes bleached prints in the sun in order to make them more attractive to those Europeans who preferred the soft colors of faded prints and who, out of ignorance, were prone to suspect forgery if the colors were fresh.[11] Eighteenth- and early-nineteenth-century ukiyo-e are printed with vegetable pigments that are highly light sensitive. Exposure to light (or moisture) for even short periods will initiate a gradual and dramatic alteration of color tones. Bright purple fades to light brown, for example, and blue to a pale buff. It is known that some greedy Japanese dealers soaked prints in tea or soot water to get the proper aged look for the foreign market. Many Americans, however, were increasingly conscientious about condition—namely wear, tear, dirt, and fading. They preferred bright colors, and this later got Wright into trouble.

The critics went wild; their enthusiastic reviews of Wright's exhibition far surpassed anything published at the time about the early Chinese painting, sculpture, and jade from the world-class collection of Charles Freer, which went on view—not coincidentally—three days later a block down the street at the Art Institute.

"Probably the finest collection of Japanese color prints in the country is now on exhibition at the Arts club," wrote a reviewer for the local paper.[12] It helped that the members of the Arts Club included the movers and shakers of the local art world: Mrs. Potter Palmer, Mrs. John Winterbotham, Alice Roullier (who had a gallery for old master prints on the seventh floor of the Fine Arts Building), and so on. The opening tea reception hosted by the ladies in the galleries was praised in the society and entertainment section of the *Chicago Daily Tribune* as "one of the most beautiful settings the Arts club has ever had."[13]

On 18 November Mme. X, society columnist for the *Chicago Sunday Tribune*, raved that "Such an alive, attractive, smart, and altogether up to date institution as the Arts club is these days it would be hard to find anywhere else. Frank Lloyd Wright's collection of Japanese prints is a thing of joy to the connoisseur

92.
Exhibition at the Arts Club, Fine Arts Building, Chicago, 1917. Installation designed by Wright

A fifth-century Chinese stone Bodhisattva stands at the entrance to the Club Room, beside a Japanese print. A Japanese screen of bamboo and a fence is mounted flat in a wood frame flanked by two square pillars topped with planters.

and to the rank outsider a collection to wonder over." Given the prevailing ignorance about Japanese art, it is not surprising that she referred to images of prostitutes and courtesans as "high bred exquisite women." More telling is the undercurrent of racial prejudice, also typical of the times. On the basis of what she saw in the prints she lamented the "utter inscrutability" of the Japanese, and described their minds as "a glittering, unfathomable blackness, a something we shall never understand."

Wright's exhibition had the added attraction of a Japanese dancer expressly imported from New York. Mme. Kimura, billed as "Dai Nippon's most famous dance artist, an enchanting young woman who looks as if she had stepped from the emperor's most beautiful screen," performed twice for club members. As if this were not enough to enhance the "utterly oriental atmosphere of the occasion" the organizers also brought in a young Indian singer, Ratan Devi, who "croons Hindoo and Persian folk songs in a soul stirring manner."[14] This was obviously the perfect venue for a showman like Wright.

For scale and drama he tarted up the rooms in the Arts Club with several Japanese screens and a variety of Chinese art, which he brought from Taliesin (ill. 93). In the Large Gallery he did something novel, even radical. At opposite ends of the room

93.
Anonymous, Kano school. *Maple Trees and Chrysanthemums*. Late Momoyama period, early seventeenth century. Six-panel screen; ink, color, and gold leaf on paper, 60⅜ x 141¹³⁄₁₆ in. Private collection

Passed down in the family of Wright's youngest sister, Maginel, until it was sold a few years ago, this is probably one of the screens Wright included in his 1917 exhibition at the Arts Club in Chicago and described in his catalogue as "a six-fold gold Momoyama screen of maple leaves in gilded goffrage [*sic*] characteristic of the period."

he bent a pair of screens into semicircles, or what he called "hemicycles," reflecting his love of geometric forms (ill. 91). In medieval times Japanese folding screens were often set out in a kind of casual semicircle to subdivide space in a large room (or out of doors) or to ensure privacy for amorous couples. Wright's later low-budget Usonian houses were designed in shapes he called "solar hemicycles." ("Usonian" is a partial acronym for the United States of North America.) Each of Wright's screens was framed with a pair of rectangular pillars, anchoring it in an architectural setting. The unit of enclosure created by this arrangement stood on a painted (or lacquered) wood platform.

Wright identified these screens as "grapes in gilded goffrage [sic] on plain copper-green ground." Grapevines, probably in two shades of gold, are silhouetted against a rounded hillock, which must have been painted a dark malachite green. (Planters of trailing vines on the adjacent pillars artfully echo those in the painting.) He described the paintings as Momoyama-period works from a palace in Nagoya, "a period in art when nearly everything done was full of life and strength." Judging from the installation photos the screens are more likely from the Edo period, perhaps late seventeenth- to early eighteenth-century. The "palace" in Nagoya is presumably a reference to the castle of the Owari branch of the Tokugawa family built in 1609–14 by the shogun Tokugawa Ieyasu (1543–1616) and decorated with sliding-door (fusuma) paintings and murals by Kano-school painters. (Wright may have visited the castle during one of his visits to Japan: he was in Nagoya in 1905.) Wright's grapevine screens are not in Kano style but in the more abstract, decorative Rimpa style (Rimpa means "school of Rim"; the "rim" or "rin" is a syllable in the name of Ogata Kōrin, and "pa" means school).

One of Wright's favorite Buddhist sculptures, a fifth-century Chinese Northern Zhou stone Bodhisattva, stood near the entrance to the Club Room (ill. 92). He made use of the architectural features of the Club Room, positioning a six-fold screen of bamboo, fence, and ivy leaves in gold leaf against a dark blue and green ground so that stalks of bamboo echo the pilasters. Wright identified the painter as Kano Eitoku (1543–1590), the famous Momoyama-period artist active in the last quarter of the sixteenth century, but the work is more likely eighteenth or nineteenth century. An attribution to Eitoku is wishful think-

ing but typical of the state of scholarship at the time. Both Japanese and American art dealers were fond of attributing "old" paintings to Eitoku, an artist with plenty of name recognition. Few early attributions have stood the test of time. Wright did later acquire a screen that may be the work of Eitoku (see ill. 157).

In another room, Wright mounted a two-panel folding screen above a banquette (ill. 94). Titled Summer Moon, it was painted in color on silver leaf by the lacquer artist Shibata Zeshin (1807–1891). A Japanese bamboo basket with an arrangement of pine branches overlaps the screen slightly, echoing the rhythmic sway of the autumn grasses depicted in the painting. Wright reveals himself here as both decorator and collector. His juxtaposition of unrelated objects and cultures (an archaic Chinese bronze beside eighteenth-century Japanese prints) is daring in terms of museum display, which tends (then as now) to be very conservative. The full moon in Zeshin's screen resonates a few yards away in the large, round form of a lidded pou, a Chinese ritual vessel dating from the Spring and Autumn period of Eastern Zhou (late seventh–early sixth century B.C.). This rare piece has a row of round bosses in a band around the shoulder and the handles are comprised of conjoined double links with a ring attached to two loops on the body. The surface appears to be covered with a heavy encrustation. (Somehow, this vessel later made its way into the renowned collection of the MOA Museum of Art in Atami, Japan.)[15] The heavy, globular form of the pou contrasts with the elegantly attenuated Tang-dynasty (618–906) ceramic tomb figure of a court official placed above on a free-standing partition wall that closes off the gallery space. (The partition was intended to mask from view a row of glass doors.) Hanging clusters of foliage link these two objects visually.

Behind the Chinese bronze Wright mounted three hosoban actor prints by Katsukawa Shunshō with their mats overlapping as though they were a triptych. They signal the leitmotif of his catalogue essay, "Shibaraku" (ills. 95, 96). Shibaraku (Stop right there!) is the name of a bombastic scene inserted into "opening-of-the season" productions of kabuki theater in the eleventh month of the year. The role of the hero, dressed in a voluminous brick-red costume, was the special preserve of the Ichikawa Danjūrō actor lineage and the actor's robe is decorated with a gigantic version of the white triple-square (mimasu) crest of the

94.
Exhibition at the Arts
Club, Fine Arts Building,
Chicago, 1917. Installa-
tion designed by Wright

The prints shown here
on the left were sold to
the Metropolitan Muse-
um of Art the next year
(ills. 95, 96). A Chinese
Tang tomb figure stands
like a sentry; Wright displayed it with similar flair
at Taliesin (see ill. 82).

95.
Katsukawa Shunshō. *The Actor Ichikawa Danzō IV in a "Shibaraku" Role as Arakawatarō Makezu in "A Dandyish Brocade: Opposing Warriors"* (*Date-nishiki tsui no yumitori*). 1779. Color woodcut, *hosoban*. The Metropolitan Museum of Art, New York, Purchase, Joseph Pulitzer Bequest, 1918 (JP 345)

Wright sold this print to the Metropolitan Museum of Art in 1918 for $60.

Ichikawa family, a design Wright loved. With cries of "Stop right there!" or "Wait a moment!" the actor would stalk forward from the rear of the theater along the raised walkway (the *hanamichi*, or "flower path") that leads to the stage. Unsheathing his massive curved sword he would then rescue a hapless victim, and good would triumph over evil once again. Trying to force a favorite theme, that of democracy in art, Wright ventured the skewed explanation that "To all who would 'look', this is the 'wait and listen' moment to let it be said that in ancient Tokyo an art was born nearer 'democratic' than ever seen."

Not one to miss a golden opportunity, the architect gave an afternoon lecture titled "The General Principles of the Prints" to club members, illustrated with ukiyo-e from his own collection. The talk was advertised with much fanfare in the society pages of the *Tribune*.[16] Wright's lectures were usually extemporaneous but this one seems to have been thought out in advance. He may even have read from a handwritten manuscript about "the principle of the print" dated Taliesin, 15 November 1917.[17] Opening with praise of Harunobu and Hiroshige, whom he extolled for their subtle rhythms and "spiritual" appeal, he glided ingeniously into a diatribe against "realistic" art, against art and architecture (especially that in America) inspired by the European Renaissance, and against professional decorators who create soulless "period" interiors. Here, again, he offered the "humble Japanese print" not simply as icon of modernity but as antidote to all the evils of the modern world. It was during this talk that Wright mentioned Fenollosa as his first contact with Japanese prints.

Wright sold a number of the Katsukawa *hosoban* from this exhibition (and many of the Hiroshige as well) to the Metropolitan Museum of Art the next year, possibly on the strength of this exhibition.[18]

FREER AND LAUFER: THE CHINESE CONNECTION

Wright's inclusion of a few fine Chinese objects may well have been a response to two major loan exhibitions of Chinese art at the Art Institute. From mid-November to early December 1917, Chicagoans could hear the great Swedish art historian Osvald Siren (1879–1966) lecture on Chinese painting, and could view paintings, sculpture, ceramics, and archaic jades on loan from Freer and Dikran G. Kelekian (1868–1951), a major New York dealer who supplied Freer, among others, and whose finest pieces were later sold to the Cleveland Museum.[19] We know that Freer and Wright met during the course of their mutual exhibitions that fall: there is a copy of Wright's catalogue inscribed "To Mr. Charles Freer from FLLW, November 29, 1917" in the archives of the Freer Gallery of Art.

Freer, who died two years later, was by this time recognized world-wide as a collector and connoisseur of Asian art (ill. 97). He had made five trips to Asia and had already promised his collection to the Smithsonian. He sounds weary and a bit cynical in a 1916 letter from New York addressed to Gookin that describes his efforts to stave off greedy dealers from around the world. "It would surprise you to know of the unusual and even dastardly attempts being made by a certain crowd of Japanese and Chinese outcasts, centering temporarily here, to unload rubbish from all parts of the universe, even Japanese and Chinese 'masterpieces' manufactured not ten miles distant from the Plaza Hotel."[20] Although there were no ancient bronze ritual vessels in his Chicago exhibition, Freer had purchased a great many in 1915 and they were loaned to the Metropolitan Museum of Art

97.
Edward Steichen (1879–1973). Charles Lang Freer. c. 1915. Gelatin silver print, 13¹³⁄₁₆ x 10¹³⁄₁₆ in. George Eastman House, Rochester, New York

Opposite

96.
Katsukawa Shunshō. *The Actor Ichikawa Danjūrō V as Hannya no Gorō.* 1776. Color woodcut, *hosoban*. The Metropolitan Museum of Art, New York, Purchase, Joseph Pulitzer Bequest, 1918 (JP 368)

Wearing costume and makeup designed to startle the audience, the actor strikes a pose on the stage of the Ichimura Theater in Edo. He applied grotesque red and white facial decoration, attached pleated sheets of paper to his wig, and tied on a samurai hat. His voluminous, brick-red costume is decorated with the Ichikawa crest, and he carries extraordinarily long swords. Wright sold this print to the museum in 1918 for $60.

in January 1916. According to Thomas Lawton, former director of the Freer Gallery of Art, it "marked the first time that ancient ritual vessels of such quality had ever been shown in the United States. Their exhibition was a milestone in the beginning of Western understanding of Chinese culture."[21] Archaic bronzes had only begun to emerge from excavations in China around the turn of the century; in New York they were sold by C. T. Loo (1880?–1957) and Yamanaka. Most Americans—Henry O. Havemeyer (1847–1907), the "Sugar King," in New York and William T. Walters (1819–1894) in Baltimore, for example—had been collecting the later archaistic bronzes or the elaborate nineteenth-century Japanese bronzes featured at the Philadelphia Centennial.

Freer's friend Berthold Laufer (1874–1934), a German-trained ethnologist who had been appointed curator of Asiatic ethnology at the Field Museum in Chicago in 1908, is credited with shifting the taste of local collectors away from the decorative arts of the late Ming (1369–1644) and Qing (1644–1912) dynasties to archaeological material (ill. 98). In the words of the art historian Elinor Pearlstein, he was "America's pre-eminent authority on the myriad facets of Chinese civilization—art, archaeology, science, technology, linguistics and folklore."[22] Laufer acquired an enormous collection of Han and Tang pottery for the museum, the result of two major purchasing expeditions to China, in 1908–10 and 1923. He assisted Gookin with loan exhibitions at the Art Institute in 1916, 1917, and 1918 that featured Han- and Tang-dynasty ceramic tomb figures from local private collections (that of architect Samuel A. Marx [1885–1964], for example) shown in combination with objects from the Field Museum.[23] It is logical to conclude that Wright's growing accumulation of ancient Chinese art was closely tied to these contemporary collecting trends in Chicago.

In addition to a fine Han-dynasty bronze *hu*, or wine vessel (see ill. 3), Wright owned at least nine green lead-glazed, earthenware *hu*. He kept one beside his daybed in his private study-bedroom at Taliesin (ill. 99). The primary appeal of these archaic vessels to the architect must have been their simple, geometric forms and spare, green glazes, qualities he valued as "organic." This again represents a departure from the prevailing American preference for decorative enameled wares and colorful, late monochromes in shades known as ox-blood, robin's egg-blue, and peach bloom; there was little interest in archaeological wares until Western railroad engineers began unearthing Chinese tombs at the end of the nineteenth century.

Wright's 1917 exhibition attracted the attention of Louise Norton Brown, a remarkable collector of Japanese illustrated printed books. Brown, a painter and illustrator who had studied at the school of the Art Institute of Chicago, lived in Lockport, Illinois. On a trip to Japan in 1913 she "fell a victim to the fascinating hobby of book-collecting" and traveled there many times subsequently.[24] She is best known for her *Block Printing and Book Illustration in Japan,* published posthumously in London in 1924 with a preface by William Spaulding.[25] A week after the opening of the exhibition, Brown wrote the architect to question his attribution of two black-and-white woodcuts to Nishikawa Sukenobu (1671–1751).[26] Whether Wright responded to this scholarly inquiry is not known.

Soon after his exhibit closed, the architect was hard at work on drawings for the Imperial Hotel. He had three young draftsmen at Taliesin assisting him in 1918: two Japanese from Tokyo, Endō Arata (1889–1951) and Fujikura Goichi (1888–?), and a Viennese architect who had been working in Chicago, Rudolph M. Schindler (1887–1953).

98.
Berthold Laufer, posing beside a rhinoceros horn, holds an eighteenth-century Chinese carved rhinoceros-horn libation cup. early 1920s

Opposite

99.
Wright's study-bedroom with a view onto the balcony. Taliesin III. 1952.

The architect placed a third-century Chinese earthenware jar on a ledge to the right of his daybed. To the left is the oarlock of a Venetian gondola. A paper mobile hangs from the skylight. The view through a plate-glass window illustrates Wright's idea that walls are vanishing, and that walls themselves will become windows.

One local Japanese art dealer with whom Wright was especially friendly was Shigehisa Mori, who arrived in Chicago no later than 1915, the year he sold his first prints to Kate Buckingham, and who died around 1957 at the age of about eighty. He styled himself S. H. Mori, creating two initials from his first name, so as to sound more Western. By 1916, when he was doing business in suite 801 of the Fine Arts Building, a large, high-ceilinged corner room on the eighth floor, Miss Buckingham was already one of his regular customers. Her invoice books in the archives of the Art Institute show that she purchased numerous examples of later Chinese decorative arts, mostly snuff bottles, as well as two green-glazed Han-dynasty jars from Mori beginning in March 1916.[27]

Mori's calling card identifies his stock as "rare and unique objects of Chinese, Japanese, and Korean arts of all descriptions, dating from B.C. periods to 18th century, including a very important collection of Japanese color prints and temple brocades, also charming lamps of artistic distinction with fascinating gauze silk shades." Apparently he had to cater to the decorator trade, as did all of his colleagues at the time. (The Yamanaka galleries in New York and Boston both had lamps prominently displayed in their shop windows.) Mori did not have walk-in trade

100.
Frank Lloyd Wright. Writing desk for S. H. Mori Gallery, Fine Arts Building, Chicago. c. 1915. Stained pine top, 24 x 42 x 24 in. University of Illinois at Chicago Art Study Collection, Gift to the University from Mary Diamond Stein, 1969

Opposite

101.
Frank Lloyd Wright. Armchair for S. H. Mori Gallery, Fine Arts Building, Chicago. c. 1915. Oak with pine seat, 26¼ x 22 x 19 in. University of Illinois at Chicago Art Study Collection, Gift to the University from Mary Diamond Stein, 1969

on the eighth floor. One customer likened him to a dried-up old prune who sat there like a boa constrictor, waiting to swallow whole and slowly digest the occasional Marshall Field or Kate Buckingham. The Oriental magnate of Chicago had good things. He surrounded himself with beautiful and costly treasures— prints, bronzes, ivories, jades, crystal balls, and porcelains. His rooms were only lit when a client came in.[28]

Mori seems to have been a very private person; virtually nothing is known about his background or training in Japan, but judging by comments of those who knew him, he spoke fluent English with a British accent and was an influential and well-liked individual as well as "one of the most reliable of the Japanese dealers."[29] His much younger Japanese counterpart at Yamanaka and Company in Chicago around 1930 remembers him as a patient, scholarly teacher and an outstanding connoisseur with special expertise in the field of ukiyo-e prints; Mori's clients included eminent local Asianists. He was a lender to an exhibition of ukiyo-e paintings and prints organized by Gookin at the Art Institute in 1923 and he participated in the exhibition of modern Japanese prints sponsored by the ambitious Tokyo print publisher Watanabe Shōzaburō (1885–1962) for the Toledo Museum of Art in 1930. On a more personal note, Mori lived in one of the furnished rooms at the Japanese Y.M.C.A. in Chicago. He is remembered as being obsessively meticulous in his habits—in the morning his bed looked as if he had not slept in it, his newspaper always lay folded in the same place, and not an article in the room was out of place, including the contents of his closet.[30]

Perhaps on the basis of Wright's earlier commissions in the Fine Arts Building, but also owing to their mutual love of Japanese art, Mori hired Wright, whose office was on the eighth floor of Orchestra Hall, two blocks north, to remodel an existing space for him and to design his furniture. Although the gallery was disassembled (Mori later moved to a smaller space), the fur-

niture has survived intact (ills. 100, 101). It is plain and functional job-built millwork, not the work of a studio craftsman. Mori was working on a tight budget. The most unusual piece is a rather elegant desk with a stained pine top and vaguely Chinese forms (spandrel, struts, and legs that terminate in outward-turning feet) created for Mori's private office. In a curtained-off space with windows at the end of the gallery special clients would sit around a large, oak work table and view prints or objects that Mori kept in his display cabinets. The table also served as a storage facility. It has a lower cupboard with double doors on both the front and the back. The armchairs and stools are low and small, as though designed to the scale of a Japanese body. (They are also rather flimsy and uncomfortable.)

Mori stored his matted prints in waist-high wooden cabinets fitted with doors and shelves; the shelves were exactly the right size to hold matted prints. On top of the wood table cases and cabinets were glass display cases for fine quality Chinese and Japanese ceramics, sculpture, and lacquer. Wright's drawings show a counter running the length of both long walls in the main gallery space.[31] Above the counters were fabric-covered sloped decks, ideal for displaying prints. Wright used a similar concept in his 1914 design for a Spaulding print room (see ill. 78).

The relationship between Wright and Mori is difficult to document. There is no known correspondence between them until 1944, when Wright paid a visit to Mori's shop (still in the Fine Arts Building, but on the sixth floor), renewing their acquaintance after a long hiatus and purchasing some books on Japanese art published by the Japan Tourist Bureau, as well as a contemporary print by Kaburagi Kiyokata (1878–1973). "As instructed," Mori wrote, "I am shipping to you today express paid the masterpiece by Kiyokata who is the Harunobu of our time. Mr. Spaulding has a copy and admires it immensely." Mori clearly knew which buttons to push with Wright. Alas, two weeks later Wright's check for forty-five dollars bounced.[32]

WRIGHT AND HASHIGUCHI GOYŌ

One of Wright's mentors in Tokyo was the great Japanese print-maker Hashiguchi Goyō (1880–1921). Goyō began as a student of Western painting at the Tokyo Art School, and he developed a reputation as a poster designer and illustrator. But he also became increasingly fascinated with ukiyo-e, began to study prints seriously, built up a large personal collection, and soon became an authority on the subject with many publications to his credit. He made his first woodcut on commission for Watanabe Shōzaburō in 1915. Then there was a hiatus until 1918 when he again resumed printmaking, this time supervising block carvers and printers himself and acting as his own publisher. He is known for his homage to the sensuous bust portraits of beautiful women by Utamaro, complete with a pale silver mica ground. Because of his training in Western art, however, and the careful pencil studies that preceded his final designs, his work, unlike that of Utamaro, has a subtle overtone of realism, a hint of three-dimensional pink shading in the skin that is decidedly modern. He also became involved in the world of print replicas; between 1916 and 1920 he worked with several

102.
Hashiguchi Goyō in the parlor of his home in Akasaka, Tokyo. 1917.
From *Ukiyo-e no kenkyū*, October 1921

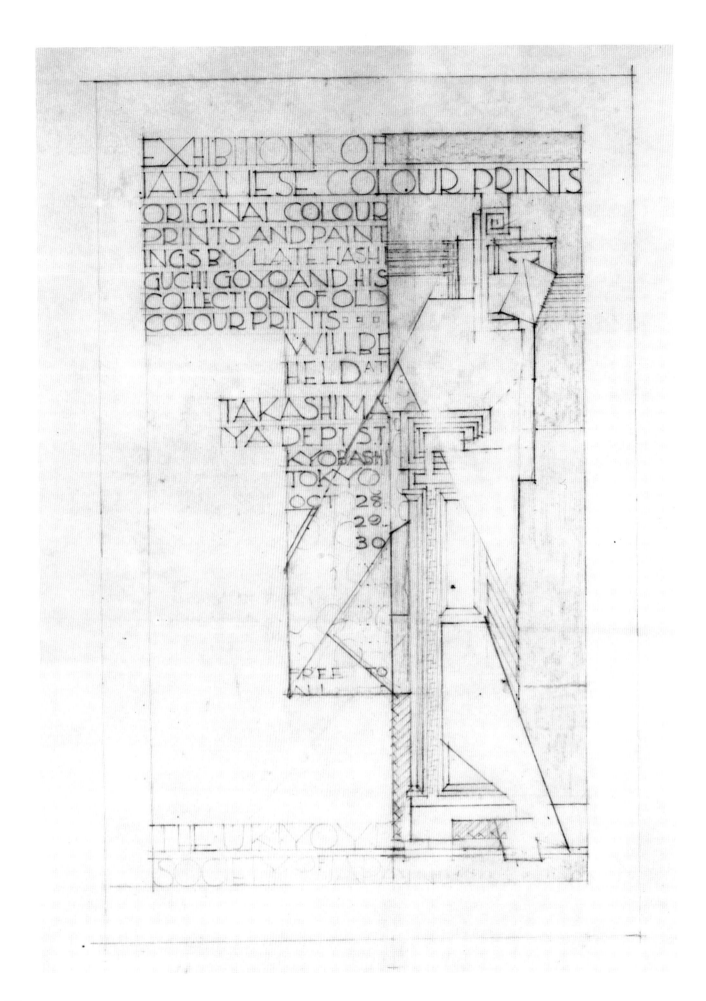

EXHIBITION OF
JAPANESE COLOUR PRINTS
ORIGINAL COLOUR
PRINTS AND PAINT
INGS BY LATE HASHI
GUCHI GOYO AND HIS
COLLECTION OF OLD
COLOUR PRINTS
WILL BE
HELD AT
TAKASHIMA
YA DEPT ST.
KYOBASHI
TOKYO
OCT 28.
29.
30

FREE TO
ALL

THE UKIYOYE
SOCIETY OF

Tokyo publishers making facsimile editions of masterpieces by Harunobu, Utamaro, and Hiroshige. His Hōeidō Tōkaidō was published by Iwanami Shoten in April 1919.

In a 1917 photo Goyō sits in the inner parlor of his home in the Akasaka ward of Tokyo, posing as a man of refined taste (ill. 102). A book is open on his elegant Chinese-style table and his elbow rests on the edge of a large hibachi. There is a fancy lacquered display stand on the left and a display alcove (*tokonoma*) with a hanging scroll on the right. A framed image of Hiroshige's *Full Moon at Ryōgoku Bridge* from the *Famous Views of the Eastern Capital* (*Tōto meisho*) series of c. 1831 is conspicuous above his closet, an insight into the stature of the once lowly print.

Goyō was extremely loquacious, discoursing with visitors far into the night on the state of the arts, both East and West. Guests sat on contemporary Austrian furniture fashionably arranged at one end of a Japanese room that doubled as a print studio.[33] He counted among his close friends in the foreign community John Stewart Happer and Wright.[34] We can imagine Wright seated in the reception room with the scholarly Goyō, chatting about Hiroshige and ukiyo-e prints. Happer was a shrewd New York businessman who moved to Kobe in 1891 to work as an agent for Standard Oil of New York. During his more than forty years in Japan he taught at Waseda University in Tokyo and wrote for *Japan Advertiser*. Happer put Hiroshige on the map in the West when he sold 700 of his 3,000 images at auction in London in 1909. He made his reputation as an authority on Hiroshige, calling himself "Hiroshige Happer." Fluent in Japanese, he was on intimate terms with the Tokyo print merchants, stayed over at their homes for days at a time, and paid them good money to hunt up prints for him.

Goyō published only sixteen of his own designs, in limited editions. Because the craftsmanship was so fine, they were from the start very expensive. At that time a print by Goyō cost ¥60, whereas one of Hiroshige's *Hundred Views* could be had for ¥3 to ¥5 and even *Sudden Evening Shower at Ōhashi Bridge*, the most coveted image in the set, cost only about ¥20.[35] Wright is not known to have owned a single example of Goyō's work.

Goyō was plagued by illness and died quite suddenly from tympanitis complicated by meningitis in February 1921 at the age of only forty-one. Wright, who spent most of that year in Japan, was evidently moved by his friend's death; in his honor

Opposite

103.
Frank Lloyd Wright. Drawing for Goyō exhibition poster (ill. 104). 1921. Graphite and colored pencil on paper, 19½ x 13 in. Prints and Photographs Division, Library of Congress, Washington, D.C., Donald D. Walker Collection, Gift 1986

he designed a colorful poster, which was displayed at the entrance to the commemorative exhibition of Goyō's work, the first annual show sponsored by the Ukiyo-e Society of Japan at Takashimaya Department Store in Tokyo in October 1921 (ills. 103, 104). The members of the Ukiyo-e Society were baffled by this image; they assumed that Wright gave it to them thinking they would want a very modern design. There was speculation at the time among members of the society that the architect had been inspired by a courtesan in a print by Kitao Shigemasa (1773–1820); Wright had mentioned to his friends in the Japanese print world that he was intrigued by the unusual figure of a beauty in a Shigemasa print he owned.[36] The poster could certainly be interpreted as a highly stylized female figure in a long-sleeved kimono stepping to the right. An obvious stylistic comparison is the abstract mural Wright designed over the fireplace in the living room of Hollyhock House in Los Angeles, completed that same year (see ill. 149). He used the identical vocabulary of overlapping, interlocking geometric forms for both. These motifs also show up in Wright's drawings for perforated tile ornaments for the interior of the Imperial.[37]

The poster did not survive but it was published in the 1922 members' quarterly of the Ukiyo-e Society of Japan. This was a society of print lovers (private collectors and scholars) who deplored the fact that appreciation of ukiyo-e was less widespread in Japan than in the West; the organization was apparently formed out of a sense of patriotic duty. Its founding fathers included Shugio Hiromichi and Hayashi Aisaku, and both Wright and Gookin were members.[38]

Congratulatory remarks by Kuki Ryūichi (1852–1931), an important art patron, were published in the first issue of the society's journal. Kuki had been a government emissary to Washington, D.C., in the 1880s, and served as senior official in the Ministry of Education and director general of the Imperial Museum, a distinguished career that ended around 1900 when he was pushed out of power. As a member of the Privy Council he continued to receive a modest annual salary of ¥5,000–6,000. Wright was attracted to aristocratic and cultivated men like Kuki. They met in the spring of 1913 when Kuki, pleased to hear of Wright's interest in Japanese art (probably via Shugio), sought out the famous architect and invited him to an "old-fashioned tea ceremony" in Kyoto followed by a private viewing of Kuki's collection of Japanese paintings at his country home in

105.
S. C. Bosch Reitz in
Austria. c. 1936

106.
S. C. Bosch Reitz.
Japanese Garden. 1900.
Color woodcut, 7¼ x
6¼ in. Private collection, Holland

Arima hot springs, near Kobe. Wright suffered through a good many tea ceremonies. He remembered,

> On tortured knees…I have painfully participated in this "idealized" making of a cup of tea following a Japanese formal dinner, trying to get at some of these secrets if secrets they are. I confess that I have been eventually bored to extinction by the repetition of it all and soon I would avoid the ordeal when I could see an invitation coming. And I freely admit, such discipline is not for us. It is far too severe. Yes, far too severe![39]

The Baron also invited Wright to see more of the collection at his home in Kojimachi in Tokyo. "On reverent knees" Wright admired the traditional architecture of Kuki's home and no doubt benefitted from his host's social connections. He perceived "poor old Baron Kuki," now long past his prime, as a "lonely aged diplomat still celebrated for his cuisine and his 'collections.'"[40] Kuki had loaned over twenty paintings, including some ukiyo-e subjects, to the Japan-British Exhibition in London in 1910; his collection was sold at auction in Japan after his death.

NEGOTIATING WITH THE METROPOLITAN MUSEUM OF ART

In the summer of 1917 Wright opened negotiations with the Metropolitan Museum of Art for a series of major print sales. Over the next five years he corresponded regularly with S. C. (Sigisbert Chretien) Bosch Reitz (1860–1938), known informally as "Gys," who had been appointed the museum's first curator of Far Eastern art in 1915 (ill. 105). Bosch Reitz lived and worked in Laren, in northern Holland, and was descended from Dutch nobility, an old and cultured family of art lovers. Trained as a landscape painter at the Académie Julian in Paris in the 1880s, he evolved into a Japanophile after his return to Holland, and spent the year 1900 in Japan. While there he immersed himself

107.
Katsukawa Shunshō.
The Actor Nakamura Tomijūrō I in a Female Role Dancing. c. 1775.
Color woodcut, *hosoban.*
The Metropolitan Museum of Art, New York, Purchase, Joseph Pulitzer Bequest, 1918 (JP 381)

Wright sold this print to the Metropolitan Museum of Art for $45. The seal in the lower right corner is that of the museum.

108.
Utagawa Hiroshige.
Peacock on Maple Tree and Poem. c. 1833.
Color woodcut, medium *tanzakuban*. The Metropolitan Museum of Art, New York, Purchase, Joseph Pulitzer Bequest, 1918 (JP 269)

The Metropolitan Museum of Art purchased this print from Wright in 1918 for $75.

in the study of Japanese art, bought prints at ridiculously low prices (¥5 for an Utamaro), studied wood-block printing techniques under the tutelage of another European, the Bohemian-German graphic artist Emil Orlik (1870–1932), and made at least one color woodcut of his own (ill. 106). In 1909 he began to devote his time to the study of East Asian ceramics. He was about to accept a position at the Louvre but with the outbreak of World War I he found himself in New York instead. He had a good eye and catholic tastes, and although known as a connoisseur of Chinese ceramics, he was, until the time of his retirement in 1927, remarkably active in the acquisition of Japanese painting and ukiyo-e for the museum's permanent collection. The walls of his bright office in the museum were sparsely decorated with Japanese prints and with photographs of Buddhist temples taken during his travels in East Asia.[41] He was a delightful raconteur with a great store of vitality and an ease of speech tinged with a warm accent.

The bulk of the museum's roughly four hundred prints with Wright provenance was purchased in two separate transactions in July and October 1918 for a total of $20,000 (ills. 107, 108. See also ills. 51, 95, 96).[42] Wright assured the curator that he had marked the prices very low (he sold the museum 227 Katsukawa *hosoban* prints at sixty dollars each, less than half of what he had charged the Spauldings in 1916) but Bosch Reitz drove a hard bargain. He selected (on the advice of Howard Mansfield) only one-third, or eighty, of the 271 Hiroshige that Wright had sent on consignment, pricing them all at $62.50 and dismissing the rest as too expensive without being very special. Wright was at first unwilling to have his collection creamed; these were prints he had been accumulating as a reserve, he said, over a period of twenty-five years. Spaulding paid much more and "he has the only ones that compete with these. But I am offering them in War times and under duress which makes a difference." Wright vowed that he would hold on to them or offer them elsewhere, because "there is nothing better anywhere and in most cases nothing equal."[43] But Bosch Reitz received a desperate-sounding note from Taliesin shortly before Wright's departure for Japan in September 1918: "Take what prints you will at the

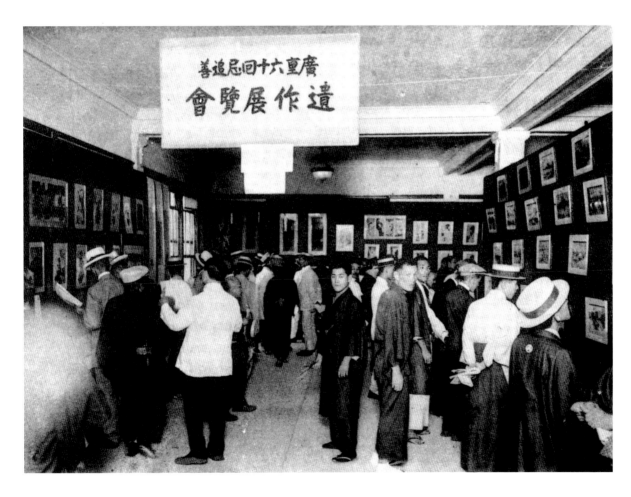

109.
Crowd of visitors at Hiroshige Memorial Exhibition, Takashimaya Department Store, Tokyo. September 1917. From Watanabe, *Catalogue of the Memorial Exhibition of Hiroshige's Works on the 60th Anniversary of His Death*, 1918

price you think is fair. I hope you will take many because I am sure the Museum will not have such an opportunity again—and I need the money." When he filed his tax return, the architect reported a net profit of only 10 percent on this sale.[44]

HIGH TIMES IN TOKYO

Wright sailed for Japan with Miriam Noel on 30 October 1918 for a ten-month stay and at once resumed buying Japanese art. His Tokyo bankbook lists a dozen vendors: Haibara, Nomura (either Nomura Yōzō of the Samurai gallery in Yokohama, or the textile dealer Nomura Shōjirō in Kyoto), Matsuki (probably Matsuki Zen'emon), Hayashi, Yamanaka and Company, Shinbi Shōin, Noda, Naitō, Nishizawa, Takashimaya [department store], Uchida, Nakaya, Nakamura, Suzuki, and "auction."[45] The present owner of the Nakazawa print gallery, founded in 1916 and until recently located beside the Imperial Hotel, remembers that his father, Nakazawa Murato (1892–1974), spoke of visits from Wright, who would appear at the end of the day still in his work clothes, dust from the construction site in his hair, eager to buy paintings and prints.[46]

In January 1919 Wright sent Bosch Reitz a note that confirms his mind was not focused exclusively on the Imperial Hotel:

> Since my arrival here, I have been deep in the print world, for recreation as usual. A distinct surprise in Hiroshige prices awaited me. No good copy of any desirable subject can be had for less than 100 yen [about $50].... The Hiroshige Sarubashi [*Monkey Bridge*] sold at the recent auctions for ¥5600. The Japanese are awake to Hiroshige now. The catalogue of the recent [Hiroshige] memorial exhibition here may not have reached you so I am sending a copy of the English edition. Read M. Yoneguchi's [*sic*] article. It is worth reading. I sold my Hiroshiges to the Metropolitan for half the price I should have.[47]

The exhibition of prints, paintings, and illustrated books commemorating the sixtieth anniversary of Hiroshige's death had taken place on the third floor of Takashimaya Department Store in downtown Tokyo on 6–8 September 1917, almost a year and a half earlier (Wright was not in Japan at the time). Watanabe Shōzaburō masterminded this extravaganza and published the English edition of the catalogue, edited by local Hiroshige collector Happer, in 1918.

Despite unbearable late-summer heat, sixteen thousand visitors had thronged the small exhibition hall over a three-day period (ill. 109). They ran the gamut from peerage to government officials, business magnates, and artists. On the occasion of his visit to Takashimaya, Ōkura Kihachirō, chairman of the board of the Imperial Hotel, wrote a comic poem (*kyōka*) in honor of Hiroshige, whom he claimed to have known personally—they had the same poetry teacher (see ill. 61). Ōkura actually took the *kyōka* pen name "Wakanomon Tsuruhiko" at the age of only fourteen. A serious art collector, he opened his own museum of East Asian antiquities (the Ōkura Shūkōkan) in 1917. Among the promoters and lenders to the show were Wright's friends Hashiguchi Goyō and Shugio Hiromichi (both contributed a set of the Hōeidō Tōkaidō) and all of the Tokyo dealers.[48] This was a blockbuster, and it is no wonder that Hiroshige prices were driven up even further.[49] The accolades that the Japanese themselves now offered up to Hiroshige, a painter of Japanese scenery in "pure Japanese style," are in tune with the nascent nationalism of the Taishō period (1912–26). Poet and print collector Yone Noguchi (1875–1947) commemorated this sixtieth anniversary celebration of the artist's death with the proclamation: "We are already all Hiroshige."[50]

Wright was in the vanguard of Hiroshige aficionados beginning with his first exhibition in 1906. In 1917 he said he believed "the subject matter of the figure pieces [i.e., prostitutes] is still offensive to Japanese polite society. Not so the landscapes of Hiroshige and Hokusai; and as the art and institutions of Old Japan give way to uglier Western models the Japanese gentleman of leisure now sees the most valuable poetic record of a beauty fast passing away forever from him and from his land.... Hiroshige is the latest arrival in the sacred places of upper printdom."[51] From about 1918 annual exhibitions of ukiyo-e prints were shown in the large hall of the Tokyo School of Fine Arts (Tokyo Bijutsu Gakkō) in Ueno Park, and by 1921 the Ukiyo-e Society of Japan was publishing a scholarly journal, *Ukiyo-e no kenkyū* (Ukiyo-e studies). Prints had gained a foothold among legitimate art forms in Japan.

Wright had several irons in the fire in the spring of 1919. In his 14 January letter to Bosch Reitz he comments on the exciting news that the great Parisian jeweler Henri Vever (1854–1943) had sold the bulk of his famous print collection to the Japanese shipping magnate Matsukata Kōjirō (1865–1950)—the first major "homecoming" for ukiyo-e prints. (The sale was mediated by Yamanaka's London agent.) Wright thought he might have a chance to design the Matsukata museum: "I am going to try to build the building that will contain [the collection]," he confided to Bosch Reitz. "I wish I had some financial backing here at the moment." Matsukata did commission a design for a museum in Tokyo but it was meant to house his Western art. He chose as his architect his friend from London days, English artist Frank Brangwyn (1869–1956). Those plans fell through. The 1927 bank crisis in Japan caused the industrialist to lose most of his business and personal assets. Ironically, Hayashi Aisaku wrote in 1932 to alert Wright to an incredible opportunity: the Matsukata collection of 8,204 Japanese woodblock prints was in the hands of the Fifteenth Bank in Tokyo and was available to the highest bidder.[52] Unfortunately, Wright had no assets at that moment, either. Matsukata's ukiyo-e prints ultimately found their way into the Tokyo National Museum.

The Imperial Hotel project was in the meantime lagging far behind schedule: Wright had initially estimated that it would take two years to build but the foundations were still being dug in 1919. It is not surprising that the savvy board of directors, all of them high-powered business tycoons (among them Ōkura, Shibusawa Eiichi, Asano Sōichirō [1848–1930], whose fortune was in cement, and Murai Kichibei [1864–1926], with tobacco interests), refused to allow their architect to accept offers to start building hotels elsewhere in Japan.[53] Wright did, in fact, make a perspective drawing and two site plans, one dated 1922, for a resort hotel in Odawara, not far from Tokyo (ill. 110). It was to have been a two-storied wooden building with a red tile roof but the project never reached fruition.[54]

Wright took on other commissions while he was in Japan and Japanese architects helped by promoting his name and work. Takeda Gōichi (1872–1938), a professor of architecture at the Kyoto School of Arts and Crafts whom Wright had met earlier, either in Japan in 1913 or in San Francisco at the Panama-Pacific Exposition in 1912, brought out a Japanese version of the Wasmuth portfolios in the spring of 1916. Takeda was a talented architect who had studied in Britain and was among the first to introduce Art Nouveau and the Secession to Japan. In November 1917 the journal *Kenchiku gahō* (Architecture pictori-

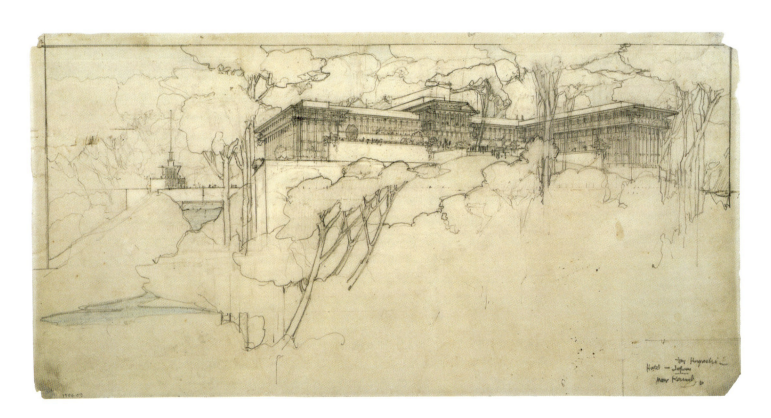

110.
Frank Lloyd Wright.
Odawara Hotel
(project), Odawara,
Kanagawa prefecture,
Japan. c. 1917–19.
Perspective; graphite
and colored pencil on
tracing paper, 12 x
24½ in. The Frank Lloyd
Wright Foundation
(1706.003)

al) devoted an entire issue to Wright, with pictures of Taliesin and the large plaster model of the Imperial (ills. 111, 112). Takeda is quoted as citing the influence of both Japanese architecture and prints on Wright's work, an insight Wright might not have appreciated. He points out that Wright has visited Japan many times, collects Japanese prints, and has studied the traditional architecture of Japan, all of which helped create a new style that benefits from the simplicity of Japanese models. According to Takeda, it is Wright's draftsmanship that most clearly shows the influence of his hobby, the prints.[55]

In an interview published in the February 1917 issue of the architecture journal *Kenchiku sekai* (World of architecture), Wright shared his thoughts about Japanese architecture and the Imperial Hotel. The introduction describes him as one of the finest architects in the United States and well known to most Japanese architects.[56] Wright's own remarks are typically self-serving: he deplores all recent Western-style architecture in Japan as unsuited to the topography and customs of the country (the buildings are too high and too Eurocentric), implying that he alone has found the solution to this dilemma. Ironically, he also castigates Japan's new Western-style buildings for their excessively high construction costs.

Wright designed several private residences and a school in Japan. The luxurious two-story mansion for Inoue Tadashirō (1876–1959), who had served as ambassador to Great Britain from 1913 to 1916, was never built (ill. 113). The architect's son John remembered working on the drawings in 1918—his last assignment in Japan:

> Sometime in the early morning my telephone rang. It was a cable from Dad, requesting me to collect a payment from Viscount Inouye for a residence we were to build for him and his British-educated wife. Inouye was a former ambassador to Great Britain.
>
> I worked all the next day and night to complete the sketches for the layout Dad had left with me, delivered them to the Viscount the next day and collected two thousand dollars on account. After deducting twelve hundred dollars for salary due me, I cabled the remaining eight hundred to Dad.
>
> The next day I received a cable: *"You're fired! Take the next ship home."*[57]

Wright did build a residence for Hayashi Aisaku, manager of the Imperial Hotel, in Tokyo in 1917, and a country villa in Hakone

111.
Cover of *Kenchiku gahō* (Architecture pictorial), vol. 8. November 1917. Prints and Photographs Division, Library of Congress, Washington, D.C., Donald D. Walker Collection, Gift 1986

This issue was devoted to Wright and the Imperial Hotel.

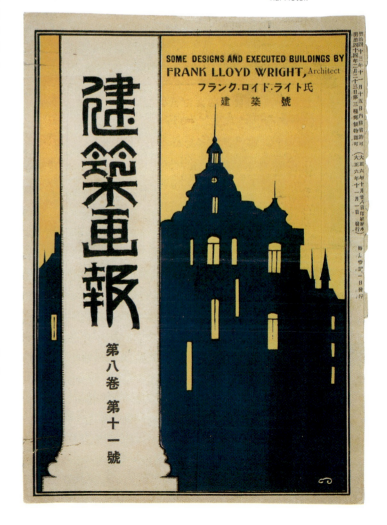

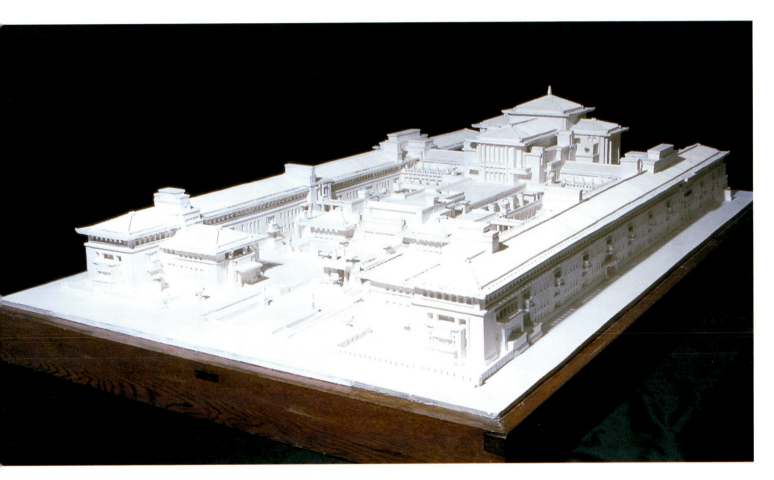

112.
Frank Lloyd Wright.
Model for the Imperial
Hotel. 1917. Plaster,
15¾ x 43⁵⁄₁₆ x 67 in. Collection Kyoto University
School of Architecture

113.
Frank Lloyd Wright.
House for Inoue
Tadashirō, Tokyo (project). 1918. Perspective;
graphite and colored
pencil on paper, 17⅝ x
26½ in. Private collection, Switzerland

114.
Frank Lloyd Wright.
School of the Free Spirit
(Jiyū Gakuen), Tokyo.
1921–26

for Fukuhara Arinobu (1848–1924), founder of the Shiseidō Company, in 1918. The latter was completed in 1920 or 1921. Both have been described as following in the style of Wright's Prairie Houses. The Fukuhara residence, however, was leveled in the earthquake of 1923; this is not mentioned in Wright's autobiography. Two small masterpieces Wright designed in Japan were completed soon after he left in 1922. Endō Arata, one of the young Japanese architects who worked closely with him on the Imperial, supervised construction of the house for the sake brewer Yamamura Tazaemon (1873–1944) in Ashiya, in the hills above Kobe, and the private school for girls in Tokyo called School of the Free Spirit, or Jiyū Gakuen (ills. 114, 115). Miraculously, this simple but elegant wood and mortar structure is still standing in the Mejiro section of Tokyo.

By July 1922, when Wright left, the north wing of the Imperial was finished. This marked the conclusion of what he called his "Oriental Symphony" and he never returned to Japan. Although he had unbuilt projects for Venice and Baghdad in the 1950s, no other foreign commissions came his way, much as he longed for them.[58]

115.
Wright with students and staff of School of the Free Spirit, Tokyo. 1922

CHAPTER FIVE

THE PRINT SCANDAL

116.

Japanese print dealers in the garden of the Man'anrō, Tokyo. c. 1913

Murata Kimbei is standing on the bridge with two young apprentice geisha. To his right, seated left to right: Shintomichō Ofumi, Shintomichō Oshin, Murata Kinnosuke XI, and Fukuda Asajirō; standing left to right: unknown man, Kakuwa Zenjirō, Yokoyama Tetsusaburō, and Kondo Toyotarō. To Murata's left, bottom row, left to right: Watanabe Shōzaburō (seated), Hirakawa Ken'kichi of Yamanaka and Company (seated), and Segawa; middle row, left to right: Nomura Tokusaburō, Maebane (Yoshida Takejirō), Sakai Shōkichi of Sakai Kokodō, Ono Harukichi, Sakai Fumisuke, Takagi, Yamanaka Sadajirō, Suwa Matsunosuke, Kōmyō Giichirō, and Hattori Hyō'e; top row, left to right: Hayashi Kyūkichi (or possibly Hayashi Kyūgo, Wright's nemesis), Murata Kōkichi, unknown woman, Mizutani Seitarō, Matsuki Zen'emon, Inoue, Shimizu Tadaji (or Naoji), Matsuki Kihachirō, unknown woman, Satō Shōtarō, Yasui Yoshimatsu, and Nakamatsu.

It all ended badly with a scandal. Writing to S. C. Bosch Reitz in January 1919, Wright hints of things to come, mentioning two remarkable opportunities: hitherto unknown and untouched collections of rare and lovely things that will rival even Vever's. He senses that he is always lucky in the print world: "My close touch with it and the large sums I have expended these past 13 years seems to have by the natural law of gravitation, started the flow toward me irresistibly."[1]

Then, on 15 March 1919 Wright alerted his draftsman in Chicago, R. M. Schindler, that "I have found rare collections of prints this time and helped myself to financial embarrassment as usual. But I believe in them as an investment for me. We shall see."[2] A month later he sent a revealing letter to his former mentor, Louis H. Sullivan, apologizing for not writing more and for not sending some money, which he knew Sullivan needed badly:

When not engaged in preparation for building, all Japan seems hunting me up with the enticing "Nishikiye" [literally "brocade pictures," or color prints] which are a pursuit in themselves absorbing and financially devastating….

I have had remarkable success this time with two old families—securing treasures the dealers never set their fakey old eyes on before. I shall make a commotion in the print world when I return—and hope to do so to my financial advantage in cold blood and perfect form.

You might help me at the Cliff Dwellers by dropping the hint to [Howard] Shaw and others that I have a collection made in the past six months that Monsieur [Henri] Vever himself would envy! An exhibition at the Art Institute [of Chicago] in September or October might be arranged—for the finest things of the kind in the world? Then I might send them on to New York and sell them there. Meantime I am broke but as I have my living here and transportation home I am sure to arrive in fairly well-fed condition.

You will find it difficult to believe, but I have succeeded in putting into this thing more than ¥170,000 or

117.
Suzuki Harunobu (c. 1725–1770). *The Crow and the Heron.* late 1760s. Color woodcut, *chūban*

Wright exhibited this print in an exhibition in Tokyo in May 1919 commemorating the 150th anniversary of the death of Harunobu. It was featured in the August 1919 issue of *Bijutsu gahō* and is the only print in Wright's collection published in Japan during his lifetime.

over $85,000. That is quite a sum and scares me when I think of it. My eggs are all in one basket.[3]

The Cliff Dwellers, a private men's club for artists and art lovers in the penthouse of Orchestra Hall, was a center for literature and the arts. Among the original 195 members, 36 were architects. Howard Van Doren Shaw (1869–1926) designed the interior of the club. Shaw, a Chicago architect with Yale and MIT credentials, and a trustee of the Art Institute, specialized in summer homes for the local gentry and churches in Gothic style. Wright knew of his colleague's interest in Asia: the two men were on the same steamer out of Yokohama in the spring of 1917, Shaw having just completed a tour of China and Japan.[4] Wright and Sullivan were also club members. Sullivan, who was at the end of his career and had given up his office, was living in a single room in a run-down hotel. Occasionally he slept on the couch at the Cliff Dwellers.

Wright made a number of purchases that spring; in addition to the two "very secret" private collections mentioned above, he is said to have purchased all of the prints offered at auction in Tokyo in April from an important old daimyo collection, that of Marquis Ikeda of Okayama, for about $85,000, the same amount he quoted Sullivan.[5] (Wright could have attended a closed dealers' auction but only by invitation. A dealer might have taken him, for example, and would have charged him a small commission.) In his letter to Sullivan Wright explains how he was able to fund such ambitious deals:

> The Hotel people here have helped me by advancing my entire commission so I might speculate with it and double it—as the work drags here frightfully and I am going to lose any compensation I might have had for my own time....
>
> I wanted to put a check in this letter as I fear you may be needing it in spite of your cheerful letters, but I can't now—it reposes along with other prospective pleasures and pressing obligations in the profound heart of the Nishikiye!

Not only does Wright have the audacity to enlist poor Sullivan's aid in the print business, but he also admits to speculating his entire Tokyo honorarium on prints. By the time Frederick Gookin sent him a stern letter of warning in 1920, a year later, it was much too late: "And now," Gookin wrote, "in view of the strained credit situation throughout the world, let me urge you most earnestly not to tie up all your available resources in prints, much though you love them. In the past you have been extremely lucky, but don't keep on taking chances."[6]

Investing in prints, a game at which he had been quite successful thus far, seemed to Wright an obvious solution to his financial difficulties. "I tried to increase my fee," he later explained to Darwin Martin, "by mixing my brains with my money, buying things I knew the quality and value of—cheap—hoping to realize a good profit on them when I came back."[7] Wright had spent the money with which he should have paid off his long-standing debt to Martin, a debt he had conveniently forgotten. It was at this very moment, in the spring of 1919, that Martin threatened he might have no alternative but to take the infamous box of prints he was holding as collateral and auction them off on the steps of the Cook County Court House. Wright worked his magic: he convinced Martin to "keep cool" a year longer with a guarantee that the 110 Hiroshige contained in that box were increasing in value by 20 percent every year. And once again he begged Martin to simply take the prints and forgive the debt.[8] Martin always kept his sense of humor; he now spoke of the box of prints as "umpty thousand dollars worth of the finest Japanese art extant."[9]

The print dealers' association in Tokyo was a tight-knit group of twenty to thirty members who got together once a month to study and comment on their merchandise over dinner (ill. 116).[10] They didn't like Wright and he knew it; he went behind their backs in search of print sources and had offended nearly all of them. Gookin had little doubt they would "'put up a job on him' if they could."[11] Wright was, in fact, defrauded by an unscrupulous Tokyo dealer, Hayashi Kyūgo (?–1947) in a classic scam: Hayashi led him by train and rickshaw to a little house hidden ("*very, very secret!*") in the woods on the outskirts of Nikkō, a few hours north of Tokyo. Wright and Miriam Noel checked into the Kanaya Hotel in Nikkō on 18 December 1918—this may have been the trip with Hayashi.[12] Hayashi had a branch store at the Nikkō Lakeside Hotel on Lake Chūzenji, a popular tourist resort. The prints belonged to the widow of an artist, he told Wright, and had been in her storehouse for many years.

> There we found the "collection." My God! I thought I had seen every subject extant by now. I hadn't. There were things in that collection still unique—things like

a large-size Harunobu (printed in gold leaf in heavy goffered paper) that later brought twenty-five hundred dollars at [the 1927 Anderson galleries] auction in New York…. Suffice it to say that this clandestine collection beggared imagination and so description…. I, still the hungry orphan turned loose in the bakeshop, spent about two hours there and bought it all for fifty thousand dollars. They needed money badly.[13]

Hayashi received a check for ¥1,157 from Wright on 14 May 1919; perhaps this was his commission.[14] He was the *bantō* or gofer for Murata Kimbei, one of the senior print dealers in Nihonbashi, the commercial heart of Tokyo.[15] Murata was the sponsor of continuous auction sales of prints in Tokyo beginning at least as early as 1913.

Wright never mentioned an ominous incident that foreshadowed the messy tale of revamped prints. In May 1919 he contributed a number of prints to a Harunobu exhibition vetted by a committee of Tokyo dealers including Watanabe Shōzaburō, Suwa Matsunosuke, and Sakai (either Saikai Shōkichi of Sakai Kokodō, or Sakai Tōbei). During the exhibition a story was put out that 80 percent of Wright's entries were overprinted fakes; John Happer snidely reported that they were "the laughing stock of the exhibition."[16] But Wright was now a serious contender: in August 1919 his impression of Harunobu's *The Crow and the Heron,* as the Japanese call the lovers under the umbrella on a winter day, was featured in *Bijutsu gahō* (Art pictorial), a Japanese art journal (ill. 117). In this special "Harunobu" issue of the journal, however, the subject of "revamped" prints was addressed head-on by one critic, Shishi Saian (probably a pseudonym). He was seriously distressed by the trend to "improve" an old, faded print by stripping or washing it (admittedly a legitimate conservation technique), tracing the original design on the fragile, worn paper in order to cut new color blocks, and then reprinting with contemporary pigments so as to make the image look bright and attractive and thus enhance its market value. Prints, after all, were rising in value faster than any other form of Japanese art, and print dealers, motivated by profit, were now improving even examples that did not really require touching up. But who knows, Saian argued, what deleterious effect modern pigments might have in the long run when applied to an old print? Not to mention the fact that new pigments

could never replicate the subtle color harmonies of old prints. Most revamped prints were going into the hands of ignorant foreigners—an unethical business. "When I went to the Harunobu exhibition," he concluded, "I saw the revamped Harunobu prints owned by a certain foreigner. The color looks marvelous now, but I fear that it may look different later and regret very much that masterpieces by Harunobu are being reprinted with new color."[17]

Wright knew to target Howard Mansfield as his most likely client for a big sale. He wrote the New York lawyer on 25 May "from the Draughting Room on the field of action—here in Tokyo," confiding that he had bought *five* private collections, including that of a Nagoya potter and a Kyoto artist's widow "that have been in hiding for a long time. Most of the prints I have bought this time, Tokyo, or any other, dealers have never seen."[18] The prints are in the finest condition, unique, rare, perfect, and so on—the usual hype. He could bring them to New York and asks Mansfield's help in disposing of them for somewhere between $250,000 and $500,000. Gookin helped fill in some details of the collection of the old potter in Nagoya in a subsequent letter to Mansfield. "Wright saw the boxes holding his prints brought out from his kura [storehouse] and unpacked. They were just as they had lain for many years and those in one box were mostly spoiled by moisture that had got in at one corner and caused damage by mildew."[19]

Wright came back from Japan in September carrying 1,500 prints, which he studied and gloated over during the tedious ocean crossing. On a stop-over in Los Angeles he first offered the collection to William Spaulding, now living in Santa Barbara. Spaulding, who had acquired the best of Gookin's collection of Harunobu a month earlier, apparently balked at the staggering asking price but did eventually succumb to a modest purchase; in December he paid Wright $5,000 for newly acquired prints.[20] Mansfield was most definitely interested and immediately set about organizing a consortium of collectors who, by mid-September 1919, were prepared to make a counteroffer of $60,000, each contributing around $15,000. Because Mansfield had already heard rumors that Wright had been "fooled by clever frauds," he responded to the architect in carefully worded legalese, requesting guarantee of title to the prints and "guarantee that there are no reprints or faked or altered or fixed prints in the collection, but that all the prints are old and genuine and that none of them has been tampered with."[21] Wright, forgetting for the moment that he had already admitted to going in debt over this purchase, was incensed at the implication he might not have paid in full:

> Well—I hasten to go on record here and now with absolute assurance that each and every print I have has been *bought outright* by me and *paid for* out of my own earnings in Tokio!
>
> No one, *whatsoever*—has any interest with me of any nature *whatsoever*. I have bought them too with what expert judgement Japan afforded me and that I felt I could trust. *Always accepting or rejecting it according to my own judgement*. My methods (going behind the dealers) has naturally antagonized them.

As for Mansfield's stipulation that the collectors be allowed to view the prints in privacy, without Wright in the room, the architect declared himself unwilling to

> expose myself and my treasures to the usual form of 'back-stairs assassination' practiced in the 'collectors' world.... If I go to you with these prints, into which I have put nearly everything I have, and submit to whispers and 'secrecy' (which is never narrower in its effects than the whole print-world), and come away with a cloud on the character of the prints, a cloud formed in this despicable and cowardly fashion—I shall suffer unjustly.[22]

Mansfield ignored this huffy tirade.

118.
Mary A. Ainsworth.
c. 1940

DOUBLED HIS INVESTMENT

In Chicago, Wright spent two days classifying and matting the prints with the help of Gookin, then doubled his investment when he took them to New York in October for a print party with Mansfield and some other collectors at the Hotel Astor. "The group called in experts...and excluded me from their conference, which hurt me.... I couldn't understand. Finally Howard, pencil and paper and lists in hand, offered me forty-five thousand dollars for about half of the collection. Make it fifty thousand, I said. Agreed." Wright misremembered the amount of the sale as $50,000. Mansfield mentions the sum of $60,000 more than once in his letters. When justifying his income tax returns for 1918 and 1919, Wright pretended to have sacrificed his prints for less than half their market price, with no profit to declare.[23]

The others assembled by Mansfield were Mary A. Ainsworth, Charles Hibbard Chandler, Miss Osborne, and Louis Ledoux. Ainsworth, an independent lady with ample means, was always willing to pay high prices (she was the terror of the New York auction rooms) (ill. 118).[24] Chandler (1859–1946), a pioneer merchant in Chicago, was a partner in Thayer and Chandler, an artists' materials and supplies company on West Van Buren Street, which he founded with Henry Thayer in 1880 (ill. 119). He said it was an exhibition of Japanese illustrated, printed books at the 1893 World's Fair that aroused his curiosity for prints (family lore has it that he purchased an entire room of antiques and furnishings at the fair), but he was influenced also by his neighbor in Evanston, Charles J. Morse. He bought from Ito Tokumatsu in Chicago as well as at auction in New York. Family lore also has it that the 1909 addition to Chandler's Queen Anne house, now an Evanston landmark, was built by a local carpenter from a design Wright sketched for the collector on a napkin. The napkin no longer exists.[25] About Miss Osborne (who married the following month and became Mrs. Kellogg), nothing is known at present.

Ledoux (1880–1948) was Mansfield's most gifted disciple in the study of Japanese art (ill. 120). Mansfield always relied on him in matters of print authentication. Educated at Columbia University, Ledoux was president of Ledoux and Company, expert assayers and chemists for mining and metallurgical firms. Described by some as a nervous aesthete, he had lean good looks and an air of elegance. Ledoux was a promising lyric poet and a collector of rare books when he met Mansfield, who treated the younger man almost like a son (Ledoux sometimes stayed at Mansfield's apartment). Ledoux and his wife made the first of several trips to Japan in 1920 and the experience confirmed him as a serious scholar of Japanese prints. Reviewing the April 1926 Utamaro exhibition in Tokyo sponsored by the Ukiyo-e Society

120.
Alexandre Iacovleff (French, 1887–1938). Unfinished portrait of Louis V. Ledoux. 10 May 1936. Sepia on paper, 14 x 13½ in. Collection Mr. and Mrs. Louis Pierre Ledoux, Cornwall-on-Hudson, New York

119.
Charles H. Chandler. c. 1915

Seated in the front sun porch on the second floor of his home at 1733 Asbury, in Evanston, Illinois, Chandler poses with a mid-eighteenth-century hand-colored print by Okumura Masanobu of a young samurai on horseback. He purchased the print at the 1896 Fenollosa/Ketcham sale in New York (see ill. 12), and it is now in the Michener Collection, Honolulu Academy of Arts. Chandler matted and hinged all his prints himself.

121.
Suzuki Harunobu. *Shimizu*, from the series *The Seven Komachi in Fashionable Dress* (*Fūryū nana Komachi*). late 1760s. Color woodcut, pillar print (*hashira-e*). Elvehjem Museum of Art, University of Wisconsin-Madison, Bequest of John H. Van Vleck, 1980 (1980.728)

The colors in this work are reprinted. Judson Metzgar told E. B. Van Vleck that this was one of the prints Mary Ainsworth bought from Wright in a New York hotel in 1919 (Van Vleck Ledger Book 1, p. 29, Elvehjem Museum of Art). When the Bank of Wisconsin sold thousands of prints from Wright's vault in 1928, this and many others like it entered Van Vleck's collection.

of Japan, he noticed that the Japanese had some twenty private collections to draw on, unlike the handful available in New York. In Tokyo,

> the attentive, studious crowd that filled the galleries were making notes of the poems, copying the designs, enjoying the references in titles and descriptions; while with us even the most habitual lover of prints, the most studious observer, sees only line and form and colour, and if he wishes to understand the frequent implications he must turn to a Japanese friend for help. It made me very humble and gave me an uncomfortable feeling of being an outsider in a world that I have loved and with which I am, after all, more familiar than most.[26]

Ledoux met Frank Lloyd Wright in the summer of 1918 when the architect was negotiating his first sale to the Metropolitan Museum of Art. Wright gave him a print and the two men traded copies of their publications—Wright's 1912 *The Japanese Print* in exchange for a book of verses.[27]

Ledoux, with Mansfield acting as his agent, came away with at least one print from the 1919 print party.[28] He was no random accumulator. More than any of his predecessors, he was a specialist, meticulous about maintaining the high quality of his collection. He did so by fastidiously rejecting any prints that were not "perfect" and by deliberately limiting himself to 250 prints, a number he had already attained by the early 1920s. Thereafter he was obliged to sell one for every new example he acquired. This selectivity was a practice inspired by his mentor, Mansfield, and sets him apart from others, like Chandler and the Spauldings, who collected in bulk.

Judson Metzgar, who had a limited budget, was not asked to join the now-famous print party, nor was Arthur Ficke. (The latter, just back from two years in Paris with the U. S. Army, may have lost touch with Wright. Or he may have sensed that the market had peaked, because he sold his entire personal collection in two auction sales in 1920 and 1925.) Metzgar learned of the party from Ainsworth, his close friend and neighbor in Moline, who asked him to look at her prints:

> The instant my eye caught them, I knew they were the revamped type. They were unmistakable. I was dumbfounded. I sat down and looked at them in silence.... Being slow to express my opinion under such circumstances, in fact not wanting to express it at all unless

asked, I could say nothing beyond remarking on the beauty of the designs. Finally she asked me just what I thought of the prints; and when I told her, she replied: "But that is impossible. There was not only myself, but Mr. Blank, and Mr. Blank and the others who bought a lot just like them. They surely can't all be wrong." However I maintained that I was right and suggested that Mr. Ficke be called in to look at them....

When Mr. Ficke saw them he reached the same conclusion that I had. The owner consulted me again and, feeling that she had been imposed upon, asked me as her lawyer to handle the matter for her; but I advised her to leave it in the hands of one of the five collectors who had been a member of the print buying group and was a prominent New York lawyer [i.e., Mansfield].[29]

It is profoundly interesting that Metzgar, like Gookin before him, noticed the "beauty of the designs" in describing prints selected by Wright.

A large number of these prints did turn out to be revamped. The skill of the Japanese printers was so great that many experts both in Japan and the West were fooled. This is a complicated and murky story, not easy to untangle. It plagued Wright for the next three years.

From the beginning there was speculation that the dealer Hayashi worked in tandem with Takamizawa Enji (1870–1927), a collector who made prints—facsimiles and fakes—as a hobby. Takamizawa had artisans working for him carving new color blocks, and eventually he began to sell his creations, which were so good that even the most experienced Japanese dealers were deceived. He was considered something of a genius by his contemporaries. The late ukiyo-e scholar Shizuya Fujikake is said to have confessed: "I couldn't tell Takamizawa's creations from original prints."[30] Gookin was fooled, too. He had spent two days looking over Wright's prints in the architect's Monroe Street sky parlor prior to the New York sale and found that "most of them have the colors almost if not quite as when first printed." He was not able to discover the slightest trace of revamping or faking of any sort. He thought rumors were being spread by dealers who were "trying to discredit [Wright] be-

122.
Sir Edmund Walker.
c. 1923

cause he has in a measure cut the ground from under their feet by seeking out their sources of supply."[31]

In the meantime, an agitated Ainsworth had express-mailed three of the prints questioned by Metzgar and Ficke to Mansfield, who went over them with his protégé, Ledoux (ill. 121). They saw no reason for complaint but sent them along to Gookin for his opinion. Gookin in turn showed them to William Spaulding, who happened to be passing through Chicago in mid-December, having already heard about these prints from Ficke. The situation was now fraught and Gookin found himself having to defend Wright to Ainsworth:

> As you speak of his reputation for dishonesty I want to say that while I hold no brief for him and have no thought of condoning his conduct in his domestic relations, I have never seen the slightest reason to consider him dishonest in money matters. He sells prints for high prices and like most dealers praises his wares to the sky, and he is an exceedingly clever salesman: but I do not think he would knowingly sell a faked print…. Despite the views of the Japanese dealers who are at outs with him, he is an excellent judge of prints and many of the finest in our collections have passed through his hands.[32]

One of Wright's visitors in Tokyo in the spring of 1919 had been the eminent Sir Edmund Walker (1848–1924), president of the Canadian Bank of Commerce. During the last fifteen years of his life, beginning around 1909, he used his spare time to put together an outstanding collection of some 1,000 Japanese prints, with emphasis on Harunobu and the earlier eighteenth-century masters (ill. 122). These he left to the Royal Ontario Museum, Toronto, where he was the first chairman of the board of trustees. In 1919 he was made honorary consul-general of Japan for Toronto.

Walker set off for a long tour of East Asia in March 1919 armed with letters of introduction from his friend and close advisor, Gookin. The latter had often acted as Walker's agent at New York sales. Letters went off to Yamanaka Sadajirō in Osaka,

and to Happer ("Happer has done more than any other person to develop interest in prints among the Japanese") and Wright in Tokyo:

> Frank Wright I think you know something about. He is a fascinating, adorable, and utterly irresponsible genius, full of magnetism, selfish to the extent of violating all the conventions if he sees fit; and an artist to his finger tips. I know of no better judge of the quality of prints, though I think he sometimes overvalues those he happens to own—a not uncommon trait against which one has always to be on guard.[33]

In December, some months after his return to Toronto, Walker found time to report back to Gookin: "I heard much about Mr. Wright's wonderful prints and indeed I saw most of them…. I fear he has been the victim of cleverly planned frauds in reprinting in whole or in part the coloured parts of otherwise fine but faded prints."[34] Gookin responded at once with a vivid glimpse behind the scenes into the ruthless, cutthroat jungle of the Tokyo print world:

> Since you left Tokyo the dealers have united in an association the members of which pledge themselves not to exhibit or sell any overprinted prints, and severe financial penalties are provided for any infractions of the compact. How efficacious it will prove remains to be seen. There was quite a row before everyone was brought into line. Murata Kimbei was forced to refund some thousands of yen and to take back a lot of the faked prints under threat of criminal prosecution. Now the association has elected Messrs. Watanabe, Sakai and one other to pass upon prints and certify to their genuineness and integrity. Frank Wright wants to know where they will acquire the necessary discernment, since every one of them admits having been "caught" at one time or another in recent months….
>
> Now as to Frank Wright. He is an extraordinarily keen judge and while he admits having acquired some overprinted prints, most of them were bought knowingly and others were returned when he examined them carefully and discovered the fraud. I have exam-

ined a large number of the prints he brought back with him in October [sic]…without finding any trace of anything wrong with the Wright prints….

There are people who hold that Wright may himself have participated in the frauds by getting Mura-Kim [Murata Kimbei] to do overprinting for him and under his supervision…. I do not believe he is so devoid of ordinary common sense, for he sells prints to the leading collectors and he knows that they would be sure to discover the fraud were it committed and would make him pay heavily for it. I tell you of this not to prejudice you against Wright, but to let you know the stories that are traveling about.[35]

FALLING BEHIND SCHEDULE IN TOKYO

Wright went back to Japan again in mid-December 1919, after only three hectic months in the States. In Tokyo he became severely ill, so much so that his aged mother, Anna Lloyd Jones Wright (1838/39–1923), who was past eighty, actually came over with a doctor, Emily Luff, and stayed at the Imperial Hotel with him from March until June 1920. She kept a journal in which she made note of how much she enjoyed the emperor's lavish garden party during cherry-blossom season in early April, and an excursion to Kamakura in the Country Club Overland that Wright had shipped over.[36]

Within the first two weeks of her arrival she had received visits from hotel manager Hayashi Aisaku and his wife, and Shugio Hiromichi and his wife, and had befriended Noémi Raymond, the French wife of Antonin Raymond (1888–1976), a young Czech-American who was Wright's chief draftsman and who stayed on to build his own architectural practice in Tokyo. She also noted among Wright's circle of acquaintances the Austrian painter Friedrich (Fritz) Capelari (1884–1950). Under the supervision of Watanabe Shōzaburō, Capelari had many of his watercolors of popular Japanese subjects turned into color woodcuts in the "new print" (*shin hanga*) style between 1915 and 1922, when he returned to Europe. Watanabe initiated the new-print movement in an effort to revive the creative spirit of

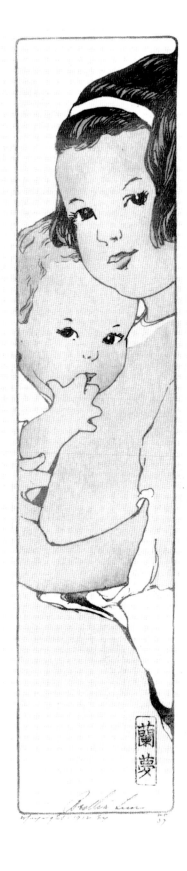

123.
Bertha Lum. *My Children*. 1912. Color woodcut, 10½ x 2³⁄₁₆ in. The Minneapolis Institute of Arts, Gift of Ethel Morrison Van Derlip, 1916 (P65)

the ukiyo-e tradition. Capelari and Goyō were among his two first recruits.[37] Another exponent of Japonisme with whom Wright was spending time in Tokyo that spring was Bertha Lum (1879–1954), a print artist from the Midwest described by Wright's mother as "a very interesting lady with two dear little girls" (ill. 123).[38] Wright took his mother and Lum and her two daughters Catherine (?–1983) and Bettina ("Peter Boy," 1911–1983) on outings in a park in the countryside more than once.

His mother's visit no doubt added some stress to Wright's life. She was bedridden with sciatica and other ailments almost immediately, and was in fact deeply unhappy for most of her stay. She spent four full weeks in bed. In her own words: "The food and climate so differant [*sic*]. All I have to say is I suffered oh I suffered I tried to hide it all."[39] If this were not enough, Wright was also having serious problems with Miriam Noel. Jealous of what she perceived to be another woman in his life (apparently one of the Russian aristocrats staying at the Imperial), she moved in July to Ikao, one of Japan's celebrated hot spring tourist resorts, within easy reach of Tokyo. Wright sent abject letters begging her to return.

Worse than all of these personal and family problems, of course, was the fact that Imperial Hotel construction was way over budget and still behind schedule (ills. 124, 125, 131). It had only reached the site preparation stage and completion was several years off. Fortunately for Wright, in 1919 the hotel had hired the experienced German-born construction engineer Paul Mueller (1857–1931?), who had worked first for Sullivan, and, after setting up shop on his own in Chicago, had done jobs for Wright. Wright's team in Tokyo included Mueller, Raymond, several young Japanese architects—notably Endō Arata and Tsuchiura Kameki (1897–1996)—and the Canadian William Smith, Wright's secretary and general assistant.

In late December 1919, just days before Wright arrived, the annex of the old Imperial had burned. The hotel asked him to design a two-story wooden replacement and it began housing guests by May 1920. Wright filled his own rooms in the annex

124.
Hayashi Aisaku looking pensive on the Imperial Hotel construction site. c. 1920

On the far right is Paul Mueller, Wright's structural engineer, who arrived in Tokyo in June 1919.

Opposite

125.
Wright with his assistants and Imperial Hotel staff at a Tokyo restaurant. c. 1920

Wright is seated at the center, with Hayashi Aisaku to his proper left. Paul Mueller is seated fifth from the left, his son is at the far left. Antonin Raymond, Wright's architectural assistant, is third from the left and the young Japanese architect Endō Arata is seated fourth from the left.

with every kind of Japanese and Chinese art, most of it later shipped to Spring Green. In his penthouse studio-bedroom, reached by means of a small stairway, he had an eight-panel Japanese genre screen over the fireplace and a seated wooden Buddha on a ledge at the head of his bed (ill. 126). A green silk textile embroidered with large white chrysanthemums was draped beside the bed. "I slept there," he said, "and had set up my drawing board there where I could work disturbing no one and could tumble into bed when tired out."[40] The Buddhist art in his small living room included a Japanese wooden statue of Monju (Manjushri), Bodhisattva of Wisdom, on the grand piano and a fourteenth-century Japanese hanging scroll depicting the welcoming descent of Amida (Amitabha), Buddha of the Western Paradise. On the long wall opposite the fireplace, where he kept a fire always burning, he installed a decorative Rimpa-school screen of autumn grasses (ill. 127). Miriam Noel summed up their lifestyle quite nicely: "At Tokyo we took a five-room apartment in the old Imperial Hotel. We were surrounded with lovely

126.
Imperial Hotel Annex,
Tokyo. Studio-bedroom
in Wright's apartment
with Japanese art.
1920–22

On the wall is a photo-
graph of the playhouse
Wright built for Mr. and
Mrs. Avery Coonley in
Riverside, Illinois.

127.
Imperial Hotel Annex,
Tokyo. Living room in
Wright's apartment with
Asian art. 1920–22

東京帝國ホテル
IMPERIAL HOTEL, TOKYO, JAPAN.

128.
Imperial Hotel, Tokyo.
Guest suite. 1920s

and costly things. Frank has a remarkable genius for creating an unusual and artistic environment. No family ever lived in greater luxury and splendor than we."[41]

Wright's new Imperial turned out to be lavish and exotic, if not especially Japanese. Still, it is tempting to point out at least one possible hint of Japonisme. The motif Wright adopted for the carpets in the guest rooms bears an uncanny resemblance to the concentric squares of the Ichikawa family crest so familiar from Katsukawa actor prints, especially the *Shibaraku* role (ills. 128, 129). Wright and Noel traveled to Beijing together in 1918 to award the contracts for the carpets, and Miriam later wrote that they were the most expensive rugs made and cost the hotel $350,000.[42]

129.
Ippitsusai Bunchō (active c. 1765–92). *The Actor Ichikawa Danjūrō IV in a "Shibaraku" Role*. c. 1768. Color woodcut, *hosoban*. Elvehjem Museum of Art, University of Wisconsin-Madison, Bequest of John H. Van Vleck, 1980 (1980.612). Ex coll. Frank Lloyd Wright; E. B. Van Vleck

130.
Frank Lloyd Wright. Imperial Hotel, Tokyo, as it looked around 1967 (it was demolished in 1968). Postcard

131.
Wright (far left), an
unidentified Japanese
man (perhaps Endō
Arata), Paul Mueller, and
Antonin Raymond pos-
ing with the thirteenth-
century Great Buddha
(Daibutsu) in Kamakura.
c. 1921

VAMPS EXPOSED

Several months after the purchases at the Hotel Astor, and after Wright had returned to Japan, Mansfield was showing off his newly augmented collection to a Japanese dealer, Matsuki Kihachirō (1879–1942), in whose judgment and honesty he had confidence, but whom he had never previously consulted as an expert. Matsuki, an aspiring artist in his youth, was the youngest of three sons, all art dealers. He joined his brother Bunkio in Salem, Massachusetts, in 1895, enrolling that year in Salem High School. Their twenty-year-old sister came along to help prepare their meals. Fluent in English, the two brothers were in business together in Boston from about 1900 to 1909, when Kihachirō returned to Japan to sell prints with his oldest brother, Matsuki Zen'emon (1864–1949), who had a business in Kyoto (ills. 132, 133). In 1917, in need of money to support his growing family, he came back to the States to spend two

and a half years working for Morimura Brothers, importers of "Japanese and Oriental Goods" (meaning fancy china and dinner ware) on West Twenty-third Street in New York. He traded on the side in Japanese prints, and was considered an expert and a "shrewd buyer" in this field.[43]

Matsuki questioned the integrity of several of the recent acquisitions from Wright. When Gookin was in town for the February 1920 Ficke sale at the American Art Galleries, he and Ledoux went over the Mansfield prints with fresh eyes and they were now convinced that some had pinpricks, evidence of re-vamping, while others were simply modern replicas. (Pinholes were used to align registration for cutting new color blocks. Guidelines for the tracer, they are the surest clues to a reworked print.) Mansfield was not one to rush to judgment, but with this new evidence, added to the doubts already raised by both Chandler and Ainsworth (only Mrs. Kellogg turned out to be perfectly satisfied with her purchases), he finally found it neces-

132.
Matsuki Kihachirō in New York. c. 1919

133.
Matsuki Zen'emon print shop, Kyoto. 1910s

sary to send off a letter to Wright divulging for the first time the names of the other members of the original consortium (they would have to present their claims individually) and requesting restitution for all of them in the form of either an equal exchange or money back.[44]

The fateful letter was waiting for Wright when he returned to Spring Green in July, as was this letter of commiseration from Gookin, offering to help prepare a strategy to salvage the architect's reputation:

> That the contents of Mansfield's letter will be a great shock to you "goes without saying." It was a knock-down blow to me to discover that both you and I as well as Mansfield had been taken in by the extraordinary re-vamping of a lot of the prints that Mansfield bought from you for himself and several of his friends. As he says in his letter you may hesitate to accept his statement. Nevertheless with the prints before you, and having knowledge of what to look for, there is no getting away from the damning evidence….
>
> You will perhaps remember that one reason why I failed to see anything wrong with the Kiyonaga diptych was—apart from its undoubted beauty—that it seemed incredible that anyone would take the risk of spoiling a print of such value, which risk would be disproportionately great because of the difficulty of getting exact register. Now, however, we know that the method of getting the register is such as to involve no risk whatever. If you will make an effort to get at the secrets of the processes, and have not alienated such men as Watanabe and the other reputable dealers, I think you can be put straight about the whole game.[45]

Mansfield was seriously annoyed that his Kiyonaga diptych, which depicts a group of courtesans and geisha entertaining a young man at a teahouse in Shinagawa, was not right (ill. 134). It had cost him $3,500 and was his favorite of the entire group, the reason he had put himself out to arrange the sale in the first place. He and Gookin compared it with a faded impression the Metropolitan Museum of Art purchased from the Spauldings in 1914 and the published Vever impression and found that while all had slight differences in the key block, only Mansfield's copy showed variation in the color blocks. Moreover, the color blocks used for Mansfield's print were judged to be less charming and

more coarsely carved, the drawing stiffer. An unmistakably modern yellowish-green tint had been printed over the water of Tokyo Bay. Not to mention the pinholes.

Gookin deduced that the Tokyo dealers who had been spreading rumors about Wright's prints had deliberately entrapped him by planting the "re-vampers" in such a way that the architect thought he was buying a private collection, and he urged Wright to make the dealers disgorge some kind of settlement. He also admits to being deeply chagrined that he did not himself discover the faking in October of the previous year, when he had been called to vet the prints; it would have saved much unpleasantness for all. "To some extent," he tells Wright, "my confidence in your knowledge and judgment influenced my opinion," but the fact is that the revamping was so diabolically clever that anyone might have failed to discover it even when looking for it. Apparently even Murata Kimbei was "hoist by his own petard," unwittingly buying one of his own revamps, to the great glee of all the other Tokyo dealers.[46]

This formal typewritten letter, which Gookin thought Wright might wish to use as an aid in getting restitution from "the chap that sold you the revamped prints" was enclosed with a more personal handwritten note:

> Now, my dear fellow, I don't need to tell you how sorry I am that we should have been taken in…. I have been lucky enough to escape, though I acquired two very beautiful specimens of revamping about two years ago knowing that something had been done to them though I was not at the time able to discover what it was….
>
> I am glad to hear that you have brought some more great treasures back with you. With them you should be able to satisfy Mansfield and his associates. My advice to you is not to haggle about the settlement. If the prints have not been revamped you can certainly afford to take them back; if they have been *you cannot afford not to take them back*. So you see that it is clearly for your interest to make a prompt settlement. Should you show any hesitation about it I doubt whether you would ever again be able to sell a print in the United States.[47]

Gookin regretted that he had not alerted Wright to the problem while he was still in Japan, but Mansfield had prudently asked him to wait until all of his prints were inspected by a third party. Also, they knew Wright had been ill and did not want to worry him on his sickbed. Mansfield was reportedly as sorry for Wright as he was for himself and his fellow collectors. In the meantime Gookin and Mansfield were both off for long summer holidays. Gookin was nervous about Wright's sensitive ego. "I am sure you will not find Mansfield unfair," he continued, "and I know he does not question your good faith. And I am sure that you will not disagree with us as to the revamping when we can go over the prints together and compare them with untouched impressions." He also pointed out that there had been a lot of revamped prints in the Matsuki Bunkio auction at the Anderson Galleries in New York in January 1920. (The prints are billed in the Matsuki catalogue as coming from "the collection of an old samurai family in Tokyo.") It was Gookin's opinion that if the revamps could no longer be marketed in Japan, Japanese dealers would inevitably find a market for them in the United States or in Europe.

Wright's reaction is predictable: he strongly doubts the truth of the accusations, demands proof, and protests his innocence. He has prints but no money, he says, and will make an exchange but only if a conscientious third party gives a fair valuation.[48] But within a few weeks he was feeling frisky again: "Hereafter, why collect mere originals?" he inquired of Mansfield.[49]

134.
Torii Kiyonaga. *Gentleman Entertained by Courtesans and Geisha at a Teahouse in Shinagawa,* from the series *Twelve Months in the South* (*Minami jūniko*). c. 1783. Color woodcut, *ōban* diptych. The Metropolitan Museum of Art, New York, Gift of Frank Lloyd Wright, 1921 (JP 1268)

Howard Mansfield bought this print from Wright in New York in October 1919. By June 1920 it had been denounced as reprinted with fresh colors. Wright took the print back from Mansfield in October 1921 and gave it to the Metropolitan Museum of Art that same year, presumably for educational use.

On the weekend of 15–16 October 1920 Wright threw open his vault at Taliesin to Gookin, Mansfield, and Chandler and one other for what he called "'The Print Party' but in reverse." Gookin was present at the request of Mansfield; surprisingly, it was his first visit to Taliesin, and he was glad of the opportunity. It is not clear whether the fourth collector was Ledoux, to whom Wright had extended an invitation, or Ainsworth; Mansfield had advised Ainsworth to leave the twenty-six prints she wished to exchange in Chicago with Chandler. Among them was the notorious Harunobu *The Crow and the Heron,* for which she had paid $825, but which turned out to have renewed embossing as well as renewed red and black color (see ill. 117).[50]

With the exception of Gookin, the collectors would have much preferred to meet in Chicago rather than make the long pilgrimage to Spring Green, but Wright was anxious to put himself in the best possible light and he was always at his best as

135.
Aerial view of Taliesin III
with the Wisconsin
River visible at top.
c. 1945–50

country gentleman, master of his own beautiful estate (ills. 135, 136).[51] Visitors from afar were always impressed by Taliesin. The British architect and designer C. R. Ashbee wrote his wife in 1916 that it was "a rather splendid establishment but quite unconventional, and very beautiful in its bohemian and original way," noting especially "the print room [the loggia] where we look at Hiroshige and Utamaro—the choicest Yoshiwara drawings."[52] Darwin Martin once told Wright that his brother had visited Taliesin while the architect was in Tokyo. He was "shown your cache of Oriental splendor, and his eyes popped so that I do not know if he has looked natural since."[53] The Viennese architect Richard J. Neutra (1892–1970) likened Taliesin to a Japanese temple district and Wright's sister Maginel detected a distinctive smell, a mixture of wood smoke, dried pennyroyal and "the faint elusive fragrance that emanates from oriental *objets d'art*."[54]

A vivid contemporary description of the impact Taliesin made on outsiders is given by twenty-seven-year-old Pauline Schindler (1893–1977) in her letters to her parents in Chicago in

136.
Taliesin II. Living room. 1924 or early 1925

This view of the living room includes two Japanese folding screens, one with white chrysanthemums (see ill. 4), and a small one with a large gourd filled with flowers. At the rear left is a Chinese Han-dynasty jar (see ill. 137) with dried flowers (these jars are porous) and a Chinese Buddhist stone sculpture (possibly Sui dynasty, late sixth–early seventh century) as well as the head of a Chinese Buddha. A contemporary Japanese bamboo shade (*sudare*) hangs in the window.

1920. Newly married, she had accompanied her husband that summer when he moved from Wright's Chicago office to Taliesin, where he was working feverishly on the drawings for Aline Barnsdall's Hollyhock House. Also present, in addition to farmhands and carpenters, was Will Smith, Wright's secretary. "Although Taliesin is ten years old," Pauline wrote on 24 July,

> it is still always continuing to be built. Last fall they were at work on two extra studios just off the main drafting room,—one for drawing perspectives, and one, a study in which Mr. Wright examines Japanese prints. He is the greatest living authority on Japanese prints,—and to play among his possessions is to touch very rare and precious things. I wandered about in the vault today, looking at exquisite Japanese embroideries and all sorts of things I had never dreamed of as existing. Of course my eyes are still asleep and untaught about them. One screen I thought rather ugly was worth sixteen hundred dollars; another, worse, is two thousand. Rare things lie all about us,—and so carelessly prodigal is their possessor that he goes off for months or years leaving many thousands of dollars worth of all sorts of art objects, mouldering in some subterranean room.[55]

Sunday was their day to play. On 29 September Pauline describes Wright at home with his Asian treasures:

> Last Sunday morning we were wakened by the voice of Mr. Wright,—"Come on. Here's a trunk from Japan to unpack." An hour later we were all in the studio, Mr. Wright, Smith, and ourselves,—parading up and down in wonderful mandarin coats,—R. M. S. [Rudolph Schindler] in a sweeping mightiness of blue, with golden dragons ramping all over him; Smith, and Mr. Wright, each in a purple satin gown, with peacock-blue lining; for me, a transparent blue silk, embroidered brilliantly with blossoms. We roared at ourselves,—we looked so impressive. And just at the height of our fun,—we looked at a window, and saw a silent group of heads peering in at us,—a dozen of the usual Sunday visitors, gaping with amazement!

She announces Mansfield's impending visit, describing the pains Wright took to present his prints to best advantage:

> [Important guests] are coming to buy Japanese prints,—from the "print-god". Did I tell you that he is called in Japan, "Wright-o-san the print-god," and "Wright-o-san the high-think-maker of the building?" For two weeks on end Mr. Wright has been playing around with his print-room,—manipulating light-effects; arranging screens and rugs and lacquer cabinets and Chinese vases dating a hundred years before Christ,—all with relation to their modification of the prints…. The great thing in showing prints, is to choose their order rightly. Never show a brightly-colored one immediately after a subtle, toned, quiet print. The folk who come…from New York, will really make or unmake Mr. Wright's finances. Of course he makes little financial profit from architecture,—he spends too much at it. But he has a hundred thousand dollars' worth of prints here in the studio,—and rejoices in finding a man who knows how to buy them with understanding.[56]

Judging by these remarks, it seems to have been common knowledge that Wright made better money as an art dealer than as an architect. Wright did have a reserve: he told Gookin that he returned from Japan that summer with another $45,000 worth of fine prints.[57] A week later Wright and Smith were still mounting and arranging Japanese prints, staging several dress rehearsals with a critical eye toward the effects of lighting and sequence. The architecture historian Kathryn Smith, in her study of the Barnsdall commission, Wright's only major American project at this time, suggests that his architectural drawings in the fall of 1920 are uncharacteristically clumsy in details owing to his preoccupation with Mansfield's visit.[58]

Wright estimated that about one-third of the prints he had sold in New York had been revamped.[59] In the adjustment process that ensued, Ainsworth acquired, among other things, a tall, wide "primitive" in not too fine condition for the sum of $2,500. As Metzgar later noted, however, it was expensive "but it was genuine."[60] News of the exchange of prints traveled quickly through the ukiyo-e grapevine. William Spaulding

137.
Jar. China, Han dynasty. c. first century B.C.–A.D. second century. Earthenware with iridescent green glaze and hunting scene molded in high relief around shoulder, 13¾ in. high.

The Frank Lloyd Wright Foundation sold the jar in 1967 at Parke-Bernet Galleries, New York (sale 2636, lot 387), for $1,100.

heard about the reunion at Taliesin from Gookin. He wrote from southern California to congratulate Wright on the extremely sportsmanship manner in which he dealt with the matter.[61]

But this was not the end of the affair. On 21 July 1921, during the brief mid-summer interlude when Wright was back from Japan, Mansfield wrote with bad news. He had hired Matsuki to evaluate his entire collection of Japanese prints and the result was very disheartening: after examining them by strong daylight, the Japanese expert condemned as revamped no fewer than seven prints that had come from Wright in October 1919 in New York and October 1920 at Taliesin, including some of the most expensive: two Utamaro and an Eiri (active 1890s), three Hiroshige bird-and-flower prints, and Kitao Masanobu's *Two Geisha*, for a total cost to Mansfield of $4,995. Both Matsuki and Ledoux could see pinholes.

Mansfield returned the prints to Wright so that he could take them back to Japan. He notes that while he declined to take a commission from the architect (or anyone else in the consortium), he did interest

three other collectors in making a purchase in which we all supposed that, buying from you as a professed expert, we were acquiring prints of unimpeachable integrity. Well, you know what happened.

Of course, in making choices, I took my chances with the others, except in having the first chance and taking the Kiyonaga diptych, which turned out to have been revamped, and thus losing my chances at one of the three fine prints which I greatly desired to have, and which my associates have now.... Of the fourteen prints that I thus acquired on competitive choices, I have had to return ten, keeping only four, and only one of the four very important, and one of the other three chosen for Ledoux!...

Thus I have been paying out a great deal of good money and getting a large number of bad prints, and while I have been holding the bad prints, you have been having the use of the good money....

I do not recall among the prints you recently brought to my apartment any that I would consider accepting on exchanges for the seven prints except the Utamaro "Girl with Umbrella" (mica ground), and possibly the large actor print by [Utagawa] Toyokuni

相観 歌麿考画

婦女人相十品

138.
Kitagawa Utamaro.
Woman with Parasol,
from the series *Ten
Classes of Women's
Physiognomy* (*Fujō
ninsō juppon*). c.
1792–93. Color wood-
cut with white mica
ground, *ōban.* The Met-
ropolitan Museum of
Art, New York, The
Howard Mansfield Col-
lection, Rogers Fund,
1936 (JP 2730). Ex coll.
Frank Lloyd Wright

that was among the actor prints that were submitted to Dr. [Arthur B.] Duel. I am willing to accept in part exchange his Utamaro at the price of $3650 which you have put upon it, although I regard the price as very high, and I ask that you instruct William Smith to send to me at 535 Park Avenue, that Utamaro, and such other Toyokunis of that type as you may have, and such other top notch prints as you have.[62]

Arthur B. Duel (1870–1936), who appears in this letter as one of Wright's print clients, was a successful eye, ear, nose, and throat surgeon with a degree from Harvard Medical School and a practice on East Sixty-fifth Street in New York. Both Mansfield and Ficke (who moved to New York in 1923) were among his patients. When he took out Ficke's tonsils, Duel "said he would be glad to pay for the privilege, but was finally persuaded to accept some erotic prints instead."[63] Duel's daughter recalled that Wright had been a visitor to their summer home, Laurelwood, a white frame house on a 2,000-acre, wooded estate at Pawling, New York. Wright's carping criticism of their conventional country house turned the visit frosty.[64]

The lovely Utamaro *Woman with Parasol* with white mica ground, which had been turned down by Duel but which Mansfield was willing to pick up for $3,650, is now in the Metropolitan Museum of Art (ill. 138). Mansfield sold it to the museum in 1936 for $2,500. The original cost to Mansfield was high, but the set to which it belongs is one of Utamaro's earliest masterworks and the value today would easily be a hundred times greater than what Wright was asking. (One print from this set sold at Christie's, New York, in 1987 for $197,000; it was subsequently resold privately for more than double that amount.)[65]

Wright's income of $3,650 for one print should be measured against his architect's fee of $2,700 for the Henry Allen house in Wichita, which took three years to build, from late 1915 through the end of 1918.[66] The print sale does not represent a pure profit, of course, but neither does the architectural fee, which went toward staff salaries, overhead, engineering expenses, and the like.

The final exchange of prints with Mansfield (totaling $3,495) could not be made until more than a year later, in the fall of 1922, after Wright returned from his last trip to Japan. By this time Wright had a fresh lot of prints with which to tempt the rich New Yorker, who spent an additional $1,000. He sent off a group of over thirty-six prints to Ledoux as well, who was annoyed when Wright tried to enlist Bosch Reitz to authenticate the lot for him.[67]

It is surprising that works by Hiroshige (relatively late and certainly modest in price) were judged as revamped. Since Murata Kimbei, Goyō, Watanabe, and others were all making high-quality facsimile replicas, one wonders whether these Mansfield prints were true vamps (old prints with new color) or simply excellent facsimiles. (Watanabe made his Hiroshige replicas from a set of original blocks he borrowed from Happer.) Wright himself commissioned facsimile replicas of sets of Hiroshige prints and gave the Metropolitan Museum of Art albums of reprints in 1918.[68] Facsimiles of Harunobu and Utamaro were being expertly made in the late nineteenth century using some (but not necessarily all) of the original blocks. There are examples of this type in the Clarence Buckingham collection, some purchased in the 1890s.[69] This subject has yet to be carefully studied. Certainly the revamping business was blown out of all proportion by Wright's detractors. The high price of prints when the market was peaking in the mid-Taishō period must have contributed to the surge in revamping and forgeries. Around 1919, when a bowl of soba noodles cost only 5 sen (a tiny fraction of ¥1) and a house could be built for ¥1,000, one wealthy Japanese collector spent ¥8,000 on a Harunobu print.[70]

An interesting footnote to this affair concerns the print by Kitao Masanobu (1761–1816) identified by Mansfield as "Two Girls" (ill. 139). Wright kept this small print when Mansfield returned it, and, together with the other "vamps," it later found its way into the Van Vleck Collection in the Elvehjem Museum of Art in Madison. The print depicts two geisha strolling in a garden, from the series *A Competition among Geisha* (*Geiko iro kurabe*) dating from the 1770s. On a piece of paper pasted on the back of the print the following inscription is written in English with a pencil: "This old print has been restored with new color blocks on faded colors. Judged by Tokyo Old Prints Society. Sep. 8, 1921" (ill. 140). Here is evidence that Wright did indeed take the Mansfield revamps back to Tokyo with him in July 1921 to submit to review by the association.

Mansfield, however, discarded many perfectly good prints by mistake. He gave back what must have been an extremely rare Eiri bust portrait of a teahouse waitress with fan on a mica-

140.
Inscription and seal on the reverse of ill. 139

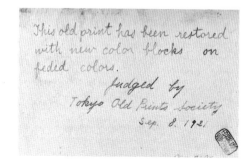

covered black ground; only three or four impressions of this print are known.[71] It has very little color, and thus not much to "revamp." The overly cautious experts were probably misled by its rarity and/or fine condition.

Prior to his final sale to the Metropolitan Museum of Art in November 1922, Wright explained the entire sorry story to S. C. Bosch Reitz:

> I lost at that time—by means of restitutions I felt bound to make—about $30,000, which I had earned by my work on the Imperial Hotel…. Upon my return to Tokyo I got after the principal dealer with all my resources—kept him out of business for two years on probation while the procurator had him in his toils—got the backing of the court with the help of Japanese friends in Tokyo and finally sold him out, home and all and took what he had which netted the munificent sum of Yen 3500.00. He went out of the country.[72]

In his autobiography, Wright later gave the following version of this saga of vengeance:

> Wrieto San had fallen. I went after the ring, wiped it out, got the ring-leader (he was Hayashi) in jail. After he had been there a year his case came up. The court sent for me. The police brought Hayashi to me where I was sitting in court at a small table to judge him. The court wanted to know what I wanted done with him. He knocked his forehead to the floor and begged for mercy as tears streamed from his eyes. I said "Take everything of the sort he has away from him. Forbid him to ever deal in color prints again and let him go." This was done. He had very little of anything. They would have hanged him if I had said so, for the Japanese authorities were furious. The trickery greatly humiliated them. So I had "cleaned up the market" in quite another way than I originally intended.
>
> The Japanese authorities openly apologized. The dealer was banished. He was last heard of in London.[73]

Various Rashomon-like stories—perhaps apocryphal—have circulated among ukiyo-e dealers in Japan concerning this unsavory incident. The tale was even cited in a 1926 diary entry by the popular novelist Nagai Kafū (1879–1959), who was himself a

141.
Katsukawa Shunshō. *The Actors Ōtani Tomoemon I and Bandō Mitsugorō I.* c. 1775. Color woodcut, uncut "double" *hosoban.* The Metropolitan Museum of Art, New York, Rogers Fund, 1922 (JP 1366)

Ōtani Tomoemon, whose crest is a cross within a circle, is on the right. Wright sold this print to the Metropolitan Museum of Art in November 1922.

serious print collector; he gives a figure of ¥200,000 (roughly $100,000 at that time) as the amount Wright lost on revamped prints purchased in 1919.[74] According to old-timers in the Japanese print world, Wright actually locked the villain in a hotel room and confronted him at gunpoint, demanding a confession and restitution before taking him to court. Hayashi implicated Takamizawa Enji, who was also summoned to the district attorney's office.[75] Hayashi never spoke of the incident, which was a very painful experience for him. His daughter says that Wright did drive the dealer out of the country temporarily, perhaps to Hong Kong, but not as far as Europe.[76] Hayashi landed on his feet. In 1923 he opened his own gallery, the Marumiya, in the Marubiru in the Marunouchi district of downtown Tokyo.

Be that as it may, the architect assured Bosch Reitz that since then "not one print which is in any way bad has been purchased by me nor knowingly presented to me for consideration—and I think in Tokyo among all the dealers the matter is settled and most anyone now safe from imposition." He announced his imminent arrival in New York to try and dispose of enough prints to meet the deficit caused by operating expenses at Taliesin. "My work in Tokyo was successful—the Japanese were more than appreciative and kind to me. They paid me much more than my due to prove it—but the work was so long drawn out that it was not profitable to me." In concluding his sales pitch, Wright confessed: "In this matter I am a merchant and expect to be treated like one—I have little use for the 'gentleman' dealer in works of art. He bores me."[77] An interesting remark; at least he knows he is on one side of the court.

The Metropolitan Museum of Art paid Wright $4,000 for seventy-four prints ranging from early "primitives" to Hokusai. "As a matter of fact," a pleased Bosch Reitz confided to the president of the board of trustees in October 1922, "the price offered is extremely low and was accepted on Mr. Wright's side because he badly wants the money and wants it as soon as possible."[78] Wright again accepted sixty dollars for each of his Katsukawa prints (ill. 141). But the Harunobu pillar prints were also a mere sixty dollars, the marvelous Utamaro large-head portraits with mica ground were $250 (quite a difference from the Utamaro he had sold Mansfield for $3,650 in 1921), and the excellent examples of Hokusai's *The Thirty-six Views of Mount Fuji* were practically given away at ten dollars each (ills. 142, 143). Back in 1909 Wright had sold prints from the *Thirty-six Views* to Sallie Casey Thayer for eighty-five dollars each. By way of comparison, at the height of the bubble market in 1990 a great impression of the Hokusai *Red Fuji* from this set sold at a Tokyo dealers' auction for $460,000 and in 1991 the *Great Wave* sold at Christie's, New York, for $220,000.[79]

Hearing that Bosch Reitz had questioned one of his prints as "too good to be true," he points out that he had it passed by the Old Prints Society in Tokyo. Several of Wright's prints purchased by the Metropolitan Museum of Art in 1922 do bear the seal of authentication of this newly formed dealers' association dedicated to ferreting out revamped prints and guaranteeing the authenticity of others. An Utamaro bust portrait of a prostitute, a diptych of women in the kitchen, and a single-sheet figure print by Torii Kiyonaga of the brine gatherers Matsukaze and Murasame, all of outstanding quality, have a paper seal affixed to the back reading, in English and Japanese: "The Old Prints Society, Tokyo: Certified Genuine" (ills. 143, 144, 145). The association did not trouble itself with later, less valuable works by nineteenth-century artists such as Hokusai and Hiroshige.

Nonetheless, Bosch Reitz was compelled to admonish Wright for retouching prints he sold:

> I dread to think what your feelings are going to be after reading what I have to say. However here it is: I went over the prints you left here and found that two of the early [Hiroshige] Toto Meisho [Famous Views of the Eastern Capital] set are revamped, all of the classic signs are there, pin holes, bright pink clouds, etc.... Further I found that of two Shunshos one background had been painted up with yellow and the other refreshed with blue.

142.
Kitagawa Utamaro.
High-ranked Courtesan
(*Oiran*), from the series
*Five Shades of Ink in
the Northern Quarter*
(*Hokkoku goshiki-zumi*).
c. 1794–95. Color
woodcut, *ōban*. The
Metropolitan Museum
of Art, New York,
Rogers Fund, 1922 (JP
1368)

A courtesan from the
Yoshiwara pleasure
quarter in the northern
section of Edo wets the
tip of her brush in
preparation for writing
a letter to a favored
client. The cartouche
with the series title at
the upper right is in the
shape of an ink stick.
Wright sold this print to
the Metropolitan Muse-
um of Art in November
1922 for $250.

If you allow me to give you a tip you should tell your man to take off the mats when he retouches the prints; painted lines which continue on the mat are a terrible give away.

Well now the worst is said, fume as you like.[80]

Wright, insulted by the accusation, replied:

There is no intention on my part to deceive you or anyone else—I think you know this. Kindly forward suspected prints at once for inspection and comparison. I have never changed the values in any of my prints. As all collectors do and will do I have worked on them sometimes with color to retouch spots, clean surfaces, put the print into condition but very little even of that…. Long ago some fooling with some of my prints was done by my studio boys who had always access to them as to a kind of library—for their education and pleasure. But that was ten years ago or more and rejected long since. I have gone through the remaining prints carefully to eliminate the "taint" or the "vamp…."

N. B. Since the "re-vamping" came to light I have preferred to let my prints strictly alone—even to stains or worm holes or "*pressing*"—. And most of my prints acquired since that time are "as found" without the customary conditioning given by Gookin and others.[81]

Wright's point is well taken: the always respectable Gookin was never reproached for *his* restoration of prints, which involved, at the very least and by his own admission, cleaning, straightening, touching up, and patching.[82] Wright was often observed drawing on woodcuts that he retained in his personal collection. The architect Antonin Raymond was amused to find Wright "improving" his color woodcuts with colored pencils and crayons, and John H. Howe (1913–1997), Wright's head draftsman from 1932, confirmed that Wright "occasionally touched up Japanese prints with colored pencils, but these were poor quality prints to start out."[83] William Wesley Peters (1912–1991), who worked with Wright continuously from 1932, became his son-in-law, and eventually served as chairman of the board of the Frank Lloyd Wright Foundation and Taliesin Associated Architects, remembered that

Mr. Wright would never have considered altering a fine print in the pristine condition that its creator envisioned. However, I have several times seen him use colored pencils to bring back the miscolored sky or faded "notan" [graduated shading] of a less than good or damaged print that failed to attain the effect that characterized finer examples of the same subject. He also sometimes sketched on poor copies of prints modules or lines that showed the proportion and structure of the concept.[84]

In the end, making the best of a bad situation, Wright was good-humored about offering to lend the Metropolitan Museum of Art a group of sixty finely executed "vamps" ("true vampires," as he called them, "convicted and generally admired as such") for a study exhibition that Bosch Reitz had in mind.[85] Ironically, Wright had sent the museum a group of revamped old prints for study purposes as early as September 1918, long before the "scandal," and Bosch Reitz had found them "most instructive, invaluable as studies."[86] The curator had a keen interest in this matter of revamping. In the fall of 1920, around the time of "the print party but in reverse," he had staged an exhibition in which he hung revamped prints side by side with the real thing "in order to put the collector on his guard."[87] One such vamp, a legacy of the Tokyo scandal, was accepted by the museum as a gift from Wright in 1921 (a rare philanthropic gesture), presumably for educational purposes. It is none other than Mansfield's beloved Kiyonaga diptych (see ill. 134). The unprinted areas of sky and faces are heavily soiled and worn, yet the fugitive blue and purple in the robes and along the horizon, as well as the red, another sensitive color, appear incongruously fresh, as though in pristine condition. When the print is viewed from behind, numerous pinholes are indeed visible. In addition to the revamping, facial outlines have been strengthened with a single-hair brush, and numerous large holes have been cleverly patched from behind. It was an image that had long appealed to Wright: the left side of an impression of this diptych was propped up on the print table in his library in Oak Park at the turn of the century (see ill. 17).

143.
Kitagawa Utamaro.
Comparison of Beauties of the Southern Quarter (*Nangoku bijin-awase*). c. 1793–94. Color woodcut with white mica ground, *ōban*. The Metropolitan Museum of Art, New York, Rogers Fund, 1922 (JP 1367)

This beauty is a high-ranking prostitute in the Shinagawa pleasure quarter on the southern outskirts of Edo, or Tokyo. The irreverent poem on her fan, decorated with a landscape of Shinagawa, contains a reference to nearby Kimono-sleeve Bay (Sodegaura) and the many clients who find refreshment there. While in Tokyo, Wright had this print "certified genuine" by the Old Prints Society. They stamped their seal and affixed a paper certificate numbered 48 on the reverse. The architect sold this print to the Metropolitan Museum of Art in 1922 for $250.

Wright was an immodest foreigner operating outside the guidelines of the closed community of Tokyo print dealers. He flaunted his money and exuded the thinly veiled bravado of the ace dealer. Prices were escalating, the stakes were high, and his jealous rivals were no doubt pleased to take him out of the game. Revamping was a new technique, totally unexpected. Greed and anticipation of huge profits had made him careless.

Wright continued to acquire Japanese and Chinese art until the end of his life but his days as a major player in the Japanese print world were effectively over. The taint of the "faked" print clung to him, inevitably, and without trips to Japan he was unable to renew his inventory. His real competitors were Japanese dealers; those living in America had the advantage of a direct pipeline to a business partner back in the home country, much as Shugio once serviced Wright. One last fling was a large purchase of prints, a screen, and two wooden Buddhas for almost ¥9,000 (about $4,500) from the Y. Nakagawa Gallery in Yokohama on the eve of Wright's embarkation in 1922. A year later he still owed a balance of ¥4,994 and in 1924 he had to return some of the prints.[88]

It had been an interesting chapter in Wright's life but a difficult one as well, if only from the point of view of the amount of working time the prints consumed. While he was drawing for the Imperial Hotel, art merchants were lined up around his drafting board interrupting him throughout the day. His son John remembered that "Dad was buying so many works of oriental art that vendors poured in every day and stood in line in the lobby of the hotel from morning until night. It kept him jumping from his stool at the drafting board to examine these antiques as they were presented to him."[89] In the end, however, the exhilaration of the search and the pride in forming a number of great American collections must have outweighed the sense of frustration or disappointment.

If we count only his documented sales of Japanese art between 1906 and 1928 (many sales were not recorded) Wright earned at least $300,000 from his "avocation." His own com-

144.

Torii Kiyonaga. *Parody of Brine Gatherers Matsukaze and Murasame*, from the series *Elegant Customs, Eastern Brocades (Fūzoku Azuma no nishiki)*. c. 1785. Color woodcut, *ōban*. The Metropolitan Museum of Art, New York, Rogers Fund, 1922 (JP 1373)

The brine-gathering maidens at the beach of Suma carry buckets of salt water by yokes over their shoulders, an allusion to the famous noh play *Wind in the Pines (Matsukaze)*. In the play the sisters are the ghosts of Matsukaze and Murasame, once loved and then forsaken by the courtier and poet Ariwara no Yukihira (818–893). During a brief period of exile from the capital he helped them carry brine to the salt kilns on the shore at Suma. Wright sold this print to the Metropolitan Museum of Art in November 1922 for $90.

pelling argument in favor of print selling, beyond getting himself out of debt, was that it allowed him to refuse any work that did not interest him, a dream of long standing, and one that any architect would envy.[90]

"It is perfectly true that my work will never bring me financial reward," he confessed to Martin in August 1922. "My taste and connoisseurship will have to come to my aid in financial matters. But I am through collecting—it has rather become a burden. I already have too much and it worries me. When I have put the things I have into good hands I shan't pursue that any further." The good hands he had in mind are those of Bosch Reitz at the Metropolitan Museum of Art and, of course, the Martins themselves. His revealing statement sums up his situation: a brilliant career stymied by financial concerns but anchored in taste and driven by connoisseurship. Caught up in a slow evolution as a major print dealer, Wright probably didn't appreciate the enormousness of his own efforts back in 1912 when he said "No, I am not a business man, Mr. Spaulding." Almost a decade later, in correspondence with Bosch Reitz in 1922, he was fully self-aware when he admitted to being a merchant with little use for the gentleman dealer in works of art. The period from 1912 to 1922 was the decade of his greatest success as an entrepreneur.

He shamelessly admitted to Martin that instead of satisfying his creditors he reinvested sixty or seventy thousand dollars earned on the Imperial job in works of art. He argued that he invested both his and Martin's money in "true 'collector's'" pieces, prints worth anywhere from $75 to $3,500, but averaging around $250 to $350 or more, "although of course I have a lot of cheap prints thrown together in a pile. The fine things are

the only good investment and my dear man they work for you while you sleep—they have trebled in value in five years." Thanks to the "best of expert advice" not to mention his own experience of over twenty years he could offer treasures such as gold-leaf screens, Chinese paintings, sculpture, small Chinese antique rugs, bronzes, pottery, embroideries, as well as the prints. He estimated that the better part of this collection would bring him at least $150,000. "I do not need to ask extravagant prices because I did not buy unless the opportunity was favorable for rare things at a low price—but I did not buy *cheap* things—only distinguished things. I could sell you priceless things for a reasonable sum."[91] On his way to see Bosch Reitz in October 1922, Wright passed through Buffalo with treasures in hand and did, in fact, manage to sell Mrs. Martin a selection of seven Japanese brocade priests' robes (*kesa*), a blue satin embroidery, a gold lacquer dipper, and a pair of screens at $2,650 for a total of over $3,700.[92]

Wright's divorce settlement with Catherine Wright in November 1922 easily ate up what profits he had made that fall from Martin, Mansfield, and the Metropolitan Museum of Art. He was required to pay Catherine a $10,000 cash settlement, $150 monthly alimony payments as long as she should live (she died two months before Wright in 1959), and education and child support for his youngest son, Llewellyn (1903–1986), a minor still in the custody of his mother.[93] (Wright sent ninety-six Hiroshige bird-and-flower prints worth $13,678 to Gookin in December, perhaps one last big push in his "selling campaign.")[94]

Wright moved to Los Angeles in January 1923 with the hope of initiating a bold new phase of his career. He also began a practice of experimenting with a new structural system using concrete blocks. Tsuchiura Kameki, who had helped with the Imperial Hotel, and his wife, Nobu, were brought over from Tokyo to assist Wright and his eldest son, the architect Lloyd Wright. By summer their office was on Barnsdall's Olive Hill estate. As it turned out, this was just the beginning of what was, truly, one of his worst periods of escalating personal and financial trauma. In the case of the Alice Millard house in Pasadena, known as La Miniatura, he actually waived the standard architect's fee so that building could continue; he wanted desperately to prove that this novel system of standardized construction would work. La Miniatura was the first of his designs for concrete-block houses and it was a small masterpiece. The surprisingly delicate structure is beautifully sited beside a pond (created by Wright) in a ravine framed by eucalyptus trees. The effect of interior light coming through pierced blocks at night is described as "one of the great thrills of twentieth-century architecture."[94] During the 1920s almost none of his designs were built. His concrete-block houses in Los Angeles were a financial disaster.

CHAPTER SIX

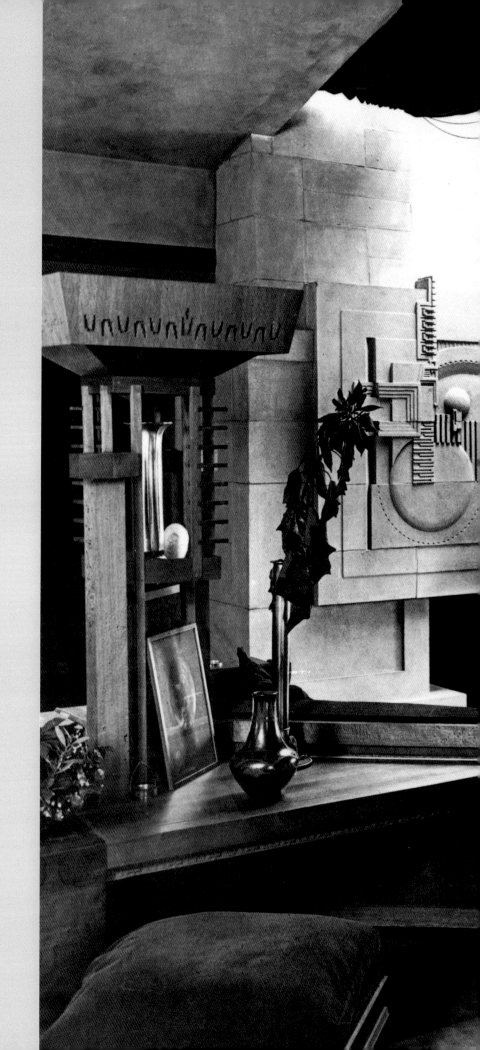

ENTR'ACTE: MAKING SPACE FOR JAPANESE SCREENS

In 1914, around the time Wright met Aline Barnsdall (1882–1946), daughter of a Pittsburgh oil magnate, she was working as codirector of a small experimental theater in the Fine Arts Building in Chicago (ill. 146). A rebel, highly unconventional, rather lonely and insecure, she soon commissioned the architect to design a theater and a house for her. Hollyhock House, set on a thirty-six-acre site known as Olive Hill high above Hollywood Boulevard in Los Angeles, has a heavy, massive solidity that some have compared to Mayan architecture, and others to the mesa pueblos of New Mexico.

Wright's preliminary drawings of 1916–18 for Barnsdall's house, before she had even acquired the site below the Hollywood Hills, show a preoccupation with mountains, prompting speculation about Wright and Hokusai: "Wright placed the building, theoretically designed for a flat lot, in an imaginary setting on an axis with the base of a gently sloping mountain," writes Kathryn Smith (ill. 147). "In so doing he recalled the work of Hokusai, one of his favorite Japanese printmakers, in his famous *Thirty-six Views of Fuji*. Although Wright conceived of the Barnsdall House as a Mayan mountain, it is probable that he was also recalling his impressions of Mount Fuji."[1]

In January 1920, a year before the house was finished, Barnsdall reminded Wright that the living room area was to have wood treatment "combined with the soft purple I showed you in your Japanese prints, and a touch of gold to link it with the screens. You will remember there will be screens along the two big expanses of wall—built in—so the woodwork may be designed to meet them."[2] Barnsdall had probably seen Wright's color woodcuts during her several trips to Chicago in the fall of 1919, following his return from a long trip to Japan with several thousand prints. Around this time Wright prepared a colored elevation drawing for the northwest wall of the living room showing a screen in exactly the location described by Barnsdall (ill. 148). Wright sold her the pair of screens, of course; she asked him to send them out to California in the fall of 1920.[3]

Barnsdall clearly wanted a house that would be "theatrical and luxurious."[4] Wright called it his California Romanza, using a musical term meaning "freedom to make one's own form." According to a report in the 2 September 1921 *Hollywood Citizen News*, the month the house was finished, her color scheme was an autumnal blend of gold and green (Wright's favorite colors); the plaster walls were of unevenly tarnished gold and the ceiling a light green. The living room walls were de-

146.
Aline Barnsdall. c. 1914

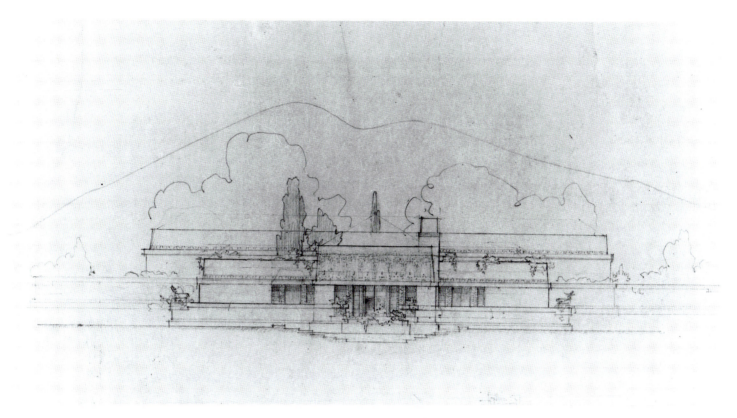

147.
Frank Lloyd Wright.
Aline Barnsdall resi-
dence, Hollyhock
House, Los Angeles,
California. 1916–18.
Front (west) elevation;
graphite and colored
pencil on tracing paper,
11 x 21 in. Collection
City of Los Angeles
Recreation and Parks
Department and Depart-
ment of Cultural Affairs,
Gift of Aline Barnsdall

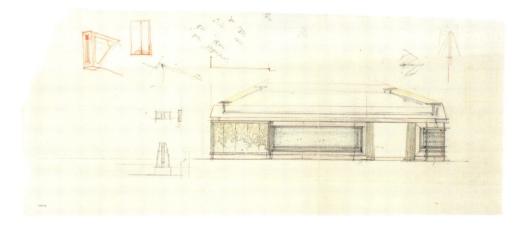

148.
Frank Lloyd Wright. Hollyhock House. Living room
north wall with Japanese screen. c. 1920. Interior section; graphite and colored pencil on paper, 13½ x 33¼
in. The Frank Lloyd Wright Foundation (1705.039)

Wright drew five panels of a screen at the left of the
wall section. The sixth panel (not shown) would wrap
around the northwest corner of the room (see ill. 150).

scribed as "inset on two sides with antique Japanese screens of green and gold brought from the Mikado land by Mr. Wright, and themselves almost priceless" (ills. 149, 150).[5] The screens may have cost Barnsdall $3,500. Correspondence between R. M. Schindler and Wright late in September and early October 1921, after the house was finished and the grapevine screens installed, indicates that she was dragging her heels making a decision to buy a screen that Wright had agreed to sell her for that amount.[6]

Unfortunately, these paintings are not known to have survived, but a 1925 interior view showing the screens in situ reveals them to be the very same paintings of grapevines against rolling hillocks that Wright featured as the centerpiece of his 1917 exhibition for the Arts Club in Chicago (see ill. 91).[7] Barnsdall's screens were installed opposite one another on the long walls of her rectangular living room, flanking the wall of

glass doors and windows at the west end leading to the terrace. The last or sixth panel of each screen wrapped around the northwest and southwest corners of the room, effectively eliminating the corners, to make the space flow more "naturally." (Wright often chose to abut windows at corners for the same effect.) The soft, fluid curves of the painting soften the hard-edge, rectilinear patterns of Wright's own design elements, notably the lighting fixtures and fireplace mural. The Japanese painting, moreover, is essentially flat and abstract, in tune with Wright's emerging modernism. Wood trim that harmonizes with the architectural setting was used to frame the painting and hold it in place.

A six-panel, eighteenth-century Edo-period screen with a flowering cherry tree and pheasants was mounted on the gold-tinted wall on the south wall of the alcove off the living room (ill.

149.
Hollyhock House. Living room with Japanese screen, view looking southwest. c. 1921–27

151). This space, which was twelve feet wide (just right for a single screen) and finished in matte gold, became, in the words of the Wright historian Donald Hoffmann, a place of "pause and great serenity." Hoffmann also claims that on the west wall of the small music room to the north of the living room Barnsdall proposed to hang her Monet painting of water lilies but "Wright prevailed, and a Japanese screen was installed instead."[8]

Wright placed a Buddhist sculpture at the exterior entrance to the Barnsdall house. It is a large Chinese marble statue of a standing Bodhisattva, decorative (probably modern garden sculpture), set off originally in a slender, deeply recessed niche that marked the beginning of the long entry axis.[9]

Sadly, although the project had cost her hundreds of thousands of dollars, Barnsdall decided that the house was too ornate and too big for her and gave it up after only two years. "My heart was not in it," she said.[10] In 1927 the City of Los Angeles accepted the house and eleven surrounding acres as a gift and it became a municipal art park. Later it was leased to another cultural foundation.

An odd but not at all surprising footnote to the Barnsdall story concerns a lawsuit filed by Wright on 28 February 1924 for architectural and other fees, including the cost of some personal property, namely woodblock prints and "one pair of six-fold gold screens, ornamented with pine trees, mountain streams and white cranes," which Barnsdall held as security on a loan. In the legal document Wright placed a value of $5,000 on the screens, but in a private notation that he made on the back of a letter from his lawyer dated 18 March 1924, he figured the cost of the screens as $2,683, which was most likely their real worth.[11] Even at $5,000 the screens were not necessarily overvalued. In 1915

150.
Hollyhock House. Living room with Japanese screen, view looking northwest. c. 1921–27

Bosch Reitz had convinced the Metropolitan Museum of Art to pay Yamanaka and Company in New York $11,000 for a single, anonymous late-seventeenth-century screen depicting an autumn landscape for which Yamanaka had paid 50,000 francs (approximately $28,000) in a bidding war at auction in Paris in 1904.[12]

A month earlier Barnsdall had taken a stand. She wrote to say that she would not return the screens until all adjustments had been made regarding the prints: "One expert has told me the Japanese prints I took on loan last spring were worth only $25 to $30 apiece…instead of the $120 you asked for them. That is the reason I want to make the exchange to the screen. I am afraid you were cheated on them."[13] The truth is, of course, that he always asked top dollar. Kathryn Smith suggests that the $4,615 demanded by Wright for causes unspecified may represent his valuation of the prints.[14] On 6 February 1925 (a year later) an itemized list of eighty-six prints was sent from Taliesin to Wright's eldest son, Lloyd, who had been supervising the construction of Hollyhock House on site in Los Angeles. This could be Wright's own accounting of Barnsdall's prints, which were most likely returned to him later.[15] Each print on this list is individually priced, for a total of $1,733. They do, indeed, average about $25 to $30 each. The oil heiress was correct in thinking that Wright was bilking her. The highest price for any individual print was the $75 valuation for a Katsukawa Shunkō portrait of a kabuki actor. Three-quarters were by Hiroshige.

Wright was incensed (and possibly embarrassed) that Barnsdall not only dared to accuse him of swindling her but also had been openly checking up on him. He repossessed the screens—a sheriff actually entered her home and woke her up to locate them—but she quickly posted a $10,000 bond and took them back. These screens apparently remained in the house: their description fits the pair of eighteenth-century Kano-school screens of cranes and pine trees by a stream that now decorate the living room as reconstructed in 1990.[16] Painted in ink and color on paper with gold leaf, they are visible in photos dating from the time of the first renovation in the mid-1940s, and were presumably the only ones that were given to the city with the house. Although they are very much in the Frank Lloyd Wright taste, they are less appropriate to their setting than the sensuous grapevines they replaced.

The case was finally settled out of court on 24 January 1927, two weeks after the Bank of Wisconsin forced Wright to sell

151.
Hollyhock House. Living room alcove with screen on south wall.
c. 1921–27

several hundred of his best prints at auction in New York, a result of his deteriorating financial situation—a drama described in detail in chapter 7.[17]

Following this stormy, embittered interlude, Barnsdall and Wright soon reconciled (she offered him more work), and her daughter joined the Taliesin Fellowship in the early 1930s. Barnsdall actually bought one or more additional screens from Wright during these lean years even though, by then, she had no place to show them. In 1940 she loaned five screens to the old Los Angeles County Museum and asked Wright to provide captions for label copy. (There was no real curator of Asian art at the museum until the arrival of the young Harvard-trained Henry Trubner in 1947.) At the time of her death six years later, when her estate was appraised, the five screens were still listed in her collection, including those with the green and gold grapevines.[18]

Wright loved Japanese screens and gave serious thought to the ways they might be displayed effectively in a Western setting. In Japan, recessed display alcoves (*tokonoma*) set off hanging scrolls, which are brought out for viewing on special occasions and then returned to their compact wood storage boxes. Screens are sometimes flattened against a wall but the individual panels are hinged in such a way that they bend backward and forward, allowing them to be free-standing. They fold up and are moved easily from room to room, but the hinging also permits easy storage (important in Japan where there is so little space) until the seasonal motifs or a specific occasion make it appropriate to place them on view. They can serve as room dividers in a zig-zag formation, or they can wrap around into

some form of U shape to ensure an additional degree of privacy.

In a Western-style home filled with furniture, screens (commonly composed in pairs) are not at all practical. They can be raised off the floor and mounted flat on an expanse of wall, but a single six-panel screen measures twelve feet across. Its installation in this manner is a serious and fairly permanent affair. The placement of Japanese screens in the Venetian-style palatial museum designed by Isabella Stewart Gardner (1840–1924) at Fenway Court in Boston gives a clear idea of the fashion of the times (ill. 152). Gardner had superb European holdings, but she traveled to Japan in 1883 and, like so many Bostonians, became an aficionado of East Asian culture. Most of her Asian art came from the Boston galleries of Yamanaka and Company and Matsuki Bunkio between 1901 and 1903.[19] A photograph taken in 1904 of the one space devoted to an Asian theme, her Early Chinese Room (which later became the Italian Room), shows a seventeenth-century Japanese screen illustrating the *Tale of Genji* mounted far above eye level, in hopeless competition with an eclectic medley of Asian textiles, curio cabinets, Venetian chinoiserie furniture, florid wall sconces, and even a portrait of the owner by Anders Zorn (1860–1930). Carved Japanese architectural elements appear throughout the upper reaches of the wall. In the relatively small and dark spaces of the second- and third-floor passageways, she hung other screens in two rows reaching to the ceiling, with the uppermost screens barely visible.

Wright's use of screens in the Barnsdall house has many precedents, the earliest being his 1906 proposal for the remodeling of the Peter A. Beachy house in Oak Park, where two six-

152.
The Early Chinese Room, with Japanese screen, Isabella Stewart Gardner Museum, Boston. 1903–4

panel Japanese screens are built in so as to create one continuous twelve-panel mural along the side wall of the dining room (ill. 153). His drawing shows a painting of a river landscape with birds and flowers framed by two blossoming trees against a background of silver leaf. (Wright ruled off small squares to indicate the sheets of silver leaf.) The architect was prepared to cut down the four center panels of the screen where the lintel of the fireplace mantel protruded. He created a similar effect a few years later in the Avery Coonley house in Riverside, Illinois, when he had the Milwaukee interior decorator George Mann Niedecken (1878–1945) design a mural of birch trees and prairie ferns. Flanking the Coonleys' living-room fireplace, the horizontal composition suggests a pair of screens in the style of early Edo-period Rimpa masters. Niedecken and Wright also worked together on the Frederick C. Bogk house in Milwaukee, which was completed in 1916. Mrs. Bogk filled her home with all manner of orientalia, and Niedecken designed overtly Japonesque light fixtures for the house.[20] Wright either gave or sold the Bogks (there is no surviving documentation) a fragment of a seventeenth-century Chinese handscroll painted with palace ladies and plum trees in color on silk and had it built in to good effect over the sideboard in the dining room (ill. 154). The scroll bears the signature of a famous Ming-dynasty artist, Tang Yin (1470–1523), but dates from at least a century later.

153.
Frank Lloyd Wright.
Peter A. Beachy House,
Oak Park, Illinois. Dining
room wall elevation
showing placement of a
pair of Japanese
screens. 1906. Elevation; graphite and colored pencil on tracing
paper, 12¼ x 27⅜ in.
The Frank Lloyd Wright
Foundation (0601.001)

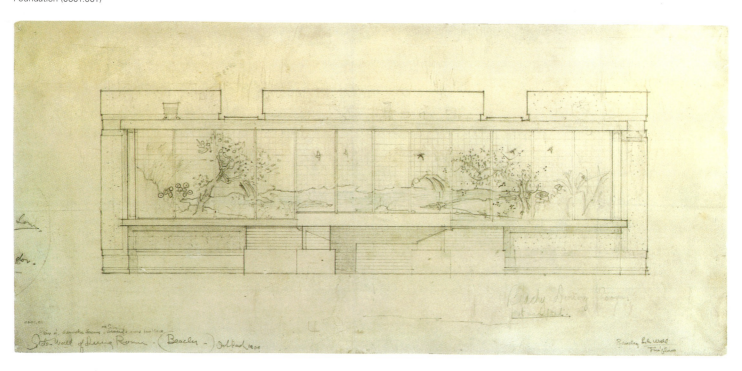

154.
Frank Lloyd Wright.
Frederick C. Bogk
House, Milwaukee,
Wisconsin. 1916. Dining
room with eighteenth-
century Chinese hand-
scroll mounted over the
sideboard

In his inscription on the Beachy drawing Wright identifies the artist as Kano Sanraku (1559–1635), an important figure in late Momoyama–early Edo-period painting. Perhaps he was hoping to sell a pair of Sanraku screens to his Oak Park clients. Judging by his own collection, the architect had a lifelong preference for colorful paintings by Kano-family artists, especially those with big pine trees boldly stretching their trunks across a background of gold leaf. (With very few exceptions, Wright did not collect ink paintings or calligraphy.)

The Beachy design was rejected, but Wright continued to work with screens—in the 1917 Arts Club exhibition, at Hollyhock House, and then at his own home at Taliesin, where wall spaces (in the loggia, living room, and studio, for example) are perfectly suited to the proportions of a single Japanese screen (ill. 155).[21] The method of installation was not sophisticated (and not acceptable by museum standards): some screens were nailed in place, others rested on a wooden ledge, still others were probably held in place by strips of wood molding nailed over the frame of the screen, rather like the print stands he had created as architectural "frames." Their installation being cumbersome, screens were rarely rotated.

The loggia, or reception room, at Taliesin was always a vibrant focal point for Wright's Asian collection. From an early date he mounted a Japanese screen above the banquette. A photograph taken in the early 1920s shows a screen of egrets and willow in snow; the other half of the pair of screens belonged to the Boston Impressionist painter Edmund C. Tarbell (1862–1938) (ill. 156).[22] A smaller Japanese folding screen with gourd and flowers is standing on the floor, wrapped around the corner of the room. Wright moved this screen around to create a dramatic photograph; it appears in a view of the living room as well (see ill. 136). The banquette is flanked by a Han-dynasty ceramic wine vessel holding dried flowers and a Chinese stone Bodhisattva (seen also in ill. 92). A Japanese nineteenth-century stacked lacquer food box beside the Chinese vessel adds to the artfully cluttered look. The architect spread a Chinese pillar carpet on the floor and draped a Japanese textile on the table, where he displayed a Chinese cast-iron head of a Bodhisattva and an American Tecoware vase, the only non-Asian piece in evidence.

After the fire in 1925 Wright redesigned the loggia and the living room, raising the ceilings and adding a balcony and second-floor bedroom. With a wall surface twelve feet eleven inches wide, he could now use a full-size six-panel screen measuring the standard twelve feet in width above the banquette in the loggia. The painting he chose, a pine with cherry blossoms and birds against a ground of gold leaf in the conservative, academic style of Kano Yasunobu (1613–1685), is still in the collection of the Frank Lloyd Wright Foundation (ill. 157). The architect removed the textile border and lacquer frame. He mounted the individual panels on plywood and actually built them into the wall. Years of exposure and pillows that invite guests to lean back have conspired to cause damage. The screen is no masterpiece, however, and Wright surely intended it as pure decoration, knowing full well that it would see some wear and tear. Recently, in an act of historical revisionism, this mediocre screen was removed from the loggia and replaced with the most important example in the collection, *Old Pine,* possibly a work by the

155.
Frank Lloyd Wright. Taliesin III. Mid-1940s. Plan; graphite, colored pencil, and ink on tracing paper. The Frank Lloyd Wright Foundation (2501.060)

On this plan yellow highlights show the locations of screens mounted on walls.

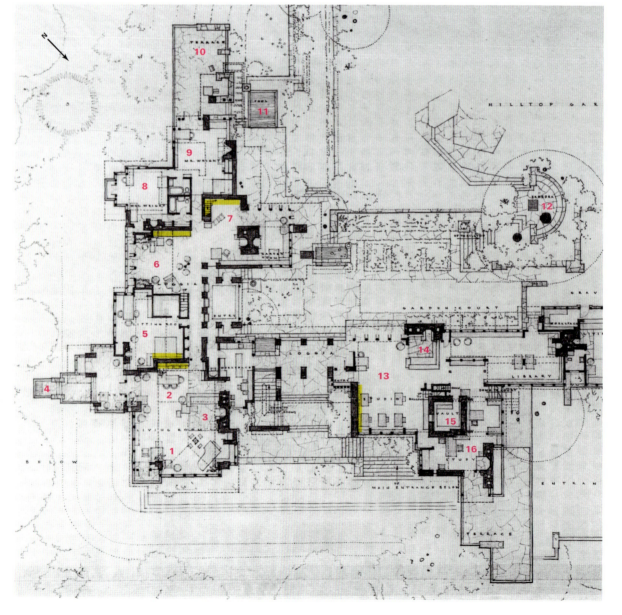

1. Living room (ills. 82, 136, 187, 201, 216)

2. Dining alcove, with screen (ills. 81, 159)

3. Living room fireplace (ill. 212)

4. Bird walk

5. Main guest room, screen above the bed (ill. 164)

6. Loggia, with screen (ills. 156, 157)

7. Loggia fireplace alcove, with Chinese screen

8. Mrs. Wright's bedroom

9. Wright's study-bedroom (ills. 6, 99)

10. Terrace

11. Pool

12. Tea circle with Chinese bell

13. Drafting studio, with screen (ills. 161, 188)

14. Studio fireplace (ill. 218)

15. Print vault (ills. 7, 160, 184)

16. Wright's private office

158.

Anonymous. Kano school. *Old Pine* and *Cranes Nesting in Pine Trees*. Momoyama period, late sixteenth century. Sliding doors (*fusuma*) remounted as two six-panel folding screens; ink, color and gold leaf on paper. Approx. 60¾ x 138¾ in. each. The Frank Lloyd Wright Foundation (1185.022–023)

The "big tree" of the Momoyama period extended its branches across the walls of public reception rooms. Cropping the tree at top and bottom increased the impression of its size. Recent scholarship indicates that *Old Pine* may have been part of a commission for the reception room of the Tenzuiji, a sub-temple of Daitokuji, an important Zen temple in Kyoto. Tenzuiji, built around 1588 for the mother of the great Momoyama-period general, Toyotomi Hideyoshi, was decorated by the painter Kano Eitoku but was destroyed toward the end of the nineteenth century.

Opposite

157.

Taliesin III. Loggia with Japanese screen, nineteenth-century Chinese lady's informal robe, and Chinese Han-dynasty ceramic wine vessel with dried flowers. c. 1935

159.
Taliesin III. View from the living room to the dining alcove. c. 1929

The small eighteenth-century screen mounted on the wall of the dining alcove shows silk cultivation in the four seasons, one of a pair by a follower of Kusumi Morikage (active first half of the seventeenth century). See ill. 81 for another screen mounted in dining alcove before the 1925 fire. The view shown here was published in *Liberty*, 23 March 1929.

160.
Taliesin II. Studio. 1924 or early 1925

From left to right: Wright, Japanese apprentice Tsuchiura Kameki, German architect Werner Moser, Viennese architect Richard Neutra, and Tsuchiura Nobu. A nineteenth-century Japanese Buddhist temple banner hangs from the balcony behind Wright, draped over a Persian carpet, one of dozens Wright collected for Taliesin. Although badly damaged by constant exposure (and guano), the banner, made of blue silk with orange silk trim and brass fittings, is still in the collection of the Frank Lloyd Wright Foundation. Also visible on the balcony is an early Chinese Buddhist statue. The Tsuchiuras were at Taliesin from October 1923 until just after the fire in April 1925. The vault for print storage is enclosed by the stone wall at the left (see also ills. 6, 184).

Opposite

161.
Taliesin III. Studio with Japanese screen and print stand. 1929

The draftsman on the far right is Vladimir Karfik, a Czech who was at Taliesin in 1928–29.

162.
Anonymous. *Ten Symbols of Long Life.* Korea, Choson period, nineteenth century. Six-panel folding screen; ink and color on silk, 60 x 126 in. Collection Nicholas, Robert, and Oliver Gillham

The symbols of longevity allude to a Daoist land of the immortals first conceived in China. The ten symbols are sun, clouds, water, rocks, deer, cranes, tortoise, pines, bamboo, and sacred fungus. Deer and cranes are both companions and messengers of the Daoist immortals. Korean screens with this theme are most commonly eight or ten panels (Wright's screen was cut down) with a continuous composition combining the ten symbols in a landscape paradise reminiscent of the conventional Island of the Immortals. The screen remains in the family of Wright's sister Maginel.

Momoyama-period master Kano Eitoku (1543–1590), a screen Wright acquired in the 1950s and never displayed (ill. 158). The present policy of the Frank Lloyd Wright Foundation is to use photo murals instead of paintings where appropriate and to rotate a selection of the most important screens each year, but only in summer when the building is in use and the humidity high.

At the beginning of each summer Wright had an apprentice bring out one of his antique Chinese or Japanese silk robes from the vault to be draped "just so" over the banquette: an eighteenth-century noh robe seen in several 1930s views of the loggia is still in the collection as is a late-nineteenth-century embroidered Chinese robe (ill. 157).

The wall area available for a screen in the dining cove in the living room is considerably narrower and shorter, limited by a shallow built-in cabinet for glassware overhead. The height of the available wall space was only three feet six inches and the width ten feet four inches (a small table built into the corner has now reduced the width to eight feet). A 1928 photo shows the right-hand screen of a small pair dating from the second half of the seventeenth century and depicting silk cultivation in the four seasons (ill. 159). It remained in situ for decades and suffered damage from tearing and clumsy restoration (some restoration on screens was done by Wright's staff). He used additional screens in bedrooms.

In the studio he installed a screen high on the east wall as a source of inspiration to the draftsmen, whose tables faced it (the wall is twelve feet three inches wide). A 1929 view shows three light fixtures mounted on a shallow ledge below the screen, for nighttime illumination; there is also a small, vertical print stand on the ledge in the corner by the window (ills. 160, 161). All drafting was done in this studio until the fall of 1939. Later Wright used the room as his office. The screen he chose for this spot (judging by period photographs it was never removed during his lifetime) is an anonymous seventeenth-century Kano-school painting in color and gold leaf on paper depicting a pine tree with pheasants, ducks, and flowers associated with spring and summer. It is a strong albeit conventional design.

Wright also liked the clean lines and colorful, decorative designs of Korean painting. A screen picturing the *Ten Symbols of Long Life* still has a Railway Express tag on the back addressed to Wright in Spring Green, and the original yen price tag (the equivalent of $50) (ill. 162). Family lore has it that he bought the Korean screens, which he gave to three of his children, in Seoul, possibly in 1913.[23] His son David, a contractor and concrete-block manufacturer, received in the 1930s a nineteenth-century eight-panel screen with scenes of farming in the four seasons. He loaned it to enliven the living room of the Malcolm Willey house in Minneapolis when the Hedrich-Blessing studio photographed it for the January 1938 issue of *Architectural Forum* (ill. 163). David later displayed the screen in his own Wright-designed living room in Phoenix, then gave it to the Milwaukee Public Museum in 1976—a well-traveled screen.

163.
Frank Lloyd Wright.
Malcolm Willey House.
Minneapolis, Minnesota.
Living room with a
Korean screen. 1937

CHAPTER SEVEN

LOSING THE COLLECTION

Auction sales of single-owner print collections were an established custom during these early years; everyone from the Spauldings to Gookin had gone this route. When Wright found himself in a difficult financial situation, it was perfectly natural that he and his creditors should turn to this venue.

After moving to Los Angeles in the spring of 1923, Wright tried hard to build a practice in southern California, but finding insufficient clients for his visionary dreams, he was disillusioned and returned to Taliesin in the fall. Wright and Miriam Noel were finally married that November, when his divorce was finalized. Marriage did not improve the couple's complex, troubled relationship. Miriam, a tortured and emotionally disturbed woman with a morphine addiction, left Taliesin in May 1924 and moved to Chicago. By 1925 they were corresponding over grounds for divorce and Wright had taken up with a beautiful Montenegrin émigré, Olga (nicknamed Olgivanna) Lazovich Hinzenberg, who was thirty-one years his junior. Daughter of a supreme court judge, she was aristocratic and mysterious. Wright was captivated. Olgivanna had been in Paris from 1917 to 1924 studying dance with G. I. Gurdjieff, the Russian mystic and founder of the celebrated human potential movement. When she came to Chicago in 1924 in her mid-twenties, it was to seek reconciliation with her husband, a Russian architect, from whom she was separated. She apparently met Wright at a performance of the Petrograd Ballet in Chicago. In September 1926 a vindictive Miriam filed a $100,000 alienation of affections suit against Olgivanna, forcing Wright and his companion (now divorced) to flee across state lines to Minneapolis, taking with them their daughter, Iovanna, born out of wedlock the year before, and Svetlana, Olgivanna's nine-year-old daughter. In a raid initiated by Miriam's lawyer, Wright was arrested there on 20 October on a charge of violating the Mann Act for adultery and actually spent a few nights in the Hennepin County jail.[1]

Miriam went on to stir up the immigration authorities in her attempt to hound Olgivanna. These unfortunate love tangles were of course reported ad nauseam by the press.

In the meantime Taliesin burned to the ground a second time, in April 1925, in an electrical fire; only the drafting studio, which was separated from the main living quarters, was saved. Insurance did not cover the hundreds of thousands of dollars of damage and Wright was forced to sell his old Oak Park home inexpensively, going further into debt. No lives were lost and valuable Japanese prints and textiles, stored in the fireproof vault in the studio, were spared. The many Chinese marble Buddhist sculptures that had graced Wright's living quarters, however, were reduced to calcified, scorched fragments. "I had been poor trustee for posterity," he wrote. "I had not protected them. Never mind. They should live in me, I thought, because I could prove their life by mine. I had loved and understood them. They had become part of me and should live in what I did."[2] In a bizarre, sentimental gesture, he picked them out of the debris and imbedded several into the walls of his home as he rebuilt it for the third time—they became emblems of the periodic cycles of destruction and renewal at Taliesin (ill. 164).

In November 1925 Wright tried in vain to inveigle Darwin Martin into the purchase of prints and screens. He owed Martin a considerable sum on past loans. "I am stalled and helpless for the time being," he wrote. "I don't know the way through with my load—yet. Would you then buy some of these treasures of mine at prices low enough as such things should go—and so enable me to get over the fence at the top of the hill? Once over I can go…. My chief assets as print purchasers—three of them—dead!" Unlike his wife, Martin did not relish the purchase of antiques, even those belonging to Wright. His response sounds mean-spirited: "Your letter postmarked Nov. 1st received today. It would draw money from a stone image—but I am harder than that."[3] Around this time he returned to Wright the box of prints he had been holding as security since 1911; Wright had hoped

for a sale.⁴ Martin did indulge Wright, however, by asking him to design a two-story lakeshore house and even a mausoleum.

On 12 December 1925 Wright went to New York to see Mitchell Kennerley (1878–1950), British-born president of the Anderson Galleries (later Sotheby Parke-Bernet), an ornate building conveniently located on Park Avenue at Fifty-ninth Street. Kennerley agreed to hold a portion of his print collection for a future sale and advanced him $25,000. A publisher of more than 400 books, a prominent bibliophile, and sympathetic friend of modern art and literature, Kennerley had known Wright personally for twenty-five years. In his experience, the famous architect had always had ample funds for adding prints to his collection, but this was a loan the auctioneer came to regret.

In June 1926, to prevent Noel from making off with any valuables, Wright executed and delivered to the Bank of Wisconsin in Madison a chattel mortgage on all personal property at Taliesin. He then informed Kennerley that he had pledged his entire print collection (including those that were to be sold in New York) to the bank and to Joseph M. Boyd (1862–?), president of a mortgage and loan company in Madison and chairman of the board of the Bank of Wisconsin, for loans in the sums of $49,076 with interest and $3,500 with interest, respectively. The bank and Boyd both had right of foreclosure on the collateral (i.e., the prints) subject to the prior claims of the Anderson Galleries.⁵

At the time these loans were being made, it was assumed that a print sale would net around $100,000. This proved to be overly optimistic. The architect obviously convinced the bank that there would be ample surplus to reimburse everyone. The Bank of Wisconsin now held a mortgage on Taliesin real estate for $25,000 and a chattel mortgage on all that Taliesin contained. On 6 September 1926 the bank foreclosed on the $25,000 mortgage. To protect its interests (Wright still owed them tens of thousands of dollars) the bank took legal possession of his estate with the intention of auctioning the personal property the next year. In addition, the bank held in its vaults in Madison art valued by Wright at $150,000: on 1 October as partial security for their large loan, bank officials removed miscellaneous personal possessions from the vault and residence at Taliesin. They took embroidered bedcovers, nineteen Chinese paintings, fifteen packages of Japanese prints (for which a five-page list was compiled), as well as a Chinese chest inlaid with mother-of-pearl that contained even more prints—for a total of more than 5,000 prints.⁶

Now the bank possessed all of Wright's property, with the exception of a portion of the collection (the McFetridge prints), which is discussed below. Hoping to reduce the bank's risk on its sizable loan, R. L. Hopkins, president of the Bank of Wisconsin, deemed it advisable to proceed immediately with Wright's plan of selling prints at auction in New York.⁷ In the meantime, Wright was still getting shipments from Japan, but was unable to claim them, having fled to Minnesota. A customs agent in Milwaukee notified Wright in 1929 that a shipment consigned to him from Yokohama had been sitting unclaimed in their storage since 17 December 1926.⁸

In November 1926, at the very moment when he was supposed to be in New York assisting with the writing of the Anderson Galleries catalogue, Wright was hiding out in Wildhurst on Lake Minnetonka, twenty miles southwest of Minneapolis. An energetic Kennerley tracked him down at the Minneapolis Athletic Club and offered him a room and stenographer if he would come to New York for one or two days to make the final selection of prints and complete the catalogue. "So far this season all good things have sold for more than last year," he wrote, "and I have great hopes of your Prints, but we must hold the sale early in January to catch the market. If you cannot come on, I shall have to have the work done by Fukushima, which I should regret."⁹ Wright, who liked to write his own material, would certainly have regretted it, as well, although Otto Fukushima was well qualified. A successful long-time Asian art dealer on Fifth Avenue (he had taken over Shugio Hiromichi's Japanese trading company in 1890), he was an advisor to Howard Mansfield. Wright was in competition for the market share with his old friend S. H. Mori, the Japanese art dealer from Chicago, who offered a large selection of 497 ukiyo-e paintings and prints, as well as some stencils at the American Art Galleries on Madison Avenue in early December, with a catalogue prepared by Gookin. Concerned that collectors would spend all their money at the Mori sale, Kennerley wanted to announce Wright's sale at once. Mori got himself some favorable pre-sale publicity; his Hiroshige landscape paintings were written up by the Wisconsin illustrator and author Gardner Teall (1878–1956) in an article for the November issue of *International Studio*.¹⁰ (Teall compared Hiroshige with Claude Lorrain and Turner.)

On 6–7 January 1927 the 346 Wright prints (approximately two-thirds of the group Wright had left with Kennerley a year earlier) were sold at Anderson Galleries without reserves

by order of the Bank of Wisconsin.[11] Although Wright and Olgivanna had left Minnesota for La Jolla, California, where they spent the winter, the architect did rush off to New York for a few days just before Christmas, and the catalogue bears his inimitable personal touch. A few egregious errors—Hokusai's famous *Great Wave* (lot 174) from *The Thirty-six Views of Mount Fuji* is attributed to Hiroshige, for example—suggest there was no time for proofreading. Just before the Hiroshige bird-and-flower prints (lots 236–68) came up, a saleroom announcement alerted bidders that Wright had refused $10,000 for this group in Japan.[12] Half of the prints in this sale were by Wright's beloved Hiroshige, and some of these fetched high prices. The celebrated *Monkey Bridge*, a double vertical *ōban* that is still the most desirable of this artist's oeuvre, went to Arthur B. Duel for $1,550 and is now in the collection of the Harvard University Art Museums (ill. 165). The auctioneer made a saleroom announcement that Wright had originally paid $2,400 for it.[13] Duel made a good buy. In early 1919 Wright had bragged to Bosch Reitz that an impression of this print had sold at auction in Tokyo for ¥5,600; Yamanaka paid ¥5,000 ($2,500) for this image in 1920 at auction in Japan.[14] Another point of comparison would be an impression from the estate of Wright's friend, the New York collector Carl W. Schraubstadter (1862–1947). His example of *Monkey Bridge* sold at Parke-Bernet in January 1948 for $850—by far the biggest price in that sale; and the very same image from Schraubstadter's collection brought $60,000 when it reappeared at Christie's, New York, in September 1983.[15] Schraubstadter, whose father made a fortune in the 1880s operating large type foundries in St. Louis and Boston, learned wood engraving as a boy, then spent many years in the business of furnishing tools and supplies for the graphic arts, retiring in 1908. On his third trip to Japan, in 1915, he extended his stay for three years owing to the difficulty of travel during the war. He took lessons in block engraving and printing in the Japanese manner, started to collect ukiyo-e prints, and became a habitué of the Tokyo auction world. Wright was very likely one of his sources; the architect joked with him about getting together for a "print fest." In 1932 a fellow collector described Schraubstadter as "a crotchety old duffer." Instead of enjoying the portfolios of prints that he

165.
Utagawa Hiroshige.
Monkey Bridge in Kai Province (Kōyō Saruhashi no zu). 1840s.
Color woodcut, double vertical *ōban*. Arthur M. Sackler Museum, Harvard University Art Museums, Gift of the Friends of Arthur B. Duel (1933.4.1243)

Arthur Duel paid $1,550 for this print in the 1927 Anderson Galleries, New York, sale of the Wright collection (lot 39).

would bring out to show his guests, he would go off into a far corner of the room and puff away on a cigar, warming to his audience only when it came time to dine. His other hobby was food, and he took great pride in his vast collection of menus and recipes from around the world, with ingredients stored in row after row of sealed Mason jars, ready for preparation by his Japanese chef.[16]

The adjectives "flawless" and "perfect" are sprinkled with abandon throughout Wright's catalogue. The lavishly printed Utamaro *Preparing Sashima*, which he had exhibited at the Arts Club in Chicago in 1917, is "in fine condition" despite a very long wormhole by the signature and several other holes or tears (ill. 166). To be fair, Wright points out in the catalogue introduction that he disregarded wormholes in describing condition. "If desired, they can easily be filled by an expert, leaving no trace." His sales pitch includes the judgment that "in this entire collection it is only fair to say that there are *no* inferior prints." Perhaps he is right when he assures the buyer that "the examples brought together here are extraordinarily fine, most of them the very finest obtainable by a search lasting more than twenty years…by one who has been more intimately in touch with the Japanese print collections of the world during those years than almost anyone else." The Spaulding collection is as usual cited in passing, as is that of the Metropolitan Museum of Art. He even points out that one print by Utamaro (lot 65) bears the seal of Shugio, "distinguished Japanese connoisseur." On the issue of investment value, he makes good sense: "[Fine] specimens of this art and craft are practically extinct; so that 'market values' so-called, if ever they existed, have ceased to exist, and the supreme thing of its kind is priceless."[17]

All parties were disappointed when the sale brought in $36,975. Anderson Galleries took the position that the auction was adversely affected by the embarrassing notoriety and flurry of publicity broadcast in the papers thanks to another contender for the proceeds, Miriam Noel Wright, the architect's estranged wife. Miriam's Chicago lawyer caused a disturbance when he attempted to take possession of the prints at the auction house four hours before the sale. (Of course, a sale may also fail because the collector has a bad *odeur*.) "Conditions at the sale were very bad," Wright reported to Martin from his room at the Hotel Brevoort in New York. "No collectors in New York or Chicago were bidding at all. The prints went practically on to a market of the amateurs and casually interested…. What then would they have bought if the sale had been held at the proper

166.
Kitagawa Utamaro.
Preparing Sashimi.
c. 1798–99. Color
woodcut with mica,
ōban. Private collection

This print sold for $230
in the 1927 Anderson
Galleries, New York,
sale of the Wright col-
lection (lot 58).

167.
Kitagawa Utamaro. *The Barber,* from the series *Fashionable Five-needle Pine (Fūryū goyō no matsu).* c. 1797–98. Color woodcut, *ōban.* Print Collection, Miriam and Ira D. Wallach Division of Art, Prints and Photographs, The New York Public Library, Astor, Lenox and Tilden Foundations

Louis V. Ledoux purchased this print for $380 in the 1927 Anderson Galleries, New York, sale of the Wright collection (lot 50).

time properly attended? At least double."[18] Years later, in his revised autobiography, Wright elevated the supposed value of these prints to several hundred thousand dollars.[19] It should be noted that the successful bidders did, in fact, include some of the big names in the print world: Duel (ill. 165), Louis V. Ledoux (ill. 167), Charles Chandler (ill. 171), the young Richard P. Gale (1900–1973)—a future Minnesota congressman—(ill. 168), the Boston businessman Gilbert E. Fuller (1882–?), the New York dealer Kano Oshima, H. E. Howley, and Yamanaka and Company.[20] Wright later confessed to his cousin Richard Lloyd Jones the surprising fact that he had himself been a bidder at the sale, albeit anonymously: working through an agent he bought back the very rare Utamaro heptaptych for $900 because he thought it worth at least three times that amount.[21] His creditors would not have been pleased that he was still buying prints.

As for the relative success or failure of the auction, the *New York Herald* commented on the "impressive prices for works by the early masters" and it certainly did much better than the Mori sale a month earlier, which brought in just over $20,000.[22] The Arthur Davison Ficke sale at the Anderson Galleries two years earlier, on 29–30 January 1925, with a comparable 362 lots, brought in only $31,642. Wright, who removed some of the best prints at the last minute, did not really have cause for complaint.

168.
Katsushika Hokusai.
Umezawa Manor, Sagami Province (*Sōshū Umezawa-zai*), from the series *The Thirty-six Views of Mount Fuji* (*Fugaku sanjūrokkei*). c. 1830–31. Color woodcut, *ōban*. The Minneapolis Institute of Arts, Richard Gale Collection (74.1.234)

Richard Gale paid $150 for this print in the 1927 Anderson Galleries, New York, sale of the Wright collection (lot 161).

Miriam had filed suit for $50,000 on the first day of the Anderson Galleries sale in order to divert payment for the prints to herself on grounds that she was part owner and that the prints had been bought with a loan of $35,000 supplied by her.[23] She asked for the attachment on the grounds that if any of the proceeds were paid to her husband he would most certainly not apply them on the $15,000 he owed her for maintenance support under their separation agreement. Wright naturally claimed that the prints had been acquired solely with his money, and that many were purchased years before he had met Miriam.[24] Immediately following the sale the beleaguered Kennerley initiated legal action to counteract Miriam's suit. He successfully sued for repayment of his own loan, with interest, as well as his commission fee and various catalogue expenses that amounted to an additional $7,500. The *New York Times* reported that he took all the proceeds from the sale. Wright complained in his autobiography that Kennerley had taken a commission of nearly 35 percent.[25]

To support herself and pay her legal fees, Miriam was forced to sell 250 Japanese prints, valued by her at $15,000, which she had been given by Wright. The "wretched creature," as Wright called her, sold her prints at public auction in February 1928 in the office of the bailiff of the Chicago municipal court in order to raise the $5,000 she owed her divorce attorney, Harold Jackson. Bidding against six other interested parties, Jackson purchased the prints for only $1,000, thinking to sell them for a big profit.[26] Commenting on this development and thinking of his own prints held in the vaults of the Bank of Wisconsin, Wright sent an emotional and reflective plea for help to Martin:

> If Jackson could sell the wrong Mrs. Wright's prints for $5,000, mine in our hands would bring fifty times that sum.... Trust my statement as to the value of the collateral the bank proposes to slaughter. That collateral alone will pay you back and all the stockholders. I have said this until I am sick of saying it.[27]

Wright had long felt that if he were quietly established at Taliesin he could—as he had in the past—dispose of prints and screens to good advantage. "By having the people interested come here—(they have done so) and see the treasures in a proper atmosphere—knowing them protected from sacrifice or slaughter—else—the wolf the collector is by nature—is roused. If only we could get possession of the property [i.e., the collection] I could start immediately."[28]

MRS. AVERY COONLEY: CLIENT AND COLLECTOR

Wright, Inc., a Wisconsin corporation, was organized in 1927 to bail out the architect. It consisted of a small group of about ten friends and relatives who were willing to buy shares of $7,500 each at considerable personal risk. (They would never see their money again.) Wright was put on an allowance, or "salary," and the fruits of his professional services were intended to pay off his merciless load of debt and reimburse the stockholders. Among the incorporators were former clients Martin and Mrs. Avery Coonley, the New York critic Alexander Woollcott, Professor Ferdinand Schevill (1868–1954), an eminent historian at the University of Chicago whom Wright claimed as his "best friend," the great New York designer and architect Joseph Urban (1872–1933), and Wright's sisters, Jane Porter (1869–1953) and Maginel. Jane and her husband, Andrew, who lived in Philadelphia, were reluctant participants who feared the investment "would be a total loss" unless the Japanese prints were sold.[29] Maginel, widowed in 1925 after a brief second marriage to a prominent New York lawyer and international financier, Hiram Barney, mortgaged her home to raise her seventy-five shares.[30]

Philip Fox La Follette (1897–1965), a member of one of Wisconsin's most prominent political families (his father had run

169.
Philip La Follette on the campaign trail. 1930

for president three years earlier), was retained as counsel for the corporation (ill. 169).[31] Phil, as everyone called him, received his law degree from the University of Wisconsin in 1922 and became a partner in the Madison law firm of La Follette, Rogers and Roberts in the Bank of Wisconsin Building. He is described variously as either genial or a prima donna.

Avery (1870–1920) and Queene Ferry (1874–1958) Coonley were among the architect's most enlightened and sympathetic clients. The masterful Prairie House that he designed for them in Riverside, a suburb of Chicago, was begun in 1907 and practically completed in 1909 when Wright set off for Europe. The Coonleys moved to Washington, D.C., in 1917, but Mrs. Coonley, who was widowed shortly thereafter, remained devoted to Wright throughout the many hardships that plagued him during the years following.

In the summer of 1927, when she happened to meet Wright on the street in New York, he tried to sell her a block of color woodcuts in exchange for a subscription of $7,500 to Wright, Inc. "Personally, I do not want them," she confided to Martin.[32] Wright kept after her, however, calling on her at her home in Washington. By 1935 she had acquired about seventy-five prints, primarily Hokusai and Hiroshige landscapes, as one would expect, but including one eighteenth-century actor print by Shunshō, and an especially rare and beautiful winter landscape in vertical *ōban* diptych format by Keisai Eisen (1790–1848). The collection passed to the Coonleys' daughter, Elizabeth Coonley Faulkner (1902–1985), and was exhibited at the Octagon in Washington, D.C., in 1983.[33] Dispersed after Mrs. Faulkner's death, some of the prints are now in the Frances Lehman Loeb Art Center at Vassar College, Queene Coonley's alma mater.

WILLIAM AND BLANCHE McFETRIDGE: A LOAN THAT PAID OFF FORTY YEARS LATER

When the estate of the late Blanche B. McFetridge (1875?–1966) was sold by her nephew at public auction at the Parke-Bernet Galleries in New York in November 1969, it consisted of 433 Japanese prints said to have come from the collection of Frank Lloyd Wright. The catalogue introduction played up the Wright provenance, pointing out that the prints sold at the Anderson Galleries in New York in 1927 formed only a part of his whole collection. "Many prints were not included, and passed from his estate on his death into other hands. A large number of them are being offered in this sale." While these prints certainly did come from Wright, they did not pass from his estate at the time of his death. They were already in the hands of William and Blanche McFetridge as early as 1926—another interesting "dark tale."

After the death of their father in 1893, William H. ("Will") (1870–1926) and Edward P. (d. 1963) McFetridge took over his interest in a woolen mill in Baraboo, Wisconsin. William had attended the School of the Art Institute in Chicago, and Edward, a graduate of the University of Wisconsin-Madison, had been working at the Baraboo National Bank (ill. 170). In 1901 the brothers became full owners of the business, the largest textile mill in Sauk County, and named it the Island Woolen Company. William was a particular friend of Wright, who is said to have designed the charming pair of lookout platforms for the dam the McFetridges installed at the mill around 1912–13. William McFetridge later returned the favor by giving Wright instructions on how to build a dam and hydroelectric plant at Taliesin. Bad health forced him to retire in 1917 and move to San Diego with his children and his wife, Blanche. There he was a member of the San Diego city planning commission and helped found the Fine Arts society, where he was active as a critic, collector, and patron. He died at the Mayo Clinic in Rochester, Minnesota, on 29 December 1926. His brother Edward was president of the profitable Island Woolen Company until it was sold in 1951, and he served on the board of directors of the Baraboo National Bank from 1908 until his death in 1963.[34]

Sometime in 1926 William loaned Wright $5,000 to tide him through a major crisis, namely the impending loss of his home and possessions to the Bank of Wisconsin. To secure this loan, Wright followed a practice that had worked for him in the past: he placed into the hands of his friend a large quantity of prints.[35] On 19 October 1926, only two months before his untimely death, William McFetridge wrote to the Long Sang Ti Chinese Curio Company at 323 Fifth Avenue in New York offering to sell a two-panel Japanese screen by Shibata Zeshin, each panel measuring 57 x 34 inches. The condition, he said, was "slightly marred. The man who brought it from Japan some several years ago informs me it can be perfectly restored and from my limited knowledge I believe it can be."[36]

His description of a realistic painting on a silver-leaf ground makes it likely that this is the very same Zeshin screen displayed by Wright in his 1917 Arts Club exhibition in Chicago (see ill. 94). McFetridge mistakenly identified the artist as "Zishen," which sounds suspiciously Chinese, and which may explain why he addressed his letter to a Chinese curio shop. It is not clear whether this screen was among the objects Wright used to secure his loan, or whether he turned it over to McFetridge for the express purpose of effecting a sale (and keeping it hidden from the Bank of Wisconsin).

McFetridge went on to say he was acting as agent for Wright, who, unbeknownst to him, was at that moment about to be jailed in Minneapolis. McFetridge had authority to sell not only the Zeshin screen

> but other larger antique Japanese six-fold screens and some several thousand Japanese prints.
>
> I also am indirectly interested in the probable ultimate sale of large collections of Oriental antiques. Most of these are held in vaults of a Wisconsin bank. The collection consists of prints, paintings, porcelains, stone, glass and tapestries.
>
> I am wondering if you might be interested in these collections. If you are I could send you a list of such part of them as the owner, whom I have known for thirty-six years, has given me.
>
> A considerable part of the collections my friend has had the desire to keep in perpetuity but my own belief is that the bank which holds them as collateral may eventually have them sold at public auction.[37]

The list McFetridge mentions must be the one compiled a few weeks earlier for the Bank of Wisconsin following foreclosure on Wright's mortgage. Presumably McFetridge was unsuccessful in his effort to help raise money for Wright. The fate of the

170.
William McFetridge at
Taliesin. 1926

Zeshin screen is not known. It is possible that Wright had given McFetridge permission to sell the prints and screen (or screens) as a means of canceling his debt.

In August 1927 Wright was granted a divorce from Noel, which simplified his personal life. Wright, Inc., paid the divorce settlement. Under the laws of the state of Wisconsin, Wright would be free to remarry after waiting a period of one year. Unfortunately, he was still unable to repay his debts and in May 1928 the bank, having giving the architect a full year's grace, foreclosed on the chattel mortgage and held a public sale of some personal effects and farm machinery. As arranged in advance with Wright, Inc., they bid the property in for $3,000. The bank, which had now purchased Taliesin and all of its contents, was ready by July to begin foreclosure on the prints it held in its vaults. (Wright himself was in La Jolla with Olgivanna waiting for construction on the Arizona Biltmore to begin.) Wright, Inc., was slow in raising the funds needed to buy back the property. By 7 September the bank, obviously weary of further delays, had struck a deal on its own with an individual (Professor Van Vleck of Madison) who paid $4,000 for a bulk sale of prints.[38] Wright, Inc., purchased the remaining art objects and personal property from the bank on 12 October.

In their search for bankable assets, the corporation was also alerted to the prints in the McFetridge estate, which Wright now valued at $25,000.[39] Martin speculated in private that this might be the very same box of prints that he himself had held as security for at least thirteen years (it was not).[40] As expected, Blanche McFetridge agreed to send the prints back from California but only if the original loan were to be repaid with interest, which, as of 15 June 1928, represented a total of $5,859.24.[41] Although the corporation saw the prints as a valuable asset, it was not willing to buy them back. What would it have used for funds?[42] La Follette, who seems not to have had the slightest idea of the value or importance of Japanese prints, obviously (and understandably) did not trust Wright's high appraisal. This was probably a costly error in judgment on his part: the print market was still relatively strong.

In August 1928 Wright married Olgivanna in California, and in September, after nearly a year in the West, the joyful little family was permitted to return at last to Taliesin, now wholly owned by Wright, Inc., thanks to an additional $20,000 paid into the corporation by its most generous shareholder, Martin. Living now in genteel poverty, Wright diligently commenced efforts at fund-raising (to pay off the Martin loan, taxes due on the farm, and so forth) through the sale of prints, hoping still to get his hands on the McFetridge lot. When he tried to interest Edward McFetridge in a "business proposition," suggesting that they collaborate in selling the prints, he was quickly rebuffed.[43]

In early November the architect sent off a veritable blizzard of letters to museums across the country. Horace H. F. Jayne (1898–1975), curator of Eastern art at the Pennsylvania Museum in Fairmount Park, Philadelphia, was interested in hearing more about the Momoyama-period screens and Dorothy L. Blair (1890–1989), assistant curator of Asian art at the Toledo Museum of Art, wanted an itemized list of his prints and sculpture.[44] A letter went to Henry J. Allen (1868–1950), a former architectural client in Wichita who had prospects (so Wright thought) as a patron of the new Wichita Museum. He hoped the Allens would take over a block of prints as a gift to the museum. "I know you don't know much about them, Henry," he wrote, "but you live in a beautiful home quite in keeping with such things, and if your financial situation is as much improved as I should think it would be now, would it be straining the point too much to become a patron of the Arts to a modest extent? It seems to me it would be quite becoming. In that way, too, you could help your recreant Architect without hurting your conscience."[45] There is no indication that Allen replied.

On 8 November 1928, the same day he wrote Edward McFetridge, Wright sent off begging letters to several former print clients. His old friend Frederick Gookin, whom Wright had not seen for years, was gravely incapacitated with an eye infection in Winnetka, where he had moved in 1923. This took him out of the running.[46] Mansfield in New York received this letter:

> My dear Howard Mansfield:
>   I wonder how you are. Last time I saw you, you were about to take to the water, but fortunately not to the very deep water I found myself in at the time. Finally we have made the shore. We are back again in

171.
Ishikawa Toyonobu.
*Sanogawa Ichimatsu I
as Soga no Gorō
Disguised as the Dyer
Karigane Bunshichi and
Onoe Kikugorō I as Kyō
no Jirō Disguised as the
Cake Seller An no
Heiemon in "Ume-
wakana futaba Soga"*
(Plum Blossoms and
Young Herbs: The Bud-
ding of the Soga Broth-
ers). 1756. Color wood-
cut, *ōban benizuri-e.*
Honolulu Academy of
Arts, Gift of James A.
Michener, 1991 (21,652)

Charles H. Chandler
acquired this print from
the 1927 Anderson Gal-
leries sale in New York
(lot 9) for $2,500.
James A. Michener
later bought the entire
Chandler collection.

Taliesin and in possession of what I have always rather humorously referred to as my "Collection." It is rather substantial still, and in it are many things that I think you might be interested in, although I don't know.

I remember the Zesschin [*sic*] Screen was one of the things you very much liked. I wonder how much you liked it. And there is a group of four Utamaros that ought to go very high in somebody's collection,—and many others of course.

It is going to be necessary to dispose of "The Collection" to compensate my friends for their faith and financial loyalty.

Kindly give my regards to Mrs. Mansfield and to Louis Ledoux.

Louis and I had rather a run-in during the trying period of the New York sale, and I guess in the desperation that had me in its grip then, I did him an injustice…. I shall see him again sometime and do my part to straighten it out…. It takes a good many kinds of us, kindred or not, to make up the collection we call humanity, and after all Louis is a pretty darned fine specimen whatever I might say to the contrary notwithstanding….

I hope we may see one another again. There is probably nothing in my experience that I have enjoyed more than our fussing over Japanese prints.[47]

The nature of Wright's "run-in" with Ledoux in New York is not known. In December 1928 (a month after the above letter was sent) the entire Ledoux collection, supplemented by examples from Mansfield and Arthur Duel, went on loan to the Metropolitan Museum of Art for a series of rotating exhibitions that continued into the spring of 1929. In 1927 the Japan Society, New York, published Ledoux's *The Art of Japan*. Wright at once wrote a vicious review (unpublished and heretofore overlooked) castigating the book as pedantic, old-fashioned, and even inaccurate. "Such appreciation as we find is condescending. The well-made smoothly written little book is a snob—." No wonder he and Ledoux were not on the best of terms. Ledoux spoke of metalwork as a "minor art" but Wright counters that "art is art in a sword guard as in a great painting or statue, n'est ce pas?" It did not help that Ledoux praised a competitor, the architect Ralph Adams Cram, for his appreciation of Japanese architec-

ture. "No man who understands Art ever copies it," Wright scoffed.[48]

There is no record of Mansfield's reply to the appeal from Wright, but Chandler, known for having one of the finest and largest collections of both Sharaku and Hiroshige in America, responded so promptly that he took Wright by surprise. Chandler had exhibited his forty-six Sharaku at the Art Institute of Chicago a year earlier (and sold them to Kate Buckingham in 1934 for $30,000). Despite the occasional print party, ukiyo-e remained an elite and exotic hobby. Sounding disillusioned, Chandler (founder of Chicago's Japan-America Society in 1931) was heard to remark: "Nobody is interested in Japanese prints, and I never show mine to anyone."[49]

In any case, it was not possible for Wright to get hold of anything to show Chandler when he materialized from Evanston less than two weeks later. Wright explained to La Follette on 23 November 1928,

> We entertained him overnight, showed him what few things were around here and he went home pleased with his experience.
>
> Some little things in the vault, just little odds and ends of no consequence, pleased him and he bought them for $241. I was not even aware of the fact that I had them.
>
> He is a good prospect but more especially for the things in the McFetridge lot. I wonder if it would be possible to get hold of some of those prints now. I am afraid that they are in California, however.
>
> I should not be surprised if we sold Mr. Chandler between $5,000 and $10,000 worth of prints.[50]

He was probably right about Chandler, who spent over $4,000 on twenty-two lots the year before at the New York auction of the Wright collection. Chandler had paid $2,500 for an early eighteenth-century two-color actor print by Ishikawa Toyonobu (1711–1785) (ill. 171). The price seems high but at the sale the auctioneer had announced that Wright paid $3,400 for this print.[51] Wright described it in the catalogue with some hyperbole as "the noblest design of the primitive period in flawless state and one of the noblest Japanese prints of any kind in existence." By the early 1940s Chandler, who was then president of Chandlers, Inc., a university bookstore in Evanston, was an invalid and had stopped collecting. In 1957, a decade after

Chandler's death, his nephew Jared Johnson, who took over the family business, lived in the Chandler home, and served as trustee of the estate, sold the remaining 4,533 prints (over half of them works by Hiroshige) to the author James A. Michener (1907–1997). Michener, who published a novel about Japan, *Sayonara*, as well as the first of several books on Japanese prints, *The Floating World*, in 1954, had been called in to appraise the collection but ended up taking out a loan in order to purchase it himself. The Michener print collection is now in the Honolulu Academy of Arts.[52]

Wright claimed that his "selling campaign" was undermined by La Follette, who would not release the prints to him. The prints that Wright, Inc., had received back from the Bank of Wisconsin (the bank's "loot," Wright called them) were still in a vault at the bank in Madison, without a proper inventory. La Follette, as lawyer for the corporation, was understandably unwilling to turn them over to the architect without a formal, written agreement that the proceeds of any sales would immediately be turned over to Wright, Inc. He even had some difficulty about the payment into the treasury of the proceeds from the few articles Wright sold Chandler. As soon as the architect had money he began to disregard the corporation and spend the income himself.[53]

Nothing came of the letter Wright sent Emil Lorch (1870–1963), professor in the College of Architecture at the University of Michigan since 1906 and a longtime admirer of Wright's work with a strong personal interest in Asian art and culture. In 1930, when Lorch approached the university's small museum on Wright's behalf, there were no funds. (The museum had just made a big purchase of Asian art at the sale of the Louisine Havemeyer estate in New York.) "If we hadn't spent practically everything we had we would certainly want some of the screens and prints, knowing how sound your selection would be. Nevertheless, I hope ere long to see what you have."[54] About this time Wright offered a gilt statue of a Buddha to George S. Parker of Parker Pen in Janesville, Wisconsin, a small subscriber to Wright, Inc.[55] Wright even asked his cousin, the well-to-do Tulsa newspaper publisher Richard Lloyd Jones, to take a few valuable Japanese prints as collateral for a loan of $1,500 in 1929.[56] Jones, who had commissioned a house from Wright, sent the money but did not want the prints.

As for Blanche McFetridge, she never did relinquish her prints. In 1955, when she heard that Wright was to give a lecture in San Diego, she wrote asking him whether he might like

172.
Kitagawa Utamaro. *The Lovers Umegawa and Chūbei* (*Umegawa Chūbei*). c. 1798. Color woodcut, pillar print. Max Palevsky Collection

This print was one of a large group Wright gave William McFetridge in 1926 as collateral for a loan. The loan was never repaid, and the print was sold by the estate of McFetridge's widow in 1969. The lovers are shown in the elopement scene from a kabuki play featuring Chūbei, a farmer's son, and Umegawa, a beautiful prostitute from the pleasure quarter in Osaka. Chūbei steals money to release her from bondage. They are inevitably caught and sentenced to death.

to visit her. "Neither of us has forgotten the security in prints, etc. I have held here in Bank Storage so many years—nor the debt of $5000 Will lent to you. It is now outlawed—yet it still remains an honor debt—we both know that (maybe we could waive the interest)."[57]

She had never unpacked the prints from their original steamer trunk.[58] Certainly she would have been stunned had she known their value. Although it was a mixed batch, of uneven quality and not assembled by Wright as a "collection" per se, their sale at Parke-Bernet in 1969 made $108,675.

Of the 433 lots, nearly half (194) were by Hiroshige, which is no surprise. One of these, the Kiso Gorge triptych (lot 431), much beloved by collectors, brought $4,400. There were well-known sets by Hokusai—*The Thirty-six Views of Mount Fuji* (including two impression of the *Great Wave*)—as well as many of Hokusai's long *surimono*, of which Wright had a seemingly limitless supply and which did very well. As one would expect, knowing Wright, there were large numbers of Katsukawa actor prints, many unfaded and in perfect condition. There were also numerous pillar prints, including the cover image (lot 138), a ravishing Utamaro of lovers sharing an umbrella in the snow, which fetched $3,500 (ill. 172). In 1988, almost twenty years later, this print resurfaced at auction in New York.[59] This time the pristine colors aroused suspicion and it was subjected to careful scrutiny. In the end it was declared to be a "vamp," a legacy of the Tokyo scandal, and was sold as such for $3,300 to a Los Angeles collector receptive to the beauty of its design. This is a print with a history: Mary Ainsworth had purchased it from Wright in New York in 1919 for $150 and had traded it back in 1920 after Matsuki identified it as revamped.

PROFESSOR VAN VLECK TAKES ADVANTAGE

It is clear that Wright had many distractions in the late 1920s: divorce, remarriage, a brief return to Taliesin, exile and threats of foreclosure, a prolonged illness in the winter of 1928, travel to California with his young bride in January 1929, then on to Arizona to pursue what he hoped would be a major commission for a resort hotel. It was not until he returned to Taliesin in the summer of 1929 that the bank finally released his prints and screens, thanks to the intercession of Martin.[60] By August Wright realized that the bulk of the collection of well over 5,000 prints, which he had placed in storage in the vaults of the Bank of Wisconsin in the fall of 1926, and which he now valued at $40,000, had been sold to Professor Edward Burr Van Vleck (1863–1943) in the interim for $4,000, or less than a dollar for each print.[61] Wright had tied up an immense amount of capital in his print inventory and, as we shall see, it was certainly worth many times more than his self-appraised $40,000. A point of comparison is the sale of the Duel collection a few years later at the low point of the Great Depression. Duel was new to collecting in 1921, when he was first buying from Wright, but by the time he was forced to sell in 1932 in order to bail himself out of economic setbacks resulting from the Depression, he had amassed 4,000 Japanese prints (955 of them *surimono*). He sold them for $200,000 to a group of his friends who gave them in his name to the Fogg Art Museum at Harvard University (see ill. 165). This was a solution Wright would have envied.

The list of prints removed from Taliesin by the Bank of Wisconsin on 1 October 1926 itemizes 5,243 individual prints and twenty-two sets or albums, each of which would include dozens of additional prints. Seventy-nine of the prints were identified as "reproductions." As for Hiroshige, there were 2,184 single-sheet prints, eight books and one set. (The word "book" was probably used to mean an album of single-sheet prints.) The bill of sale to Van Vleck (dated 10 September 1928) gives him clear title to "certain Japanese prints and works of art contained in packages 1 to 15 inclusive, one inlaid chest and contents, and certain Japanese prints known as the New York prints, purchased by the Bank of Wisconsin at public sale August 25, 1928."[62]

Wright had all along been under the impression that the bank had sold only the so-called "New York prints" for $4,000. These were in a portfolio originally sent to New York for the Anderson Galleries sale but removed by Wright at the last moment. By his calculation they were the best (and most valuable) of the lot, worth $20,000 by themselves.[63] That the professor had made off with most of the inventory, however, was another story.

Bank officials had permitted Van Vleck and two Japanese to visit the vault for the purpose of making a survey and identifying valuable pieces. The bank paid Van Vleck $243 for his appraisal.[64] On Wright's copy of the bank's bill of sale to Van Vleck he penciled in the comment that in addition to the sale as represented by La Follette, there were another 553 prints of fine quality, 196 vertical Hiroshige, 250 *surimono*, and twenty-nine old printed books, more than 1,000 items.[65] "I can't tell you how outrageous this whole thing seems to me," he wrote Martin, his confidant and the chief supporter of Wright, Inc. "It is rank robbery and concealed by the indifference of LaFollette or his carelessness at the time in getting no details of the transaction. For the first time LaFollette and Rogers have seen the bill of sale to Van Vlack [*sic*]. Van Vlack made a clean-up in collusion with the Bank. What can I do now? Anything?—This seems quite too much."[66]

The much-maligned La Follette responded to an inquiry from Martin as follows:

> Mr. Wright deposited his prints with the Bank of Wisconsin as security for his loans. The loans came due. Mr. Wright and everyone concerned were given ample notice. Finally, after much solicitation for prospective buyers, the Bank sold at sale a block of the prints to Prof. Van Vleck, who was the only bidder. The Bank of Wisconsin took a loss of some $20,000 on its transaction with Mr. Wright.... Pure self interest, aside from any business honesty, makes apparent the groundlessness of any supposition that the bank sold collateral for less than it was worth when it took such a substantial loss. In addition, the fact remains that, if the prints had a market value anywhere in excess of $4,000, some purchasers could have been found. Mr. Wright's prints may have value in his hands under *favorable* conditions. The Corporation has owned a block of these valuable prints but has been unable to raise any money from them. Perhaps when Mr. Wright's affairs are in better shape and he is in a position to give more time to the matter, these prints can be worked out, but that still remains a matter for the future to disclose.[67]

By curious coincidence, one of the subscribers to Wright, Inc., Professor Schevill, ran into Van Vleck's daughter-in-law while on vacation in Cody, Wyoming, that August. In all innocence and with no intention of boasting, she "declared that her father-in-law had acquired one of the finest collections in the world for a paltry sum through his knowing the banker of Frank Lloyd Wright."[68] It was around this time that La Follette offered to resign as counsel for the corporation. His mind was in any case on bigger and better things: the next year, at the age of thirty-three, he became the state's youngest governor.

173.
Edward Burr Van Vleck. 1920

Van Vleck was at the right place at the right time. A professor of mathematics at the University of Wisconsin at Madison from 1906, he was also a serious collector of Japanese prints (ill. 173). Two of his sisters, Jane and Anna, collected prints, and he received his first example as a gift from Jane around 1899. His purchases were sporadic at first but he began the formation of a proper collection in 1916, when he acquired 149 prints from a private source in Connecticut. From that time on he was very active in the tight little circle of American print collectors, spending substantial sums in Europe, at the New York auctions (usually through Lucy F. Brown, a Japanese print dealer on Fifth Avenue), and buying in Chicago from dealers such as Mori and Ito. Between 1916 and 1921, for example, he spent $4,526 on prints. He stopped collecting in 1941 but toward the end of his life he carefully transcribed his meticulous notes into thirteen ledger books, describing each print and recording its cost and provenance. Comments by visiting scholars such as Gookin and Metzgar in the 1930s are recorded as well. Metzgar was in fact paid to help arrange and catalogue the Taliesin prints, which came with little documentation.[69] Van Vleck left his collection to his son John Hasbrouck Van Vleck (1899–1980), Nobel Prize-winning professor of physics at Harvard. When the latter died in 1980 he bequeathed the core collection of about 2,874 prints to the Elvehjem Museum of Art at the University of Wisconsin-Madison, his alma mater. On the death of John Hasbrouck Van Vleck's widow in 1984 another 1,062 that had been set aside by Edward Burr Van Vleck because they were duplicates, modern reprints, or of lesser quality were given to the museum. About 2,260 prints, more than half of the Elvehjem's Van Vleck collection—ranked among the top eight collections of ukiyo-e in America today—, is a legacy of the 1928 purchase. It is one of the largest extant repository of Wright prints.[70]

E. B. Van Vleck and his wife had already visited Taliesin on 1 May 1926, and received two Hiroshige prints as a gift from the architect: one from the vertical Tōkaidō series and one from the *Sixty-nine Provinces* series. This was probably a courtesy gift in exchange for Van Vleck's purchase of a fine Utamaro for $150 (Wright told them it was worth $300) (ill. 174).[71] Mrs. Van Vleck

174.

Kitagawa Utamaro. *The Middle Class (Chūbon no zu),* from the series *Elegant Customs of Three Ranks of Young Women (Fūzoku sandan musume).* c. 1794–95. Color woodcut, *ōban.* Elvehjem Museum of Art, University of Wisconsin-Madison, Bequest of John H. Van Vleck, 1980 (1980.3216)

E. B. Van Vleck purchased this print for $150 when he and his wife visited Wright at Taliesin in 1926.

selected and purchased one print by Hiroshige II (1826–1869) for $10.[72] About a year later Van Vleck picked out a rare Utamaro triptych at Kroch's bookstore in Chicago for $75. He was told that it came from "the final balance of Frank Wright's collection" and that Wright, who valued it at $250, thought it the only copy in existence.[73] It is interesting to find a print dealer trading on Wright's name.

By the spring of 1928 Van Vleck must have known that he might have a shot at buying the Wright collection: that April he went to Winnetka to meet with Gookin and study his collection. Van Vleck was surely the only serious print collector in Madison, and when the Bank of Wisconsin needed a buyer for the prints stored in their vault, he was ready, having already ap-

175.
Utagawa Hiroshige. *Salmon Fishing in the Snow in Echigo Province* (*Hokuetsu setchū shōryō no zu*). late 1830s. Color woodcut *aiban*, fan print. Elvehjem Museum of Art, University of Wisconsin-Madison, Bequest of John H. Van Vleck, 1980 (1980.1983). Ex coll. Frank Lloyd Wright; E. B. Van Vleck

praised the prints for them. A letter from La Follette to Martin on 7 September 1928 reveals that Van Vleck actually made the bank a second offer to purchase the remainder of the prints for another $4,000.[74] Luckily for Wright, the bank did not act on that offer.

Van Vleck kept a ledger with a running account of subsequent transactions relating to his Wright prints. In October 1928 he spent two days with Gookin in Chicago reviewing his new acquisitions and determining which prints might be deaccessioned. By April 1929, less than a year later, he had made back his entire investment by selling off 532 Hiroshige prints to friends and colleagues. (He gave away a great many as well.)

Van Vleck retired that spring and made his first trip to Japan and China in the fall. (Hayashi at Nikkō is listed among the dealers he visited. Perhaps this is the Hayashi who was Wright's nemesis.)[75] By 1938 he had sold more than 2,000 of the Wright prints to eighty-six clients for a total of $11,299, tripling his initial investment.[76] He reinvested the profits by enlarging his collection, concentrating on works by contemporary Japanese artists.

Van Vleck had inadvertently acquired more than one hundred of Wright's notorious revamped prints, most of them pillar prints by Koryūsai and Harunobu. He was not aware of this until alerted later by Judson Metzgar and Gookin and he never sold them. Many pages of Van Vleck's notes are devoted to discussion of pinholes and telltale evidence of new color blocks.

Even though 290 Hiroshige duplicates were deaccessioned in the 1980s, the museum still retains at least 1,755 Hiroshige with Wright provenance, representing the great strength of this collection (ill. 175). (Wright, as we know, was not the only one to invest heavily in Hiroshige. In 1932 Carl Schraubstadter told the architect that he had more than 4,000 works by the artist.

176.
Utagawa Hiroshige. *Fudō Waterfall at Meguro* (*Meguro Fudō no taki*); *Flower Viewing at Ueno* (*Ueno hanami*); *Maple Leaves at Kaian Temple* (*Kaianji momiji*); *Fish Seller at Nihonbashi Bridge* (*Nihonbashi*), from the series *A Collection of Assembled Pictures of Famous Places in Edo* (*Edo meisho harimaze zue*). 1857. Color woodcut, *ōban*. Elvehjem Museum of Art, University of Wisconsin-Madison, Bequest of John H. Van Vleck, 1980 (1980.2076)

E. B. Van Vleck acquired four identical images of this print in his 1928 purchase of more than 5,000 prints from Wright's collection. Wright also owned a nearly complete set of the wood blocks used to print this image. The blocks are still in the collection of the Frank Lloyd Wright Foundation.

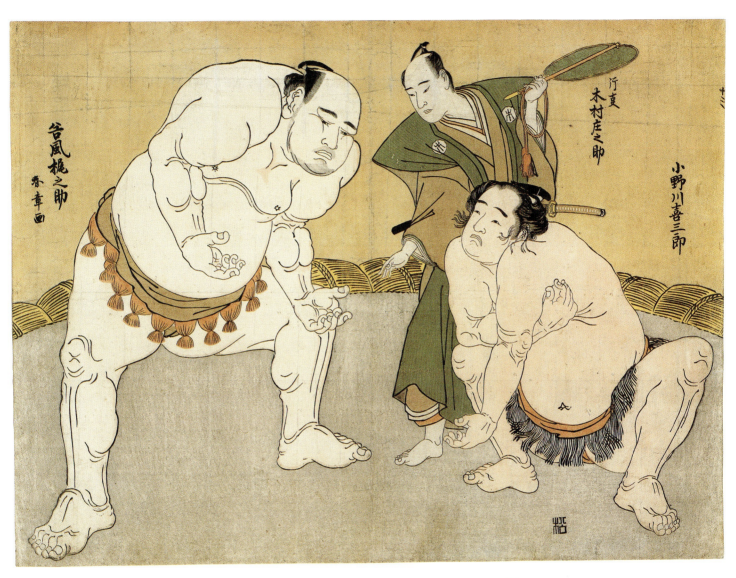

谷風梶之助
春章画

行司
木村庄之助

小野川喜三郎

十三

177.
Katsukawa Shunshō. *The Wrestlers Tanikaze
Kajinosuke and Onogawa Kisaburō with the Referee
Kimura Shōnosuke.* 1783. Color woodcut, double
ōban. Elvehjem Museum of Art, University of
Wisconsin-Madison, Bequest of John H. Van Vleck,
1980 (1980.3037). Ex coll. Frank Lloyd Wright;
E. B. Van Vleck

Wright's response: "I'm glad the compression didn't flatten out your hobby.")[77] The Elvehjem has complete or near complete examples of most of Hiroshige's important sets, and many rarities, including several unrecorded designs for fans, which may be unique.

During his visit to Japan in 1913 Wright acquired an almost complete set of nine keyblocks and forty-one color blocks for Hiroshige's 1857 *harimaze* series *A Collection of Pictures of Famous Places in Edo* (*Edo meisho harimaze zue*). He owned most of the prints for this series as well (ill. 176). The blocks were preserved at Taliesin in their original wrapping of Japanese newspapers dated Tokyo, June 1913. Shugio evidently shipped them to Spring Green in the summer of 1913 after Wright's departure but they were not unpacked until "rediscovered" a few years ago.[78] There are 115 different Hiroshige *harimaze* images in the Van Vleck collection, not including duplicates (sometimes as many as five duplicates). This is surely one of the largest collections of its kind in the world. Wright obviously bought in bulk and the fact that he had multiple copies suggests that they were dealer's stock; these are probably the very same *harimaze* he tried so hard to sell William Spaulding in late 1913 and 1914.[79] Wright was unique in his encyclopedic collection of *harimaze*; most collectors then as now have considered the individual images too small and sketchlike, if not downright boring. They were probably intended to be seen as a kind of album or portfolio of the artist's work. The collage effect of *harimaze* composi-

178.
Katsukawa Shunshō.
*The Actor Ichikawa
Danjūrō V as a Samurai
in a Wrestling Arena
Striking a Pose on a
Go Board.* c. 1780.
Color woodcut,
hosoban. Elvehjem
Museum of Art, University of Wisconsin-
Madison, Bequest of
John H. Van Vleck, 1980
(1980.3026). Ex coll.
Frank Lloyd Wright;
E. B. Van Vleck

At a climactic moment
in the play the actor
faces off against his
opponent by stepping
onto the *go* board and
scattering the *go* stones
on the ground.

179.
Katsushika Hokusai.
*A Simplified View of
Tago Bay near Ejiri on
the Tōkaidō Road*
(*Tōkaidō Ejiri Tago no
Ura ryakuzu*), from the
series *The Thirty-six
Views of Mount Fuji*
(*Fugaku sanjūrokkei*).
c. 1830–31. Color wood-
cut, *ōban*. Elvehjem
Museum of Art, Univer-
sity of Wisconsin-Madi-
son, Bequest of John H.
Van Vleck, 1980
(1980.2406). Ex coll.
Frank Lloyd Wright;
E. B. Van Vleck

180.
Utagawa Toyoharu.
The Eight Views of Ōmi
(*Ōmi hakkei no zu*),
from the series *Per-
spective Pictures of
Japan* (*Uki-e wakoku no
keiseki*). 1770s. Color
woodcut, *ōban*. Elve-
hjem Museum of Art,
University of Wisconsin-
Madison, Bequest of
John H. Van Vleck, 1980
(1980.3102). Ex coll.
Frank Lloyd Wright;
E. B. Van Vleck

tions in which many miniatures are grouped together was in vogue in the nineteenth century among both print artists and painters.

It comes as no surprise that other strengths of the Wright prints at the Elvehjem are kabuki actor portraits and sumo wrestlers by the Katsukawa artists (ills. 177–179). According to the print historian Roger Keyes, approximately seventy-five of the figure prints in the Elvehjem collection are unrecorded and unknown elsewhere; many of these may be unique.[80]

Wright was attracted to the linear abstraction of complicated architectural views and the collection includes a stunning group of forty-three "perspective pictures" (uki-e) in Western style by Utagawa Toyoharu (ill. 180; also ill. 33). More unexpected are the forty-seven evocative landscapes by Kobayashi Kiyochika (1847–1915) (ills. 181, 182). It seems that Wright's eclectic interest in landscapes carried over into the work of this contemporary artist. Kiyochika's night scenes of 1880–81 have dazzling chiaroscuro lighting effects derived from Western photography

and engravings. They capitalize on new trends in Westernization and modernization in the Meiji period; some of the prints depict brick structures: the Bureau of Industry Building, or Shimbashi train station in Tokyo, for example. Wright rarely if ever made reference to any artist later than Hiroshige, who died in 1858, but he must have enjoyed Kiyochika's views of modern architecture. Perhaps S. H. Mori had some influence on him. The Mori auction in New York on 9–10 December 1926 featured fifty-one prints by Kiyochika, an artist the Japanese dealer obviously favored.[81]

It is clear that the Bank of Wisconsin, with the consent of La Follette, acted foolishly and with total ignorance of market values when it struck the deal with Van Vleck. Wright was quite justified in his frustration and anger. However, the bank was tired of waiting on Wright and could not be expected to see into the future. It is perhaps poetic justice that the Bank of Wisconsin failed and was liquidated during the Depression.

182.
Kobayashi Kiyochika.
Shimbashi Train Station, Tokyo (Shimbashi suten-shon). 1881. Color woodcut, *ōban*. Elvehjem Museum of Art, University of Wisconsin-Madison, Bequest of John H. Van Vleck, 1980 (1980.2480). Ex coll. Frank Lloyd Wright; E. B. Van Vleck

大 池の端 火

182.
Kobayashi Kiyochika.
Fireworks at Ikenohata
(*Ikenohata hanabi*).
1881. Color woodcut,
ōban. Elvehjem Muse-
um of Art, University of
Wisconsin-Madison,
Bequest of John H. Van
Vleck, 1980 (1980.2483).
Ex coll. Frank Lloyd
Wright; E. B. Van Vleck

CHAPTER EIGHT

TRADES, GIFTS, AND PARTIES: THE FELLOWSHIP YEARS

SELLING PRINTS IN DENVER

In the early 1930s, during the Depression years, work was scarce and Wright was all but unemployed; only two commissioned projects were constructed between 1928 and 1935. It was not until the Johnson Wax commission in Racine, Wisconsin, begun in 1936 and finished in 1939, that Wright returned to world prominence in architectural practice following a decade almost without work.

The publication of *An Autobiography* in 1932 was meant to stir up interest (and architectural clients) for Wright. As he explained it, "We are only hoping that the book won't be too much like begging in the market place with my heart on my sleeve and a sob in my throat."[1] He devoted several lengthy sections of the book to his years in Japan and to the privileged status that allowed him to search out the finest and rarest Japanese prints, thereby highlighting his expertise as a collector.

Wright began not only to publish profusely but also to travel constantly from coast to coast lecturing on architecture at museums and universities. As his biographer, Robert Twombly, noted, these speaking engagements brought him public exposure he obviously enjoyed and cultivated. "He acquired a reputation, which he did nothing to discourage, for visiting a city and ridiculing its architecture."[2] This was the beginning of Wright as celebrity and media star, a calculated public flamboyance that helped attract apprentices and, eventually, clients. His travels often gave him the opportunity to seek out new print collectors as well.

In November 1930 he was approached by Cyril Kay-Scott (1879–?), an artist and director of the Denver Art Museum, and agreed to give two lectures on modern architecture for $500, the fee suggested by Wright. The president of the board of trustees, George E. Cranmer (1884–1975), offered to put up Mr. and Mrs. Wright during their visit.[3] The lectures took place in early December and were widely reported in the *Denver Post*. Deliberately provocative, Wright offended his audience of local architects, artists, and members of the city planning commission with a vitriolic attack on their newly opened city and county buildings, which he labeled atrocities.

The architect seems to have hit it off well with the Cranmers, both of whom were from old Denver families. In 1917 they had built themselves a luxurious twenty-two-room house in a mixture of Spanish and Italian Renaissance styles with a lovely garden and Denver's first outdoor swimming pool. The Cranmers habitually entertained visiting celebrities and musicians. Jean Chappell Cranmer (1886–1974) had two years of violin training in Dresden, Germany, as a young woman. The public musicales hosted by the Cranmers eventually led to the formation of the Denver Symphony Orchestra. Mrs. Cranmer had money of her own. In 1922 she and her brother had given the Denver Art Museum (then known as the Denver Art Association) its first permanent home, Chappell House, their family mansion. George Cranmer, a Princeton graduate, did so well as a stockbroker in the 1920s (he had his own firm) that he was able to retire in 1928 at the age of forty-four. An entrepreneurial type of many talents and great vision, he was appointed manager of parks and improvements for the city of Denver in 1935.[4]

Wright targeted Cranmer as a potential print client. On Christmas eve, 1930, he took the liberty of sending him "a collection of remarkably fine Japanese Prints...never offered for sale before." Wright's pushy sales pitch touched on connoisseurship, quality, authenticity, condition, investment opportunity, and educational value. He reminds Cranmer that he was instrumental in forming the Buckingham, Spaulding, and Metropolitan Museum of Art collections. "I feel that if I know anything, I know Prints, and my advice in that connection good." He confesses that he is being forced to sell even though the market is weak.

> I am asking one third less in the first instance than I have been accustomed to get for similar things—, and there is another reduction for "quantity."

This is all rather sudden. I hadn't expected to do this when in Denver.

I needn't tell you that nothing would do your young [art] students as much good as these Prints which lie right at the root of our whole modern culture in Art. They are not a passing fad, but intrinsic. They will be worth a great deal more than I am asking for them in the near future.[5]

When a week went by with no response, Wright fired off the following succinct note: "My dear George Cranmer: ? Anxiously yours, Frank Lloyd Wright."[6] Cranmer, who had been distracted by his wife's need for emergency surgery, graciously offered to talk to some of his friends. Wright in turn begged for any substantial offer at all, claiming that his situation had "gone from bad enough to far worse."[7] By late March 1931 Wright was so desperate that he wrote directly to Kay-Scott, asking him to intercede with Cranmer. The sale was needed, he confessed, to avoid an imminent bank foreclosure. The bank had, in fact, begun to threaten foreclosure in the summer of 1930. The interest payments on a five-year mortgage on Taliesin held by the bank since November 1928 were not being met and Wright was delinquent on county taxes.[8] The prints, Wright suggested, should remain in Denver so as to benefit the museum. Again he offered to reduce the price if necessary. "If the price is seriously standing in the way and a further reduction would save the situation—I would rather make it than start out all over again in another direction." In late April he wired Cranmer: "Can anything be done with the prints. If not would you be willing to lend me half their value for six months." A beleaguered Cranmer cabled back: "WE HAVE SOLD OVER FIVE HUNDRED DOLLARS WORTH AND ARE MAILING YOU CHECK DO NOT KNOW WHERE I CAN SELL ADDITIONAL PRINTS NOW BUT WILL BE GLAD TO TRY MAKE IT AN INVARIABLE RULE NOT TO LEND ANY MONEY."[9]

Wright's inventory lists for the five groups of prints mailed to Denver show that he was asking a hefty total of $6,240.[10] Group one included five triptychs for $1,850—three Utamaro (one of these was "unique," so he claimed), one Katsukawa Shunzan (active c. 1782–98) ("a prize for any collection"), and one Utagawa Toyokuni I (1769–1825). The other four groups contained forty-nine images by Hiroshige. In group two there were thirty-one of *One Hundred Views of Famous Places in Edo* for a total of $2,475; they were priced at $75 each except for *Fox*

Fires at Ōji Inari Shrine and *Sudden Evening Shower at Ōhashi Bridge*, which were $125 and $175 respectively. He prefaced the typed price list for this group with the usual immodest claim that they were "Superior by comparison with nearly all those in existence. The best subjects of the last and greatest series by the great Master.... This, by the Japanese connoisseur Shugio is considered the work upon which Hiroshige's fame will ultimately rest. Have been saving these fifteen years, and believe the prices asked for such examples—less than half their value— even at the present time." Group three was a miscellaneous assortment of Hiroshige images priced at anywhere from $40 to $125 each, the group at $1,305. Four prints from Hiroshige's Reisho Tōkaidō series of c. 1850 at $65 each made up group four ("This Tokaido is rare. Prints of this quality still more rare.") The Reisho Tōkaidō, named for the clerical script (*reisho*) of the title cartouche, was published around 1851. It is actually inferior to the Hōeidō set, as Wright would have known, but the set is, in fact, relatively rare, indicating that only a small number were printed. Group five consisted of Hiroshige's three famous triptychs from the so-called S*now-Moon-Flower* (*Setsu-gekka*) series, priced at $1,350 for the lot. He was asking $450 for the ever-popular Kiso Gorge snow scene and added in a postscript that he had seen $800 paid for it in New York. (An impression from his own collection sold at the 1927 Anderson Galleries sale in New York for $500.)

In the end the museum notified Wright of the sale of nine of the Hiroshige and returned the balance of the prints. Mrs. Cranmer had purchased one of the Reisho Tōkaidō images, and her friends Mr. and Mrs. Paul Mayo had acquired eight prints from the *Hundred Views*, including the *Fox Fires* and *Ōhashi Bridge*. Paul T. Mayo (1894–1940), a wealthy former diplomat who collected etchings, was a benefactor of the University of Denver and served on the faculty as an instructor in English literature. The museum took a commission of 20 percent, netting Wright a total of $652.[11] Wright assured Cranmer that they had sold enough for Taliesin to function for several more months; the foreclosure was still pending, he said. "I am sorry to have been so insistent and to have thrown myself on you as a 'prospect,'" he wrote. "It is the penalty a man like you pays for his fine qualities where men like me are concerned, in such circumstances as mine."[12]

The Cranmers and the Wrights remained warm friends. Jean Cranmer took the time to visit the Wrights at Taliesin in August 1931 and her husband encouraged Wright to design a set of silverware to be manufactured by Cartier in New York.[13] Cranmer and his family impressed Wright. He said that his visit to the Cranmers, whom he perceived as the "ideal American family," inspired his House on the Mesa, an unbuilt project for Denver. The design was an example of what he called American machine-age luxury and he created it specifically for the historic *Modern Architecture* exhibition organized by Philip Johnson and Henry-Russell Hitchcock for the Museum of Modern Art in New York in February 1932. It was his response to the International Style of his European colleagues.[14] Not surprisingly, the people who earned Wright's respect were the ones who would not lend him money.

KROCH'S BOOKSTORE AND ART GALLERY

The unsold prints were immediately sent off to Chicago on consignment to Adolph A. Kroch (1882–1978), an Austrian bookseller with a store at 206 North Michigan Avenue and a branch on North La Salle Street.[15] (In 1955 he created Kroch's and Brentano's, Inc., the largest bookstore in the world.) One feature of Kroch's establishment was an art gallery; over the years it provided an outlet for many of Wright's prints. On 26 December 1930, for example, only two days after first broaching the idea of a sale to Cranmer, Wright sent a rather similar appeal to Kroch. The tone of this letter is very defensive and suggests that Kroch had already complained about Wright's prices.

> Dear Kroch: Concerning prices for Japanese Prints—this for the record. As you may find out—Fine prints are now finished as a market commodity....

I don't know of any source of supply in the world from which fine prints could be bought for love or money at the present time or in the near future. Yamanaka and Mori have a few rejects from the greater collections for sale—usually. But not many even of these. So, fine prints today are, commercially speaking—extinct....

Sometimes a print or two can be picked up for little or nothing. It was so because of general ignorance of the whole matter. It is not so now. Rarely only can a fine thing be picked up that way now, except as I offer these prints at what seems to me, in the light of what I know about prints and prices, at extremely low prices, owing to hard times and my own necessity.[16]

In September 1931 Kate Buckingham acquired from Kroch one of the Utamaro triptychs that Wright had first offered to the Cranmers (ill. 183).[17] She paid $425, exactly the amount Wright had been asking of both Cranmer and Kroch, but her invoice indicates that it was "reduced from $850." Perhaps Kroch did not make any profit on this sale.

In January 1932 Wright mailed a collection of about fifty Japanese printed illustrated books and single-sheet prints bound or mounted as albums, primarily works by Hiroshige and Hokusai, to his friend and associate in Chicago, the architect and professional renderer Charles Morgan (1890–1947), for delivery to Kroch. (Kroch had exhibited Morgan's own watercolors, lithographs, and etchings two years earlier.) The group was valued by Wright at $1,228 and it was hoped that Kroch would advance an amount equivalent to two payments on Wright's car, which was in danger of being repossessed.[18]

Kroch tried to maintain a businesslike attitude. A year later, in early January 1933, he received a shipment of eighty-nine prints and twenty-one books priced by Wright at $2,820. The books included albums of single-sheet prints as well as printed illustrated books such as the Hokusai *Manga* and Hokusai's *Manual of Drawing*.[19] He immediately notified Wright that

> While I find the books extremely interesting, the prints are certainly not up to your usual standard. They are, in many instances, poor impressions and in not very good condition. I presume the selection was not made by you personally.
>
> There is, of course, not a remote possibility of selling the material at the prices indicated by you but we will try to sell them at the best prices that the market will bring.[20]

The proceeds from the sale were to be on a fifty-fifty basis, with Wright's 50 percent to be credited to his account. (He owed Kroch $350 from previous advances.)

Kroch found a client for Wright's set of fifty-eight small Tōkaidō prints by Hiroshige, and priced them at $6 each. As a favor, he lowered his commission to 35 percent, less than his usual, offering Wright $4 for each print sold. He begged Wright to lower the prices of the remaining prints so as to make them more saleable. "My dear Kroch," Wright responded petulantly, "You may sell the prints. Can't you wipe out my debt to you and forget the commission on this deal? I've lost heavily on all print transactions with the house of Kroch and received no discount on books although I have bought heavily from you."[21]

Kroch had been a loyal Wright supporter. He had distributed the *Wendingen*, the 1925 Dutch publication of Wright's work up to 1923, and had actively promoted sales of the *Autobiography* in 1932. He remained unfailingly civil: "I regret your statement that you have lost heavily on dealings with me. The fact is that I still have a large collection of prints on hand of which I was unable to dispose and for which I paid you over two years ago. I never would have brought this up if it were not for your own statement."[22] Wright kept other avenues for print sales open: even as he was negotiating with Kroch, he was contemplating selling a block of the Kroch prints through an auction house in the Fine Arts Building in Chicago because their commission was lower.[23]

In the fall of 1934 Wright tried to lure Paul Gardner (1894–1972), the newly appointed director of the Nelson Gallery of Art in Kansas City, Missouri, to Taliesin. He was offering one hundred prints from Hiroshige's *Hundred Views of Edo* at $42.50 each, a "rare opportunity" if compared with the $76 on average he had billed the Spauldings for similar pieces. Gardner politely passed Wright along to his "Oriental advisor," Langdon Warner (1881–1955) at the Fogg Art Museum, Harvard University. Warner had the prints vetted by Chie Hirano (1878–1939), Japanese print specialist at the Museum of Fine Arts, but neither the Fogg nor the Nelson had money for Japanese prints during these hard times (the Fogg had not made any purchases of Asian art in three years).[24]

Opposite

183.
Kitagawa Utamaro. *Cherry-blossom Viewing at Gotenyama.* 1806. Color woodcut, *ōban* triptych. The Art Institute of Chicago, Clarence Buckingham Collection, 1932 (1932.15)

This may be one of Utamaro's last prints (published a few months after his death) or it may be the work of Utamaro II (?–1831). Wright sold the print to Kate Buckingham through Albert Kroch, a Chicago book dealer, in 1931.

Meanwhile, in October 1932, in the midst of the Great Depression, Wright and Olgivanna established the Taliesin Fellowship, a residential group of student apprentices, each of whom paid an annual tuition of $1,100. This was exactly the cost of tuition, room, and board for one year at Harvard College in 1932. Wright's two hundred acres of pastoral land required constant attention, both physical and financial. At the age of sixty-five he was also in need of a new stimulus to enliven the creative environment at Taliesin.

From the beginning he involved the apprentices with his print collection. He kept his Japanese prints (as well as his

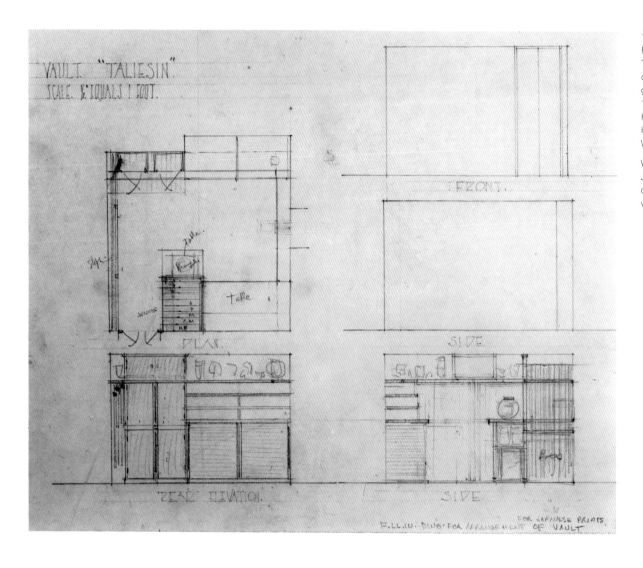

184.
Frank Lloyd Wright. Taliesin III studio vault. c. 1933. Elevation; graphite on paper, 16½ x 13¼ in. John Howe Collection, State Historical Society of Wisconsin, Madison

Wright stored his Japanese prints and other Asian art in the vault in his studio.

prized collection of Sullivan drawings) on shelves in a stone, fireproof vault adjacent to the drafting studio and his office at Taliesin (ill. 184). Some were in albums, others in folders or matted, but most were neatly tied in unmatted bundles, arranged by artist and series, and stacked on shelves, which were carefully labeled. Because of their close proximity to the work space, he would at times bring out prints for informal perusal and talk about them. Elizabeth Bauer Kassler (1911–1998), a charter apprentice in 1932, recalls that on Sundays, if there was a drafting table free, Wright liked to bring out two or three prints and look at them simply because he loved them so. An apprentice who happened to be passing by would stop and look; soon a group would have formed around the master, and he would talk about the prints, bringing out a few more. "He let us share his pleasure if we were of that mind," says Kassler.[25]

The fellowship was soon centered in the refurbished Hillside Home School building that Wright had inherited from his aunts, Jane and Ellen Lloyd Jones, three-quarters of a mile over the hill across his land from Taliesin. This had been the site of his grandfather's farm. In the summer of 1934 he upgraded Hillside to include a theater, dining room, and kitchen, as well as a large drafting studio flanked by apprentices' rooms and two galleries. The Dana Gallery (named for Wright's early patron Susan Lawrence Dana) was for display of architectural models (the utopian Broadacre City, for example) and drawings, while the Roberts Room (dedicated to the patronage of Mr. Charles E. Roberts, a well-to-do Oak Park client and Isabel Roberts's father) was used for exhibitions of Japanese prints and screens.[26] (In naming galleries for his patrons, Wright was adopting a strategy used with success by most museums.) A charter applicant to the fellowship, Robert K. Mosher (?–1992) of Bay City, Michigan, reported that truckloads of Asian art, architectural models, and drawings were moved to the new galleries from storage at Taliesin.[27] The general public was welcomed on Sunday afternoons to watch foreign films in the Playhouse theater and to chat with the master himself over a cup of tea. For fifty cents visitors were given an apprentice-guided tour, which began in the Taliesin drafting studio and continued on to the Hillside

building group. A museum of sorts, Taliesin and its exotic collection of Japanese prints, Buddhas, wood carvings, and pottery became a growing local tourist attraction.[28]

Wright used the Dana Gallery for informal Tuesday evening talks to the fellowship. Topics were varied and spontaneous but often included the merits of the Japanese print. For the first talk, on the evening of 2 August 1934, Wright's theme was one of his favorites: the ability to express the inner spirit of the drawn object. He argued that Asian art, which is inherently abstract, could serve as a model, and he illustrated his talk with prints by Hokusai and Hiroshige and with designs by the early-eighteenth-century Japanese painter Ogata Kōrin. The latter were probably images of Kōrin's work in printed books, of which Wright had many.[29] In the audience that evening was Ernest L. Meyer (1892–1952), staff columnist for the *Madison Capital Times*. He and his family came in late July to spend a week "vacationing" at Taliesin, living and working alongside the thirty apprentices. In reporting on the experience, Meyer concluded his review of an exhausting day tilling the soil and tarring the drafting-room roof with this picture of Wright as teacher:

> After supper, the master invites all apprentices to the newly-completed art gallery. He lectures on Japanese prints drawing from Oriental art illustrations for his theory of craftsmanship. He pleads with his apprentices to see—as the Japanese masters saw—more than the surface of the world around them…. Once they have probed the complex texture of the world, he says, they can begin to interpret it through art and through building…. He speaks quietly, convincingly, directly, and with power.[30]

"At Taliesin," a column assigned to apprentices, but heavily edited by the master himself, ran intermittently in both Madison newspapers and later in several rural weeklies between January 1934 and January 1938. Wright's print talks are often the subject of these columns. His thoughts about the "romance of the Japanese print" are reported with a kind of wonder and awe.[31]

PRINT PARTIES

In later years woodcuts continued to serve a didactic function for the Taliesin Fellowship at Spring Green. There were occasional "print parties" in the summer, which are fondly remembered by those who worked with Wright in the 1940s and '50s (ills. 185, 186). Curtis Besinger (1914–2000), professor of architecture at the University of Kansas, remembered three or four such parties during his years in the fellowship, one in the summer of 1940, one in the fall or winter of 1942, and one in the early 1950s. He recalled that these events were planned several days in advance since they required some culinary preparation. The sukiyaki dinner was prepared and served out of doors, on the terrace adjacent to the studio:

> Everyone sat on the floor on cushions (no tatami and no kimono!) in groups of four or five people seated around one gas stove. Each group had dishes of meat and vegetables and containers of soy sauce, etc. I think that we had cast iron skillets that we cooked in. Once the "mix" of liquid (don't ask me the make-up of this "mix") began to boil we filled it with meat, vegetables, etc. And waited for it to become cooked. After which everyone helped themselves to a "helping" and more meat, etc., was put in to cook.
>
> After the meal…Mr. Wright "talked" about the prints…. It was certainly not as formal as a "lecture." He must have at least one or two of these "parties" explained the process of making the prints. And [there were] copies of prints in various stages of printing which he showed and explained.
>
> It seems to me that what he talked about were "ideas" or principles that he saw at work in the prints and which he used as the basis for his work. And also, somewhat more nebulous and more difficult to explain, were certain "experiences" that one had from viewing a print which he attempted to translate into three (or four?) dimensional experience in architecture.[32]

Typically, Wright would set out print easels and line up many impressions of the same subject by Hiroshige for comparison (ills. 187, 188). Standing in front of them, he would discourse at leisure, beginning with a detailed explanation of

185.
Wright hosts a print party at Taliesin III. 1957

Young apprentices grouped around Wright include, from right to left, David Dodge, an unidentified man, Antonio Elmiger, Vernon Swaback, and Sara Logue (or her twin sister, Minerva Montooth).

Opposite

186.
Taliesin III. Loggia with Japanese screen, prints, Chinese ceramics, Chinese painting (far right, obscured by ferns), and Chinese carpet. 1937

the technique of the printing process, and going on to suggest the value of prints for students of art and architecture. His passion for the color woodcut never diminished. "Well, boys," he said at a print party in September 1950, "Hiroshige did with a sense of space, very much what we have been doing with it in our architecture. Here you get a sense of tremendous, limitless space, instead of something confined within a picture.... That's a great lesson for you boys to learn." (By "limitless" he meant the effects of abrupt cropping and diagonal asymmetry exploited so effectively by Hiroshige and others.) In reality, few apprentices could articulate what "lesson" they may have learned from prints. Besinger, puzzling over this matter years later, concluded that just as the print compositions appear to "reach out" and continue beyond the actual margins, so too "a house could, by its design, extend or be seen as extending, into the space around it, and by so doing make its site seem larger by reaching beyond the boundaries of the site."[33] One Taliesin architect, Charles Montooth (b. 1920), believes it was worth being there ten years just for one of those print parties. As a draftsman, he was impressed by the linear abstraction and the clarity and precision of drawing that he saw in prints.[34]

In any case, Wright encouraged the study of prints. Less than two years before his death he told his apprentices, "If any

187.
Taliesin III. Japanese prints in the living room. 1950s

230

of you boys will get together with Gene [Eugene Masselink (1910–1992)], at any time you want to see them, there they are, that is what they are for. Ask to see the prints in order that you may have the same refreshment and inspiration to your vision that I myself have had."[35] Wright believed Japanese woodcuts would teach abstraction and simplification, qualities he valued in architecture. Pulling out Hiroshige's scene of *Ōhashi Bridge* for the assembled apprentices, he said: "You see how they indicate the rain? It's abstract. When you once start with these prints, you never look at nature the same way after.... Certain realistic things disappear, and the whole scene becomes more effective and simple. "[36]

"I have never confided to you the extent to which the Japanese print per se has inspired me," he announced to a group

188.
Taliesin III. Japanese prints displayed in the studio. 1 August 1957

The prints are from Hokusai's *The Thirty-six Views of Mount Fuji*. For a 1929 view of the same screen mounted on the studio wall see ill. 161.

in June 1954. "I never got over my first experience with it and I shall never, probably, recover. I hope I shan't. "[37] Wright's tone as he speaks (several of these sessions were taped, the last in October 1957) is confident, casual, and knowledgeable. He makes jokes and has a good sense of timing. Apprentices interrupt to ask about technical matters and their questions are always answered clearly and with patience. He is the seasoned teacher, drawing in the students for slow, thoughtful study of individual prints with comments like "Look at that!" or "Can you see the boats in the river and the birds in the sky?" And he speaks of the prints and artists with real affection, as if referring to old friends. ("What you see here is always something you could keep looking at for weeks, literally. Exquisite things you never dreamed could exist.") He has either memorized or can actually read some signatures and is apparently able to distinguish between the various Katsukawa artists. When discussing his special "finds" he is boastful and proud, justifiably so. ("I selected them for their quality, myself.") He brings out a first-edition Hōeidō Tōkaidō, for example, mounted as an album: "an extraordinarily valuable thing…one of the finest things I found, and I guess the only thing of its kind in existence. Because, when we see the prints now, they don't come in this style. They're all taken off, mounted, pressed, fixed—so you see there—the original." An apprentice asks, "Mr. Wright, have you always had that book?" "Yes," he replies, "I brought it back from Japan with me when I came home…. As a collector's item it would be almost priceless." (Two Hōeidō Tōkaidō albums sold at Christie's, New York, at the peak of the "bubble" market in 1990 for just under half a million dollars each.)[38]

He moves on to Hiroshige's last great work, the *Hundred Views* of 1857–58, which, he says, up to the time he started collecting "nobody had thought much of, nor seen much of. And old Shugio, the emperor Mutsuhito's connoisseur, who had charge of all the exhibitions, was my friend in Japan, and he said something to me one time: 'Wright, never miss one of those. Someday it will be recognized as Hiroshige's greatest work.'" Wright liked to promote Shugio from government official to personal advisor to the emperor.

He points to *Sudden Evening Shower over Ōhashi Bridge and Atake* (ill. 189): "There's the one that Van Gogh has copied—'after Hiroshige,' he called it—but I couldn't see that it was anything but just an oil painting of this print. I don't think he did a good job of it either. The print was so far superior that it was too bad to look at what he did."

Opposite

189.
Utagawa Hiroshige. *Sudden Evening Shower over Ōhashi Bridge and Atake (Ōhashi Atake no yūdachi),* from the series *One Hundred Views of Famous Places in Edo (Meisho Edo hyakkei).* 1857. Color woodcut, *ōban.* The Metropolitan Museum of Art, New York, Purchase, Joseph Pulitzer Bequest, 1918 (JP 643)

Wright sold this print to the Metropolitan Museum of Art in 1918 for $62.50. He was very fond of the image and owned many duplicate examples. He liked to compare variations in printing. In a later state of this print, for example, the gray block for houses and trees on the horizon was re-engraved without the two boats at the upper right. At the same time a plug was inserted to cover an unintentional blank area among the pilings of the bridge.

Turning to Utamaro, he brings out an untrimmed *ōban* heptaptych of c. 1799 showing women imitating a procession of the Korean embassy, explaining that he bought it from a Russian Jew in Yokohama on his first trip to Japan:

> Never been cut. It has faded a little since I've had it....
> In perfect condition you see. The French loved Utamaro more than any of the other artists; he was a trifle dissolute, always graceful. He lived in the Yoshiwara with prostitutes, which would commend him to the French, I would think.[39]

He goes on to show them some of Hokusai's *The Thirty-six Views of Mount Fuji*, describing this artist as more of an architect and a dramatist. "He never drew Fujiyama [Mount Fuji] honestly.... He always lied about it—he liked to make it pointed. He thought it was too heavy and too flat, so he improved on it. That's the way he thought it ought to be, and that's the way he drew it."

Wright then brought out illustrated printed books—the Hokusai *Manga* and the *One Hundred Views of Fuji*—("I have thousands of these books"). And as his finale he produced a box of *surimono*, a precious collection of prints that is still preserved in the archives of the Frank Lloyd Wright Foundation in Scottsdale (ills. 1, 190, 191).[40] With reverence in his voice he points out the luxurious special effects such as gaufrage and metallic powders, and the beautiful colors: "My God, what a color that is! That's *beni*—unfaded *beni* [safflower red]. That's the way it was when it was perfectly unfaded. The sharpest red in the world, isn't it.... This costs a lot of money." He is always appraising the collection with the eye of a dealer:

> Well, now, here's a rare print. I think that there are only two in existence. Vever in Paris has one, and the Spaulding collection in Boston has one. Now I made the Spaulding collection, and I think most of the prints in the Metropolitan were once mine. Most of those in the Art Institute [of Chicago], and most all of those in the Kansas City Museum [he means the Spencer Museum of Art in Lawrence] were once mine. Japanese prints practically built Taliesin II and III. [Laughter can be heard on the tape.][41]

191.
Kubo Shumman (1757–1820). *Lacquer Picnic Box in a Draw-string Pouch, Violets, and Dandelions.* c. 1818. Color woodcut with gaufrage, *shikishiban*. The Frank Lloyd Wright Foundation (3007.041)

One of the poems in this print is by Masagoan Michimori (?–1819):

Opening the lunch box
for a picnic in the fields,
they find boiled greens
from waters of the marsh—
asters and dandelions.

Opposite

190.
Yashima Gakutei (1786?–1868). *Woman with Poem Card and Writing Brush.* c. 1825. Color woodcut with gaufrage, brass ground, and bronze and silver powders, *shikishiban*. The Frank Lloyd Wright Foundation (3010.032)

Seated beside a desk with stacks of books, an elegant beauty prepares to inscribe a poem card. Three humorous poems (*kyōka*) by friends of the artist allude to the art of composing poetry.

The gallery at Hillside was used for display of screens as well as prints. One pair of screens exhibited there belonged to Mrs. Darwin D. Martin. In 1938, three years after the death of her husband, Isabelle Martin was feeling hard pressed for cash and asked Wright what value he would place on the pair of screens of persimmon trees in snow that she had purchased from him in 1922 for $2,650.[42]

It may seem surprising that Mrs. Martin would be in need of money. The bulk of Martin's assets, $2–3 million, was held in Larkin Company stock. He redeemed the stock after he retired in 1925 but became entangled with the Internal Revenue Service, eventually losing everything. By the late 1930s his estate was insolvent, and there were still large unpaid tax claims against it. Martin's son spent many years unsuccessfully attempting to recoup the approximately $38,000 his father had loaned the architect.[43]

Mrs. Martin was reluctant to part with the screens. They had always given her a great deal of inspiration and joy but now she was forced to put the Jewett Parkway house up for sale, and had moved into an apartment. She hung one half of the pair of screens in her living room, and put the other on loan to what is now the Albright-Knox Art Gallery in Buffalo.[44] Wright offered to sell them for her at $2,500. He tried without success to interest Aline Barnsdall and Herbert Johnson (his two wealthy clients) in the screens. In his pitch to Barnsdall he claimed that the Metropolitan Museum of Art had been interested in this "stunning" pair of screens after Martin had taken them. "I think you would like them better than any you have and there is nothing like them to be had for money in the world."[45]

By February 1941 Isabelle was being forced to move in with her daughter in Buffalo, and notified Wright that she hoped for an immediate sale of the screens, even if they were to bring less than $2,500.[46] In the meantime, the director of the Albright Art Gallery, Gordon Washburn (1904–1983), had obtained a professional evaluation for Mrs. Martin. He sent the screens to the Museum of Fine Arts in Boston, where they were reviewed by the curator of Asiatic art, Kojiro Tomita (1890–1976).[47] In Tomita's opinion, they were mid-seventeenth-century in date, and the work of a Kyoto Kano-school painter. Of average quality and in poor condition, they had been further ruined by an unskilled restorer some one hundred years ago. He felt they were priced "somewhat higher" than a dealer would ask for the pair.[48] "I think he is showing considerable Japanese restraint in this remark," Washburn reported back, "and I would take it to mean not 'somewhat' but 'considerably' higher…. I am inclined to advise you to put the screens in Mr. Wright's hands if you are satisfied that he can be relied on to dispose of them for you. I must say in confidence that such an act sounds somewhat 'chancy' to me knowing as I do something of Mr. Wright's effervescent character." Washburn firmly but politely declined to purchase the screens for his own museum.[49] (Washburn is best remembered for his distinguished service as director of the Asia House Gallery in New York from 1962 to 1974.) Isabelle took the news in stride. "I have always suspected," she replied, "that Mr. Wright overestimated their value and charged us accordingly."[50] She closed the big lakeshore house in Derby, moved into the garage apartment, and let go the chauffeur and gardener.

Wright, who was not told of the Tomita appraisal, sensibly advised Mrs. Martin that it was not possible to make further progress unless she sent him the screens so that he could actually put them on display in the gallery at Hillside: "If I could show them I am sure I could sell them and would guarantee $1,000 for them from some source or other if you sent them on to me at Taliesin."[51] The following spring he again urged her to send the screens since it was not possible to find a prospect for them "unsight and unseen." Wright clearly viewed this sale as a labor of love. "I do wish I could do something to discharge the obligation I feel I owe to you and Darwin D. Martin," he wrote. "It wasn't enough to build your homes for you since D. D. was so very generous to me."[52]

In May 1941 the screens were finally at Hillside. By September, Isabelle was so desperate that she offered to accept $750 for an immediate cash payment. Keeping up the pressure, she added, "Do you remember that the man who did the work on the central fireplace in Jewett Parkway (I think his name was Giannini) told me you were 'the most magnetic devil' he had ever known. I expect you to use this occult power on some of your clients with whom to effect an immediate sale." "You'll hear soon," Wright assured her.[53]

He put the pair of screens in his exhibition gallery where he took people to see them, but it was now wartime and the sale of Japanese art was obviously more difficult than ever. "The same old silly prejudice against an enemy nation prevails I suppose," he wrote her. "Many admire but hesitate to buy. But something may turn up."[54] In July 1943, during the tourist season at Taliesin, he again reported an offer of $500 for the screens, but hastened to assure her that the low price did not mean that he was trying to buy them himself (at less than market value). Isabelle was learning the hard way that art is not a liquid investment: "When I consider that you charged us $2,600 for them, and the high value you placed on them of art and antiquity your offer would seem meagre indeed to a connoisseur, wouldn't it?"[55]

It was not until 7 December 1943 that she received her pitifully small check for $500, with this note of apology: "The screens went to a young man with a great appreciation for beautiful [*sic*] but afflicted with the usual champagne appetite and beer income but this is at last yours and I am glad of it." The identity of the young man with champagne appetite is unknown.[56]

GIVING AWAY PRINTS

From the beginning Wright involved his apprentices with the prints through lectures but also in more tangible ways. Around 1938 he hung eight groups of prints from his collection in each of the two corridors off the apprentices' rooms flanking the drafting studio at Hillside. These single-loaded passageways have wall-mounted light fixtures and three prints were grouped around each fixture. In each group two horizontal prints from Hiroshige's Hōeidō Tōkaidō flanked a vertical, large-head actor portrait by Utagawa Kunisada (1786–1865) from the popular 1852 series *The Sixty-nine Stations of the Kisokaidō*. (The latter were mass-produced in Kunisada's busy studio with the help of his pupils.) The prints were mounted onto cardboard, and the boards adhered to the plaster wall surface, with a trim piece of ½ x ½-inch dark stained oak. There was little daylight here, but fortunately Wright did not choose fine prints for what became essentially a permanent installation. They were dismantled by Bruce Brooks Pfeiffer (now archivist at the Frank Lloyd Wright Foundation) in 1968. "How they survived the thirty or more years at Hillside," he recalls, "with us kids running up and down to the showers with towels around our waists and not too much concerned about Japanese works of art along the way—is a miracle, to say the least!" The prints, which are badly faded, trimmed, foxed, mildewed, and in some cases torn, were finally ruined by smoke and water damage from a fire in 1952.[57]

Wright often gave prints as gifts at Christmas (a custom he initiated at least as early as 1929), or as a reward for a job well

192.
Edgar Tafel at home
with Japanese prints.
1989

done, especially if the apprentice put in long hours of over-time.[58] For the first fellowship Christmas in 1932, he selected a print for each of the apprentices. Elizabeth Bauer Kassler re-ceived one that was inscribed on the back: "Hiroshige, Plum Blossom Festival at Sunset. To Betty Bauer, Christmas 1932, FLLW and Olgivanna."[59] Later, if there were ten apprentices on hand at Christmas, Wright would typically bring out fifteen prints selected from middle-quality duplicates, put them all out on view and the group would draw straws, thus ensuring that no one got a bum deal. After an apprentice chose a print, Wright explained the subject matter so that it would be fully appreciated, and then inscribed the print in pencil.[60] The print-giving was discontinued in the late 1940s, probably because the number of apprentices increased dramatically after the war.

Edgar Tafel (b. 1912), a young apprentice at the time, remem-bers a visit to Taliesin by Ludwig Mies Van der Rohe (1886–1969) in the 1930s. As a gesture of friendship Wright brought out a group of prints and offered Mies a choice. Mies took his

193.
Frank Lloyd Wright and a model of the Herbert F. Johnson residence, Wingspread. 1940

194.
Utagawa Hiroshige. *Susaki in Fukagawa and the Hundred-thousand* tsubo *Plain* (*Fukagawa Susaki Jūmantsubo*), from the series *One Hundred Views of Famous Places in Edo* (*Meisho Edo hyakkei*). 1857. Color woodcut, *ōban*. Collection Karen Johnson Boyd, Racine, Wisconsin

This print was a Christmas gift from Wright to Mr. and Mrs. Herbert F. Johnson, commemorating the beginning of construction and the naming of their house, Wingspread, in Windy Point, Wisconsin, in 1937. Wright's penciled inscription was pasted on the back of the print: "'Eagle and Floating Cask of Wine,' Hiroshige Snow scene, Printed 1839 [*sic*], 'Wingspread,' Mr. and Mrs. Herbert Johnson—ergo 'Jane and Hib,' From Mr. and Mrs. Frank Lloyd Wright or Olgivanna and Frank, Christmas 1937."

time making a selection. Suddenly Wright said, peevishly, "Oh, I didn't think I had put *that* one out."

Tafel was Wright's construction manager on many projects and labored with three other apprentices on the drawings for the Johnson Wax building in the 1930s (ill. 192). He recalls that

> one night at about 10 o'clock, just before all the drawings were completed, Mr. Wright went into the vault, and came out with four Japanese prints, one for each of us, and placed them on our respective tables, saying they were gifts showing his appreciation of our efforts.... I still have this thin, long print, where I see it every day at home. It gives me a wonderful feeling of being mine—an accomplishment.[61]

Tafel has given away fifty or sixty Japanese woodcuts to his clients over the years since he has been a practicing architect, a habit he picked up from the master.

Wright also gave prints (usually by Hiroshige) to his architectural clients as house-warming gifts or Christmas presents. A classic example is the one he selected for Mr. and Mrs. Herbert Fisk Johnson in 1937 in honor of the naming of their home. Johnson (1899–1978), grandson of the founder of the S. C. Johnson Wax Company in Racine, Wisconsin, had commissioned Wright to build the company's now-famous Administration Building (1936–39). Johnson also asked Wright to build him a house on a farm he owned nearby (ill. 193). The spot they chose was intended to be a bird refuge. Johnson had dammed up a pond in a ravine and stocked it with fish to attract pheasants, ducks, and geese; Canada geese flew overhead. The owner was himself a pilot, and the children requested a "lookout" tower on top with radio and weather station so they could contact their father when he was flying. Last but not least, the house was designed with four long wings radiating like a pinwheel from a central core. During discussion of the plans with its extended wings, Wright named the house Wingspread. That Christmas he gave the Johnsons an appropriate Hiroshige from the *One Hundred Views*—a golden eagle with outspread wings in a winter landscape (ill. 194). After the house was completed in 1939 Hib Johnson hung the print in the entry hall and then later in his bedroom.[62]

The young newspaperman Herbert Jacobs moved into his revolutionary new Usonian house, an early experiment with low-cost housing, in Madison in November 1937. "I put in a mailbox on a rack which joined those of half a dozen other residents along the street on a rack two blocks away," Jacobs recalled. "At Christmas time the mailman delivered there, unknown to us, one of Wright's choice Hiroshige prints from his vast collection of Japanese prints. I say unknown to us, because it fell off the mailbox, being too big to go into it, and got buried in the snow for four days before we found it."[63] The Jacobs hung the print on the wall of their living room (ill. 195). Prints sent in a moment of generosity often went missing. Giuseppe Samonà (1898–1983), dean of the School of Architecture in Venice, was helpful in bringing the large one-man show of

195.
Frank Lloyd Wright.
Herbert Jacobs House,
Madison, Wisconsin.
Living room with a
Hiroshige landscape
print, a gift from Wright,
on the wall. 1940

196.
Frank Lloyd Wright. Unitarian Meeting House, Madison, Wisconsin. Corridor with Hiroshige prints, a gift from Wright. Photographed in 1992

Wright's work to the Palazzo Strozzi in Florence in June 1951. He received this message from Wright the next year: "I want you all to know that when we returned home I went into my collection of antique Japanese prints, picked out one for each of my Italian friends and their wives—eight in all—sent them care of [Carlo Ludovico] Ragghianti care Palazzo Strozzi and have just learned (nearly a year later) that they were confiscated by the Italian Government. How to trace them now is the question."[64]

A very public example of Wright's magnanimous giving of prints (not without an element of self-interest) can be seen in Madison. The First Unitarian Society of Madison commissioned Wright, one of their life-long members, to build them a new church in 1946. The architect was so enthusiastic about this project that he donated his time and that of his apprentices, as well as materials from Taliesin. His one-floor Meeting House, famous for the prow that soars above its auditorium, opened in 1951. The building is simply furnished with wood benches and triangular wood tables. The educational area is a long extension with a wide corridor and seven classrooms set on an angle to the corridor. Here, in each of the seven triangular bays outside the Sunday school classroom doors, Wright hung framed Hiroshige landscapes chosen from his own collection, pairing a vertical and a horizontal in each bay (ill. 196).[65] The prints are a miscellaneous group, from a variety of different series. They hang opposite a wall of windows and have faded, but they are almost all good impressions.

George Banta, Jr. (1893–1977), was the son of the founder of the George Banta Publishing Company in Menasha, Wisconsin, one of the largest printing companies in the country. He served both as president and as chairman of the board of that firm and was well known for his philanthropic work through the Banta Company Foundation. (He later served as a director and officer of the First National Bank of Menasha and as a director of First National Bank of Appleton.) He was obviously an easy-going fellow and financially secure, for he readily (and foolishly) agreed to Wright's proposal to swap prints for labor.

In October 1934 Wright alerted Banta that he hoped to use Japanese prints to pay off his debt for the cost of printing thousands of copies of the prospectus and applications for the Taliesin Fellowship as well as envelopes, letterheads, and postcards. The handsome red and white graphic designs by Wright had proven to be quite tricky for the printer to reproduce, resulting in much haggling back and forth over details. When it came time to pay the bill, Wright tried an old ploy:

> You know I still have a fine collection of the finest rare Japanese "prints" in the world. A group of these on your walls at home and in the office too would have intrinsic value in every way and I would mark them down to you in the circumstances, to one half what the Metropolitan Museum of New York, the Boston Museum and the Chicago Art Institute and many other famous collectors have paid me for precisely similar ones some years ago. Will you trade?[66]

After months trying to collect on an overdue bill, Banta seems to have resigned himself to the inevitable. The prints were very slow in coming, however. Wright postponed the selection several times owing to his hectic travel schedule. First there was "an important business trip" to Pittsburgh (the Kaufmann commission for Fallingwater), several trips to the East coast, a visit to Arizona, and then, in January 1935, two lectures in Kansas.

Wright's secretary, Masselink, contacted Banta in mid-January, when Wright was already in Kansas, advising him that to make the selection simpler the prints were divided into groups, the "fine specimens" ranging from $35 to $65, and the "specimens not so fine" from $5 to $15. Wright wanted to send some of each quality marked accordingly up to the sum owed Banta. "The prints that remain in Mr. Wright's collection," wrote the dutiful Masselink, "are among the finest to be had anywhere," ranking them yet again in a now familiar litany alongside those in the Metropolitan Museum of Art, the Spaulding, and the Buckingham collections. "Making a selection from prints that are all of fine quality is difficult and therefore if you would rather have Mr. Wright do that here please make some indication of about how many of the more expensive prints are desired and then the amount can be filled out with the others."[67] It was not until 30 December 1935, more than a year after the original offer to swap, that Masselink was finally able to send off the long-promised parcel to Banta. Banta acknowledged receipt of sixteen prints on 3 January 1936.[68]

The legacy of this trade-off is a group of twelve prints now in the Wriston Art Center at Lawrence University in Appleton, Wisconsin, not far from Menasha. Banta, who had attended Lawrence Seminary and was serving on the university's board of trustees, gave the prints to the university in 1936, within months of receiving them. Apparently there had been some thought in his mind that he could sell the prints to friends and recoup his losses that way. Perhaps that explains the four missing prints. It is difficult, however, to account for the low or merely average quality of the twelve prints, which consist of ten works by Hiroshige (a few each from the Hōeidō Tōkaidō, Gyōsho Tōkaidō, *Famous places in the Eastern Capital* [*Tōto meisho*], and *Famous places in Edo* [*Edo meisho no uchi*] series), one by Yamamoto Shoun (1870–1965), dated 1906, and one modern replica of a print by Ishikawa Toyomasa (active 1770–80). One hopes these were among the group priced at $5. For one thing, Wright wrote captions and comments directly onto the margins of the prints with pencil. He may have begun this practice when he opened his gallery at Hillside in 1934, thus providing the public with ready-made label copy in the master's own hand. Presumably he limited this practice to "specimens not so fine." (Notations in the margin, however, would not actually affect the value of the print.) Most of Banta's prints were chosen from somewhere close to the bottom of Wright's stockpile. *Mishima, Morning Mist,* from the 1834 Hōeidō Tōkaidō set is, to be sure, a strong, evocative image, but Banta's example is not only a late impression (the seals are blurred), but also dirty, stained, rubbed, and worn around the edges, not to mention scarred by a wormhole (ill. 197). The black keyblock lines are worn and broken, and the colors are muddy. One cannot help but feel that Banta, who was evidently not a print connoisseur, was duped.

Wright had a gift for retaining friends even after abusing their generosity. In 1939, on the occasion of the eightieth anniversary of the charter of Wisconsin Beta at Lawrence College, Banta urged Wright to come up and accept a Phi Delta Theta Golden Legion certificate from the alumni.[69]

197.
Utagawa Hiroshige. *Mishima, Morning Mist* (*Mishima asagiri*), from the series *Fifty-three Stations of the Tōkaidō* (*Tōkaidō gojūsan tsugi no uchi*). 1833–34. Color woodcut, *ōban*. Lawrence University, Appleton, Wisconsin, Gift of George Banta, Jr. (36.111)

Wright pencilled the following notation in the upper margin: "Late impression Tokaido series Misty morning Hiroshige." Dirty and torn, this print was among those Wright traded Banta in exchange for money owed the Banta Publishing Company for printing services.

LECTURES IN KANSAS

In January 1935 Wright had a speaking engagement at the University of Kansas at Lawrence. Afterward he and Olgivanna continued on to Wichita, where he had been invited to give two lectures, one addressing the subject of architecture, the other a supplementary talk on Japanese prints, for a combined fee of $150. The Wrights were house guests of former clients Elsie (1869–1951) and Henry Allen. The Allen house (now the Allen-Lambe House), designed by Wright in 1915 and completed no later than December 1918, a month before Allen was elected governor, was a product of the architect's Japan years, and subtle Japanese influence is especially notable in the large, sunken water garden, the wood and mulberry-paper light fixtures, which are markedly architectural in feeling, and the detailing of the expansive tiled roof. What gives the roof its Asian look is the ornamental, crenelated ridge and the illusion of a curve in the turned-up end of the tiles along the drip line, or lower starting course. Wright considered this, the last of his so-called Prairie Houses, "among my best" and regretted that he had been carried to Japan as it was being built.[70] At the time of the architect's visit in 1935 Allen was chairman of the board of the Wichita Beacon Publishing Company and president of the Beacon Building Company.

The architect had previously suggested to Mrs. Allen that he would like to bring prints to Wichita for an exhibition. Elsie was able to persuade the new president of the Wichita Art Association (which she and her husband had been instrumental in founding) that this was a worthwhile project.[71]

The Wrights arrived in Wichita on Thursday, 17 January (ill. 198). They visited Wichita University and were feted that evening at a convivial dinner for local high society at the Hotel

FAMED ARCHITECT AND WIFE

Preceding the lecture that he will give Friday evening at East High School under the auspices of the Wichita Art Association, Frank Lloyd Wright, internationally noted architect, and his charming wife, are being lavishly entertained and feted by Wichita society. They are house guests of Mr. and Mrs. Henry J. Allen, whose residence on North Roosevelt was designed by the architect.

Frank Lloyd Wright to Talk Friday Night

198.
Mr. and Mrs. Wright on tour in Wichita, Kansas. From the *Wichita Beacon,* 18 January 1935

Lassen, at which Mrs. Allen and several other ladies presided. After dinner there was an exhibition of "rare objects of art" in one of the hotel suites. Wright was described by an enthusiastic reporter for the *Wichita Beacon* as a man having the appearance of one twenty years younger. "Of slightly above average height, he stands erect, walking with sprightly step. His iron grey hair is heavy and well-groomed. His dress is immaculate. He wears a natty blue shirt and collar in informal garb. His tie is a neat bow. His grey business suit was in a happy color combination as would befit one famous in the arts."[72] In short, a description of the classic guru. Among the distinguished guests that evening was the painter and printmaker B. J. O. Nordfeldt, who, like Wright, had been deeply touched by Japanese prints during his years in Chicago. Nordfeldt was now a teacher at the Wichita Art Association.

The fruit of Elsie's labor was a reception and tea in Wright's honor in the ballroom of the Hotel Lassen on Friday afternoon. As reported the next day in the *Wichita Eagle*, the ceiling was festooned with vines and colored balloons, and on the walls were Japanese prints from the "rare collection of Mr. Wright."[73]

Wright delighted the members of the Wichita Art Association (now the Wichita Center for the Arts) and the Wichita Junior League with his talk on Japanese prints, some of which may have been purchased by Mrs. Allen herself; she and her husband were already serious collectors of prints by regional Kansas artists. As early as December 1918, when the house was first built, there was an eighteenth-century Japanese pillar print hanging on a brick pier in the living room of the Allen home; one wonders whether this might have been a house-warming gift from their architect (ill. 199).[74] Early views of the interior of the Allen house indicate that Mrs. Allen accumulated quite an assortment of Asian items, from coromandel screens to hanging scrolls. At least seven Japanese woodcuts were among a group of prints donated in 1971 to the Wichita Center for the Arts by the Allen's daughter, Henrietta Allen Holmes (?–1972). It was a collection formed by both the Allens and their daughter but there is speculation, without documentation, that some or all of the ukiyo-e may have been purchased at the time of Wright's 1935 visit. The prints themselves are rather disappointing: three are by Hiroshige, one by Kunisada, one by Utagawa Toyohiro (1773–

199.
Elsie Allen and her daughter, Henrietta, in the living room of the Allen house, December 1918, on the eve of the inauguration of Henry Allen as governor of Kansas

1828), and one by Keisai Eisen. On Friday evening Wright lectured on his "organic" architecture in the auditorium of East High School. Louise K. Hoult attended the lecture, resulting in a commission for the C. H. Hoult house, which, while never built, was the prototype for his "Usonian" house, realized in many variations throughout the country over the next two decades (see ills. 195, 205).[75] Much later, in 1958, Wright was hired to build an education center for the University of Wichita; it was completed after his death.[76]

A HŌEIDŌ TŌKAIDŌ FOR DALLAS

A few months later Wright was again making good use of his print collection. H. Stanley Marcus (b. 1905) had commissioned a modest home from Wright. In his 1974 memoir, *Minding the Store*, he recalled that the architect made frequent appeals for financial assistance. On a visit to Dallas in January 1934 Wright saw the family department store, Neiman-Marcus Company, and sized up Marcus's father ("Senior"). He incorrectly concluded that the son wasn't of the modest means that he had represented himself to be. "I don't see why a young man situated in life as you are shouldn't have the very best of every kind of material," he wrote Marcus.[77] In the end the house Wright designed was never built owing to cost estimates that burgeoned from $15,000 to $60,000, too much for a Depression-era budget. According to Marcus "almost every letter contained a request for a contribution of a further advance" to support the Taliesin Fellowship. In late April 1935 Wright asked for a "Marcus Fellowship" to pay for the tuition fees of one Taliesin apprentice. "If we had $1100 at the moment," Wright begged, "what a burden would be lifted and how much we could do with it."[78] The young Marcus, anxious about the spiraling cost of his new house, declined, but a week later Wright asked for a loan of $750, "for which I would send you super-fine prints as security to several times the amount. The sum to be deducted eventually from fees due me or if the sum not paid back in eighteen months the prints to be yours. I am asking this because our work is held back and our farm lying half productive for the lack of even so small a sum as that." Wright pressed hard with a follow-up note, stressing that

the entire fellowship was counting on Marcus to make the advance "as a good sport, a good Samaritan and a good friend. In other words Stanley, you can help us."[79] Marcus remembered that

> Financially extended though I was, I couldn't turn down this urgent plea, little knowing the nature of the prints he was planning to send. In due course a large and heavy case arrived containing a complete set of the prints comprising "The Tokaido" by the Japanese master printmaker Hiroshige. Later Mr. Wright explained that at the time he was building the Imperial Hotel in Tokyo, he acquired a set, and that later he either bought or received another set as a gift from Mrs. Spaulding of Boston. Which of the two sets he sent to me, I never knew. He never did redeem it, so it became ours.[80]

Marcus waited ten years, and when he wasn't paid he took ownership of them in his own mind and notified Wright to that effect. There was no acknowledgment from the architect.[81] As we know, this Hōeidō Tōkaidō was actually one of dozens, if not hundreds, of similar sets that passed through Wright's hands. It is now in the collection of the Dallas Museum of Art, a gift from Mr. and Mrs. Stanley Marcus (see ill. 29). There are three duplicates in addition to the usual fifty-five prints that comprise the series; Wright must have assembled the group in great haste from the seemingly limitless bundles in his storage vault: some are from very late editions, many have wormholes or other damage. The "Nihonbashi" subject was defaced by a red Japanese seal stamped all over the surface. When he put the set together, Wright numbered each print (each station of the Tōkaidō) sequentially with pencil in the lower right corner. The red seal of the Japanese dealer Hayashi Tadamasa appears on one of the finest in the set.

Marcus and his wife did enjoy the prints and always had one hanging on display. Wright had recommended that Marcus show them on a low easel in the living room, reminiscent of his display technique at Taliesin.[82] The quality of the group is just average, but they cost Marcus only $12.93 apiece, definitely a good investment.

A HŌEIDŌ TŌKAIDŌ PORTFOLIO FOR ALEXANDER WOOLLCOTT

Wright and Alexander Woollcott (1887–1943) met for the first time in April 1925, only hours before the second Taliesin fire. The writer, who happened to be in Madison on a lecture tour, was curious to see the home such a man would build for himself. His account of the visit was published five years later in a laudatory profile for the *New Yorker*, an essay Wright was proud to send out whenever advance publicity was called for.[83] At a moment when Wright's fortunes were very low, Woollcott had championed the architect, extolling him as the only living American genius. The architectural critic Herbert Muschamp has pointed out that Woollcott was a man who habitually sought his own solitary crusades, and in this instance he took up the cause of Frank Lloyd Wright. "What Wright gave Woollcott, to his delight, was a chance and a half to perform a selection of his most cherished public roles: champion of the underdog, connoisseur of the arts, foe of the philistine, sentimental milkman of human kindness. What did Woollcott offer Wright? Support both public and private, financial and moral."[84] Woollcott was among the small group who gave money to create Wright, Inc., in the late 1920s for the purpose of paying off Wright's debts. In short, they were great, good friends.

In April 1937 Woollcott wrote to announce his intention of visiting Taliesin in the fall. He reminisced about his last, unfortunate meeting with Wright: "I have not laid eyes on you since you invaded my privacy on the train going to Chicago, now more than two years ago. I count on train trips for solitude and would shoot any intruder were he three times as entertaining, twice as instructive and five times as attractive as you are. If, as I suspect, I seemed singularly unamiable at that time, it was because I was sick and, being unfamiliar with sickness, thought I was merely tired."[85] Woollcott also described a house he was building for himself on Neshobe Island in Lake Bomoseen, Vermont, to be laid out like Taliesin, along the ridge of a hill. Wright shot back this response:

> Dear Alex: The only man three times as entertaining, twice as instructive, and five times as attractive as I am is you. So what blame to you for preferring yourself?
>
> Call it privacy—
>
> But intruder? Hell—you invited me to dine with you on the train—and all I saw was a waiter pushing into your privacy with a tray [with] enough food on it to founder a horse. So I sat at your door angry and sweetly played my little melodeon.... I've never done a damn thing to please you. So before I get too far gone I am having the boys put something into shape for that new house of yours. Don't be alarmed—you'll like it for it will be something worthy [of] myself and yourself and not too personal to either.[86]

It took longer than planned for Wright to get together his surprise gift, a special portfolio of the Hōeidō Tōkaidō. According to Tafel, Wright still felt some remorse at having hu-

200.
Frank Lloyd Wright. Title sheet for Alexander Woollcott's portfolio of the Hōeidō Tōkaidō series. 1937. Black ink and red gouache on medium wove paper, 20 x 26 in. Cincinnati Art Museum, Gift of Dr. Gustav Eckstein, 1970 (1970.731b)

THIS JAPANESE CLASSIC
COMPLETE IN ORIGINAL STATE
FIRST NUMBER OF FIRST AND SECOND EDITIONS
PUBLISHED A CENTURY AGO

TO
ALEXANDER WOOLLCOTT

A TOKEN OF AFFECTION
FROM FRANK LLOYD WRIGHT

TALIESIN — AUGUST 1937

miliated his friend in public on the train. He asked Masselink to get from the vault an entire set of Hiroshige's *Fifty-three Stations of the Tōkaidō* and then had it boxed beautifully. "I hurt his feelings and he's a good friend," Tafel recalls Wright saying. (Tafel also recalls thinking that *one* print would have been quite enough.) Wright and Woollcott often traveled together between New York and Chicago in a Pullman. Exactly what transpired on this occasion is unclear but Wright accepted blame for a "trying imposition of bad manners."[87]

The gift was not only magnanimous but was also packaged in a unique fashion. The prints, individually matted, are contained within two hinged wooden covers. The front cover was inscribed with the series title, "The Fifty-three Stations of the Tokaido by Hiroshige." The letters were incised and then colored in with red pencil. The hand-lettered dedicatory page was inscribed: "This Japanese classic complete in original state, first number of first and second editions, published a century ago. To Alexander Woollcott, a token of affection from Frank Lloyd Wright, Taliesin, August 1937" (ill. 200). The "first number of first and second editions" referred to Wright's inclusion of two states of the first print in the series, *Nihonbashi, Morning View,* for a total of fifty-six rather than the usual fifty-five prints. (The second state includes more travelers.) The mats, which were cut (sometimes rather crudely) at Taliesin, were individually titled in ink. A first draft of the titles was written out in pencil, and is occasionally still faintly visible under magnification. Wright obviously composed the individual legends, and even added his initials after one of the more lengthy annotations. He described Mishima (Station 14), for example, as "Always in a 'mist'" (see ill. 197), Hamamatsu (Station 30) as "Coolies warming up," and Kameyama (Station 47) as "At the castle gates on a frosty morning" (see ill. 29).[88] Two of the images in this set protrude into the print margin—the peak of Mount Fuji in Hara (Station 14) (see ill. 9) and the kite in Kakegawa (Station 27). Wright loved this playful disregard for conventional boundaries (he often tried it in his own drawings), and he cut out the mats to accommodate Hiroshige's vision.

The portfolio, weighing thirty-one pounds and valued for insurance purposes at $3,500, was sent off on 27 August by Railway Express with Wright's excited letter of explanation:

> I know of nothing in the world so intrinsic in value as these prints by one of the greatest artists who ever lived. The craft that produced them is [an] all-time high in craftsmanship too.
>
> I could think of nothing less for you to have by you in your new home. I hope you will take the box of prints to your table occasionally and make the trip with the diamya [*sic*; daimyo] procession down the Tokaido with Hiroshige to show you the sights—starting at dawn from the Nihombashi bridge at Tokyo (then Yedo) and after making many stations that used to take some weeks to make, go across the bridge to Kyoto, the ancient capital, at sunset.
>
> When the series of views was made by Hiroshige eternity was now.
>
> So, I think it is destined to endure longest of any graphic masterpiece whatsoever. In it a unique civilization lives for posterity. But for this record by a native son that civilization will have vanished before long.
>
> The complete journey is rare now in any state. I know of seven in the world of which yours is one…. The designs (all are designs portraying actual places) you like most at first will probably not be those you eventually like best. But no one of them is empty. Their significance has changed the Western art world for the better in the elimination of the insignificant so badly needed.
>
> Cherish them for that if for nothing else.[89]

The flabbergasted recipient assured Wright that he intended to keep the prints in a place of honor in his new home. "I don't know quite what to say, which is not a characteristic difficulty," he wrote.

> It isn't enough to call the Hiroshige portfolio a handsome gift. I'd say that of a bowl of chrysanthemums or a case of wine, which would both be gone before Christmas. So I'll just say that it is a gift drawn to the scale of the giver and let it go at that.
>
> Since the prints came, I have already made the journey three times. I hope to make it next under the guidance of Dr. Gustav Eckstein of Cincinnati. He's the minute and astonishing teacher from the medical school there, who once wrote a play called "Hokusai" and is best known, I suppose, as the biographer of Noguchi [Hideo].[90]

It may have been the "journeys" down the Tōkaidō that inspired Woollcott to reminisce, in this same letter, about his own annual pilgrimages to the family home for the Christmas holidays. He describes reaching the station five miles away in the early dark of a winter afternoon, hiring a "smelly hack," and driving over rutty roads with the sound of hoof beats echoing on bridges.

Wright sent a follow-up note to explain that the box "is to be taken to a table and the lid dropped to make a kind of easel hanging over the edge (supported from behind by a hassock or something similar) into which you can set up the prints to view them…. Your acceptance was a lovely one (literature of the sort only you can make)."[91]

Only four years later Woollcott gave the portfolio away to his good friend Dr. Gustav Eckstein, Jr. (1890–1981), whom he mentioned in his letter to Wright. Eckstein was a brilliant author, scientist, and humanitarian. A professor of physiology at the University of Cincinnati College of Medicine, he had a keen interest in Japan, having written a group of stories based on his travels through Japanese villages, followed by a best-selling 1931 biography of the Japanese bacteriologist Noguchi Hideo, and the 1935 play *Hokusai*. Eckstein in turn gave the Tōkaidō set to the Cincinnati Art Museum in 1970, claiming that it had been given to Frank Lloyd Wright in 1922 by the emperor to congratulate the architect upon the completion of the Imperial Hotel. He also remembered hearing that the emperor had seven complete Tōkaidō sets in his possession in the 1920s (Wright had mentioned seven known sets in his letter to Woollcott).

One, he said, went to the Museum of Fine Arts in Boston, one to Wright, and at least one stayed in the imperial collection.[92] Roland Koscherak, the New York art dealer who appraised the prints for the museum in 1970, was asked to comment on the hearsay provenance: "My experience in this field would lead me to believe that any Imperial gift would be of impeccable quality. These prints are not."[93]

The prints are in fact of uneven quality, having been assembled from various groups or lots (they are not all from the same set). Most have fairly fresh color but are soiled, damaged, or trimmed and some have bad centerfolds. As there was no time (or talent) available for proper conservation, Wright dealt with the matter of holes in a manner common among collectors. To prevent the white mat paper from showing through a hole, an appropriately colored pencil was used on the mat itself directly under the hole. This technique did not damage the print in any way. Although the original mats have now been replaced with acid-free paper, they are still preserved in the museum, complete with Wright's legends and the traces of colored pencil.

There are two relatively early impressions in the group, and the others are average to late. Hiroshige's Hōeidō, or Great Tōkaidō was reprinted endlessly: only the first hundred or so printings, now very rare, are considered "fine." The next several hundred are "early" impressions, the next lot "average," and the remainder "poor" or "late." Until recently, Japanese prints were never numbered, but it is assumed that the Hōeidō series might have gone as high as ten thousand. The blocks continued to be printed well after the time of the first "edition," indeed even after the artist's death. At auction today, as in Wright's time, early impressions fetch multiples of the late ones. The Great Tōkaidō is timeless, and continues to be appreciated as much as it was in 1834.

PRINT EXHIBITIONS FOR THE MIDWEST

It has been said that every small museum within easy driving radius of Taliesin is likely to have prints from the Frank Lloyd Wright collection. Caroline L. Burr, of the Fine Arts department at Beloit College in Beloit, Wisconsin, invited Wright to lecture to the Beloit Art League in November 1934 on "the new architecture which you have given the world."[94] Taken aback when Wright offered to talk about his pet subject, the Taliesin Fellowship, she recommended something with more public appeal. In June 1935, when she asked him for an exhibition to be shown in Art Hall, he agreed on the grounds that it would feature the work of the fellowship, i.e., drawings and furniture. At the last minute, however, he told her that he was adding a group of "fine Antique prints" as well. Burr agreed to display the Japanese prints in the small Print Room adjoining the main gallery.[95]

A second Beloit exhibition, featuring photographs of Wright's work, was planned for November 1937. Again there was a last-minute change of plans. The photographs were not available and Masselink wrote Burr (who was not really much of an Asian art enthusiast): "We are terribly sorry to disappoint you again and are sending you by express today a group of thirty-three of the finest Hiroshige prints in Mr. Wright's collection to take the place of the exhibition you wanted." There is no record of Burr's reaction. A three-page exhibition checklist prepared by Masselink lists the thirty-three prints, including eighteen from Hiroshige's *One Hundred Views*. *Sudden Evening Shower at Ōhashi Bridge* was among the loans.[96]

In the early years Wright had built two houses in Grand Rapids, Michigan. On the occasion of a lecture there in 1937 he met a real art lover. Otto Karl Bach (1909–1990), director of the Grand Rapids Art Gallery (now the Grand Rapids Art Museum), later became director of the Denver Art Museum. He was genuinely excited by the possibility of buying some of Wright's Japanese prints. To raise funds for this acquisition, he hit upon the idea of staging a small display, with the hope that a donor would come forward to purchase them for the gallery. Wright was of course receptive, expansively assuring the director that "out of the finest collection of Hiroshige in the world from which came the collections of the Boston Museum—the Metropolitan—the Chicago Art Institute and Kansas City, you ought to find something valuable."[97] The opening, originally scheduled for mid-April, was delayed until May because Wright was traveling and he wanted to make the selection himself. As his secretary explained to Bach, Wright "had no chance to make the selection of prints for the gallery. He wants to put some thought into it and send a wide variety of characteristic valuable subjects."[98] When the show opened on 12 May the *Grand Rapids Press* praised the fifty-five prints from Hiroshige's Hōeidō Tōkaidō with this bit of typical Wrightian hyperbole: "To the best knowledge of critics, Wright's collection is the only

complete series of the Tokaido in the world."[99] The gallery acquired its first Japanese prints as a gift in 1959, and there is no known connection between those prints and Wright.

COLLECTING AGAIN

Wright had begun adding to his collection again. As before, he bought extravagantly, on impulse, and on credit. In early July 1937, returning from an international congress of architects in the Soviet Union, he stopped off in Paris to seek out the foremost gallery of Asian art, Vignier, at 4, rue Lamennais. Charles Vignier, a famous Parisian dealer, began writing about Japanese prints as early as 1909 and his own collection now resides in the Bibliothèque Nationale. Drawing from French collections, Vignier and his Japanese collaborator, Inada Hagitaro, prepared six richly illustrated exhibition catalogues for the Musée des Arts Décoratifs in Paris between 1909 and 1913. These scholarly volumes immediately became standard reference works for all early collectors, including Wright.

Vignier's niece, Marian Densmore, succeeded him in the gallery in the late 1930s. Wright bought thirty-nine prints from her for approximately $288.[100] His selection was very predictable: more than half were Katsukawa actor prints, the remainder were from Hokusai's *The Thirty-six Views of Mount Fuji*.

A month later Wright wrote Densmore to offer another $288 for a small Japanese screen, and in September he had her send over $234 worth of diptychs and triptychs by Hosoda Eishi (1756–1829) and Utagawa Toyokuni (1769–1825), a complete album of Hiroshige's Gyōsho Tōkaidō series (i.e., a set of single-sheet prints mounted at some later date in album format), as well as Hokusai's masterpiece, *One Hundred Views of Fuji*, a book printed in 1835.[101]

Characteristically, however, Wright neglected to pay for the second installment of prints, and Densmore was forced to send a strongly worded letter eight months later in April 1938 asking him to either return the goods or face legal action. Wright shot back this cable: "SORRY FOR LONG DELAY. CABLING SIX THOUSAND ONE HUNDRED FRANCS. IF YOU CARE TO SEND SMALL SCREEN NOW DO SO. MIGHT BUY ALL YOUR PRINTS AND BOOKS IF FAVORABLE PROPOSITION FROM YOU."[102] At this point the gallery, wisely, was only willing to ship the screen subject to advance payment. "About my collection of Japanese prints and books," Densmore added, "it is impossible to tell you an exact price for the all, because you don't know really what I have. Since last year I have sold some of them but I have bought many others."[103] The last recorded invoice from Vignier (another $300) is dated August 1939. It lists not only a six-panel Japanese landscape screen but two later Chinese paintings (white herons at the edge of a river and a bust portrait of a young woman), and a pair of seventeenth-century Chinese coromandel screen panels with figure scenes on both sides.[104]

YAMANAKA TAKES A LOSS

In late February 1937 the Wrights stopped in at Yamanaka and Company at 680 Fifth Avenue in New York. An invoice of purchases reflects the architect's eclectic taste.[105] There were four Katsukawa actor prints (including an image by Shunshō of Danjūrō in the *Shibaraku* role), architectural elements such as five Chinese Qing-dynasty carved wood panels (listed on the invoice as Ming and costing $75), and a pair of Qing three-panel carved wood folding screens with bird-and-flower subjects

201.
Taliesin III. View from the dining cove into the living room. November 1937

Wright purchased the pair of late Chinese carved wood folding screens (far right) and many other examples of Asian decorative arts at Yamanaka and Company, New York, in February 1937. By the time this photograph was published in *Architectural Forum* a year later, he had not yet paid his bill. The Ming-dynasty sixteenth-century cast-iron statue of Guanyin at the far left was in place in 1929, when a view of the living room was published in *Liberty* (see ill. 159).

(again listed on the invoice as Ming and costing a hefty $350). There were two Chinese red silk tassles, no less than eight Japanese folding screens, and a Japanese statue of a standing wood Buddha. By mistake, Wright had even set aside a fourteenth-century Thai (or possibly Tibetan) Buddhist painting, something he later decided he did not want, owing to its poor condition. Four of the screens were also deleted from the list a few weeks later. Even so, the balance due on an invoice for $1,275 was $775.

Wright almost certainly made this large purchase in early 1937 in expectation of the important photo shoot planned at Taliesin for the January 1938 issue of *Architectural Forum*, devoted to his recent work. A view of the master bedroom shows the five smaller Chinese wood panels cleverly incorporated into the architecture, wrapping around one corner below the clerestory windows.[106] The Hedrich-Blessing photographs of the living room, taken in November 1937, feature the Qing carved wood folding screens with the caption "Living room showing furniture as a part of the building. In the manner of the buildings from 1901 [*sic*] to 1938" (ill. 201).[107] The architect positioned the screens in the southeast corner of the spacious room diagonally opposite the piano, as a backdrop to set off himself and Olgivanna when guests gathered. A future apprentice, Curtis Besinger, attended a formal Sunday evening dinner-musicale in the summer of 1939 and was struck by the thronelike placement of two upholstered chairs for Mr. and Mrs. Wright, obviously the place of honor: "The chairs were in front of an old, carved and painted, wooden Chinese screen."[108] Seats for guests were grouped nearby, within conversational distance.

It was not until mid-October 1938 that Wright finally settled his account in full with Yamanaka and Company for the February 1937 purchase. It would have dragged on even longer, but Mr. K. Tenneco, the patient Yamanaka representative in New York, finally resorted to the always effective threat of legal action. There had also been much haggling back and forth over the gilt lacquer Buddha, supposedly chosen because Olgivanna had admired it. Wright took the position that the asking price had been $75. Tenneco was adamant that the price was $100, and as late as November 1938 he was still insisting (in vain) on having this piece returned.[109]

The stoic Tenneco nonetheless continued to do business with Wright. Only a month later, on 7 December 1938, he sent some items to Wright in care of the Herbert Johnson Wax Company in Racine. A Chinese blue-and-yellow wool rug and

two pairs of Japanese six-panel folding screens identified as spring and autumn floral subjects by anonymous seventeenth- and eighteenth-century Kano-school artists totaled a hefty $6,350. Wright had also expressed interest in a Chinese Northern Wei-dynasty (386–534) pottery head for $50 and a Cambodian head for $500. When no check arrived from Wright, Tenneco sold the Cambodian sculpture to a Parisian. Wright returned the rug because it did not "go" in the house for which he intended it (presumably Johnson's Wingspread) but did offer to purchase it himself if the price were substantially reduced. He offered $200.[110] The fate of the screens is not known.

In the autumn of 1942 Yamanaka and Company went into liquidation under supervision of the Alien Property Custodian of the United States government. It took the representative of the government's Chicago office until 4 December 1943 to collect the $150 Wright owed for a Momoyama-period screen he had taken from Yamanaka in 1938.[111] On 1 December 1943 Yamanaka in New York also acknowledged receipt of $1,839.17 from Wright, the balance still due on a purchase two years earlier of a twelve-panel Chinese lacquer coromandel screen ($1,500), a large Chinese sixth-century terra-cotta figure of a standing woman ($230), a sixth-century Chinese terra-cotta head of a woman ($50), and a two-panel Japanese screen of pine tree in snow and autumn maple, with a "Sōtatsu school" attribution ($300).[112] In 1944 the Alien Property Custodian sold the remaining inventory of Yamanaka's New York, Boston, and Chicago branches at auction at Parke-Bernet Galleries in New York.[113]

When Wright began to receive commissions in northern California after the war, it became expedient for him to establish a base of operations there. He opened an office at 319 Grant Avenue in San Francisco in 1951 in association with architect Aaron Green (b. 1917), a former Taliesin apprentice, who acted as West Coast representative. During the remaining eight years of his life, Wright frequently visited San Francisco. Green accompanied him on many shopping expeditions to such places as Gump's, in the ongoing search for treasures. He had to pay many of the bills, as well. Speaking of Wright, Green remembers that "one of his pleasures was visiting the best of the oriental antique dealers both Japanese and Chinese…. We looked for and purchased screens, ceramics, textiles, and similar artifacts when he found things he favored."[114] In August 1955, for example, Gump's was holding three Japanese screens Wright hoped to place in the Harold Price house in Scottsdale—$900 total, less 20-percent discount. Wright made a gift of them but later sent

Price a bill.[115] Besinger remembers driving to San Francisco in a pick-up truck in 1955 during his apprenticeship to get parts of the glazed-tile Chinese gateway that Wright bought as decoration to be distributed around various places at Taliesin West.[116]

Wright mounted a Japanese screen on the wall of his personal office in San Francisco. That office was dismantled in 1988 under Green's supervision and is now installed in the Carnegie Museum of Art in Pittsburgh, complete with the original screen, a late and decorative painting of a plum tree. Influenced by his association with Wright, Green collected Asian art for his own residence as well as for the homes of his clients; there is a screen with pine tree on the wall of his office.

Wright made his first purchases from Gump's at least as early as 1941, at which time he had something of a run-in with A. Livingston Gump (1869–1947), the president. Gump was dunning the architect for an unpaid bill on an assortment of Chinese artifacts such as Han ceramics and Ming lacquer screens, and suggested that some of his "affluent friends" guarantee his account.[117] Wright adopted a pose of righteous indignation: "Well, I can make a mistake and so can you. I would never knowingly do any business with a man who wanted my account guaranteed by somebody.... We have had a nice time leading each other to water but neither could make the other drink. Nevertheless, even as I see you now, I still like you."[118]

Later Wright did business with Richard B. Gump (1906–1989), the son, who sold him a "Japanese gong" in the 1940s: "We hope that you find someone who will benefit the eyes and ears of the Wright Foundation by presenting you with that great Japanese gong. Why not design your next house in a pear shape to match the tone of this magnificent instrument?"[119] The item in question may be the large Chinese Daoist temple bell that hung from a tree in the tea circle on the hill garden in Wisconsin. As late as November 1958, the year before he died, Wright received this telling note from Gump: "Were you hinting for a gift of the rooster by any chance? If so, may I hint that we have a small bill past due? Then let's speak of the more spiritual aspects of gift-giving. Unfortunately we live in a very material world and our maintenance therein depends on vulgar collections. Let me hear from you with or without insults."[120]

Who could deny credit to the world's greatest architect? As Wright's lawyer observed with some scepticism in 1928: "His friends apparently feel that the best policy to pursue is to keep Mr. Wright's good will at any cost in the hope that Mr. Wright will take care of his obligations out of his generosity."[121] Martin once told Wright that he was the kind of fellow "who was always just going to have money but who never quite did."[122]

When he worked on the Guggenheim Museum commission during the 1950s Wright had a permanent base of operations in New York. He kept a grand suite on Fifty-ninth Street on the third floor at the Plaza, his favorite hotel, with a red-and-purple interior of his own design, accentuated with gold leaf (ill. 202). (Suite 223, which he called Taliesin East, was dismantled after his death.) Here he crystallized what one critic called "the posture of an iconoclast."[123] He was interviewed by newspapermen and saw clients in two rooms filled with art from his collection: his Georgia O'Keeffe oil painting, an Indian stone sculpture

from French and Company, a large Chinese Zhou-dynasty (c. 11th century–256 B.C.) bronze vessel, a Han-dynasty ceramic *hu*, and several late-eighteenth-century triptychs by Eishi, somewhat soiled and faded, set out on an easel.[124] Wright surrounded himself with what he valued so people would know how to judge him. An early eighteenth-century Korean dragon jar made a dramatic centerpiece (ill. 203). Just over sixteen inches high, this white porcelain storage jar, probably intended for court use, is decorated with a single dragon among clouds. The design is painted in underglaze iron-brown with direct, powerful brush strokes. Olgivanna and the Frank Lloyd Wright Foundation sold the jar at auction in New York in 1967 for $1,000; it was later

202.
Wright's suite at the Plaza Hotel, New York, with a Korean dragon jar on a table and late-eighteenth-century Japanese prints propped against an easel at the rear left. December 1958

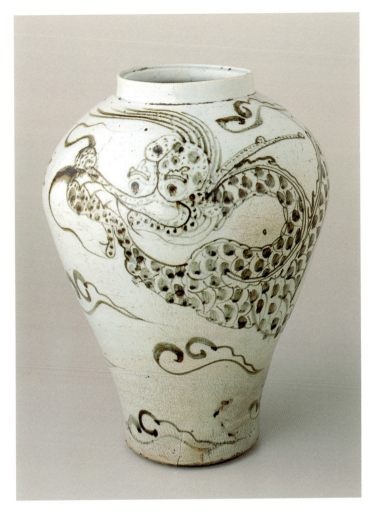

203.
Dragon Jar. Korea, Cho-
son period, eighteenth
century. Porcelain with
underglaze iron-oxide
painting, 17 x 13 in. The
Minneapolis Institute of
Arts, Gift of Louis W.
Hill, Jr.

Wright purchased this
jar in New York and
used it to decorate his
suite at the Plaza Hotel
("Taliesin East") during
the 1950s (ill. 202),
when he was supervis-
ing construction of the
Guggenheim Museum.
It was sold in 1967 at
auction at Parke-Bernet
Galleries, New York
(sale 2636, lot 342), for
$1,000.

given to the Minneapolis Institute of Arts by Louis Hill, Jr., a Saint Paul collector. Thirty years later Wright's jar probably has a market value of at least several hundred thousand dollars: in 1996 a large eighteenth-century dragon jar sold at auction at Christie's, New York, for a world-record $8 million. Had he foreseen the boom in Korean porcelains, Wright might not have filled his jar with a top-heavy cluster of flowering branches. On the other hand, he received pleasure from his collection for the very reason that he did put everything to use.

On his midtown walks the architect would stop off to visit his favorite Asian art dealers, sometimes accompanied by his friend the sculptor Isamu Noguchi (1904–1988). Between 1947 and 1952 he bought almost $12,000 worth of Chinese carpets and Ming jardinières for Spring Green from Mitchell Samuels at French and Company on East Fifty-seventh Street. Wright postponed payments as long as he possibly could, castigated Samuels for having the effrontery to send him a bill, and forced him to literally beg for even a meager down payment. Samuels was still begging in 1955. Their correspondence over "filthy lucre" is painful to read. "I wish that we went back to the wampum days," Samuels wrote, "and that seashells were legal tender."[125]

The architect started buying Chinese paintings, ceramics, and sculpture from Ralph M. Chait (1892–1975) on East Fifty-eighth Street off Fifth Avenue as early as 1945. In 1947 he ordered Chait to ship no fewer than nine Han-dynasty green-glazed ceramic *hu* to Spring Green. They were specially reduced to $1,000 each. When Chait asked him to pay the long-overdue bill the next year, Wright responded coyly: "Dear Ralph Chait: Soon—we are approaching the apple cart."[126] The architect bargained well and hard and Chait was pleased to do business with him because of his appreciation of Asian art.[127] Nevertheless, when Chait was thinking of moving to a new location in the late 1950s he turned down Wright's offer to build him a new gallery.

Wright's traveling exhibition *Sixty Years of Living Architecture* opened on 23 October 1953, on a vacant lot that was the site of the future Solomon R. Guggenheim Museum on Fifth Avenue. For this temporary display, his apprentices spent the better part of the summer and fall building a mock-up of a prefabricated, two-bedroom house (a Usonian house) that would cost its owner no more than $30,000–35,000, modestly priced for the average American family.[128] No mention was made, however, of the

204.
Olgivanna and Frank
Lloyd Wright in the liv-
ing room of the model
Usonian house, New
York, on the occasion
of the opening of his
Guggenheim Museum
exhibition *Sixty Years of
Living Architecture*.
1953

extra expense of decorating with Chinese and Japanese art. Apparently, a house was just not comfortable for Wright without Asian art. On 5 October, a few weeks before the opening, he purchased a two-panel eighteenth-century Japanese screen of geese and reeds under a bare willow in winter from Joseph U. Seo (?–1998) on Madison Avenue for $250 (ill. 204). This screen (still in the collection of the Frank Lloyd Wright Foundation) was installed flat against the brick wall at the far end of the living room of the Usonian house, abutting its fireplace. Reminiscent of Wright's brilliantly placed Hollyhock House screens, it must have been a dramatic focal point as one turned to enter the room.

The screen appears to be "framed" above by the natural-block pierced pattern along the top of the brick wall. It creates an imagined window opening onto a winter landscape, complementing the enclosed garden visible through the floor-to-ceiling glass wall on one side of the room. A fourteenth-century Japanese wood lion-dog (*koma-inu*), a Shinto sculpture, stood on a ledge overhead; it was part of the same purchase from Seo and cost $150.[129] Wright also bought a pair of massive, carved stone Chinese lions (30 inches high; 52 inches long) from Chait on 6 October 1953, for $2,000 (together with a Chinese wood statue of a seated Lohan, a disciple of the Buddha) especially for use in

205.
Frank Lloyd Wright. Entrance to the model Usonian house, New York, constructed for *Sixty Years of Living Architecture*. 1953

For his exhibition Wright borrowed the Calder mobile from the Guggenheim Museum and bought the Chinese lion from Ralph Chait in New York.

this exhibit (ill. 205).[130] The architect sent his "boys" to pick them up in a truck—they weighed about five hundred pounds each and may originally have lined the pathway to a Song-dynasty (960–1279) imperial tomb. One graced the specially designed exhibition pavilion, the other stood at the entrance to the model house. After the show closed Wright took the lions to Taliesin as garden decoration. They were sold at auction in 1967 for $1,500.[131]

Two or three times a year Wright slipped away on a secret mission to Joseph U. Seo's Oriental Art Gallery (ills. 206–208). Upon entering the sixth-floor gallery on Madison at Fifty-seventh Street he would always ask: "What do you have for me?" Wright impressed the dealer as egotistical ("he acted as though he were an expert"), authoritarian, self-centered, and extraordinary. Seo remembered the time Wright urged him to present items to the Frank Lloyd Wright Foundation as tax-deductible gifts. This was a ploy the architect had tried with Samuels as well.[132] Wright bought many Japanese prints from Seo, including a collection of fifty *surimono*, and a complete set of the so-called Reisho Tōkaidō for $400.[133] Once he came with the director of the Guggenheim Museum and tried unsuccessfully to talk him into buying a pair of stunning eighteenth-century screens of cranes associated with the style of Ogata Kōrin; Seo sold them to the Freer Gallery of Art in 1956. Wright purchased the left half of an eighteenth-century Tosa-school screen with scenes from the *Tale of Genji* from Seo in 1956 or later. The pair had been sold as individual lots at a Parke-Bernet auction in New York in January 1956: the right half went to Mary Griggs Burke, whose collection of Japanese art is now world famous.[134]

An irrepressible collector, Wright died owing money to both Chait and Seo.

MRS. WRIGHT DISPOSES

A postwar building boom made Wright prosperous but also invited the scrutiny of the Internal Revenue Service. Money was needed to pay off delinquent taxes, including penalties going

206.
School of Iwasa Matabei. *Woman Playing Shamisen and Woman Reading a Letter.* Edo period, early seventeenth century. Framed panel; ink, color, gold, and gold and silver leaf on paper, 51 x 22¼ in. The Frank Lloyd Wright Foundation (1105.015)

This painting, one of two Matabei-school paintings in Wright's collection, was probably originally mounted with others on a pair of six-panel screens as scenes of fashionable courtesans in the pleasure quarter of Kyoto. Wright purchased the two paintings from Joseph U. Seo in New York in 1954 for $150.

Top

207.
Anonymous. *Kitano Shrine in Kyoto*. Edo period, seventeenth century. Six-panel screen; ink, color and gold leaf on paper, 34¾ x 87½ in. The Frank Lloyd Wright Foundation (1185.028)

208.
Studio of Kano Motonobu (1476–1559). *The Four Worthy Accomplishments*. Muromachi period (1392–1573), mid-sixteenth century. Sealed: Motonobu. Six-panel folding screen; ink and light color on paper, 59⅛ x 134⅝ in. The Frank Lloyd Wright Foundation (1185.035)

The four worthy accomplishments of a Chinese gentleman, rooted in Daoist ideals of retirement and harmony with nature, were music, a board game called *go* in Japanese, calligraphy, and painting. Music and *go* are represented on this right-hand screen of a pair. Two attendants carry the *gin* (a relative of the Japanese koto) of the scholar, who pauses on the bridge. Wright acquired this screen in the 1950s but did not display it.

back to 1940, at which time Wright had decided unilaterally that the newly established Frank Lloyd Wright Foundation was a tax-exempt educational institution. After his death in 1959 there came a time of reckoning and the Asian collection was pressed into service. More than 150 Chinese and Japanese ceramics, lacquers, bronzes, and sculptures from Taliesin were sold at auction through Parke-Bernet in New York in December 1967 for $61,155.[135]

The sale of Wright's print collection in the mid-1960s was preceded by a show in January 1962 at the Municipal Art Gallery in Barnsdall Park, Los Angeles, the site of Barnsdall's Hollyhock House (ill. 209). Specialists in Chicago catalogued the 115 prints, which they appraised at $13,000; the architect's son Lloyd designed the installation. There was an unwelcome flurry of excitement when one dealer surfaced to insist Wright had never paid for some of the prints, a reprise of a similar unfortunate incident in 1913.[136] The subsequent sale of these prints was handled by Orrel P. Reed, Jr. (b. 1921), a fine-print dealer in Los Angeles. (According to Reed, Olgivanna cried when he balked at selling the fine Japanese screens and Chinese carpets.)[137] In 1965 trunkloads of ukiyo-e were shipped to Reed, who spent eight months cataloguing every item and eventually sold a total of nearly 6,000 prints (including "many thousands of poor prints"). In 1966 he appraised 194 illustrated books and bound series of prints at about $31,990.[138] Only a small percentage of these sales can still be tracked today. Reed sold 515 individual sheets (including the 115 prints in the 1962 Los Angeles show) to the Grunwald Center for the Graphic Arts at UCLA for high prices in 1965 and 1966.[139] These are mainly Hokusai and Hiroshige (the Hōeidō Tōkaidō, the *Hundred Views*, and so on), but there are some outstanding eighteenth-century figure prints as well (ills. 210, 211). The Pasadena Museum (now the Norton Simon Museum) also acquired 390 Wright prints through Reed, all donated by benefactors of the museum between 1966 and 1975. Of these, 299 are by Hiroshige. There are twenty-one Hokusai, and a smattering of figure prints by Utamaro, Eishi, and the Katsukawa artists, among others. Dr. Richard Lane, an ukiyo-e scholar and dealer living in Kyoto, took over $7,000 worth of prints on consignment from Reed in late 1969, mainly Hiroshige of mixed quality but the *Hundred Views* sometimes involved three or four of the same design, the best being quite good.[140] There was also a bulk sale of thousands of prints to the Los Angeles-based actor Vincent L. Price (1911–1993), the "Master of Menace," who was not only an avid collector and connoisseur, but also art consultant for Sears, Roebuck and Company. Sears sold Japanese prints through a gallery in its Chicago store.

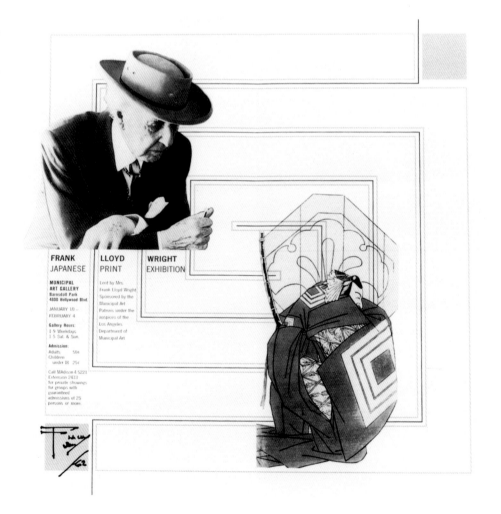

209.
Advertising brochure for *Frank Lloyd Wright: Japanese Prints Exhibition* at the Municipal Art Gallery, Barnsdall Park, Los Angeles, California, 10 January–14 February 1962. Collection of Nicholas, Robert, and Oliver Gillham

This was a posthumous exhibition of Wright's Japanese prints, preceding their sale.

210.
Katsukawa Shunshō.
"The Red Danjūrō":
Ichikawa Danjūrō V in a
"Shibaraku" Role. 1777.
Color woodcut,
hosoban. Collection of
the Grunwald Center for
the Graphic Arts, UCLA,
1965 (1965.30.11). Purchased from the Frank
Lloyd Wright Collection

Danjūrō V, the leading
actor of the 1770s and
1780s, is shown from
an unconventional viewpoint, silhouetted
before the divided curtain bearing the large
gingko-leaf crest of the
Nakamura Theater. (The
curtain has faded from
blue to a dull buff color.)
Danjūrō is hunched over
like a coiled spring,
preparing to shout out
"Shibaraku" (Wait a
moment), the dramatic
highlight of the play.

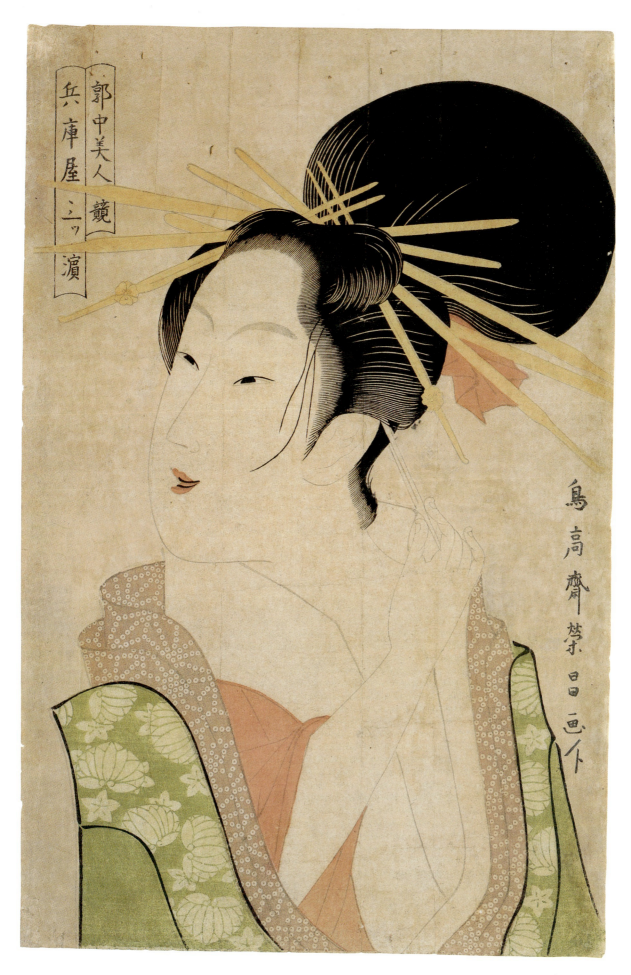

郭中美人競
兵庫屋
三ッ濱

鳥高齋榮昌画

211.
Chōkōsai (Hosoda)
Eishō (active
1780–1800). *The Cour-*
tesan Mitsuhama of the
Brothel Hyōgoya (*Hyō-*
goya Mitsuhama), from
the series *A Competi-*
tion of Beauties from
the Licensed Quarter
(*Kakuchū bijin kurabe*).
c. 1795. Color woodcut
with mica ground, *ōban*.
Collection of the Grun-
wald Center for the
Graphic Arts, UCLA,
1965 (1965.30.23). Pur-
chased from the Frank
Lloyd Wright Collection

JAPAN AS REFUGE

For Wright, Japan was an arena where he could excel both as an architect (the Imperial Hotel project came at a time when commissions at home were rare) and as a competitive businessman. "America…has taken to prints as she takes to everything," he once said, "reckless of cost and determined to win—whatever that may mean."[141] He recognized the opportunism of his acquisition of woodcuts in Japan at a time when money was scarce there, but he also had the perception to acknowledge an element of escapism in the lure of the East. "I wanted to get away from the United States," he wrote of his 1917 trip to Japan:

> I still imagined one might get away from himself that way—a little. In spite of all my reasoning power and returning balance I was continually expecting some terrible blow to strike. The sense of impending disaster would hang over me, waking or dreaming.… I looked forward to Japan as refuge and rescue.[142]

Wright found solace in Asia. He described the collections formed in the early twentieth century (including his own) as

212.
Wright with a sixth-century Chinese marble Buddhist triad in the living room at Taliesin II. 1924

"shrines for the artist pilgrims in need of worship or in search of light."[143] His preoccupation with the natural beauty of Japan and what he perceived to be the spirituality of its people has much to do with his ethnic roots in the "Driftless Area" of southwest Wisconsin, a region with rolling green hills and fantastic rock formations that was miraculously saved from glacial destruction and residual drift. Taliesin lies twenty miles from Richland Center, the place of his birth in 1867. Most of his life was connected in some way to the land of his family, his own paradise.[144]

Throughout his life he surrounded himself with Asian art, tangible evidence of an exotic, idealized culture that captured his imagination and appealed to his romantic sensibility and love of nature. His preference for images of preindustrial Japan is understandable in a man of his generation. Vincent Scully has said of Wright that his "time, his day, his age" were those of late nineteenth-century America. "He was the embodiment of its most tenacious attitudes: of its supreme confidence in the common future, and of its desperate, complementary yearning for pre-industrial, sometimes pre-civilized, images and symbols to root itself upon."[145]

213.
Taliesin II. Loggia with an eighteenth-century Japanese wood sculpture of Amida, Buddha of the Western Paradise. c. 1915–25

214.
Olgivanna Wright with
Chinese Ming-dynasty
cast-iron Guanyin in the
pose of "royal ease," at
Taliesin III. 1936

A few years ago the
statue was vandalized;
the missing head has
been replaced by a
replica.

Wright was also attracted to the spiritual side of Japan and wrote about it with painfully muddled sentimentality: "I went to Japan sufficiently alive to our sins and shortcomings as material people," he wrote in 1906. "I came back believing the Japanese a truly spiritual people…. To contrast their pure and delicate art with the mass of Western art is to contrast the spiritual lines and exquisite grace of the single flower with the material richness of the much cultured rose: to contrast the symbol with the literal; the sensuous with the sensual; chastity and restraint with incontinence and gluttony…." He thought the life of the Japanese was harmonious with "the heart of Nature."[146] In his autobiography he professed that "spiritual significance is alive and singing in everything concerning the Japanese house…. The Japanese lavish loving care on their beautiful things. To them beautiful things are religious things and their care is a great privilege."[147]

It is impossible to ignore the proliferation of Buddhist painting and sculpture in his home and studio, often close to the hearth, the symbolic household center (ill. 212). He created visually exciting ritual spaces by carefully placing Buddhist devotional icons in almost every room, often mounted appropriately high on a ledge and in key locations in the garden (ills. 81, 164, 213, 214, 216). Wright had no religious affiliation; he liked to say his church was "Nature." That he surrounded himself with Buddhist art in no way betrayed a serious commitment to the religion. Apart from having visited many temples and shrines in Japan (probably with an eye to their aesthetics of structure and shape) there is no evidence that he studied or discussed Buddhist doctrine—it was more a vague aura of "spirituality" that energized him—but he was refreshingly open-minded in an era when most would have called these alien images pagan.

215.
Head of the Bodhisattva Guanyin. China, Ming dynasty, c. 1500. Cast iron, 13¾ in. high

Wright displayed this head in the living room at Taliesin. It was sold by the Frank Lloyd Wright Foundation in 1967 at Parke-Bernet Galleries, New York (sale 2636, lot 142), for $1,000.

Occasionally he would quote hoary phrases from the Daoist sage Laozi, which he gleaned from *The Book of Tea*, written in Boston in 1906 by the Japanese art critic and connoisseur Okakura Kakuzō (1862–1913). When Wright began to speak of houses as vessels of space in the 1920s, he credited Laozi.

Dominating the sight lines in the living room like the figurehead on the prow of a ship is the Ming-dynasty standing figure of the compassionate Bodhisattva Guanyin (Avalokiteshvara in Sanskrit and Kannon in Japanese), an image that gives the large room a "buzz" of sanctity (ills. 201, 216). Wright called it the "spirit of the place." Like many Westerners, he was quite attracted to this androgynous Buddhist deity, perhaps because it was so accessible, compassionate, and feminine, qualities also associated with the familiar figure of the Virgin.[148] Early photos of the fireplace in the drafting studio at Taliesin show a Japanese Buddhist painting directly above the hearth. It is the descent of

216.
Taliesin III. Living room with a Chinese statue of the Bodhisattva Guanyin, a Japanese screen, and a lampshade Wright made from a fragment of an eighteenth-century noh robe. c. 1937

Amida, Buddha of the Western Paradise, the most desireable of the Buddhist paradises, and his heavenly host—an image more appropriate to deathbed rituals, but what Westerner would care about the actual meaning? There was also a Japanese wood statue of the Thousand-armed Kannon and a Chinese Ming-dynasty cast-iron head of a Buddha (ills. 218, 219). Wright liked to imagine that the "Studio Buddha," as the head was known, conveyed wise thoughts to the draftsmen as they worked. In his "dialogue" with the Buddha published in *Architectural Forum*, January 1951, he said that "in Oriental Art the great Buddha taught his prophets other words to use than 'repose.' Some of them are familiar in the drafting room at Taliesin. Some of them we do not yet understand. But the expression of this ancient cast-iron head of the Studio Buddha, changing with the sun, sometimes pervades our thought." Asked what it had meant to Wright—what hidden meaning this Buddhist image might have had for the architect—a wise Edgar Kaufmann, Jr., gave this prosaic explanation: "Oh, Wright had lots of those things; he liked them because they were cheap in those days."[149] Whether a Buddha or a Momoyama screen, "those things" did have magical powers in Wright's mind. "If the eye rested on some ornament," he said of his collection, "it could be sure of worthy en-

Opposite

218.
Taliesin III. Studio fireplace with Buddhist art. late 1920s

The eighteenth-century Japanese painting *Descent of Amida, Buddha of the Western Paradise, and Attendant Bodhisattvas* was framed by Wright and placed above the fireplace mantel in his studio by 1924. Also visible are a Japanese wood statue of the many-armed Kannon, the Buddhist deity of compassion and wisdom, and a Chinese head of a Buddha known as the "Studio Buddha" (ill. 217). The architectural models are two early unbuilt commissions, the Chicago Abraham Lincoln Center and the *San Francisco Call* Building.

217.
The "Studio Buddha."
Taliesin III

This head of a cast-iron Chinese Buddha dates from the Ming dynasty, sixteenth century, and measures 18 inches high. Wright displayed it in the drafting studio at Taliesin (ill. 218) and featured it in several publications, including *Architectural Forum*, January 1948. Today the head is on view in the Cabaret Theater at Taliesin West in Scottsdale, Arizona.

tertainment. Hovering over these messengers of Taliesin from other civilizations and thousands of years ago must have been spirits of peace and goodwill. They seemed to shed fraternal sense of kinship."[150]

Wright's collection, which he always touted as "extremely rare" or "unique," defined his status and confirmed his self-image as a genius, a man of truly superior insight and refinement. Much like van Gogh in Arles with his horde of Japanese prints, it set him apart as an initiate into the esoteric and rarified aesthetic of another culture. "The Japanese print," he assures us "is one of the most amazing products of the world, and I think no nation has anything to compare with it."[151] His preconceptions about Japanese art led him to describe prints in terms of every noble value he espoused as his own—democracy, spirituality, purity, and harmony with nature.

Wright moved easily between high and low art and valued screens and prints alike as stunning abstract designs. He knew how to pick them and it is fair to say that during the years he was building the Imperial Hotel his escalating involvement with Japanese art not only drove up the value of prints on the international market, but elevated him to the status of a discerning and much admired figure in the world of Asian art connoisseurs in America. Mansfield included Wright among the important collectors of Asian art in America in 1915, Frederick Gookin knew of "no better judge of the quality of prints," and Judson Metzgar believed that Wright, despite fierce competition, brought more and finer Japanese prints to America than anyone else, with the exception of Ernest Fenollosa.[152] This was a remarkable achievement for an architect. While it has been said that Wright's architecture, notably the Imperial Hotel, had little if any influence in Japan, Japan had a profound impact on Wright.

Opposite

219.
Anonymous. *Descent of Amida, Buddha of the Western Paradise, and Attendant Bodhisattvas.* Edo period, early eighteenth century. Three hinged panels; ink and color on paper, 50¾ x 44½ in. The Frank Lloyd Wright Foundation (1185.025)

NOTES

ABBREVIATIONS

AB	Aline Barnsdall
ADF	Arthur Davison Ficke
AG	Aaron Green
ALG	A. Livingston Gump
AAK	Adolph A. Kroch
AM	Alfred MacArthur
AW	Alexander Woollcott
BBP	Bruce Brooks Pfeiffer
BM	Blanche McFetridge
CKS	Cyril Kay-Scott
CLB	Caroline L. Burr
CLF	Charles Lang Freer
CLW	Catherine L. Wright
CS	Carl Schraubstadter
DDM	Darwin D. Martin
EA	Elsie Allen
EHH	Edwin H. Hewitt
EL	Emil Lorch
EM	Eugene Masselink
EPM	Edward P. McFetridge
EW	Sir Edmund Walker
EWUT	Sir Edmund Walker Papers, MSS. Collection 1, Thomas Fisher Rare Book Library, University of Toronto
FGA	Charles Lang Freer Papers, Freer Gallery of Art Archives, Smithsonian Institution, Washington, D.C.
FK	Fiske Kimball
FLW	Frank Lloyd Wright
FLWA	Frank Lloyd Wright Archives, Scottsdale, Ariz.
FWG	Frederick W. Gookin
FWL	Francis Little
GEC	George E. Cranmer
GB	George Banta
GNL	Gookin Family Papers, Special Collections, Newberry Library, Chicago
GW	Gordon Washburn
HA	Hayashi Aisaku
HHFJ	Horace H. F. Jayne
HJA	Henry J. Allen
HLH	Herbert L. Hahn
HM	Howard Mansfield
IM	Isabelle Martin
IW	Irwin Weinberg
JDL	John D. Larkin
JTS	John T. Spaulding
JUS	Joseph U. Seo
KEJ	Karl E. Jensen
KJB	Karen Johnson Boyd
KR	Kuki Ryūichi
KS	Katrina Spaulding
KT	Tomita Kojiro

KV	Katrina Veerhusen Collection, Chicago, courtesy of Pamela Veerhusen
LKH	Louise K. Hoult
LHS	Louis H. Sullivan
LNB	Louise Norton Brown
LVL	Louis V. Ledoux
LVM	Elvehjem Museum of Art, University of Wisconsin-Madison
LW	Langdon Warner
MA	Mary Ainsworth
MWB	Mary W. Baskett
MD	Marian Densmore
MIA	Archives, Minneapolis Institute of Arts
MK	Mitchell Kennerley
MMA	The Metropolitan Museum of Art Archives, New York
MS	Mitchell Samuels
MSG	Marie Sieboth Gookin
OKB	Otto Karl Bach
PFLF	Philip Fox La Follette
PG	Paul Gardner
RBG	Richard B. Gump
RK	Roland Koscherak
RLH	R. L. Hopkins
RLJ	Richard Lloyd Jones
RMC	Ralph M. Chait
RMS	Rudolph M. Schindler
SCBR	Sigisbert Chretien Bosch Reitz
SH	Shugio Hiromichi
SHM	S. H. Mori
SM	Stanley Marcus
SPS	Sophie Pauline Gibling Schindler
ST	Darwin D. Martin Papers (MO355), Stanford University Libraries, Department of Special Collections
SUNYB	Frank Lloyd Wright-Darwin D. Martin Papers (MSS. 22.8), University Archives, State University of New York at Buffalo
WBG	Walter Burley Griffin
WEM	William E. Martin
WHM	William H. McFetridge
WLK	William Lawrence Keane
WSS	William Stuart Spaulding
WSSA	William Stuart Spaulding Archives, Santa Barbara, courtesy William Stuart Morton-Smith
WWP	William Wesley Peters

Letters are credited to a particular collection only if they are not in the Frank Lloyd Wright Archives, The Frank Lloyd Wright Foundation, Scottsdale, Arizona. The foundation correspondence is indexed in Anthony Alofsin, ed., *Frank Lloyd Wright: An Index to the Taliesin Correspondence*. It can be accessed on microfilm at the Getty Research Institute, Los Angeles, California.

For the notes an abbreviated style is used where a source is fully cited in the bibliography.

INTRODUCTION

1. Mirviss, with Carpenter, *The Frank Lloyd Wright Collection of Surinomo*, 1995.

2. The Metropolitan Museum of Art, New York; the New York Public Library; the Museum of Fine Arts, Boston; the Art Institute of Chicago; the Minneapolis Institute of Arts; the Allen Memorial Art Museum, Oberlin, Ohio; the Spencer Museum of Art at the University of Kansas, Lawrence; the Cincinnati Art Museum; the Frances Lehman Loeb Art Center, Vassar College, Poughkeepsie, New York; the Honolulu Academy of Arts; the Dallas Museum of Art; the Wriston Art Center at Lawrence University, Appleton, Wisconsin; the Norton Simon Museum, Pasadena, California; and the Grunwald Center for the Graphic Arts, UCLA.

3. As reported by Richard's son, Jenkin Lloyd Jones, in Secrest, *Frank Lloyd Wright*, 1992, 364.

4. John Lloyd Wright, *My Father, Frank Lloyd Wright*, 1992, 116–18.

5. For illustration see Gordon, "Wright's Way with Little Things," 1959, 233.

6. *Chicago Daily Tribune*, 22 April 1925 (unpaginated clipping). ST.

7. Frank Lloyd Wright, *An Autobiography*, rev. ed., 1943, 196. The 1977 Horizon Press publication of the autobiography is considerably revised and expanded. It was published long after Wright's death with editorial changes made not only by Wright but by others as well and should be used only with caution. The 1943 revised and expanded edition of the autobiography (reprinted in 1998 by Barnes and Noble Books, with identical pagination) is preferred.

8. Lancaster, *The Japanese Influence in America*, 1963, 221.

9. Thomas E. Tallmadge, *The Story of Architecture in America*, rev. ed. (New York: Norton, 1936), 229.

10. For Mount Fuji see Levine, *The Architecture of Frank Lloyd Wright*, 1996, 122; for the pagoda theory see Lancaster (1963), 162–65; Hearn, "A Japanese Inspiration for Frank Lloyd Wright's Rigid-Core High-Rise Structures," 1991; for a monograph on Wright and Japanese architecture see Nute, *Frank Lloyd Wright and Japan*, 1993.

11. Lilien, *"At Taliesin,"* 1936, 17.

12. Frank Lloyd Wright (1943), 205.

13. Ibid.

14. Transcript of a print party talk, 29 September 1957. FLWA.

15. Howard Mansfield was treasurer and Robert W. de Forest was president. For the latter see William McBrien, secretary to de Forest, to SCBR, New York, 7 October 1918. MMA.

16. Frank Lloyd Wright (1943), 118.

17. FLW to Darwin R. Martin, Jr., Spring Green, 28 May 1938.

18. For the significance of the imperial art collection in China see Ledderose, "Some Observations on the Imperial Art Collection," 1978–79, 39. For Wright and Griffin see Brooks, *The Prairie School*, 1972, 81; also FLW to WBG, Fiesole, Italy, 16 June 1910.

19. Frank Lloyd Wright, *An Autobiography*, 1932, 204.

20. Frank Lloyd Wright, *Antique Color Prints*, 1917, unpag.

21. FLW to FK, Spring Green, 23 November 1928.

22. Frank Lloyd Wright, *Hiroshige*, 1906, 1–2.

CHAPTER 1

1. Frank Lloyd Wright, unpublished, undated essay prepared for Darwin D. Martin with a letter from FLW to DDM, Oak Park, 11 August 1906. SUNYB.

2. Quoted in Weisberg, "L'Art Nouveau Bing," 1979, 6.

3. Jōzuka, *Gashō Hayashi Tadamasa* and *Umi o wataru ukiyo-e*, 1972 and 1981; also *French Painting and Ukiyo-e: The Eye of Tadamasa Hayashi, a Bridge Between the Eastern and Western Cultures/Furansu kaiga to ukiyo-e: Tōzai bunka no kakehashi, Hayashi Tadamasa no me ten*, ed. Hasegawa Hiroshi et al., 1996.

4. For Matsuki see *"A Pleasing Novelty": Bunkio Matsuki and the Japan Craze in Victorian Salem*, 1993. For Yamanaka see Lawton, "Yamanaka Sadajirō," 1995, 80–93.

5. Theodore Robinson diaries, Frick Art Reference Library, New York, entry for 20 March 1894; Mansfield "Japanese Prints," 1899, 113; *Japanese Engravings*, 1894. In 1904 Bing sent a representative to New York to open a shop for the sale of ukiyo-e prints. For a monograph on Bing see Weisberg, *Art Nouveau Bing*, 1986.

6. The fullest treatment of Fenollosa is a two-volume study in Japanese: Yamaguchi, *Fuenorosa*, 1982. For discussion in English see Chisholm, *Fenollosa*, 1963; *Asiatic Art in the Museum of Fine Arts Boston* (Boston: Museum of Fine Arts, 1982); and scattered references in Ellen P. Conant, in collaboration with Steven D. Owyoung and J. Thomas Rimer, *Nihonga: Transcending the Past: Japanese-Style Painting, 1868–1969* (Saint Louis: Saint Louis Art Museum and the Japan Foundation, 1995).

7. Fenollosa, *Epochs of Chinese and Japanese Art*, 1912, 2: 197–99. Fenollosa's two-volume history of Far Eastern art was published posthumously by his widow.

8. Fenollosa, *The Masters of Ukioye* [sic], 1896.

9. Fenollosa, introduction to *Catalogue of The Exhibition of Ukioye* [sic] *Paintings and Prints*, 1898, 5. For Arthur Wesley Dow see Meech and Weisberg, *Japonisme Comes to America*, 1990, 163–79; Frederick C. Moffatt, *Arthur Wesley Dow (1857–1922)* (Washington, D.C.: Smithsonian Institution Press, 1977); Nancy Green, *Arthur Wesley Dow and His Influence* (Ithaca, N.Y.: Herbert F. Johnson Museum of Art, Cornell University, 1990).

10. There was a legal dispute between Kobayashi and Ketcham regarding ownership of the consignment, which was later sold by New York lawyer E. S. Hull. See Clark, *Ukiyo-e Painting in the British Museum*, 1992, 242. Buckingham eventually purchased more than forty prints from Ketcham; Freer came away with about thirty paintings.

11. Frank Lloyd Wright, *Frank Lloyd Wright, Collected Writings*, 1992, 1: 149. There are a handwritten version and undated typescript versions in the FLWA. "Twenty-five years ago" would be 1892, not 1896, but Wright was often inaccurate in remembering dates.

12. Nute (1993), 24–26.

13. Ibid., ills. 30, 33 illustrated in *Inland Architect* 34, no. 6 (1990), 5 plates.

14. Connely, *Louis Sullivan as He Lived*, 1960, 153.

15. Johnson, *A History of the World's Columbian Exhibition*, 1898, 413–16. Handy, *The Official Directory of the World's Columbian Exposition*, 1893, 468. In 1876 James Jarves claimed that architecture "in its noblest condition" is unknown in Japan. This is a sentiment that was slow to die. James Jarves, *A Glimpse at the Art of Japan* (New York: Hurd and Houghton, 1876), 21.

16. Scully, *Frank Lloyd Wright*, 1960, 13. "I knew little or nothing of the East until 1906 [sic] when I first went to Japan," Wright claimed in 1939 (see *Frank Lloyd Wright, Letters to Architects*, ed. Pfeiffer, 1984, 100). Kevin Nute suggests that the similarities between the description of a Japanese house by Morse in 1886 and by Wright in his autobiography are more than coincidental. Nute (1993), 37.

17. Brooks, *Writings on Wright*, 1981, 86–87.

18. Ibid., 187.

19. Brooks (1972), 79.

20. Frank Lloyd Wright (1932), 194.

21. The inscribed book is now in the collection of the Frank Lloyd Wright Home and Studio Foundation, Oak Park, Illinois.

22. Hanks, *The Decorative Designs of Frank Lloyd Wright*, 1979, p. 2 and fig. 1; also Quinan, *Frank Lloyd Wright's Larkin Building*, 1996, 74.

23. Guerrero, *Picturing Wright*, 1994, 30.

24. A copy of the 1902–3 brochure is in the John Howe collection at the State Historical Society of Wisconsin in Madison. It belonged to Howe's mother, who was a student at the school.

25. Mrs. Morris was the wife of a Shakespearean actor based in New York. The note was in a copy of the 1897 *House Beautiful* acquired by Kelmscott Gallery, Chicago. Scott Elliott to author, Benton Harbor, Mich., 19 September 1994.

26. The entire album of photographs is published and the views identified in *Frank Lloyd Wright's Fifty Views of Japan: The 1905 Photo Album*, ed. Melanie Birk, 1996. Tanigawa claims that although the Wrights and the Willits began the trip as a foursome, they soon parted ways and returned home separately. Tanigawa, "Wright the Tourist," 1996, 15–19.

27. Frank Lloyd Wright (1943), 194.

28. The register books with Wright's signature are illustrated in Tanigawa, *Raito to Nihon*, 1977, 49–52.

29. Transcript of a Sunday morning print party talk, Taliesin West, Scottsdale, Ariz., 5 February 1956. FLWA. The Shugakuin did not open to the public until 1906. Tanigawa deduces that Wright must have visited this garden at a later date. Tanigawa, "Wright the Tourist," 1996, 17.

30. Transcript of a Sunday morning print party talk, 21 March 1954, 8–9. FLWA.

31. Stipe, "Wright's First Trip to Japan," 1995, 22.

32. Most of the prints were loaned by Buckingham and Gookin, with a few contributed by Howard Mansfield and John H. Wrenn. For Wright's print see Gookin, "Catalogue of…Suzuki Harunobu," 1905, p. 29, no. 56.

33. Recently the architect's son David gave the Frank Lloyd Wright Home and Studio Foundation, Oak Park, about 150 prints (none particularly fine) as well as printed books and other decorative items, all a legacy of the 1905 voyage. For illustrations see *Frank Lloyd Wright's Fifty Views of Japan* (1996).

34. DDM to FLW, Buffalo, 30 December 1905. SUNYB.

35. Henry D. Smith II, "Hiroshige in History," 1997, 33–34.

36. The only evidence linking pillar prints with actual pillars is one color woodcut from the 1760s by Suzuki Harunobu. It shows a long, narrow print mounted as a hanging scroll on an interior pillar of a house. For illustration see Pins, *The Japanese Pillar Print,* 1982, 17.

37. For American Japonisme see Meech and Weisberg (1990); also Meech-Pekarik, "Early Collectors of Japanese Prints and the Metropolitan Museum of Art," 1984, for a more detailed study of Genthe and Weir.

38. For the Oak Park and River Forest events see "Unity Club of Unity Church," *Oak Leaves,* 24 March 1906, 12; "Fifteenth Annual," *Oak Leaves,* 28 April 1906, 11; Margaret Williams Norton, "Japanese Themes and the Early Work of Frank Lloyd Wright," 1981, 4.

39. Quoted in Brooks (1981), 87.

40. Frank Lloyd Wright (1943), 118–19.

41. Quoted in Brooks (1981), 91.

42. Mahony later came to dislike Wright intensely and was unwilling to share credit with him (as he with her). Defending her contribution, she claimed that all of the architects in the "Chicago school" began to collect prints after seeing the Japanese exhibit at the 1893 fair. Marion Mahony, 1940 interview with Grant Manson, Grant Manson papers, Oak Park Public Library.

CHAPTER 2

1. Martin founded a chair of mathematics at the University of Buffalo in 1928 and endowed a scholarship at Buffalo Seminary. He was, among other things, a director of Buffalo City Planning Association, Buffalo Museum of Science, Buffalo Historical Society, New York State Historical Association, Buffalo Chamber of Commerce, Buffalo Symphony Society, and president and chairman of the board of Pine Mountain Settlement School in Kentucky, an occupational guidance institution for the underprivileged.

2. WEM to DDM, Chicago, 22 October 1902. SUNYB.

3. The Larkin Administration Building, finished in August 1906, has been described as an icon of modern architecture. See Quinan (1987).

4. Manson, *Frank Lloyd Wright to 1910,* 1958, 144.

5. Ibid.; see also FLW to DDM, Oak Park, 28 December 1905. SUNYB.

6. Frank Lloyd Wright, *Ausgefürte Bauten und Entwürfe von Frank Lloyd Wright,* 1910[–11], preface.

7. Giannini and Ostertag had collaborated on a similar wisteria mosaic for one of the mantels in Wright's 1899 Joseph M. Husser house in

Chicago. The Husser house wisteria mosaic was characterized in *The Architectural Review* in 1900 as having "vine trunks and a weeping profusion of wisteria sprays and pendent blossoms upon a ground dull gold below and bright gold above a suggested horizon. The white joints have been employed with great skill to delineate dainty stems and leaves of softer green and crackled gold. The sprays of blossoms are inlays of rosy white and pearly glass which fall in the airiest, sweetest fashion from the tangle of leaves below…. No monochrome can even suggest the exquisite beauty of this facing in its splendid play of iridescent color." Spencer, "The Work of Frank Lloyd Wright," 1900, 72. A preliminary drawing of cascading wisteria for the Martin house mosaic, now in the collection of the Metropolitan Museum of Art, is attributed to Wright. The art-glass windows in the Martins' dining room also have an abstract wisteria design, and Wright planted wisteria in the Martins' garden. Years later, in 1924, he designed a wisteria mosaic for the Ennis house in Los Angeles.

8. O'Hern, "Frank Lloyd Wright's Martin House," 1988, 47–48.

9. DDM to FLW, Buffalo, 14 February 1906, and FLW to DDM, Oak Park, 1 March 1906. SUNYB.

10. FLW (per Isabel Roberts) to IM, Oak Park, 31 October 1906. SUNYB.

11. Ibid.

12. By 1912, if not earlier, Mrs. Martin had hung one of her framed Hiroshige landscapes directly on the South Room fireplace, not a felicitous solution. A photograph of Mrs. Martin seated in front of the fireplace beneath the Hiroshige print is with the Wright-Martin papers. SUNYB. The hole for a nail from which the print hung is still visible on the fireplace.

13. Sanders, *The Craftsman,* 1978, 304–7.

14. The Roberts interior is documented in a photograph (FLWA 0808.0005). For Drummond see Brooks (1972), fig. 68.

15. See Gookin, *The Chicago Literary Club,* 1926, 124–25.

16. Recollection of Kathleen Van Deusen, whose mother was a Bryn Mawr classmate of Gookin's daughter, in conversation relayed by IW to author, 17 March 1995.

17. Gunsaulus and Kelley, "Frederick W. Gookin," 1936, 19; "Frederick William Gookin," *Chicago Literary Club Year Book for 1936–1937,* 1937, 109–11; "F. W. Gookin Dies; Oriental Scholar," *New York Times,* 19 January 1936, section 2, p. 8. For a bibliography of Gookin's writing consult Green, *Japanese Woodblock Prints,* 1993. Gookin charged Charles Freer a $25 daily fee for consulting work.

18. FWG to MSG, New York, 19 April 1911. GNL.

19. In 1926 Gunsaulus joined the staff of the Art Institute of Chicago as an assistant curator of Japanese art and when Gookin died, she succeeded him as curator of the Buckingham Collection of Japanese Prints. Information on Gunsaulus can be found in the Archives, Art Institute of Chicago. See Metzgar, *Adventures in Japanese Prints,* [1944], 75–76, for an eyewitness account of a Buckingham print party. Margaret Gentles, successor to Helen Gunsaulus at the Art Institute, wrote that other guests at Buckingham print parties included Henry O. Havemeyer, George Vanderbilt, and Ernest Fenollosa. Unfortunately, she gave no documentation. Gentles, "Clarence Buckingham," 1966, 211.

20. Art Institute publications sometimes list him as keeper, sometimes as curator.

21. The prints in the permanent collection were a small part of the thousands of Asian objects given in 1900 by Mr. and Mrs. Samuel Mayo Nickerson. Nickerson (1830–1914), chairman of the biggest bank in the city, was a founding trustee.

22. For more about Dow see Meech and Weisberg (1990), 163–79. Dow published his theories of abstract design, a synthesis of Eastern and Western aesthetics, in *Composition* (1899), a how-to design manual for art students and teachers relying heavily on examples taken from Asian art. His utilitarian exercises in line, mass, and color could be applied to painting, printing, photography, textile design, metalwork, and even woodwork. The book was a huge success—it went into twenty editions by 1938. Wright no doubt benefitted from the messages contained in *Composition.*

23. Kaufmann, "Frank Lloyd Wright's Architecture Exhibited," 1982, 4–5.

24. Deakin moved several times. Thayer invoices in the archives of the Spencer Museum of Art show him both in the Fine Arts Building and on Elkhorn in 1909, and at 2236 Warren Avenue in 1911. Wright also made purchases from Deakin (Metzgar [1944], 37). There was a Toyo Art Shop in the Fine Arts Building around 1911 (see Peattie, "The Fine Arts Building in Chicago" [1911]). Thayer later bought from Yamanaka in New York, and from the Hamilton Easter Field and the Judson Metzgar sales. Carol Shankel, "History of the Collection," in Keyes, *Surimono: Privately Published Japanese Prints in the Spencer Museum of Art,* 1984, 9; also Shankel, *Sallie Casey Thayer and Her Collection,* 1976, 26–30. Keyes published several hundred *surimono* from the Thayer collection. Metzgar cites Thayer as one of the important collectors of her day in his *Adventures in Japanese Prints.*

25. Sallie Casey Thayer to FLW, Chicago, 17 September 1909, archives, Spencer Museum of Art, Lawrence, Kansas. The Thayer invoices are in the archives of the Spencer Museum of Art.

Today there are only nine of the thirty-six views in the collection; the others may have been deaccessioned by the museum. The invoice for $2,000 from the New Gallery, which took a 10-percent commission, leaving Wright with $1,800, is dated 15 January; the year is not given but must be 1910. On this invoice prints are identified only by the name of the artist—there are about nine by Utamaro, for example—and therefore cannot be matched precisely with examples in the Thayer collection. The author is grateful for the assistance of Carolyn Chinn Lewis and Midori Oka at the Spencer Museum of Art, Lawrence, Kansas.

26. This sale is cited in FLW to DDM, Oak Park, 13 January 1911: "I have concluded the deal with Mrs. Thayer today (the lady who bought before) for $10,075." SUNYB.

27. Karl E. Jensen (Wright's secretary) to Mrs. W. B. (Mary) Thayer, Spring Green, 1 July 1933.

28. The firm of Hewitt and Brown designed many of the most important buildings in Minneapolis, among them the Minneapolis Telephone Building and St. Mark's Church.

29. Lancaster (1963), 220–23; Hess, *Their Splendid Legacy*, 1985, 14; Meech and Weisberg (1990), 127–29.

30. EHH to FLW, Minneapolis, 20 June 1908. MIA.

31. EHH to FLW, Minneapolis, 17 November 1908; FLW to EHH, Oak Park, 3 February 1909. MIA.

32. FLW to DDM, [Oak Park], 16 September 1909. SUNYB.

33. CLW to EHH, Oak Park, [27 October 1909]. MIA.

34. CLW to EHH, Oak Park, November 1909. MIA.

35. Quoted in *Frank Lloyd Wright: Letters to Clients*, 1986, 17.

36. DDM to FLW, Buffalo, 17 November 1910. SUNYB. By 1917 Wright's mortgage was only one of seventeen held by Martin; apparently he favored mortgages as a form of investment.

37. DDM to FLW, Buffalo, 12 November 1910. SUNYB.

38. FLW to JDL, [Chicago], 21 October 1910; FLW to DDM, Oak Park, 25 October 1910. SUNYB.

39. "Wright and Family Apart in One House to 'Save His Soul,'" *Chicago American*, 8 September 1911, afternoon edition, 2.

40. Kaufmann (1982), 27–28. For the Littles see Heckscher and Miller, *An Architect and His Client*, 1973; also Jordy, "The 'Little house' at the Metropolitan," 1983.

41. See Lancaster (1963), pl. 4 and fig. 69, for photographs of the interior before it was dis-

mantled. Other portions of the house have found their way into the Minneapolis Institute of Arts, the Museum of Art in Allentown, Pennsylvania, and the Dallas Museum of Fine Arts.

42. Francis Little's daughter, Eleanor Stevenson, to author, Wayzata, Minn., 14 September [1981]; Olive Johnson, "Frank Lloyd Wright's Early Work in Minnesota," 1940, typescript, Grant C. Manson papers, Oak Park Public Library.

43. DDM to FLW, Buffalo, 1 December 1910, and 9 December 1910. SUNYB.

44. FLW to DDM, [Chicago], 19 November 1910; FLW to DDM, [Chicago], 29 November 1910; the comment about Buckingham: FLW to DDM, [Oak Park], 3 December 1910; FWL to FLW, Minneapolis, 23 November 1910. SUNYB.

45. FLW to DDM, [Oak Park], 3 December 1910. SUNYB.

46. FLW to DDM, Oak Park, 5 December 1910. SUNYB.

47. FWL to FLW, Minneapolis, 6 December 1910. SUNYB.

48. FLW to DDM, Oak Park, 7 December 1910. SUNYB.

49. DDM to FLW, Buffalo, 9 December 1910. SUNYB.

50. FLW to DDM, Oak Park, 30 December 1910. SUNYB.

51. DDM to FLW, Buffalo, 4 January 1911; for Wright's remark on priceless treasures see FLW to DDM, Oak Park, 29 November 1910. SUNYB.

52. FLW to DDM, Oak Park, 13 January 1911. SUNYB.

53. See *Catalogue of the Private Collection of an Importer*, 1911. The sale included a first edition set of Hiroshige's Hōeidō Tōkaidō that sold for £120 (approximately $600); FLW to DDM, R. M. S. *Lusitania*, 21 January 1911, misdated 21 January 1910. SUNYB.

54. FLW to DDM, Oak Park, 9 June 1911. SUNYB.

55. DDM to FLW, Buffalo, 1 November 1911, and 8 November 1911. SUNYB.

56. 1920 Matsuki sale, lot 208. The author is much indebted to Shonnie Finnegan, archivist, State University of New York at Buffalo, and Annegret Richards for assistance in studying the prints in the Martin house collection.

57. FLW to DDM, Chicago, [postmarked] 2 April 1912. SUNYB.

58. See FLW to DDM, Chicago, 12 April 1912. SUNYB. There is a priced inventory list of the prints on Wright's Orchestra Hall stationery dated 11 April 1912. Courtesy Scott Elliott.

59. DDM to FLW, Buffalo, 24 April 1912. SUNYB.

60. DDM to FLW, Buffalo, 25 September 1913. SUNYB.

61. In 1922 Martin sent Wright a copy of the list as a reminder with a letter dated [Buffalo], 30 October 1922. Courtesy Scott Elliott.

62. The sale in 1911 was paid in three installments—January, February, and June. There were further sales in March and May of 1912.

63. FWG to FLW, Chicago, 20 May 1912.

64. Ibid.; also FWG to FLW, Chicago, 30 June 1912.

65. Two examples of Shunshō's work with Wright provenance in the Clarence Buckingham Collection are catalogued as 1925.2477 and 1925.2448. For the importance of Katsukawa Shunshō see Clark, "Katsukawa Shunshō and the Revolution in Actor Portraiture," 1992; Clark and Ueda, *The Actor's Image*, 1994. Gookin's magnum opus on Shunshō, begun in 1921, was never published. After working on the manuscript for many years, he visited collections in London, and there he was shown several albums filled with Shunshō's images that he had never even seen before; at this, he gave up in despair. There is a copy of the 276-page typed manuscript in the department of Asian art at the Art Institute of Chicago. David B. Waterhouse to author, Toronto, 5 March 1983. See also Green, "Lost in Time," winter 1984.

66. Frank Lloyd Wright (1943), 524.

67. Fernandez, *Eastern Winds*, 1982, 7.

68. Frank Lloyd Wright, *The Japanese Print*, 1912, 5, 6, 12, 16.

69. Transcript of a print party talk, 24 September 1952, 7. FLWA. Wright had a large collection of illustrated printed books. Those that remained in his collection after his death were sold or, if damaged, thrown out.

70. Lane, *Hokusai*, 1989, 116.

71. Transcript of a print party talk, 24 September 1952, 12–13, 24. FLWA. It was probably the Boston watercolorist and society painter Charles Hovey Pepper (1864–1950) who first remarked that the primary appeal of ukiyo-e prints to Westerners is their simplicity. "They eliminate all unessentials," he wrote in his 1905 booklet *Japanese Color Prints*. Wright may have adopted this message as his own. Before he launched his career in Boston, Pepper spent a year in Tokyo in 1903 collecting prints and designing his own woodcuts. Kobayashi Bunshichi printed them for him. See Meech and Weisberg (1990), 153–63.

72. FWG to MSG, New York, 30 December 1911. GNL. Gookin is reacting to a newspaper account: "Architect Wright in new romance with 'Mrs. Cheney,'" *Chicago Sunday Tribune*, 24 December 1911, 1.

73. FWG to FLW, Chicago, 30 June 1912. Another artist who tried to sell prints to the Metropolitan Museum of Art around this time was the New York painter Francis Lathrop (1849–1909). During the last fifteen years of his

life he accumulated an astonishing total of 12,000 woodblock prints, including 4,000 by Hokusai. Unpublished letters in the museum archives show that in 1908, a year before his death, he offered to sell his entire collection to the Metropolitan Museum of Art for the sum of $150,000. Museum officials flatly refused the offer.

74. Mansfield, "Japanese Prints: an address delivered by Howard Mansfield…," 1899, 128.

CHAPTER 3

1. Obituary, *New York Times*, 16 August 1937, 19, and *Boston Evening Transcript*, 16 August 1937, 11; Spaulding entry, *Harvard College Class of 1888*, 1938, 312–13.

2. "The Spaulding Collection," *Life* (1 Nov. 1948): 76.

3. Ferre, "The House and Garden of W. S. Spaulding, Esq." (1910). Also FWG to his wife, Marie Sieboth Gookin (MSG), Prides Crossing, 10 July 1912. GNL.

4. KS to W. G. Constable, curator of paintings at the Museum of Fine Arts, Boston, New York, 11 February 1948. Archives, Museum of Fine Arts, Boston. The 1909 trip to Japan was documented with photographs that remain in the collection of the Spaulding family. Dr. William Stuart Morton-Smith, William Spaulding's grandson, provided essential documentation pertaining to the 1909 trip, including a letter of 25 June 1909 from John Spaulding to Katrina Fairlee and a clipping ("William Stuart Spauldings to renew here acquaintances in smart set") from an unidentified Chicago newspaper dated 10 January 1924.

5. WLK to WSS, Yokohama, 20 April 1911. WSSA. I am indebted to Irwin Weinberg for careful analysis of the complex Keane-Spaulding financial records.

6. WLK to WSS, Yokohama, 9 July 1913. WSSA.

7. FWG to FLW, Chicago, 30 June 1912.

8. FWG to MSG, Prides Crossing, [11 July 1912]. GNL. Gookin's letters to his wife are not dated. Dates written on the letters were supplied at a later time by family members and are often inaccurate. Postmarked envelopes do not survive. Gookin does specify the day of the week, however. Letters are datable on the basis of internal evidence and calibration with a perpetual calendar.

9. The Spaulding catalogue cards, compiled by Gookin, have an accession date of July 1912 for this first purchase from Wright.

10. WSS to FLW, Boston, 19 December 1912.

11. WSS to FLW, Boston, 31 December 1912.

12. Frank Lloyd Wright (1943), 525.

13. WSS to FLW, Boston, 10 January 1913.

14. WSS to FLW, Boston, 6 February 1913. The Hiroshige goshawk is catalogued as 1921.6886 in the Spaulding Collection, Museum of Fine Arts, Boston.

15. For the story of the Imperial Hotel see *The Imperial: The First 100 Years*, 1990.

16. FWG to FLW, New York, 16 October 1911.

17. *The Imperial* (1990), 81, 94–95; Tanigawa (1977), 89–90.

18. *The Imperial* (1990), 65. For Hayashi, see ibid., 72 ff.

19. HA to FLW, Tokyo, 6 March 1948. The painting, signed *Rifū* (Tōsendō Rifū) and with two seals, is a hanging scroll in color on paper and is still in the collection of the Frank Lloyd Wright Foundation (1105.030). Rifū was active around 1720 and worked in the style of the Kaigetsudō school.

20. HA to FLW, Tokyo, 19 August 1913. For views of Hayashi's house see *Frank Lloyd Wright Retrospective*, 1991, 156.

21. FLW to DDM, Chicago, [postmarked] 10 January 1913. SUNYB.

22. *The Imperial* (1990), 96, 102.

23. WSS to FLW, Boston, 18 January 1913. The financial agreement between Wright and the Spauldings is first alluded to by William Spaulding in a letter addressed to Wright at the Imperial Hotel, dated Boston, 14 January 1913.

24. WSS to FLW, Boston, 17 February 1913.

25. WSS to FLW, Boston, 20 February 1913. Wright missed the boat for Japan and had a two-week delay, which he spent in California, departing finally at the end of January. He arrived in Tokyo by mid-February and was back in Chicago by late April.

26. FWG to FLW, Chicago, 23 January 1913.

27. FWG to FLW, Chicago, 3 April 1913. Includes preceding Spaulding comment.

28. FWG to MSG, Boston, [29 April 1913], and FWG to MSG, Boston, [30 April 1913]. GNL.

29. FWG to MSG, Boston, [30 April 1913]. GNL. The Straus-Negbaur collection was exhibited in Frankfurt at the Städelsches Institut in 1909–10; see Julius Kurth, *Japanische Holzschnitte aus der Sammlung Straus-Negbaur in Frankfurt a. M.* (Frankfurt am Main: H. Hahn, 1909), and Glaser and Rumpf, *Sammlung Tony Straus-Negbaur*, 1928.

30. FWG to FLW, Chicago, 26 June 1913. Wright's dispute was with Katherine M. Ball, a San Francisco collector/dealer and superintendent of drawing in the public schools.

31. WSS to FLW, Prides Crossing, 16 June 1913.

32. Ibid. Spaulding says he will meet Wright at the train on 9 July; see also FWG to FLW, Chicago, 21 June 1913: Gookin tells Wright he will meet him at Prides Crossing in two weeks;

FWG to FLW, Chicago, 2 July 1913: Gookin says he is hurrying to get Mr. Spaulding's triptychs mounted and back to him by the time they all meet at his house "next Wednesday." FLWA. FWG to MSG, Prides Crossing, 10 July [1913]. GNL. Gookin does not give a year, but does give the date of "Thursday morning, July 10th," which corresponds with 1913. Gookin tells his wife that he arrived the day before.

33. Frank Lloyd Wright (1943), 526–27. In the revised 1977 edition the editor (Wright?) adds that Ficke, Mansfield, and Chandler were also present. Wright liked to substantiate his own mythology: the Who's Who of "other collectors" was invented to glamorize the occasion. They are not mentioned by Gookin, who recorded every minute of this visit in daily letters to his wife, Marie. (All three collectors were guests of the Spauldings at other times, however.)

34. WSS to FLW, Prides Crossing, 29 July 1913.

35. WSS to FLW, Boston, 24 January 1914. FLWA. For Gookin's comment see FWG to EW, Chicago, 8 March 1914. EWUT.

36. FWG to MSG, Prides Crossing, [10 July 1913]. GNL.

37. Frank Lloyd Wright (1943), 527.

38. Maginel, who later married Hiram Barney, had a large, seven-room apartment overlooking the Hudson River. See Hamilton, "Maginel Wright Barney: An Artist in Her Own Right," 1992, 7–8.

39. FWG to MSG, Prides Crossing, undated, [11 July 1913, continued on 12 July 1913], and undated, [13 July 1913]. GNL. Gookin's catalogue cards are kept with the Spaulding collection in the department of Asian and African art in the Museum of Fine Arts, Boston. The cards include the name of the vendor and date of purchase.

40. HM to Edward Robinson, director, Metropolitan Museum of Art, Peterborough, N.H., 25 September 1913. MMA. Mansfield's letter is quoted in full in Meech-Pekarik (1984), 111–12.

41. According to an interview with Shugio published in 1922, he spent those four years in America. Shugio, "Odoroku bakari no kyōki," 1922. However, Shugio's family documents indicate that he was sent to England and family oral history has it that he attended Oxford, although his name is not listed in Foster's *Alumni Oxonienses*. Apparently trivial but trustworthy evidence for his presence in England is found in *Saigetsu* (Time and tide), a historical novel by Shiba Ryōtarō published in 1969, in which Shugyō Kenkurō is mentioned in passing as an Oxford student in the early 1870s. See Shiba, *Saigetsu* (Tokyo: Kodansha Bunko, 1971), 564–65. These references were kindly provided by Shugio Ippei, nephew of Shugio Hiromichi.

42. Information about Shugio was first conveyed to the author in a letter from Shugio Ippei, Tokyo, 30 March 1983. For the Kiryū Kōshō Kaisha (sometimes incorrectly identified as Kiritsu Kōshō Kaisha) see Noguchi, *Ginza monogatari*, 1997, 228. I am indebted to Shugio Ippei for this reference. According to listings in New York residential directories for the 1880s, Shugio had both a wholesale and a retail store at 465 and 865 Broadway, respectively. There were four other Japanese working for the company's New York business in 1884. When Fukushima took over he changed the name of the company to Japanese Trading Company.

43. For the Tile Club see Millet, "The Tile Club," 1922, 78; also Ronald G. Pisano, *The Tile Club and the Aesthetic Movement in America* (New York: Harry N. Abrams, 1999), 103, where Shugio's name is written incorrectly as "Niromichi Shugio."

44. Theodore Robinson diaries, entry for 8 April 1894, Frick Collection Library. Others who acknowledged Shugio's help were the Japanophile Edward S. Morse, in the preface to his 1886 *Japanese Homes and Their Surroundings*, and the British ukiyo-e scholar Edward F. Strange, in his 1925 *The Colour-Prints of Hiroshige*.

45. SH to Weir, Georgetown, 26 May 1894, J. Alden Weir scrapbook, private collection. Doreen Bolger Burke provided this reference.

46. Kōshū, "Shugio Hiromichi shi o tou," 1911. In club records Shugio's first name, Hiromichi, is often written incorrectly as "Hiromich," probably because the final "i" is nearly silent. Shugio's sponsors for Grolier Club membership were two of the club's founders, Alexander Drake, director of *The Century Magazine*, and Samuel Marvin, superintendent of *Scribner's* manufacturing department.

47. La Farge, "La Farge on Japanese Art: In a Personal Letter to H. Shugio," *The Japan Magazine* 2, no. 6 (1911): 331. La Farge dated the letter 29 September 1898.

48. Shugio, *Catalogue of an Exhibition of Japanese Colored Prints and Illustrated Books*, 1889; reviewed in *Critic*, 13 April 1889. Shugio, *Catalogue of an Exhibition of Japanese Prints*, 1896. This summary of Shugio's career was first published in slightly more detail in Meech-Pekarik (1984), 107–9, and Meech, "Shugio Hiromichi and the Grolier Club," 1998, 79–90; for the posters see Meech and Weisberg (1990), 46. Shugio retained his membership in the Grolier Club until his death, and often sent gifts, including a marvelous large sketch for a painting of Chinese warriors by Utagawa Kuniyoshi (1798–1861). The framed sketch hangs over the fireplace in the fifth-floor meeting room of the club. For Shugio and Mansfield see CLF to SH, [Detroit], 30 September 1898. FGA, Letterpress Books, 4: 667.

49. Gookin, *The Chicago Literary Club*, 1926, 287; for Shugio's lecture see Modern Manuscripts (Chicago Literary Club), Special Collections, Newberry Library, Chicago.

50. This inscribed copy in the collection of Robert Vergez was brought to the author's attention by Professor Yamaguchi Keizaburō, Tokyo.

51. Metzgar [1944], 75–76.

52. Shugio's letter offering introductions, dated Tokyo, 18 March 1905, was first cited by Stipe (1995), 23, and is with the Lloyd Wright papers, copies of which are in the FLWA; SH to FLW, Tokyo, 1 May 1912: Shugio writes "Do let us know what you are doing and how you are since I parted with you in London two years ago. I often think of those pleasant days I spent with you there with pleasure." For Wright's stopovers in London see also Alofsin, *Frank Lloyd Wright — The Lost Years*, 1993, 61–62.

53. See Shugio, "Japanese Art and Artists Today," 1910.

54. Lawrence Binyon of the British Museum, quoted in Conant, "Refractions of the Rising Sun," 1991, 87.

55. Alofsin (1993), 62.

56. SH to FLW, Tokyo, 1 May 1912. For Shugio's essay on Hiroshige see "The Great Landscape Artist of the Ukiyoye School," *The Japan Magazine* 2, no. 7 (1911): 373–77.

57. SH to Matsuki Heikichi, Tokyo, 19 March 1913, and idem, 6 April 1913, courtesy Segi Shin'ichi, Tokyo.

58. FLW to SH, Spring Green, 22 August 1925. This is a letter of introduction for Dean Russell of the University of Wisconsin, who was on his way to Tokyo.

59. SH to FLW, Tokyo, 22 March 1921.

60. Frank Lloyd Wright (1943), 525–26.

61. Shugio assured Wright: "You are always welcome to use my godown while you are in need of it." SH to FLW, Tokyo, 19 February 1917.

62. Frank Lloyd Wright (1943), 527.

63. For the purchase see the eight-page handwritten list of prints on Imperial Hotel stationery with annotations by Wright in the FLWA (MSS. 1033.001). For Kobayashi's 1892 exhibition see Nagata, *Shiryō ni yoru kindai ukiyo-e jijō*, 1992, 105.

64. Lawton and Merrill, *Freer: A Legacy of Art*, 1993, 146; Yamaguchi, "Kobayashi Bunshichi jiseki," 1988, 7; "Japanese Prints Lost in the Earthquake," *The Literary Digest* (6 September 1924): 32. There is archival material pertaining to Kobayashi in the Freer Gallery of Art. For a good overview of Kobayashi's career, as well as the letter from Freer to Gookin dated 31 October 1900, see Clark, *Ukiyo-e Paintings in the British Museum*, 1992, 34–38. Clarence Buckingham ac-quired a number of prints from Kobayashi in November 1906. Kobayashi's printers worked for the American artists Helen Hyde and Charles Pepper. Kobayashi's Yokohama shop was the first place Arthur Wesley Dow visited the morning after docking on his 1903 visit to Japan.

65. Shugio was working out of the Taishō Exhibition Office in Tokyo, preparing for the 1914 domestic exposition. SH to FLW, Tokyo, 20 August 1913.

66. WSS to FLW, Prides Crossing, 3 September 1913; idem, 20 October 1913.

67. WSS to FLW, Prides Crossing, 26 October 1913. The income tax amendment to the Constitution was adopted by Congress on 25 February 1913.

68. WSS to FLW, Boston, 24 November 1913.

69. WSS to FLW, Boston, 11 January 1914. Spaulding includes a priced list of the prints. See also WSS to FLW, Boston, 16 January 1914.

70. WSS to FLW, Boston, 16 January 1914, and 21 January 1914. Charnley had sold the Spauldings some prints in December 1912. In the spring of 1914 Gookin arranged a similar "Print Fest" in Chicago for a small group of print devotees that included Ainsworth, Metzgar, and Ficke. They gathered in the rooms of the Chicago Literary Club in the Fine Arts Building for a one-day private exhibition of the collection of Henry Appleton, a retired British army colonel from Vancouver, B.C., who was well known as a big game hunter and a botanist. Appleton had spent several years in Japan, where he amassed prints (he had a sale at Sotheby's in London in April 1910), and he was passing through Chicago on a selling campaign. (He had success with the Spauldings in Boston in early April.) His prints, in particular his *surimono*, were known to be of exceptional quality and condition. Gookin also treated his fellow enthusiasts to a private viewing of the Buckingham prints at the Art Institute. FWG to EW, Chicago, 8 March 1914. EWUT. Gookin indicates that William Spaulding will be present but the plans may have undergone last-minute alterations because the colonel visited with the Spauldings in Boston on 7 April. WSS to FLW, Boston, 7 April 1914; see also "Japanese Color Prints Shown," *Chicago Daily Tribune*, 26 March 1914, 10.

71. For a biography of Ainsworth see Green, "Mary A. Ainsworth," 1986. Her collection was catalogued and published by Roger Keyes, *Japanese Woodblock Prints*, 1984. With only a few exceptions, it is not possible to determine which of Ainsworth's prints were acquired from Wright.

72. For a biography of Ficke see Green, "A Chat on Arthur Davison Ficke," 1983; also Metzgar [1944], 54. William Spaulding wrote Wright from Boston on 24 January 1914 to say: "We were all delighted with Mr. Ficke—he is a

thoroughly wise fellow—and most appreciative of really fine things—and he rarely slips up! Many times he wanted to keep on dreaming over certain treasures—which time forbade—but he is absolutely human and I liked him."

73. ADF to FLW, Davenport, 25 April 1916, and Wright's response written on the bottom of Ficke's letter, to be typed by his secretary.

74. SH to FLW, Tokyo, 10 June 1917.

75. WSS to FLW, Boston, 24 January 1914, and idem, 23 February 1914.

76. Twombly, *Frank Lloyd Wright*, 1979, 167.

77. John Lloyd Wright (1992), 80, 85.

78. Levine (1996), 109.

79. WSS to FLW, Boston, 7 May 1915.

80. WSS to FLW, Grand Cascapedia River, 19 July 1916.

81. FWG to MSG, Detroit, 22 October 1915. GNL. The board of directors of the Imperial met on 30 November and agreed to send Hayashi to the United States to find the best method of construction for the hotel, with final decision to be made by the board after his return. Hayashi wrote Charles Freer on 3 November to say: "I would have written you before this but the new hotel project was finally decided upon only a week ago." (HA to CLF, Tokyo, 3 November 1915. FGA.)

82. FWG to FLW, Chicago, 24 November 1915.

83. *The Imperial* (1990), 95–96; HA to CLF, Grand Canyon, Ariz., 8 January 1916. FGA. Yoshitake (Wright mistakenly calls him Yoshitaki in his autobiography) was fluent in English, having graduated with a degree in architecture from a school in Scranton, Pennsylvania. Sherman M. Booth to DDM, Chicago, 1 March 1916. ST. Kathryn Smith, "Frank Lloyd Wright and the Imperial Hotel," 1985, 299.

84. FLW to DDM, [Spring Green, postmarked], 24 April 1916. ST.

85. FLW to DDM, Chicago, 17 November 1916, and idem, 20 November 1916; DDM to FLW, Buffalo, 29 November 1916. ST.

86. "An important gift of Japanese color-prints," *Bulletin of the Minneapolis Institute of Arts* (1917). Some sixty of the remaining prints in the Little collection were sold to Steve Keye of Control Data in Minneapolis, and the rest (about one hundred faded pillar prints and Katsukawa-school *hosoban*) were acquired by London art dealer Robert Sawers from Donald Lovness, of Stillwater, Minnesota, in 1969 and again around 1976. Robert D. Jacobsen, The Minneapolis Institute of Arts, to author, Minneapolis, 6 October 1982.

87. Hiroshige designed only one other Tōkaidō set in the horizontal *ōban* format. Published around 1851 by Maruya Seijirō, it is known as the Marusei or Reisho Tōkaidō. The Tōkaidō Road, the shortest route between Kyoto and Edo (modern Tokyo), covered a distance of over three hundred miles and took at least two weeks to traverse on foot. In the summer of 1832 Hiroshige was invited to join a "travel group" on an official mission to Kyoto. Travel was becoming a national pastime and Japanese are notoriously sentimental about their famous "beauty spots." Sketches he made on this journey were reworked as designs for a series of prints loosely focusing on the fifty-three checkpoints that the military regime used to control traffic. Hiroshige skillfully evoked the pleasures and perils of the journey. He included the bridges at the beginning and terminus, the Nihonbashi (Japan Bridge) in Edo and the Sanjō Ōhashi (Great Bridge at Third Avenue) in Kyoto, for a total of fifty-five designs. The set was issued jointly in 1833–34 by two publishing houses, Hōeidō and Senkakudō, but the latter was quickly bought out by Hōeidō, and today the series, titled *Fifty-three Stations of the Tōkaidō*, is commonly known as the Hōeidō or Great Tōkaidō.

88. WSS to FLW, Grand Cascapedia River, 19 July 1916; WSS to FLW, Boston, 27 November 1916.

89. Hoffman, *Frank Lloyd Wright's Dana House*, 1996, 107, 109.

90. WSS to FLW, Boston, 19 February 1917; SH to FLW, Tokyo, 19 February 1917.

91. On 22 December, on the eve of his departure for Japan, his friends in Chicago gave Wright a farewell dinner. "Frank Lloyd Wright given farewell dinner," *Chicago Tribune*, 23 December 1916; for a careful study of Wright's voyages to Japan see Kathryn Smith (1985).

92. SH to FLW, Tokyo, undated, [spring 1917].

93. SH to FLW, Tokyo, 10 June 1917; WSS to FLW, Boston, 22 June 1917.

94. AM to DDM, Chicago, 23 June 1917. ST.

95. FLW to DDM, Spring Green, 10 July 1917. ST.

96. DDM to FLW, Buffalo, 14 July 1917. ST.

97. AM to DDM, Chicago, 8 July 1919. ST. MacArthur was general agent for the National Life Insurance Company in Chicago. For more about him see Secrest (1992), 332.

98. JTS to FLW, Boston, 17 March 1918.

99. WSS to FLW, Boston, 23 February 1914.

100. Shand-Tucci, "First Impressions on the Rediscovery of Two New England Galleries by Ralph Adams Cram" (1979), 6–9; idem, "The Time Is Wright," *Boston Phoenix*, 23 April 1999, 15. An undated letter of c. 1908 in the Archives of the Museum of Fine Arts to Dr. Arthur Fairbanks, the director, from Francis Stewart Kershaw, keeper of the Chinese and Japanese collections, and S. G. Warren, the president (who died in February 1910), documents the collaboration of associate curator Francis Curtis and Cram, with the advice of Japanese sculptor Niirō Chūnosuke.

101. WSS to FLW, Boston, 19 February 1917. FLWA. In his 1918 correspondence with the Metropolitan Museum's curator, Wright identifies these drawings as the "Spaulding print room" and as the "Exhibition Room for Japanese Prints." FLW to SCBR, Spring Green, 27 July 1918 (misdated 1917); FLW to SCBR, Spring Green, 2 September [1918]; FLW to SCBR, letter signed by Will Smith on behalf of FLW, Spring Green, 23 October 1918; Bosch Reitz, in-house memo dated New York, 6 November 1918: "I also return his drawing for a print room." All SCBR correspondence is in the MMA. The Spaulding country house was sold in 1948 and later demolished.

102. The sword fittings were most likely purchased from the Boston branch of Yamanaka and Company.

103. This feature would of course be anathema to any conservator concerned with insect infestation.

104. John Spaulding was still making purchases at the Charles Jacquin and Carl Schraubstadter sales in New York in January and February 1921.

105. A review of the catalogue is given in Metzgar [1944], 75. A marked sales catalogue in the department of Asian and African art, Museum of Fine Arts, Boston, shows that Gookin, Louis Ledoux, Mary Ainsworth, Arthur B. Duel, Yamanaka and Company, Charles Hovey Pepper, Harold Henderson, and Mrs. Carl Holmes were among the many successful bidders.

106. Memo from A. D. Larson, assistant treasurer of the Museum of Fine Arts, to E. L. Powers, Boston, 24 December 1971, Archives, Museum of Fine Arts, Boston; Tomita, "The William S. and John T. Spaulding Collection of Japanese Prints," (1922), 31; idem, "The William S. and John T. Spaulding Collection of Japanese Prints," *Bulletin of the Museum of Fine Arts*, 1941, 73; and Hickman and Swinton, *Utamaro* in *Bosuton bijutsukan 3/Museum of Fine Arts, Boston III*, 1978, 209; Metzgar [1943], 74.

CHAPTER 4

1. Chicago Architectural Club (1914), 39–40; also *The Work of Frank Lloyd Wright* (1914). Kaufmann (1982), 4–5.

2. Florence Patton, "Architects Quit Big Exhibit." *Chicago American*, 9 April 1914, home edition, section 1, p. 1.

3. SH to FLW, Tokyo, 18 March 1905. Lloyd Wright papers, courtesy Margo Stipe.

4. For Nomura see Paul, "A Creative Connoisseur," 1984, 12–21. For the January 1915 Boston auction see *Ancient Chinese and Japanese Nishiki and Kinran Brocades* (Boston: The Copley Society of Boston, 1914). The Nomura collection was featured in *Catalogue of Chinese and Japanese Brocades, Kinran, Nishiki, Tsuzure 1400 to 1812 A.D.: Collected by Shojiro Nomura* (Chicago: Art Institute of Chicago, 24 March–14 April 1915).

5. Possible evidence of a sale immediately following the show is a priced list of prints dated 26 December 1917. He priced Hokusai's *Great Wave* at $400 (FLWA, MSS. 1033.001).

6. Peattie, "The Fine Arts Building in Chicago," 1911, unpag.; Darling, "Arts and Crafts Shops in the Fine Arts Building," 1977, 79.

7. Levy (1917), 89; Wells, *The Arts Club of Chicago*, 1992, unpag. This recent history of the Arts Club erroneously suggests that there was no exhibition space until 1918.

8. Transcript of a print party talk, 24 September 1952. FLWA.

9. Frank Lloyd Wright, *Antique Color Prints from the Collection of Frank Lloyd Wright*, 1917, unpag.

10. Edgar Tafel, conversation with author, March 1994.

11. Packard, "Nihon bijutsu shūshūki," 1976, 140.

12. Louise James Bargelt, "Art," *Chicago Sunday Tribune*, 18 November 1917, part 8, p. 2; also an undated Chicago newspaper clipping (FLWA, 1025.011).

13. "Japanese Prints Background of Arts Club Opening Tea," *Chicago Daily Tribune*, 12 November 1917, 15.

14. The author is indebted to Irwin Weinberg, Chicago supersleuth, for the reference to Mme. X and many others from the Chicago press.

15. Hayashi, *Shunjū-sengoku jidai seidōki no kenkyū*, 1989, p. 136, no. 6. I am grateful to Thomas Lawton for this reference and to Yoshioka Yoji, director, MOA Museum, for confirming the identification.

16. "Frank Lloyd Wright to Lecture Today on His Japanese Prints," *Chicago Daily Tribune*, 22 November 1917, 15.

17. Frank Lloyd Wright (1992), 1: 148–53. For handwritten and undated typescript versions see FLWA.

18. The museum's curator of Asian art, S. C. Bosch Reitz, was in Chicago to see the Freer exhibition at the Art Institute in November. He would certainly have visited the Fine Arts building, as well. "Chinese Art Show Opens at Institute," *Chicago Daily Tribune*, 20 November 1917, 14.

19. Pearlstein, "The Chinese Collections at the Art Institute of Chicago," 1993, 37; Gookin, *Catalogue of a Loan Exhibition of Ancient Chinese Paintings, Sculptures and Jade Objects from the Collection Formed by Charles Lang Freer*, 1917.

20. CLF to FWG, [New York], 10 March 1916. FGA.

21. Lawton (1993), 224.

22. Pearlstein (1993), 36.

23. Marx is known as the designer of the Pullman car, as well as the fashionable Pump Room in Chicago's Ambassador East Hotel. There is considerable correspondence between Marx and Wright but it dates from the 1940s.

24. See Petteys, *Dictionary of Women Artists*, 1985; Louise Norton Brown, *Block Printing and Book Illustration in Japan* (London and New York: G. Routledge and E. P. Dutton, 1924), ix.

25. Spaulding paints a picture of a woman possessed of a passionate, fanatic devotion to her "hobby," and widely respected in academic circles in Japan. Her wide-ranging collection was purchased for the Art Institute of Chicago in 1926 by Martin A. Ryerson (1856–1937), a trustee and vice president of the museum.

26. She claimed that these full-size prints were actually book pages from a work titled *Popular Scenes of Japan Painted by Nishikawa (Fūryū yamato ezukushi Nishikawa fude no yama)*, an example of which was in her own collection. "In spite of the significant '*Nishikawa Fude*' [brushed, or painted by Nishikawa]," she wrote, "I have never been altogether convinced that the drawings were not by some earlier man, possibly one of Moronobu's [Hishikawa Moronobu, c. 1618–1694] immediate followers. I have compared them closely with many other drawings known to be by Sukenobu and there is certainly a great difference…. Will you be so kind as to let me know if you have the other prints of the series and if any one of them is actually signed Sukenobu?" LNB to FLW, 18 November 1917; despite her doubts, she did later publish this book with an attribution to Sukenobu and a date of c. 1730.

27. The Spaulding catalogue cards show that they made purchases from "S. Mori" in November 1913. Mary Jane Hamilton conveyed the information that 1916 is the first year S. H. Mori's name appears in the Chicago *Lakeside Classified Directory*. Special thanks to Elinor Pearlstein, associate curator of Chinese art at the Art Institute of Chicago, for information regarding the Kate Buckingham invoice book, March 1915–May 1923. Vendor, date of purchase, and price code were recorded by Gookin on the Buckingham catalogue cards at the Art Institute of Chicago.

28. The calling card and description of Mori are from Robert O. Muller, who visited the

Chicago dealer in 1936; Muller, telephone conversation with author, 20 April 1994.

29. Colburn, *The Story and Catalogue of the Japanese Prints Collected by Frederick S. Colburn* [1930?], 4. There was another "Mr. Mori" (Mori Tasaburō) who was the Japanese print specialist at Yamanaka and Company on Fifth Avenue in New York in 1911. Gookin was in New York for long periods during that year cataloguing the prints at the Metropolitan Museum of Art and the New York Public Library. He often visited and lunched with Mori, and occasionally was shown prints suitable for Clarence Buckingham. Mori and Gookin actually spent Christmas day, 1911, together; Mori treated Gookin to a lunch of turkey shabu-shabu at the Nippon Club. Later, before taking in a Broadway show, they rode the subway uptown to the apartment Mori shared with a Mr. Sakurai, a Japanese specialist at the Metropolitan Museum of Art, where Mori had a few prints to show Gookin. FWG to MSG, New York, 3 April 1911, 10 November 1911, 9 December 1911, and 26 December 1911. GNL.

30. Aiko Nakane, Chicago, as told to Irwin Weinberg; IW to author, Wilmette, 1 March 1994. Mori's clients included Laufer, Helen Gunsaulus, Frederick S. Colburn, and Charles Fabens Kelly (1885–1960), the Art Institute's curator of Asian art from 1923. Ōta Yoshiaki to author, Takarazuka City, Japan, 16 June 1994. For the 1923 exhibition see Gookin, "Japanese Paintings and Prints" (1923). Others who were induced to lend were Yamanaka and Company, New York, Howard Mansfield, John Spaulding, and locals such as Colburn, Charles Chandler, Mrs. George Smith, and Mrs. William Sutherland.

31. Wright's drawings for the Mori gallery are undated and there is no evidence to support the traditional date of 1914. The furniture was given to the University of Illinois at Chicago by Mori's successor, Mary Diamond Stein, in 1969. The drawings for the gallery are reproduced in Pfeiffer and Futagawa, eds., *Frank Lloyd Wright* (1984–88), 4: 10–11. See also Storrer, *The Architecture of Frank Lloyd Wright*, 1974, 183. Mary Diamond Stein, Palm Springs, who took over Mori's shop after his death, in telephone conversation with author, 9 March 1994.

32. SHM to FLW, Chicago, 22 September 1944; SHM to FLW, Chicago, 9 October 1944.

33. Ueno, "Hashiguchi Goyō koden," 1921, 4.

34. Oka, *Taishō no onna*, 1976, unpag.: see heading "*kōyū kankei* [friends]." Happer is described by Arthur Wesley Dow, who met him in Japan in 1903, in a letter quoted by Charles J. Morse in a letter to CLF, Evanston, Ill., 13 March 1907. FGA. See also Watanabe Tadasu, ed., *Watanabe Shōzaburō*, 1974, 126, and *Catalogue of the Valuable Collection of Japanese*

Colour Prints, the Property of John Stewart Happer, Esq., Sotheby, Wilkinson and Hodge, London, 14–18 June 1909. Arthur Davison Ficke should be added to the list of Goyō's American friends; he probably visited Goyō during his trip to Japan in 1917 and wrote a heartfelt memorial for the artist in the January 1922 issue of *The Arts*.

35. Oka, "Hashiguchi Goyō," 1976, 4.

36. "Honkai no posuta," 1922, 22–23 and illustration, 24. The date of this publication as given in Japanese is March 1922, but the English title page is misdated October 1921. Nos. 1 and 2 were both published in October 1921 and the same date was probably reused accidentally for no. 3 as well. The poster is also illustrated in Aoki and Sakai, *Kindai no hanga*, 1994, 62–63.

37. For an example see FLWA 1509.447. Anthony Alofsin suggests that the poster figure is derivative of the conventionalized forms Wright used first for the sculptures of winged sprites at Midway Gardens in Chicago around 1914 and that were then recycled in the courtyard of the Imperial Hotel. Alofsin (1993), 291–92.

38. The membership list was published in the November 1925 issue of *Ukiyo-e no kenkyū*. Other foreign members were Happer, Louis Ledoux, Carl Schraubstadter, the Ryerson Library of the Art Institute of Chicago, and the Museum of Fine Arts, Boston.

39. KR to FLW, Tokyo, 29 March 1913, and KR to FLW, Tokyo, 22 April 1913; Frank Lloyd Wright (1943), 199–200. Kuki is incorrectly cited as "R. Kouki" in Alofsin's index to the Taliesin correspondence.

40. Frank Lloyd Wright (1943), 200. I am indebted to Hiroko T. McDermott for sharing her broad knowledge of Kuki's career.

41. Boon, "A Dutch Artist in Japan," 1971, 41–48; also notes completed by N. A. Bosch Reitz, Melbourne, in MMA; Meech-Pekarik (1984), 113; "Young Boswell Interviews S.C. Bosch Reitz," undated newspaper clipping in MMA stamped "New York Tribune, 28 March 1923."

42. There is a discrepancy between the numbers of prints that were purchased and the numbers surviving today; some may have been deaccessioned.

43. FLW to HM, Spring Green, 10 September 1918; FLW to SCBR, Spring Green, 12 August 1918. Both MMA. Robert W. de Forest, president of the board of trustees, bought five Hiroshige from the group that were to be returned to Wright.

44. FLW to SCBR, Spring Green, 15 September 1918. MMA. For Wright's income tax return giving details of the sale to the museum see Getty Research Institute, Los Angeles, Special Collections, and Visual Resources, Frank Lloyd Wright Correspondence with R. M. Schindler, 1914–29, accession no. 960076, document #31098.

45. Frank Lloyd Wright's bank book (FLWA, MSS. 1033.003) for Mitsubishi Goshi Kaisha, Tokyo, 16 January 1917–15 May 1919. The list of names is on the last page.

46. Nakazawa Akimasa, M. Nakazawa Company (Nakazawa Shoten), on Miyukidōri in Yūrakuchō opposite the Imperial Hotel, interview with author, Tokyo, 12 July 1982.

47. FLW to SCBR, Tokyo, 14 January 1919. MMA.

48. Watanabe Shōzaburō, *Catalogue of the Memorial Exhibition of Hiroshige's Works*, 1918.

49. As just one example of what happened to the cost of prints during these years, we can trace Arthur Davison Ficke's copy of Hiroshige's small landscape titled *Bow Moon* from the time he bought it in Chicago at the shop of Ito Tokumatsu for $38 (rather steep at the time), to its sale in 1920 to Sir Edmund Walker of Toronto for $475, followed by its retrieval by its former owner in a trade, and then its last appearance in the 1925 Ficke sale, where it was knocked down to Arthur Duel for $725 (Metzgar [1944], 42–44). A Japanese dealer remembered that a set of Hiroshige's *One Hundred Views* cost ¥100 (about $50) in 1907, but had escalated to ¥10,000 ($5,000) by 1926. Watanabe Tadasu (1974), 115.

50. "Panegeryic [sic] Read by Mr. Yone Noguchi on the Occasion of the Exhibition," and translated by Noguchi himself in Watanabe Shōzaburō (1918), 12.

51. Frank Lloyd Wright, *Antique Colour Prints from the Collection of Frank Lloyd Wright* (1917), [2].

52. FLW to SCBR, Tokyo, 14 January 1919. MMA. HA to FLW, Tokyo, 23 August 1932. For Matsukata, Vever, and Brangwyn see Meech and Guth, *The Matsukata Collection*, 1988. Vever kept back several hundred prints, which formed the basis of his later collection. These were sold at Sotheby's in London in 1974, 1975, and 1997. See Hillier, *Japanese Prints and Drawings from the Vever Collection*, 1976, 3 vols.; and *Highly Important Japanese Prints from the Henri Vever Collection: Final Part*, Sotheby's, London, 30 October 1997.

53. Sherman Booth to DDM, Chicago, 1 March 1916; FLW to LHS, Tokyo, 10 April 1919, quoted in *Frank Lloyd Wright: Letters to Architects*, ed. Pfeiffer, 1984, 14.

54. According to the Wright historian Tanigawa Masami, construction on the Odawara Hotel was abandoned after it was partially built. There are no photographs showing the hotel under construction. Tanigawa, "Wright's Achievement in Japan," 1991, 59.

55. Takeda is quoted in Kusaba, "Furanko Roido Raito…," 1917, loose, unnumbered page of text.

56. Frank Lloyd Wright, "Nihon kenchiku ni taisuru shokan narabi ni teikoku hoteru no sekkei" (1917), 3.

57. John Lloyd Wright (1992), 99. Tanigawa Masami has published a tracing of ill. 113 made in April 1921 by a Japanese named Y. Tadokoro. Tanigawa, *Zumen de miru F. L. Raito* (1995), 71. The tracing is in the library of the school of engineering of Nihon University, Tokyo.

58. Wright used the term "Oriental Symphony" in a letter to the Dutch architect H. P. Berlage (1856–1934), 30 November 1922, quoted in *Frank Lloyd Wright: Letters to Architects* (1984), 54. According to a 1923 interview with William T. Evjue, Wright expected to have studios in Chicago, Hollywood, and Tokyo. *Madison Capital Times*, 18 October 1923. For Wright's unbuilt projects for Venice and Baghdad in the 1950s see Levine (1996), ch. xi; also Mina Marefat, "Wright's Baghdad," in Alofsin (1999), 184–213.

CHAPTER 5

1. FLW to SCBR, Tokyo, 14 January 1919. MMA.

2. FLW to RMS, Tokyo, 15 March 1919. Raymond and Pauline Schindler's letters are all courtesy of their son, Mark Schindler, Los Angeles. The author is grateful to Kathryn Smith for sharing these letters. Smith inserted missing dates by use of a perpetual calendar.

3. FLW to LHS, Tokyo, 10 April 1919.

4. Kathryn Smith (1985), p. 300, n. 25. Also Leonard K. Eaton, *Two Chicago Architects and Their Clients: Frank Lloyd Wright and Howard Van Doren Shaw* (Cambridge, Mass.: MIT Press, 1969), 158. Shaw's work includes the Market Square in Lake Forest, and the Goodman theater and Lakeside Press buildings in Chicago. For the Cliff Dwellers see Regnery, *The Cliff Dwellers*, 1990. I am indebted to Irwin Weinberg for this reference.

5. In 1954 James Michener quoted an unnamed Japanese source to the effect that Wright spent $87,500 on a bulk purchase at the 7 April 1919 sale of the collection of Marquis Ikeda, former daimyo of Okayama (Michener, *The Floating World*, 1954, 240). The same information is cited by Yoshida, *Ukiyo-e no chishiki*, 1963, 97, Higuchi, *Ukiyo-e no ryūtsū, shūshū, kenkyū, happyō no rekishi*, 1972, 53, and Takamizawa, *Aru ukiyo-eshi no isan*, 1978, 13. According to Higuchi, when the Ikeda collection was sold in 1919 it made ¥850,000, a record price, of which ukiyo-e paintings and prints (most purchased by Wright) accounted for ¥175,000 ($87,500). Not a single woodblock print is il-

lustrated or cited in the catalogue for this sale. There was a second Ikeda sale in October of the same year, but again there were no prints cited. For an account of the Japanese print auction world written by an American collector, see "Japanese Print Auctions Are Novel," *New York Times*, 13 February 1921, section 2, p. 4.

6. FWG to FLW, Chicago, 24 December 1920.

7. FLW to DDM, [Spring Green], 20 August 1922. ST.

8. DDM to FLW, Buffalo, 21 April 1919; FLW to DDM, Tokyo, 9 June 1919. ST.

9. DDM to Alfred MacArthur, Buffalo, 28 August 1920. ST.

10. Watanabe Tadasu, ed. (1974), 158

11. FWG to EW, Chicago, 28 December 1919. EWUT. The Walker-Gookin correspondence was published by Waterhouse, *Images of Eighteenth-Century Japan*, 1975, 15.

12. Tanigawa (1977), 49.

13. Frank Lloyd Wright (1943), 528. The large Harunobu is lot 10 in the 1927 Anderson Galleries, New York, sale of Wright's collection. It is a unique double-width pillar print with gold leaf depicting a courtesan and her attendant (*kamuro*) parading beneath a cherry tree. This print sold to H. E. Howley for $1,050. Wright was confused: it was not the Harunobu but the Toyonobu, lot 9, that sold for $2,500, to Charles H. Chandler. Information concerning the dealer Hayashi, who later changed his name to Hayashi Shōgo, is from Abe Chizuko, Hayashi's daughter, interview with author, at Marumiya, in Tokyo, 12 July 1982. Judson Metzgar gave an account of the Hayashi incident in his *Adventures in Japanese Prints*, [1944], 60; see also Tanigawa, "Iwayuru 'Raito jiken' ni tsuite" (1990), 125–28.

14. Copy of a check in Wright's 1917–19 Mitsubishi Goshi Kaisha bank book (FLWA, MSS. 1103.003).

15. Takamizawa (1978), 14.

16. Quoted in FWG to EW, Chicago, 28 December 1919. EWUT.

17. Shishi Sai'an, "Hanga no hoshoku," 1919, 13.

18. Extracts from FLW to HM, Tokyo, 25 May 1919. KV.

19. Quoted in HM to MA, New York, 6 October 1919. KV.

20. Frank Lloyd Wright (1943), 528. FLW to HM, [Chicago] undated, [c. 27 September 1919]. KV. WSS to FLW, Boston, 4 December 1919.

21. FLW to HM, Tokyo, 25 May 1919; HM to MA, New York, 14 August 1919; HM to FLW, New York, 16 September 1919; HM to MA, New York, 17 September 1919. All KV.

22. FLW to HM, [Chicago], undated, [probably 27 September 1919]. KV.

23. Frank Lloyd Wright (1943), 529. For the income tax matter see FLW to RMS, Tokyo, 30 March [1920], and worksheets for individual income tax return. Getty Research Institute, Los Angeles, Special Collections, and Visual Resources, Frank Lloyd Wright Correspondence with R. M. Schindler, 1914–29, accession no. 960076, document #31098.

24. Judson Metzgar to Harry Getz, [Los Angeles], 10 April 1950. KV. Getz was the husband of a niece of Ainsworth. Metzgar and Ficke estimated that Ainsworth spent about $10,000 but Getz annotated the letter with the comment that she actually spent more than $15,000. In this letter the Hotel Astor is given as the location of the meeting. Further documentation that Ainsworth was in New York in October 1919 is an invoice in the Ainsworth file at the Allen Memorial Art Museum for prints she purchased on 17 October 1919 from E. T. Shima, 47 West Forty-second Street, New York.

25. Morton W. Johnson, son of Chandler's nephew, and a former occupant of the Chandler house, in conversation with IW, Wilmette, Ill., 3 July 2000.

26. Ledoux, "The Utamaro Exhibition," 1926, 2.

27. LVL to FLW, [New York], 24 July 1918, and 15 September 1918. FLWA. HM to FLW, New York, 19 July 1920. KV. For a brief biography of Ledoux see Meech-Pekarik (1984), 115–18.

28. Mentioned in HM to FLW, New York, 21 July 1921.

29. Metzgar [1944], 60–61. Metzgar identifies Wright and Ainsworth by name in his 1950 letter to Harry Getz (see chapter 5, n. 24).

30. For Takamizawa Enji see Takahashi, *Traditional Woodblock Prints of Japan*, 1976, 175, and Takamizawa (1978), 14. Some have claimed that Hayashi himself was duped and may have acquired revamped prints by mistake. Watanabe Tadasu, nephew of Watanabe Shōzaburō, interview with author, Tokyo, July 1982.

31. Letter from Gookin to Mansfield quoted in HM to MA, New York, 6 October 1919. KV.

32. FWG to MA, Chicago, 7 December 1919. KV.

33. FWG to EW, Chicago, 9 February 1919. EWUT.

34. EW to FWG, Toronto, 24 December 1919. EWUT.

35. FWG to EW, Chicago, 28 December 1919. EWUT.

36. Wright identifies this as the emperor's garden party in his autobiography; his mother simply refers to it as a Japanese residence.

37. For Capelari see Meech, *Rain and Snow*, 1993, p. 61 and n. 79; Stephens, *The New Wave*, 1993, 45–46, 209–10.

38. Wright may have been introduced to Lum by his sister Maginel. Lum and Maginel Enright (later Maginel Barney) were about the same age, and both were illustrators who had attended the art school of the Art Institute of Chicago in the 1890s. After moving to Minneapolis, Lum made her first trip to Japan in 1903 to buy tools, brushes, and everything necessary for printing. In 1908 she went again to Japan and worked every day for three months in a shop cutting blocks, followed by two months working with a printer. In 1911 she took a house in Tokyo, where she had several printers working under her instruction. Soft and lyrical, her landscape prints are obviously influenced by Hiroshige. She focused on nostalgic themes that exploit the "exotic Orient" to the fullest. Returning many times to Asia, Lum eventually commuted between Peking and Pasadena. See Meech and Weisberg (1990), 127–56.

39. Yearbook of Anna Lloyd Wright (FLWA, MSS. 4021.009) and "Daily Records" of Anna Lloyd Wright (FLWA, MSS. 4021.002).

40. Frank Lloyd Wright (1943), 204; also Kathryn Smith, "F. L. Raito," 1988, 77 ff.

41. Miriam Noel Wright, "The Romance of Miriam Wright," 1932, 2. This 1928 autobiography was published two years after Miriam's death.

42. Ibid. Wright discusses in his autobiography the trip to Beijing to award contracts for the rugs. His guide was the Oxford-educated author Dr. Ku Hung Ming, former secretary to the empress dowager. Frank Lloyd Wright (1943), 531; De Long, *Frank Lloyd Wright*, 1996, p. 124, n. 52.

43. Matsuki Kihachirō to F. Holland Day, Boston, 30 December 1917; idem, New York, 12 January 1920, and 17 August 1921. Fred Holland Day Papers, Archives of American Art. I am indebted to Verna Curtis, Library of Congress, and Christine Guth for bringing these letters to my attention. Matsuki's auction room prowess is described in Green (1986). Matsuki's daughter Uchida Junko and nephew, Uehara Tomoo, also supplied biographical details. Matsuki married in 1912. His first two children were born in 1913 and 1917. When he returned to his family in Japan in 1921 he lived in Kamakura and made his way as a print dealer, sending prints to clients in Boston and New York, including Gookin, Ledoux, and Mansfield. (Matsuki to Mr. Tuttle, Kamakura, 14 March 1924, courtesy Gary Levine.) In 1925 he squired Frederick Gookin around Japan, Korea, and Manchuria. In the 1920s Matsuki and Watanabe Shōzaburō formed a partnership to open Shōbisha, an export/import print shop in Kanda, Tokyo.

44. HM to MA, New York, 16 June 1920; HM to FLW, New York, 17 June 1920; HM to MA, New York, 18 June 1920; HM to FLW, New York, 10 July 1920; HM to MA, New York, 21 July 1920. KV. Mansfield's letter to Ainsworth of 18 June 1920 includes a priced list of all prints offered by Wright and individual priced lists of prints returned by Mansfield and Ainsworth as revamped.

45. FWG to FLW, 27 June 1920. Mailed on 16 July 1920 from Estes Park, Colo.

46. Ibid.

47. FWG to FLW, Estes Park, Colo., 11 July 1920, continued on 16 July 1920.

48. FLW to HM, Spring Green, 12 July 1920. KV.

49. Telegram from FLW to HM, [Spring Green, 9 August 1920], quoted in HM to MA, New York, 9 August 1920. KV.

50. HM to MA, New York, 9 August 1920, and 9 October 1920. KV. FWG to FLW, Estes Park, Colo., 13 September 1920, and 9 October 1920. FLWA. Pauline Schindler (SPS) to her parents, Spring Green, [20 October 1920], courtesy Mark Schindler. The Harunobu is included in the list of prints acquired from Frank Lloyd Wright in autumn of 1919, including 26 "Prints Which Miss Ainsworth Wants to Return. Revamped" in HM to FLW, New York, 17 June 1920. KV.

51. HM to FLW, New York, 4 October 1920.

52. Ashbee to his wife, 14 April 1916, quoted in Brooks (1981), 4.

53. DDM to FLW, Buffalo, 28 August 1922. ST.

54. Maginel Wright Barney, The Valley of the God-Almighty Joneses, quoted in Secrest (1992), 145.

55. SPS to parents (M/M Edmund Gibling), Spring Green, [24] July 1920, courtesy Mark Schindler.

56. SPS to parents, Spring Green, 29 September [1920]. Partially published in Kathryn Smith, Frank Lloyd Wright: Hollyhock House and Olive Hill, 1992, 105.

57. Gookin quoted in HM to MA, New York, 14 July 1920. KV.

58. Kathryn Smith (1992), 105–6.

59. Frank Lloyd Wright (1943), 530.

60. Metzgar [1944], 61.

61. WSS to FLW, Montecito, Calif., 21 December 1920.

62. HM to FLW, New York, 21 July 1921.

63. Ficke's widow, Gladys Brown Ficke, quoted in Green, "Dr. Arthur B. Duel (1870–1936)," 1984, 3–4.

64. Ibid., 5–6. The Duel collection was accepted by the Fogg Art Museum in 1933 from the "Anonymous friends of Arthur B. Duel."

65. In the January 1927 Anderson Galleries, New York, sale, Wright sold another print from this set (lot 70) for $500 to a New York dealer, Kano Oshima. The retail value was presumably at least twice what the dealer paid.

66. Wright worked on a 10-percent commission. His fee for the Allen house was based on a total cost of $27,000. See Don Schuler to FLW, Wichita, 8 March 1916.

67. Wright's handwritten list titled "Prints taken by Mr. Mansfield Sept 1922," and Mansfield's handwritten list titled "Statement: Prints taken by H. M. for F. L. W. in autumn of 1922" (FLWA, MSS. 1033.001). For Ledoux see FLW to SCBR, [Spring Green, 20? November 1922]. MMA.

68. Watanabe Tadasu (1974), 126. Wright mentions the facsimiles in a print party talk he gave in the studio at Taliesin, taped on 20 September 1950. FLWA. For the gift of albums of reprints to the Metropolitan Museum of Art see SCBR to FLW, New York, 9 August 1918. MMA.

69. Two Harunobu prints in this category in the Clarence Buckingham Collection at the Art Institute of Chicago are 1925.2140 and 1925.2141. There is also a modern impression of a Torii Kiyonobu (1925.1704) said to be one of twenty made around 1915 by Murata Kimbei from the original block on old paper. Kate Buckingham purchased it from "K. Matsuki" (Matsuki Kihachirō) in November 1919.

70. Higuchi (1972), 53.

71. Vever's copy is illustrated in color in Hillier (1979), vol. 1, fig. 245. I am indebted to Sebastian Izzard for insights regarding this print.

72. FLW to SCBR, Spring Green, 17 October [1922]. MMA. The dollar amount of Wright's loss is confirmed in a letter Pauline Schindler wrote to her parents from Taliesin [20 October 1920] concerning the visiting collectors: "They bought thirty-four thousand dollars' worth of prints from Mr. Wright, who has the third finest collection in the country, and all are passionate collectors themselves." Wright also cited $30,000 in his autobiography: Frank Lloyd Wright (1943), 530. Wright had written R. M. Schindler from Tokyo on 2 October 1921: "I found nothing here as I expected to in the way of money for restitution on prints." At about the same time, on 11 November 1921, Pauline Schindler again wrote her parents that Wright had recently lost "some tens of thousands of dollars through his Japanese prints." Schindler letters courtesy Mark Schindler.

73. Frank Lloyd Wright (1943), 529–30.

74. Nagai Kafū diary entry for 21 July 1926 in Nagai Kafū nikki, 1958–59, 2: 49. Kafū misidentified the culprits as Takamizawa Enji and the book dealer Murayuki. Kafū's name and those of many other print dealers and collectors in Japan, including Shugio Hiromichi,

John Stewart Happer, William Keane, Noguchi Yonejirō (Yone Noguchi), and Hayashi Kyūgo, are listed on a woodblock-printed bansuke, or imitation sumō broadsheet, compiled as a New Year's greeting for early spring 1920. Higuchi (1972), 55.

75. Takamizawa (1978), 13–17; the print scholar/collector Charles Mitchell, interview with author, Tokyo, 10 July 1982; Kikuchi Sadao, curator of prints at the Tokyo National Museum, interview with author, Tokyo, 2 July 1982. Kikuchi claimed that Hayashi moved to Paris, where he lived near the Cathedral of Notre Dame.

76. Abe Chizuko, interview with author, Tokyo, 12 July 1982. There are those who think that Hayashi never left Japan. C. R. Boxer, a British collector of Nagasaki prints, took a generous view of the demise of another Tokyo ukiyo-e dealer, Shimizu Gensendō, who was likewise sent to jail because of a scandal: "The regrettable fact this worthy dealer was imprisoned for faking works of art on a large scale in 1934–5 does not reflect on his undoubted ability as a connoisseur of Nagasaki-e; and the present writer will long retain a grateful remembrance of this genial personage and of his tireless efforts to secure colour-prints from all quarters." C. R. Boxer, Jan Compagnie in Japan, 1600–1850. 2nd rev. ed. (The Hague: Martinus Nijhoff, 1950), p. 67, n. 1.

77. FLW to SCBR, Spring Green, 17 October [1922]. MMA.

78. SCBR to Robert W. de Forest, New York, 31 October 1922. MMA. FWG to FLW, Chicago, 9 February 1921.

79. Daiikai ukiyo-e dainyūsatsukai (First large ukiyo-e auction) (Tokyo: Nihon ukiyo-e sho kyōdō kumiai, 1 June 1990), fig. 089; Christie's, New York (sale 7236), 27 March 1991, lot 438. This copy of the Great Wave had been sold in the auction of the Carl Schraubstadter Collection in 1948 for $500.

80. SCBR to FLW, New York, 26 October 1922. MMA.

81. FLW to SCBR, Spring Green, 2 November 1922. MMA. The letter is written over a period of two days. The first part of the letter is misdated 1 November 1921.

82. FWG to MSG, New York, 19 December 1911. GNL. Lucy Rogers Hawkins, "North Shore Personalities," Winnetka Talk, 28 November 1935, 28.

83. Raymond, An Autobiography, 1973, 51; Howe to author, Burnsville, Minn., 4 May 1988.

84. WWP to author, Scottsdale, Ariz., 25 February 1985. For more on this see Menocal, Taliesin 1911–1914, 1983–84, pp. 26, 31, n. 26.

85. FLW to SCBR, Spring Green, [undated reply to SCBR letter of 26 October 1922]. MMA.

86. FLW to SCBR, Spring Green, 12 August 1918. MMA. SCBR to FLW, New York, 10 September 1918. While most FLW/SCBR correspondence is in the MMA, the handwritten note on this SCBR letter appears only on the original in the FLWA. MMA carbon copy has no note.

87. Bosch Reitz, "Revamped Japanese Prints," 1920, 281.

88. Invoice from the Y. Nakagawa Fine Art Gallery in Yokohama dated Yokohama, 1 July 1923 (FLWA, MSS. 1033.001).

89. John Lloyd Wright (1992), 96.

90. FLW to DDM, Oak Park, 13 January 1911. SUNYB.

91. For preceding quotes see FLW to DDM, Spring Green, 20 August 1922, and idem, 1 September 1922. ST. FLW to DDM, Spring Green, 20 August 1922. ST.

92. DDM to FLW, Buffalo, 30 October 1922, with Wright's itemized, priced memo dated Buffalo, 27 October 1922, courtesy Scott Elliott.

93. Sauk County Court divorce settlement, Frank Lloyd Wright vs. Catherine L. Wright, Madison, 13 November 1922, courtesy Scott Elliott. Wright paid for Llewellyn's college education (at Cornell), which he did not do for any of his other children.

94. "List of prints sent to Mr. Gookin, Dec. 29th/22" (FLWA, MSS. 1033.001). Wright sent a note to Sullivan on 30 November: "I am going to tell you a secret, which I hope you will keep—I am extremely hard up, and not a job in sight in the world. My 'selling' campaigns have failed." FLW to LHS, [Spring Green], 30 November 1922.

95. Sweeney, *Wright in Hollywood*, 1994, 40.

CHAPTER 6

1. Kathryn Smith (1992), 43; Neil Levine has also used the Hokusai/Hollyhock House comparison. See Levine, "Hollyhock House and the Romance of Southern California," 1983, 163.

2. AB to FLW, 7 January 1920; see Kathryn Smith (1992), 83.

3. Telegram, AB to FLW, New York, 6 October 1920.

4. Kathryn Smith (1992), 77.

5. "Mesas basis for perspective," *Hollywood Citizen News*, 2 September 1921, 2, courtesy Virginia Kazor, Historic Site Curator, Cultural Affairs Department, City of Los Angeles. Kathryn Smith points out that water damage to the house due to rain between November 1921 and April 1922 was so severe that it was replastered inside in the summer of 1922. It is not known whether Wright was there. He re-turned from Japan in August 1922. The actual colors of the interior thus remain quite controversial. Smith, fax to author, Santa Monica, 8 September 1994; Thornburg, "The Wright Stuff," 1990, 32.

6. Since Wright does not mention screens, only "a screen," there may have been a single six-panel screen, such as the pheasant under a blossoming cherry that was placed in the alcove off the living room.

7. Widjeveld, ed., *The Life-Work of the American Architect Frank Lloyd Wright*, 1925, 152, shows the room unfinished (or at least without furnishings) but with the grapevine screens in place.

8. Hoffmann, *Frank Lloyd Wright's Hollyhock House*, 1992, 73, 75. Virginia Kazor confirms that there was originally another screen in the center of the west wall of the music room. Kazor to Penny Fowler, Los Angeles, 4 February 1991.

9. There is no documentation in the Barnsdall house records relating to this sculpture. The iconography is confused: the hand gestures are those of a Buddha, but the costume is that of a Bodhisattva.

10. Kathryn Smith (1992), 161.

11. Frank Lloyd Wright vs. Aline Barnsdall, State of California (Superior Court) Case #138514, "Affidavit for Claim and Delivery of Personal Property," and Case #138515 "Complaint for Money and Notice to Produce Certain Documents and Writings." Documentation cited in Kathryn Smith (1992), 222, chapter 16, n. 3, and Smith to author, Santa Monica, 21 August 1994. Barnsdall received the pair of screens on about 15 December 1923 and Wright demanded their return on 26 January 1924.

12. Lawton (1995), 88–89. The screen had been published by Fenollosa in his *Epochs of Chinese and Japanese Art* (1912) with an attribution to Hon'ami Kōetsu, the early seventeenth-century progenitor of the Rimpa school of art. Today, for lack of evidence, scholars refrain from attributing paintings to Kōetsu.

13. AB to FLW, Los Angeles, 21 January 1924.

14. Kathryn Smith (1992), 193.

15. "Japanese prints sent to Lloyd Wright Feb. 6/25" (FLWA, MSS. 1033.001). Wright was in the habit of sending an occasional "block" of prints to his son Lloyd to sell in order to raise money for his Los Angeles architectural projects. See FLW to LW, Spring Green, 15 September 1924. Barnsdall did offer to return both the screen and the prints: Herbert L. Hahn, telegram to FLW, Pasadena, 11 February 1925. There were twenty-five horizontal Hiroshige (mostly from various Tōkaidō series), twenty-five vertical Hiroshige, thirteen Hiroshige, which were either still in an album or had been removed from an album of the *One Hundred Views*, six Katsukawa actor prints, two Utamaro, one Torii Kiyomine (1787–1868), and a group of fourteen *surimono*, including Totoya Hokkei's image of a kite with a portrait of the actor Ichikawa Danjūrō VII (1791–1859).

16. HLH to FLW, Pasadena, 18 March 1924. Illustrated in Levine (1996), pl. 130, and Kathryn Smith (1992), 148–49, color plate.

17. HLH, telegram to FLW, Pasadena, 11 February 1925; Wright vs. Barnsdall, Case #138514 and #138515, "Release," Los Angeles, 24 January 1927; see Kathryn Smith (1992), 193–94, for a blow-by-blow account.

18. AB to FLW, Los Angeles, 15 June 1940. There were also four Chinese paintings and five prints by Hiroshige. Her estate listed 162 works of art. See "Order settling final account of will," 19 October 1949. This document was described to me by Kathryn Smith, Santa Monica, 21 August 1994. For 1933 purchases see AB to FLW, Zuoz, Switzerland, 8 January 1933 ("I enclose check for screen"); AB to FLW, Paris, 11 July 1933 ("I couldn't possibly buy the screen"); AB to FLW, Los Angeles, 16 October 1936 ("Please let me know why you have not sent my screen"). I am grateful to Kathryn Smith and Donald Hoffmann for drawing my attention to this correspondence. The old Los Angeles County Museum later split into two institutions, the Los Angeles County Museum of Art and the Natural History Museum of Los Angeles County. Cathy McNassor, archivist at the Natural History Museum of Los Angeles County, found records in the registrar's office that show Barnsdall loaned five screens in August 1940. McNassor, fax to author, Los Angeles, 3 August 2000.

19. Weston, *East Meets West*, 1992, 10.

20. I am indebted to Barbara Elsner, current owner of the Bogk house, for sharing period photographs of the interior showing Asian art.

21. There is one photograph of the Taliesin dining area before the 1914 fire (FLWA 1104.0046), but it is not clear whether or not a screen is mounted on the wall. The May 1916 issue of *The Craftsman* recommended placing Japanese screens painted on silk or formed of a series of woodblock prints above the mantel, in front of a fireplace when not in use, or against a wall.

22. Photographs of Tarbell's screen were enclosed in a letter from Bruce W. Chambers, Berry-Hill Galleries, Inc., to Andrew Pekarik, The Asia Society, New York, 9 August 1984.

23. David Wright to author, Phoenix, 5 September 1994.

CHAPTER 7

1. Harold Jackson to Joseph Spencer, Chicago, 3 January 1927, courtesy Scott Elliot. "Police Seize Frank Wright at Minneapolis," newspaper clipping, 20 October [1926]. ST. Wright de-

scribes the incident in some detail in his autobiography.

2. Frank Lloyd Wright, "Taliesin: The Chronicle of a House with a Heart," 1929, 28; idem (1932), 260.

3. FLW to DDM, Madison, 1 November 1925. ST. DDM to FLW, Buffalo, 4 November 1925. ST.

4. DDM to FLW, Buffalo, 22 September 1925. ST.

5. Affidavit filed by Mitchell Kennerley on 13 January 1927, Supreme Court of the State of New York, County of New York, in the case of Miriam Noel Wright against Frank Lloyd Wright, courtesy Scott Elliott. See also Randolph P. Conners to Darwin R. Martin, Jr., Madison, 5 November 1941. ST.

6. Five-page list compiled for the bank titled "Inventory of 15 Packages of Japanese Prints Taken from residence and vault of Frank Lloyd Wright, To be held as security by Bank of Wisconsin, Madison, Wis. Oct. 1, 1926," MSS. SC565, presented to the archives of the State Historical Society of Wisconsin, Madison, by Joseph H. Makler, Chicago, in 1968, together with the Island Woolen Co. (McFetridge) papers but now filed under the name Frank Lloyd Wright.

7. RLH to FLW, Madison, 5 November 1926.

8. See Walter J. Wilde, Treasury Department, to FLW, Milwaukee, 5 February 1929.

9. MK to FLW, New York, 10 November 1926.

10. Teall, "The Water-colorings of Hiroshige," 1926. This reference was supplied by Edgar Tafel.

11. The figure of two-thirds is found in FLW to DDM, New York, [8 January 1927]. ST. The letter is undated but has indistinct notation by DDM "PM 1/8/27." It was misfiled in the archives as 8 January 1929.

12. Annotation in E. B. Van Vleck's copy of the Anderson Galleries catalogue in the LVM archives.

13. "155 Japanese Art Color Prints Are Sold for $23,295," New York Herald, 7 January 1927, cites the Duel purchase; the salesroom announcement is recorded in E. B. Van Vleck's personal copy of the Anderson Galleries catalogue in the LVM.

14. Marked copy of a catalogue of a Japanese print auction sponsored by Murata Kimbei on 2 May 1920 at the Chōseikan in Ōiso, Kanagawa prefecture. Library, Christie's, New York.

15. There were two sales of prints from the Schraubstadter estate at the Parke-Bernet Galleries, New York: sale 920 on 19–20 January 1948, and sale 942 on 8–9 March 1948. The sales brought $25,203 for 616 prints, of which 409 were by Hiroshige.

16. CS to FLW, St. Louis, 21 June 1929; FLW to CS, [Spring Green], 25 March 1932. Schraubstadter wrote a useful little book for collectors, Care and Repair of Japanese Prints (Cornwall-on-Hudson: Idlewild Press, 1948), with a biographical preface by Kojiro Tomita. Lilla S. Perry (1882–1971) is the collector who visited Schraubstadter in 1932. Her comments are in an unpublished memoir in manuscript form, which her son passed on to William Green, who generously shared it with me.

17. Frank Lloyd Wright, The Frank Lloyd Wright Collection of Japanese Antique Prints, 1927, passim. Referred to as Anderson Galleries catalogue.

18. FLW to DDM, New York, [8 January 1927]. ST. The letter is undated but has indistinct notation by DDM "PM 1/8/27." It was misfiled in the archives as 8 January 1929.

19. Frank Lloyd Wright, An Autobiography, (1977), 313.

20. Gale purchased lots 161, 179, and 230, now in the Minneapolis Institute of Arts. "155 Japanese Art Color Prints Are Sold for $23,295," New York Herald, 7 January 1927; see also Art News 25 (15 January 1927): 12; Mansfield does not seem to have been bidding at the 1927 sale. Priced and annotated copies of this auction catalogue are available in the LVM (the Van Vleck copy), the Watson Library at the Metropolitan Museum of Art (the Bosch Reitz copy), as well as in various other private and public collections. The author is grateful to Charles Verbeck, Washington, D.C., for assistance in identifying the bidders at this sale.

21. FLW to RLJ, Chandler, Ariz., 15 May 1929. Several marked sale catalogues and an Art News review indicate that the Bank of Wisconsin sold Wright's set of seven untrimmed sheets of this very rare subject to Noel Bradley for $900 at the Anderson Galleries, New York, sale in 1927 (lot 38). Bradley was acting as agent for Wright himself. Marked copies of the 1927 sale catalogue are in the Geoffrey Oliver Collection and the E. B. Van Vleck Collection in the LVM. See also Art News 25 (15 January 1927): 12.

22. "155 Japanese Art Color Prints Are Sold for $23,295" (1927).

23. The Wright historian Robert Twombly claims that Miriam did have considerable money of her own in the form of alimony from her wealthy first husband. Twombly (1979), 174.

24. "Charges Wright gave up wealth to defraud her," Chicago Daily Tribune, 18 February 1927, 28; "$36,975 for Wright Prints," New York Times, 8 January 1927, 12; "Backs Mrs. Wright's Claims," New York Times, 18 February 1927, 44. Scott Elliott shared the letter from Miriam's lawyer, Harold Jackson, to the New York attorney Joseph Spencer, Chicago, 3 January 1927, and Miriam Noel's affidavit bringing suit against Wright and filed

with the Supreme Court of the State of New York on 6 January 1927 as well as Wright's affidavit protesting his innocence dated 12 January and similar depositions by his sister Maginel on 12 January and his sister Jane on 15 January.

25. "Retain auction proceeds," New York Times, 20 February 1927, 6; Frank Lloyd Wright (1932), 288.

26. "Lawyer Obtains Mrs. M. N. Wright's Japanese Prints," Chicago Daily Tribune, 29 February 1928, 7; "250 Japanese Prints Sold for Lawyer's Fee," newspaper clipping [29 February 1928]. ST.

27. FLW to DDM, Phoenix, undated, [25 March 1928]. ST.

28. FLW to DDM, [Spring Green?], 2 November 1927. ST.

29. Andrew T. Porter to Alfred T. Rogers, Philadelphia, 3 November 1927. The Porters, who had a house designed by Wright on family property adjacent to Taliesin, had come to Wisconsin in 1907 to manage the Hillside Home School. For a list of subscribers see FLWA, MSS. 1033.012.

30. For Maginel's mortgage see FLW to DDM, Washington, D.C., 3 February 1927. ST.

31. La Follette's brother, Robert ("Little Bob"), was a senator from 1925 until 1946 and his father, Robert ("Old Fighting Bob"), was a hell-raising liberal who ran for president in 1924 on the Progressive Party ticket after serving forty-four years as a representative, senator, and governor from Wisconsin.

32. Queene Ferry Coonley to DDM, Washington, D.C., 17 June 1927. ST. FLW to DDM, [Spring Green], 14 November 1927. ST. Wright first invited Mrs. Coonley to acquire Japanese prints in 1911 (see chapter 2, p. 68).

33. Meech-Pekarik, Frank Lloyd Wright and Japanese Prints: The Collection of Mrs. Avery Coonley, 1983. I am grateful for information provided by Elizabeth Coonley Faulkner in 1983, when the Coonley prints were exhibited at the Octagon; the assistance of Mrs. Faulkner's daughter, Celia Crawford, is also gratefully acknowledged.

34. Island Woolen Company file, Manuscript Archives, State Historical Society of Wisconsin, Box 63. Also Goc (1990), 64, 126. Goc says that William's move to San Diego took place in 1918. He also notes that the mill itself closed in 1949. Wright designed a concrete lookout station on either end of the dam—an open structure with seats on the inside and a flat concrete roof supported by a concrete center pole into which were implanted shells. The dam and platforms were demolished around 1970. "A Touch of Wright in Baraboo," News Republic, 27 October 1983, p. 5, section B; "W. H. McFetridge, S. D. Resident, Dies in the East," San Diego Independent, 6 January 1927, gives McFetridge's birth date as 1868.

35. PFLF to DDM, Madison, 14 June 1928. ST.

36. Long Sang Ti and Company did import screens. According to an advertisement they placed in *House Beautiful* in November 1907 their main offices were in Canton, Hong Kong, and Yokohama, and they sold old prints, umbrellas, tapestries, furniture, and jewelry among other things.

37. WHM to the Long Sang Ti Chinese Curio Company, 19 October 1926. MSS. Archives, State Historical Society of Wisconsin, Box 63, folder 9.

38. PFLF to DDM, Madison, 7 September 1928. ST.

39. Wright earlier valued the McFetridge prints at $30,000. Ferdinand Schevill to the Subscribers of Frank Lloyd Wright, Inc., Chicago, 19 January 1928. ST.

40. DDM to La Follette, Rogers, and Roberts, Buffalo, 26 July 1928. ST. Martin had returned his box of Hiroshige prints in 1925 after settling all accounts on the Oak Park mortgage.

41. PFLF to DDM, Madison, 14 June 1928. ST.

42. PFLF to FLW, Madison, 18 September 1928. ST. In the summer of 1929 Darwin Martin told Wright that any earned income should be used first to pay current expenses, then to repay a new $2,000 loan from Martin himself, and only after that to repay the McFetridge loan. DDM to FLW, Buffalo, 8 July 1929. ST.

43. FLW to EPM, Spring Green, 8 November 1928; FLW to Ben E. Paige, Spring Green, 16 November 1928; EPM to FLW, Baraboo, 24 November 1928.

44. FLW to Fiske Kimball, Spring Green, 8 November 1928; FK to FLW, Philadelphia, 20 November 1928; HHFJ to FLW, Philadelphia, 21 November 1928; Dorothy Blair to FLW, Toledo, 1 December 1928. Dorothy Blair was writing on behalf of the curator, J. Arthur MacLean, who had earlier been curator of Asian art at the Art Institute of Chicago.

45. FLW to HJA, Spring Green, 8 November 1928. Wright also planned to correspond with the "new museum" in Kansas City (the Nelson-Atkins), the Minneapolis Institute of Arts, and the Albright Gallery (now the Albright-Knox Art Gallery) in Buffalo, all museums with an interest in Asian art. FLW to Ben E. Page, Spring Green, 16 November 1928; FLW to FK, Spring Green, 23 January 1928.

46. FLW to FWG, Spring Green, 8 November 1928; FWG to FLW, Winnetka, 10 November 1928.

47. FLW to HM, Spring Green, 8 November 1928.

48. Frank Lloyd Wright, "The Art of Japan by Louis V. Ledoux," typescript dated 25 October 1927. FLWA.

49. Lucy Rogers Hawkins, "North Shore Personalities," *Winnetka Talk* (1935), 33, and idem, "Local Merchant Collects Japanese Prints as Hobby," *Evanston News-Index*, 3 December 1932, 3. Gookin, "Actor Prints by Sharaku," *Bulletin of the Art Institute of Chicago* 21, no. 1 (1927): 5, and idem, "A Notable Addition to the Buckingham Collection," *Bulletin of the Art Institute of Chicago* 28 (November 1934): 78. Chandler exhibited fifty-one Hiroshige fan prints at the Art Institute of Chicago in 1938: Helen C. Gunsaulus, "Japanese Fan Prints," *Bulletin of the Art Institute of Chicago* 32, no. 5 (1938), 75–76; and "When Hiroshige Turned His Genius to Fans," *Art Digest* (1 October 1938), 18. See also Metzgar [1944], 80–81: Metzgar and Chandler exchanged prints prior to 1916. Betty Y. Siffert found information concerning Chandler's interaction with the museum in the registrar's records in the Art Institute of Chicago. He sold hundreds of prints to Kate Buckingham, which she then donated to the museum.

50. FLW to PFLF, Spring Green, 23 November 1928.

51. Reference to the auctioneer is in E. B. Van Vleck's copy of the 1927 Anderson Galleries catalogue, LVM.

52. *The Floating World*, a labor of love, was followed by *The Hokusai Sketchbooks: Selections from the Manga* in 1958 and *Japanese Prints: From the Early Masters to the Modern* in 1959. The prints in the latter were all taken from Michener's collection, which had grown to 5,400 and was valued at the time at more than $100,000. (Day, *James A. Michener*, 1964, 105; Link, "James A. Michener," 1994, 9.) For Wright's prints in the Michener collection see Michener, *Japanese Prints from the Early Masters to the Modern*, 1959, figs. 41, 73, 79, 82, 123, 133–35, 161, 205; see also Kobayashi and Link, *Prints by Utagawa Hiroshige*, 1991, 6, and White, "Hokusai and Hiroshige," 1998, 11–17.

53. FLW to PFLF, Chandler, Ariz., 4 March 1929. FLWA. PFLF to DDM, Madison, 9 November 1928; PFLF to DDM, Madison, 4 May 1929. Both ST.

54. FLW to Benjamin E. Page, [Spring Green], 16 November 1928; EL to FLW, Ann Arbor, 14 July 1930. Lorch did sponsor a lecture by Wright at the university in 1931 when Lorch was director of the College of Architecture; FLW to EL, Spring Green, 8 December 1930, and FLW to EL, Spring Green, 8 April 1931. Lorch, who attended MIT and had an M.A. from Harvard, had been a student of Denman W. Ross (1853–1935), the Harvard-trained historian who served as a trustee of the Museum of Fine Arts in Boston from 1895 until his death, and who collected everything from Japanese prints to Islamic textiles.

55. FLW to DDM, [Spring Green], 8 August 1930. ST.

56. FLW to RLJ, Chandler, Ariz., 15 May 1929.

57. BM to FLW, San Diego, 18 March 1955.

58. O. P. Reed, who catalogued the prints for the 1969 sale, conversation with author, October 1990. Roger Keyes, who helped catalogue McFetridge's prints for the 1969 sale, shared his recollections with the author. The prints in the McFetridge sale were for the most part sold to print dealers—R. E. Lewis and Dawson's Book Shop, for example—and have since been dispersed. A Koryūsai pillar print, lot 30, was acquired by Richard Gale; he gave it to the Minneapolis Institute of Arts in 1974 (1974.1.305).

59. See Christie's, New York, sale 6576, 15–16 April 1988, lot 344; and Christie's, New York, sale 6672, 7–8 October 1988, lot 287. The print is included in a priced list entitled "Prints Which Miss Ainsworth Wants to Return," drawn up by Howard Mansfield. The list is not dated but appears to have been enclosed with his letter to Miss Ainsworth, New York, 18 June 1920. KV.

60. DDM to PFLF, Buffalo, 19 June 1929.

61. FLW to DDM, Spring Green, 3 August 1929. ST.

62. There is a copy of the unsigned Bill of Sale (FLWA, MSS. 1033.099).

63. The group in question must have numbered around 150 prints: Wright sold 346 lots in New York, representing only two-thirds of the prints he originally set aside for the sale. See note 11 above. Thinking that he might still retrieve the remainder, Wright had sent the following telegram to Darwin Martin from Phoenix on 15 September 1928: "Prints returned from New York and sold by bank for four thousand dollars were kept out of that sale by me as most valuable and I can sell them for five times the four thousand they were sold for by the bank within six months. By all means let us hang on to them." See also FLW to PFLF, [Spring Green?], 28 September 1928. ST.

64. Van Vleck ledger titled *Memoranda*. LVM.

65. Wright's list of articles missing from the group he had deposited in storage at the bank includes miscellaneous household items such as embroidered bedcovers, nineteen Chinese paintings, Japanese hanging scrolls, twenty-two pillar prints, thirty actor prints by Katsukawa Shunshō, fifty bird and flower prints by Hiroshige, and an abundance of Hiroshige's Hōeidō Tōkaidō series—three sets in the form of single-sheet prints and five albums—and so on. Wright indicates that the bank had removed some Japanese prints and printed illustrated books during his absence previous to the foreclosure.

66. FLW to DDM, Spring Green, 3 August 1929. ST. Alfred T. Rogers was one of the partners in La Follette's Madison law firm.

67. PFLF to DDM, Madison, 9 August 1929. ST.

68. Schevill's letter to DDM dated Chicago, 16 August 1929, as quoted in DDM to PFLF, Buffalo, 20 August 1929.

69. *Memoranda Book* ["Memoranda relating to the Wright prints purchased by me"], 90–93. LVM. In the archives of the LVM are E. B. Van Vleck's thirteen ledger books: two locating the prints in Van Vleck's file cabinets (the location notebooks entitled on their title pages *Volume I* and *Volume II*), two tracking the finances of his buying, selling, and giving away of prints (from the inscriptions on their first pages these are called the *Accession Book* and the *Memoranda Book*), and nine that list the collection print by print (of these there are four books called *Hiroshige Book 1* through *Book 4* taking up the Hiroshige prints, and five more called simply *Book I–Book V*).

70. The author is grateful for the generous co-operation and guidance of Andrew Stevens, curator of prints and drawings, LVM. Every print in the Van Vleck collection is listed and illustrated (although multiple impressions are represented by only one photograph) in *The Edward Burr Van Vleck Collection of Japanese Prints*, 1990; LVM has compiled a separate list of the Wright prints in the collection, based on E. B. Van Vleck's ledger books. These prints were all accessioned in 1980. The provenance of the prints given in 1984 is not known. Many are duplicates or inferior, and were not recorded as assiduously by Van Vleck. Others were probably added to the collection by John Hasbrouck Van Vleck. Nonetheless, most of the prints with a 1984 accession number were probably also from the Wright collection. This group includes some fine examples from Hokusai's *The Thirty-six Views of Mount Fuji*.

71. For the Hiroshige, Van Vleck ledger titled *Accession Book*, 9; see also *Hiroshige Book III*, 17 (VV #1668) and 119 (VV #1770, or 1980.1307). For Utamaro, Van Vleck ledger *Book II*, 205 (VV #272, or 1980.3216).

72. See *Hiroshige Book IV*, 257 (VV #2308). The date of 1 May 1906 is an error in transcription. Internal evidence suggests that the date of the visit was 1 May 1926.

73. This *aiban* triptych, purchased 1 June 1927, is now in the LVM, 1980.3224abc. See Van Vleck ledger *Book II*, 247.

74. PFLF to DDM, Madison, 7 September 1928. ST.

75. Van Vleck ledger *Book IV*, 71.

76. See Van Vleck *Memoranda Book*.

77. CS to FLW, New York, 20 March 1932; FLW to CS, [Spring Green], 25 March 1932.

78. A visit to the FLWA by Keiko and Roger Keyes in 1987 provided the incentive for the unwrapping and first serious study of the blocks. See *Frank Lloyd Wright and Hiroshige/Furanku Roido Raito to Hiroshige*, 1992. The ten prints at the LVM with Wright provenance corresponding to blocks in the FLWA are 1980.2075–1980.2084.

79. See chapter 3, p. 95. WSS to FLW, Boston, 11 December 1913; WSS to FLW, Boston, 11 January 1914.

80. Roger Keyes's 1980 report on the Van Vleck Collection is in the archives, LVM.

81. See Gookin, *Ukiyo-e Paintings, Japanese and Chinese Color-Prints*, 1926, lots 360–411.

CHAPTER 8

1. FLW to Jean and GEC, [Spring Green], 8 February 1932.

2. Twombly (1979), 204.

3. CKS to FLW, Denver, 3 December 1930.

4. See Leonard and Noel, *Denver: Mining Camp to Metropolis*, [1990]. The author is grateful for assistance from Mrs. Tiny Tipps, historian for the Denver Symphony Guild; see also Bach and Chambers, *The Denver Art Museum*, 1973, 58.

5. FLW to GEC, Spring Green, 24 December 1930. In this letter Wright twice writes "Mrs. Martin" instead of "Mrs. Cranmer," probably because he was in constant correspondence with Darwin D. Martin.

6. FLW to GEC, Spring Green, 31 January 1931.

7. GEC to FLW, Denver, 11 February 1931; FLW to GEC, Spring Green, 16 February 1931.

8. Interest payments ceased and nothing was paid on the principal when it came due in 1933 nor thereafter. In 1932 the Bank of Wisconsin assigned the Taliesin mortgage to the First Wisconsin National Bank of Milwaukee. The mortgage was assigned to Olgivanna Wright in 1936, and within two weeks she in turn transferred it to William Wesley Peters, a charter apprentice at Taliesin and Wright's son-in-law. Peters foreclosed on the mortgage in the late 1940s. See James E. Doyle of La Follette, Sinkyn and Doyle to Darwin R. Martin's Buffalo lawyer, Edward H. Kavinoky, Madison, 30 March 1949.

9. FLW to CKS, Spring Green, 28 March 1931; FLW to GEC, Spring Green, 25 April 1931; GEC to FLW, Denver, 1 May 1931.

10. FLWA, MSS. 1033.007. There are two lists, one written in Wright's hand, the other typed (but with errors in transcription), probably by his secretary.

11. Rose M. Blount, secretary, office of the director of the Denver Art Museum to FLW, Denver, 7 May 1931. None of these prints was ever donated to the Denver Art Museum. Cranmer's gifts to the museum include examples of African sculpture and Native American art, as well as some European furniture. Information courtesy Michele Assaf, Denver Art Museum.

12. FLW to GEC, Spring Green, 15 June 1931.

13. Jean Cranmer, cable to Olgivanna Wright, Denver, 12 August 1931; Cartier Inc. to GEC, New York, 14 November 1931; GEC to FLW, Denver, 17 November 1931.

14. FLW to GEC, Spring Green, 8 February 1932; GEC to FLW, Denver, 17 February 1932; FLW to GC, 20 February 1932; for Wright's description of the house as "the luxurious American home" see FLW to Alice L. Felton of the Photographic Division, Metropolitan Museum of Art, [Spring Green], 25 April 1932. See also Sweeney (1994), 195–200.

15. Notation on typed copy of the Cranmer inventory list (FLWA, MSS. 1033.007).

16. FLW to AAK, Spring Green, 26 December 1930.

17. Invoice for one triptych (*Lady arriving at cherry flower picnic*) from Kroch's Bookstore, Chicago to Art Institute of Chicago, dated 28 September 1931 and paid by Kate Buckingham in January 1932. Archives, The Art Institute of Chicago. See ill. 183.

18. A two-page list of printed books titled "Books (Antique Japanese) sent to Charles Morgan Jan. 19th, 1932" accompanies Wright's cable to CM dated [Spring Green], 19 January 1932; see also "Charles Morgan, Architect, also does etchings," *Chicago Daily Tribune*, 9 September 1930; FLW to CM, Spring Green, 9 January 1932; Wright and Morgan shared an office at 333 North Michigan in Chicago and there is considerable correspondence between them from 1929 to 1946.

19. KEJ to AAK, Spring Green, 30 December [1932]. The letter is dated only by day and month but the list accompanying the letter is headed: "Japanese wood-cut folios and manuals sent to A. Kroch—December 29, 1932."

20. AAK to FLW, Chicago, 14 January 1933.

21. FLW to AAK, Spring Green, 29 June 1933.

22. AAK to FLW, Chicago, 1 July 1933.

23. Mrs. Clarence Hough to FLW, Oak Park, 9 May 1933; KEJ for FLW to Mrs. Clarence Hough, Spring Green, 15 May 1933.

24. FLW to PG, Spring Green, 3 September [1934]; PG to FLW, Kansas City, Mo., 11 September 1934; LW to FLW, Cambridge, Mass., 10 December [1934].

25. Elizabeth Bauer Kassler, telephone conversation with author, 18 April 1994. See also Pfeiffer, "Frank Lloyd Wright: Collecting Japanese Art," in Mirviss, with Carpenter (1995), 8.

26. Dana and Roberts had contributed to the creation of the new school building in 1902.

27. Henning, "At Taliesin," 1992, 63–64.

28. Earl Friar, "At Taliesin," [undated, unpag. newspaper clipping, probably *Capital Times*, 24 April 1936]. ST.

29. "Taliesin," Spring Green's *Weekly Home News*, 2 August 1934, 8; reprinted in Henning (1992), 66. Illustrated printed books with designs by Kōrin from Wright's collection are cited in a list of books compiled by O. P. Reed at the request of Olgivanna Wright on 6 October 1966 at the time the collection was being inventoried for dispersal. All were sold by Reed. A Sotheby's, London, sale on 25 October 1978 lists various woodblock printed books with Frank Lloyd Wright provenance.

30. Henning (1992), 306.

31. Twenty-three-year-old William Adair Bernoudy, an apprentice from St. Louis with a high-school education, recorded a print talk in the "At Taliesin" column in 1934. See Bernoudy, "At Taliesin," 1934, 9. Robert Twombly dismissed these fledgling journalists as pretentious and incompetent: "Having learned his jargon and his phraseology, many pint-sized Frank Lloyd Wrights attempted to bandy about the Master's ideas without bothering to digest them." Twombly (1979), 219.

32. Curtis Besinger to the author, Lawrence, Kans., 10 March 1985.

33. Besinger, *Working with Mr. Wright*, 1995, 30.

34. Besinger, telephone conversation with author, 3 December 1986.

35. Transcript of a print party talk, 29 September 1957. FLWA.

36. Transcript of a print party talk, 20 September 1950. FLWA. Eugene (Gene) Masselink, from Grand Rapids, entered the fellowship at the age of twenty-three, became Wright's secretary, and later took charge of Taliesin graphics and publications. He died at Taliesin.

37. Transcript of a print party talk, 20 June 1954. FLWA.

38. Christie's, New York (sale 7048), 29–30 March 1990, lot 558, and (sale 7176) 16 October 1990, lot 727. Other sets were sold at Christie's, New York (sale 7648), for $266,500, 27 April 1993, lot 240, and $156,500 (sale 8526), 2 November 1996, lot 649.

39. See chapter 7, n. 21. Wright had spent $900 in 1927 buying back this print from his own collection.

40. See Mirviss, with Carpenter (1995).

41. Transcript of a print party talk, 20 September 1950. FLWA.

42. Martin's son remembered the "big Japanese screen" on the wall above a sofa in a room on the first floor. Taped interview with Darwin R. Martin, October 1976 (TR 107, tape 5, side 1). SUNYB. For the original sale see DDM to FLW, Buffalo, 30 October 1922, courtesy Scott Elliott. The screens are identified by Martin only as "pair of screens" and were pur-

chased on 22 October 1922. The sale price of $2,650 is cited also by Mrs. Martin: IM to FLW, Graycliff, Derby, N.Y., dictated 1 June 1941; the screens are described by Wright in FLW to AB, Spring Green, 26 June 1940.

43. Darwin R. Martin to FLW, [Buffalo], 1 March 1938; also taped interview with Darwin D. Martin's daughter, Dorothy Martin Foster, 1972 (TR 9, tape 1, side 1). SUNYB.

44. IM to FLW, Graycliff, Derby, N.Y., dictated 19 June 1941; IM to FLW, Buffalo, 5 May 1939. There is no record of her 1938 letter to Wright; FLW to IM, [Spring Green], 14 June 1939; IM to FLW, Buffalo, 1 January 1940.

45. FLW to IM, Spring Green, 26 June 1940; FLW to AB, [Spring Green], 26 June 1940.

46. IM to FLW, Buffalo, dictated 28 February 1941.

47. Tomita, a disciple of Okakura Kakuzō, joined the staff of the museum in 1907 at the age of eighteen and retired as curator in 1962.

48. TK to GW, Boston, 6 June 1940, courtesy Archives, Museum of Fine Arts, Boston.

49. GW to Nora M. Herrick, Buffalo, 11 June 1940, courtesy Archives, Albright-Knox Art Gallery, Buffalo. (Scott Elliot first drew my attention to this and other letters pertaining to the Martins' screen.) Herrick served as Mrs. Martin's "lady's companion" for many years.

50. IM to GW, Graycliff, Derby, N.Y., 22 June 1940. Archives, Albright-Knox Art Gallery.

51. FLW to IM, Spring Green, 4 September 1940.

52. FLW to IM, Spring Green, 19 March 1941.

53. EM to IM, Spring Green, 26 May 1941, courtesy Scott Elliott; IM to FLW, Derby, N.Y., dictated 1 September 1941; FLW to IM, Spring Green, 15 September 1941.

54. FLW to IM, Spring Green, 6 August 1942.

55. FLW to IM, [Spring Green], 22 July 1943, and FLW to IM, [Spring Green], 2 August 1943; IM to FLW, Derby, N.Y., dictated 26 July 1943.

56. FLW to IM, [Spring Green], 2 August 1943; FLW to IM, [Spring Green], 7 December 1943. In an interview with the author on 18 January 1991, at Taliesin West in Scottsdale, Ariz., architect John DeKoven Hill (1920–1996), who arrived as an apprentice in 1937, said that William Wesley Peters, Wright's son-in-law, had a beautiful pair of screens from the Martin residence, which he later sold to a collector in Minneapolis.

57. Phil Feddersen to author, Clinton, Iowa, 8 April 1994; BBP to author, Scottsdale, 23 May 1994. The prints are now in FLWA in storage. Curtis Besinger also noted a few matted Japanese prints on the walls of the guest rooms of the main house at Taliesin in 1939. Besinger (1997), 11.

58. Donald D. Walker (?–1994), an architect who worked for Wright at Taliesin in 1928–29, received a Hiroshige print inscribed by Wright as a Christmas gift in 1929. It is now with the Walker Collection in the Library of Congress.

59. Elizabeth Bauer Kassler, telephone conversation with author, 18 April 1994.

60. Edgar Tafel, conversation with author, New York, 24 July 1984; John H. Howe to author, Burnsville, Minn., 4 May 1988; among Wright's prints in the Grunwald Center for Graphic Arts at UCLA is one inscribed "To Gene [Eugene Masselink], Christmas 1941." There are several similarly inscribed prints in the FLWA and no doubt in the collections of most former Wright apprentices.

61. Tafel, *About Wright*, 1993, 245.

62. Johnson's daughter, Karen Johnson Boyd (KJB), to the author, [Tarpon Springs, Fla.], 20 April 1994; KJB to author, Racine, [21 September 1994]; the author also benefitted from a lecture on Wingspread by Jonathan Lipman at the Museum of Modern Art, New York, in April 1994.

63. Jacobs, *Building with Frank Lloyd Wright*, 1978, 45–46.

64. *Frank Lloyd Wright: Letters to Architects* (1984), 191. Ragghianti was a Florentine art historian who was director of the Italian Institute of Art History, headquartered in the Palazzo Strozzi.

65. I am indebted to Mary Jane Hamilton for bringing these prints to my attention. See Hamilton, *The Meeting House*, 1991. Bruce Brooks Pfeiffer witnessed the giving of these prints in September 1951. Pfeiffer, telephone conversation with author, 26 September 1994.

66. FLW to GB, Spring Green, 8 October 1934; the debt to Banta had accumulated over a period of about one year; for stationery order see KEJ to GB, Spring Green, 3 October 1933, and J. H. Wilterding to KEJ, Menasha, Wis., 17 July 1934.

67. EM to GB, Spring Green, 14 January 1935.

68. GB to EM, Menasha, Wis., 3 January 1936.

69. GB to FLW, Menasha, Wis., 1 March 1938, and 16 January 1939.

70. FLW to EA, [Spring Green], 24 June 1932.

71. Negotiations for a lecture on architecture were initiated by Wright's secretary; KEJ to EA, Spring Green, 10 [16?] August 1934. The print exhibition is mentioned in a letter from the president of the Wichita Art Association, Maude Schollenberger, to KEJ, Wichita, 23 August 1934; and in a letter from EA to FLW, [Wichita], c. 1 October 1934.

72. *Wichita Beacon*, 18 January 1935, 11.

73. *Wichita Eagle*, 19 January 1935, 3.

74. A photo similar to this one was published in the *Wichita Eagle*, 12 January 1919. A series of photos of the exterior of the house was published on 22 December 1918.

75. LKH to FLW, Wichita, 17 February 1935, quoted in Kingsbury, *Frank Lloyd Wright and Wichita*, 1992, 22.

76. In 1957 Maude Schollenberger, who had corresponded with Wright in 1934 and was still president of the Wichita Art Association, asked Wright to design a new building for the association's art school and gallery. Maude G. Schollenberger to FLW, Wichita, 28 June 1957.

77. FLW to SM, Spring Green, 10 January 1935.

78. FLW to SM, Spring Green, 27 April 1935.

79. FLW to SM, Spring Green, 1 May 1935; FLW to SM, Spring Green, 11 May 1935.

80. Marcus, *Minding the Store*, 1974, 92–93.

81. SM to author, Dallas, 29 March 1994.

82. Ibid.; FLW to SM, Chandler, Ariz., 22 February 1936.

83. Woollcott, "Profiles: The Prodigal Father," 1930, 22–25.

84. Muschamp, *Man about Town,* 1983, 42.

85. AW to FLW, New York, 22 April 1937.

86. FLW to AW, Spring Green, 25 April 1937.

87. FLW to AW, Spring Green, 15 October 1937. Edgar Tafel gives the following bizarre account of this story: Wright utterly mortified Woollcott by demanding of the waiter on the train that his bread should be toasted on one side only. When the bread inevitably arrived toasted on both sides, Wright sent it back to the kitchen with great fanfare. Tafel, telephone conversation with author, 17 February 1994.

88. The author is indebted to Bernice Weisman for transcribing the inscriptions.

89. FLW to AW, Spring Green, 17 August 1937; Railway Express receipt addressed to Woollcott at 10 Gracie Square, New York, FLW to AW, Spring Green, 27 August 1937.

90. Telegram from AW to FLW, Bomoseen, Vt., 11 September 1937; letter from AW to FLW, Bomoseen, Vt., [undated but probably September 1937].

91. FLW to AW, Spring Green, 15 October 1937.

92. Mary W. Baskett, curator of prints, Cincinnati Art Museum, to Roland Koscherak, Cincinnati, 25 November 1970, curatorial file, Cincinnati Art Museum.

93. RK to MWB, Flushing, N.Y., 29 December 1970, archives, Cincinnati Art Museum.

94. CLB to FLW, Beloit, 28 August 1934.

95. FLW to CLB, Spring Green, 13 May 1935; CLB to FLW, Beloit, 15 May 1935.

96. EM to CLB, Spring Green, 1 November 1937; checklist in FLWA titled "Catalogue: Japanese prints loaned to Beloit College for exhibition: November, 1937." Written on the first page is the notation "Returned December 3. O.K. (Gene)"; and Railway Express receipt for one package sent by FLW from Spring Green to CLB in Beloit, 2 November 1937.

97. OKB to FLW, Grand Rapids, 30 September 1937; FLW to OKB, Spring Green, 2 October 1937; also EM to OKB, Spring Green, 12 October 1937.

98. EM to OKB, Spring Green, 27 April 1938.

99. "Japanese Art Is Shown Here: Prints from the Collection of Frank Wright at Local Gallery," *Grand Rapids Press*, 12 May 1938. This reference was provided by Luci King, librarian, Grand Rapids Art Museum. FLWA has an unsigned memorandum of prints sent to the Grand Rapids Art Gallery by Masselink dated Spring Green, 10 June 1938. According to this list, which is at variance with the report published in the *Grand Rapids Press,* he sent off fifty-two matted Hiroshige prints identified only as "16 horizontal, 36 vertical."

100. Vignier invoice dated 10 July 1937, the day Wright sailed for home on the *Bremen;* MD to FLW, Paris, 21 July 1937. Conversion rates are approximate: the invoice is for 7,500 francs, and the dollar was worth 26 francs at the time.

101. The Gyōsho or "Semi-cursive" Tokaidō is named for the style of the script used to write the title cartouche. The set was published in *aiban* format in the early 1840s. For the screen, priced at 7,500 francs, see FLW to MD, Spring Green, 17 August 1937, and MD to FLW, Paris, 10 September 1937. For the prints see Vignier invoice addressed to FLW, Paris, 6 September 1937.

102. MD to FLW, Paris, 30 April 1938; FLW to MD, [Spring Green], [undated], April 1938.

103. MD to FLW, Paris, 30 July 1938.

104. MD to FLW, Paris, 10 August 1939.

105. Invoice from Yamanaka and Company, New York, to FLW listing Wright's account balance from 20 February to 20 December 1937.

106. See Frank Lloyd Wright, "Frank Lloyd Wright," 1938, 16.

107. Now catalogued as FLWA 1186.087. Hedrich-Blessing is a photography studio in Chicago founded in 1930.

108. Besinger (1995), 17.

109. K. Tenneco of Yamanaka and Company to FLW, New York, 19 September 1938; FLW to K. Tenneco, Spring Green, 8 July 1938; EM to K. Tenneco, Spring Green, 15 October 1938; Yamanaka and Company to FLW, New York, 1 November 1938. This gilt-lacquer Buddha, which was considered Olgivanna Wright's property, is on display at Taliesin in Wisconsin. It is in fair condition.

110. Invoice for $6,350, Yamanaka and Company, New York, to FLW, New York, 7 December 1938; EM to Yamanaka and Company, Spring Green, 10 December 1938.

111. R. E. Rothblum, lawyer, to FLW, Chicago, 6 September 1939; Emmett L. Kiley, Alien Property Custodian, to FLW, Chicago, 3 September 1942, and Robert S. Neier of Yamanaka and Company, Chicago, to FLW, Chicago, 4 December 1943.

112. Invoice from Yamanaka and Company, New York to FLW, New York, 31 January 1942; E. H. Perbix, Yamanaka and Company, New York, to FLW, New York, 1 December 1943.

113. Salmony, "The Yamanaka Sale," 1944, 14.

114. AG to author, San Francisco, 13 May 1991.

115. AG to FLW, San Francisco, 9 August 1955. The anonymous eighteenth-century screens with scenes of the twenty-four paragons of filial piety were originally meant for Price Tower in Bartlesville, Oklahoma. When Wright painted a mural on the only available wall surface, they were moved to the Price home, but never exhibited. Joe D. Price to author, Corona Del Mar, 19 February 1999.

116. Besinger (1995), 281.

117. ALG to FLW, San Francisco, 6 February 1941.

118. FLW to ALG, Phoenix, 11 February 1941.

119. RBG to FLW, [San Francisco], 2 March 1948.

120. RBG to FLW, [San Francisco], 24 November 1958.

121. PFLF to DDM, Madison, 9 August 1929.

122. DDM quoted in FLW to DDM, Tokyo, 9 June 1919. ST.

123. Muschamp (1983), 106.

124. The Chinese pieces were sold at auction in 1967 and the prints were sold in 1973 to Richard Lane in Kyoto.

125. MS to FLW, New York, 7 January 1952.

126. FLW to RMC, [Spring Green], 27 January 1948.

127. Ralph Chait's son and daughter, Allen Chait and Marion C. Howe (1923–1997), conversation with author, New York, 16 August 1984.

128. Frank Lloyd Wright, *The Usonian House,* 1953, unpag.

129. In 1953 Seo was located at 598 Madison Avenue but he moved to 756 Madison Avenue the next year. Invoice from JUS to FLW, New York, 5 October 1953; also on display in the Usonian house was a spurious modern Chinese stele incised with the figure of a Bodhisattva in sixth-century style. This is now installed in the drafting studio at Taliesin, Spring Green (FLWA 1187.004).

130. RMC to FLW, New York, 6 October 1953. Wright borrowed the Calder mobile for the Usonian house from the Guggenheim collection, according to Besinger (1995), 259.

131. *Oriental Art: Snuff Bottles, Bronzes, Jades, Pottery and Porcelains, Paintings, Furniture and Decorative Objects,* Parke-Bernet Galleries, New York (sale 2636), 14 December 1967, lot 151.

132. Joseph Seo, interview with author, New York, 16 August 1984; FLW to MS, [Spring Green], 10 August 1951.

133. Invoice from JUS to FLW, New York, 5 October 1953; idem, 20 July 1954. The Taliesin fellow John DeKoven Hill took credit for introducing Wright to Seo in 1953. Hill, interview with author, Taliesin West, Scottsdale, Ariz., 18 January 1991.

134. *Chinese Art; Japanese metal work, lacquer, ivories and screens,* Parke-Bernet Galleries, New York, 4–5 January 1956, lots 449 (illustrated) and 449a. Seo paid $425 for 449a, the Wright screen now in the Frank Lloyd Wright Foundation (1185.032). For Burke screen see Burke, *Japanese Art*, 1993, pl. 3.

135. *Oriental Art* (1967). The objects were sold as "Property of an Arizona Educational Institution." For the longstanding dispute over tax-exempt status see Besinger (1997), 275.

136. Mary Diamond Stein (1909–?), Chicago art dealer, appraised the group of 115 prints in 1961. Mary Diamond, "To Whom It May Concern" appraisal, Chicago, 30 December 1961. The unwelcome excitement at the time of the exhibition was described by two individuals who remember the event: Kenneth Ross, former general manager of Cultural Affairs, City of Los Angeles, in a telephone interview with Heather de Savoye on 15 January 1999, as conveyed to the author; and Robert Haynes, in conversation with the author in Seattle, 18 October 1998. Diamond was in charge of selecting and cataloguing the prints for *Frank Lloyd Wright: Japanese Prints Exhibition* at the Municipal Art Gallery from 10 January through 4 February 1962. Lloyd Wright modeled the gallery on the exhibition pavilion constructed for *Sixty Years of Living Architecture.* For the 1913 incident see chapter 3, p. 86.

137. O. P. Reed, telephone conversation with author, 17 October 1994. In 1984, when the Frank Lloyd Wright Foundation sold a group of Wright's drawings at the Max Protech Gallery in New York, Bruce Pfeiffer, archivist for the foundation, said that Wright told Olgivanna "There are three things that will help you financially: my real estate, my collection of Japanese prints, and my drawings, which will someday be priceless." Michael Kimmelman, "The Frank Lloyd Wright Estate Controversy," *ARTnews* (April 1984): 103.

138. Reed to Richard Carney, Los Angeles, 23 March 1966; Reed to John Amarantides, Los Angeles, 23 June 1966, together with lists. Amarantides (b. 1928), who joined the fellowship in 1951, did the preliminary cataloguing at Taliesin West prior to sending the prints to Reed. The London print dealer Robert Sawers acquired a few hundred dollars' worth of the remaining few books from Reed in the 1970s. They included one book of courtesans by Hosoda Eishi, which he sold to Jack Hillier and which now resides in the British Museum.

139. On the eve of one of the sales to the Grunwald, Reed wrote to the Frank Lloyd Wright Foundation: "I may sell another seven thousand dollars worth to UCLA, and the matter is in the hands of Chancellor [Franklin] Murphy this morning as this is the meeting for the current budget." Reed to Amarantides, Los Angeles, 23 June 1966. Reed's priced lists of the prints that were in the 1962 Municipal Art Gallery exhibit are in the FLWA. Reed also sold some of Wright's prints to the renowned West Coast print collector Edwin Grabhorn (1889–1968). Reed to Carney, Los Angeles, 23 March 1966.

140. Richard Lane to author, Kyoto, 11 March 1999. The sale files are in the FLWA. Reed later sent Lane in Japan two or three faded Eishi and Eishō triptychs.

141. Frank Lloyd Wright, *Antique Colour Prints from the Collection of Frank Lloyd Wright,* 1917, unpag.

142. Frank Lloyd Wright (1943), 193–94.

143. Frank Lloyd Wright, *Antique Colour Prints....,* (1917), unpag.

144. See Beeby, "Wright and Landscape," 1988, 154 ff.

145. Scully (1960), 11.

146. Frank Lloyd Wright, unpublished, undated essay prepared for Darwin D. Martin with letter from FLW to DDM, Oak Park, 11 August 1906. SUNYB.

147. Frank Lloyd Wright (1943), 198–99.

148. The statue appears in archival photos of Wright's studio taken in 1924 (FLWA 6004.023). See Guth, "The Cult of Kannon among Nineteenth Century American Japanophiles," 1995, 28–34.

149. Edgar Kaufmann, Jr., in conversation with the author, New York, January 1985. Cast-iron Ming sculpture is still not well studied. See Albert W. R. Thiel, "Cast Iron in Chinese Art," *Oriental Art* 10, no. 3 (1964): 158–62.

150. Frank Lloyd Wright (1929), 26.

151. Frank Lloyd Wright, transcript of print party talk to fellowship, Taliesin, 20 September 1950 (FLWA 1014.007).

152. Mansfield, "American Appreciation of Japanese Art," 1915, 246–47; FWG to EW, Chicago, 9 February 1919. EWUT. Metzgar [1944], 60, 83.

GLOSSARY OF JAPANESE PRINT TERMS

Note: Prints are measured according to the size of the sheet of paper, not the image, but, as collectors know, the sheet may be trimmed. Although paper sizes remain remarkably stable, there are slight variations depending on the region of manufacture. Certain standard sizes are recognized by collectors, but there is still considerable confusion in terminology.

aiban
"medium-large block," a size of paper used for prints that measure approximately 9¼ x 12–13 in.

beni
safflower red

benizuri-e
"red printed picture," a two-color print, generally deep pink and green, popular c. 1740–55

chūban
"medium block," a print measuring half the size of an *ōban* or an *aiban*

harimaze
"pasted scraps," a print composed of many small pictures

hashira-e or *hashirakake*
literally "pillar picture" or "pillar hanging," a very tall, narrow print said to have been displayed on a wooden pillar mounted as a hanging scroll, measuring approximately 27 x 4 in.

hosoban
small, narrow print in vertical format typically measuring 13 x 5⅝ in.

kakemono-e
"hanging scroll picture," a vertical *ōban* diptych. The term was used in Western literature in the early twentieth century as a catchall to describe a variety of prints in extra-large format, including those made in the late seventeenth–early eighteenth century, which we would now call *ōōban*. Current Japanese scholarship uses the term *kakemono-e* to describe vertical *ōban* diptychs, which were popular from the early nineteenth century and which were often sold mounted as hanging scrolls.

mizu-e
"water picture," a type of full-color woodcut with color rather than black outline, which enjoyed a brief vogue in the 1760s

ōban
"large block," a print in either vertical or horizontal format and the most common size of woodcut from the 1790s through the nineteenth century. In the first half of the eighteenth-century *ōban* were printed on a half sheet of Mino paper and measure approximately 18 x 13 in. (see ill. 171). From the 1760s they were printed on half of a smaller sheet and measure approximately 15 x 10 in.

ōōban
"extra-large block," a standard format for black-and-white and hand-colored prints from c. 1670 to the mid-1710s, measuring approximately 12½–25½ x 12–13 in. A smaller sheet of paper was pieced to the bottom of the print to extend its length: close inspection will reveal a horizontal seam.

pillar print
see *hashira-e*

shikishiban
color woodcut in the nearly square shape of a poem card (*shikishi*), a format popular for *surimono* from 1810 to about 1835, measuring approximately 8¼ x 7½ in.

sumizuri-e
uncolored woodcut printed in ink (*sumi*)

surimono
literally "printed thing"; deluxe, limited-edition print, privately commissioned either for an announcement or for issue as a New Year's greeting, often including one or more poems

tan-e
woodcut hand-colored with red lead (*tan*) pigment

tanzakuban
"narrow block," a term for various sizes of paper used for prints in narrow, vertical format that measure approximately 15⅜ x 4⅛–6¹⁵⁄₁₆ in., usually a half or third of an *aiban* or *ōban* sheet; a small *tanzakuban* measures approximately 13 x 5 in., while a medium *tanzakuban* measures approximately 15 x 5 in.

uki-e
perspective print

ukiyo-e
"picture of the floating world," a generic term for Japanese woodcuts

BIBLIOGRAPHY

Alofsin, Anthony. *Frank Lloyd Wright—The Lost Years, 1910–1922*. Chicago and London: University of Chicago Press, 1993.

———, ed. *Frank Lloyd Wright: An Index to the Taliesin Correspondence*. 5 vols. New York and London: Garland, 1988.

"An Important Gift of Japanese Color-prints." *Bulletin of the Minneapolis Institute of Arts* 6 (Nov. 1917): 65–68.

Annual of the Chicago Architectural Club, Being the Book of the Thirteenth Annual Exhibition 1900. Chicago: Chicago Architectural Club, 1900.

Aoki Shigeru and Sakai Tadayasu, eds. *Kindai no hanga* (Modern woodblock prints). Vol. 12 of *Nihon no kindai bijutsu* (Modern Japanese art). Tokyo: Ōtsuki Shoten, 1994.

Applebaum, Stanley. *The Chicago World's Fair of 1893: A Photographic Record*. New York: Dover Publications, 1978.

Bach, Cile M., and Marlene Chambers. *The Denver Art Museum: Major Patrons and Donors*. Denver: Denver Art Museum, 1973.

"Backs Mrs. Wright's Claim." *New York Times*, 18 February 1927, 44.

Bargelt, Louise James. "Art." *Chicago Sunday Tribune*, 18 November 1917, part 8, p. 2.

———. "Japanese Prints and Etchings on Show at Institute." *Chicago Daily Tribune*, 7 December 1917, 20.

———. "Superb showing of Japanese prints at the Arts Club." *Chicago Daily Tribune* [c. 17 November 1917]. Clipping attached to Jane Porter's copy of Wright's 1917 *Antique Colour Prints from the Collection of Frank Lloyd Wright*, Archives, Frank Lloyd Wright Foundation, 1025.011.

Beeby, Thomas H. "Wright and Landscape: A Mythical Interpretation." In *The Nature of Frank Lloyd Wright*, edited by Carol R. Bolon, Robert S. Nelson, and Linda Seidel. Chicago: University of Chicago Press, 1988.

Bernoudy, William. "At Taliesin." *Wisconsin State Journal*, 19 September 1934, 9.

Besinger, Curtis. *Working with Mr. Wright: What It Was Like*. New York and Cambridge, England: Cambridge University Press, 1997.

Boon, K. G. "A Dutch Artist in Japan." In *The Fascinating World of the Japanese Artist*, edited by H. M. Kaempfer and W. O. G. Sickinghe. The Hague: Society for Arts and Crafts, 1971.

Bosch Reitz, S. C. "Revamped Japanese Prints." *Bulletin of the Metropolitan Museum of Art* 15 (Dec. 1920): 280–81.

Brooks, H. Allen. *The Prairie School: Frank Lloyd Wright and His Midwest Contemporaries*. New York and London: W. W. Norton and Company, 1972.

———. *Writings on Wright: Selected Comment on Frank Lloyd Wright*. Cambridge, Mass., and London: MIT Press, 1981.

Bruccoli, Mathew J. *The Fortunes of Mitchell Kennerly, Bookman*. San Diego, New York, and London: Harcourt Brace Jovanovich, 1986.

Burke, Mary Griggs. *Japanese Art: Personal Selections from The Mary and Jackson Burke Collection*. Exh. cat. Delray Beach, Fla.: Morikami Museum and Japanese Gardens, 1993.

Catalogue of a Part of the Valuable Collection of Japanese Colour Prints, the Property of Frederick William Gookin, Esq. of Chicago, U. S. A. London: Sotheby, Wilkinson and Hodge, 23–24 May 1910.

Catalogue of the Private Collection of an Importer of Japanese Products Comprising Valuable and Important Japanese Colour Prints. London: Sotheby, Wilkinson and Hodge, 24–27 January 1911.

Catalogue of the Valuable Collection of Japanese Colour Prints, Illustrated Books and a Few Kakemono, the Property of John Stewart Happer. Preface by Arthur Morrison. London: Sotheby, Wilkinson and Hodge, 26 April 1909.

"Charges Wright gave up wealth to defraud her." *Chicago Daily Tribune*, 18 February 1927, 28.

"Charles Morgan, Architect, also does etchings." *Chicago Daily Tribune*, 9 September 1930.

The Chicago Architectural Annual. Chicago: Chicago Architectural Club, 1902.

Chicago Architectural Club. *Book of the Twenty-seventh Annual Exhibition*. Chicago: Art Institute of Chicago, 1914.

Chinese Art; Japanese metalwork, lacquer, ivories and screens. New York: Parke-Bernet Galleries, 4–5 January 1956.

"Chinese Art Show Opens at Institute; Eminent Men Here." *Chicago Daily Tribune*, 20 November 1917, 14.

Chisholm, Lawrence. *Fenollosa: The Far East and American Culture*. New Haven: Yale University Press, 1963.

Clark, Timothy T. "Katsukawa Shunshō and the Revolution in Actor Portraiture." *Orientations* 23 (June 1992): 53–63.

———. *Ukiyo-e Paintings in the British Museum*. London: British Museum Press, 1992.

Clark, Timothy T., and Osamu Ueda. *The Actor's Image: Print Makers of the Katsukawa School*. Chicago: Art Institute of Chicago with Princeton University Press, 1994.

Colburn, Frederick S. *The Story and Catalogue of the Japanese Prints Collected by Frederick S. Colburn, 1915–1930*. N. p.: Privately printed by the author, [1930?].

Coleman, Oliver. *Successful Homes*. Chicago: Herbert S. Stone and Co., 1899.

Conant, Ellen P. "Captain Frank Brinkley Resurrected." In *Meiji no Takara, Treasures of Imperial Japan*. Vol. 1 of *The Nasser D. Khalili Collection of Japanese Art*, edited by Oliver Impey and Malcolm Fairley, 124–50. London: Kibo Foundation, 1995.

———. "Refractions of the Rising Sun: Japan's Participation in International Exhibitions 1862–1910." In *Japan and Britain: An Aesthetic Dialogue 1850–1930*, edited by Tomoko Sato and Toshio Watanabe, 79–92. London: Lund Humphries, 1991.

Connely, Willard. *Louis Sullivan as He Lived.* New York: Horizon Press, 1960.

Coombs, Elizabeth I. "The Role of Discovery in Conservation: Reading History from Japanese Prints." *Impressions* 21 (1999): 70–89.

Cram, Ralph Adams. *Impressions of Japanese Architecture.* First printed by The Baker and Taylor Company, 1905. Boston: Marshall Jones Company, 1930.

Daiikai ukiyo-e dainyūsatsukai (First large ukiyo-e auction). Tokyo: Nihon ukiyo-e sho kyōdō kumiai, 1 June 1990.

Darling, Sharon S. "Arts and Crafts Shops in the Fine Arts Building." *Chicago History* 6 (summer 1977): 79–81.

Darwin D. Martin Papers, Department of Special Collections, Stanford University Libraries.

Day, A. Grove. *James A. Michener.* New York: Twayne Publishers, 1964.

De Long, David G. *Frank Lloyd Wright: Designs for an American Landscape, 1922–1932.* New York: Harry N. Abrams, 1996.

[Diamond, Mary]. *Frank Lloyd Wright: Japanese Prints Exhibition.* Exh. pamphlet. Los Angeles: Municipal Art Gallery, 1962.

Dow, Arthur Wesley. *Composition: A Series of Exercises Selected from a New System of Art Education.* Boston: J. M. Bowles, 1899.

Drexler, Arthur. *The Drawings of Frank Lloyd Wright.* New York: Museum of Modern Art, 1962.

Duis, Perry R. "'All Else Passes—Art Alone Endures': The Fine Arts Building 1918 to 1930/40." *Chicago History* 7, no. 1 (1978): 40–51.

———. "'Where Is Athens Now?' The Fine Arts Building 1898 to 1918." *Chicago History* 6, no. 2 (1977): 66–78.

The Edward Burr Van Vleck Collection of Japanese Prints. Introduction by Andrew Stevens. Madison: Elvehjem Museum of Art, University of Wisconsin-Madison, 1990.

"F. W. Gookin, 82, Famous Expert on Japanese Art, Dies." *Chicago Sunday Tribune*, 19 January 1936, 16.

"F .W. Gookin Dies; Oriental Scholar." *New York Times*, 19 January 1936, section 2, p. 8.

[Fenollosa, Ernest Francisco]. *Catalogue of the Exhibition of Ukiyoe* [sic] *Paintings and Prints.* Tokyo: Bunshichi Kobayashi, 1898.

Fenollosa, Ernest Francisco. *Epochs of Chinese and Japanese Art.* 2 vols. First published by Frederick A. Stokes Company and William Heinemann, 1912. New York: Dover Publications, 1963.

———. *Hokusai and His School.* Exh. cat. Boston: Museum of Fine Arts, 1893.

———. *The Exhibition of Ukiyoye Paintings and Prints at the Yamanaka Galleries.* New York: Yamanaka Galleries, 1908.

———. *The Masters of Ukioye* [sic]: *Japanese Paintings and Color Prints.* New York: W. H. Ketcham, 1896.

Fenollosa, Mary McNeil. *Hiroshige: The Artist of Mist, Snow and Rain.* San Francisco: Vickery, Atkins and Torrey, 1901.

Fernandez, Rafael. *Eastern Winds: The Imprint of Japan on Nineteenth and Early Twentieth Century Western Graphics.* Williamstown, Mass.: Sterling and Francine Clark Art Institute, 1982.

Ferre, Barre. "The House and Garden of W. S. Spaulding, Esq." *American Homes and Gardens* (Oct. 1910): 375–82.

Ficke, Arthur Davison. *Chats on Japanese Prints.* London: T. Fisher Unwin, 1915.

———. *The Japanese Print Collection of Arthur Davison Ficke.* New York: Anderson Galleries (sale 1915), 29–30 January 1925.

———. "A Modern Japanese Print Designer." *The Arts* (Jan. 1922): 203–6.

"Fifteenth Annual." *Oak Leaves*, 28 April 1906, 11.

Finlay, Nancy. *Artists of the Book in Boston: 1890–1910.* Cambridge, Mass.: Department of Printing and Graphic Arts, Houghton Library, Harvard College Library, 1985.

Forrer, Matthi. *Hiroshige.* Munich and New York: Prestel, 1997.

Frank Lloyd Wright: Architect. Edited by Terence Riley with Peter Reed. New York: Museum of Modern Art, 1994.

Frank Lloyd Wright and Hiroshige/Furanku Roido Raito to Hiroshige. Edited by Alpha Cubic Gallery. Exh. cat. Kyoto: Kyoto Shoin, 1992.

Frank Lloyd Wright and Japan/Furanku Roido Raito to Nihon ten. Edited by Hata Shinji. Exh. cat. Tokyo: Stichting Siebold Council, 1997.

Frank Lloyd Wright-Darwin D. Martin Papers (MSS. 22.8), University Archives, State University of New York at Buffalo.

Frank Lloyd Wright: Letters to Architects. Edited by Bruce Brooks Pfeiffer. Fresno: Press at California State University, 1984.

Frank Lloyd Wright: Letters to Clients. Edited by Bruce Brooks Pfeiffer. Fresno: Press at California State University, 1986.

Frank Lloyd Wright Retrospective/Furanku Roido Raito kaiko ten. Edited by Jonathan Lipman et al. Exh. cat. Tokyo: Mainichi Shinbun, 1991.

"Frank Lloyd Wright to Lecture Today on His Japanese Prints." *Chicago Daily Tribune*, 22 November 1917, 15.

Frank Lloyd Wright's Fifty Views of Japan: The 1905 Photo Album. Edited by Melanie Birk. San Francisco: Pomegranate Artbooks, 1996.

"Frederick William Gookin." In *Chicago Literary Club Year Book for 1936–1937*, 109–11. Chicago: Chicago Literary Club, 1937.

"Frederick W. Gookin (1853–1936)." *Bulletin of the Art Institute of Chicago* 30 (Feb. 1936): 19.

Frelinghuysen, Alice Coonley, Gary Tinterow, Susan Alyson Stein, Gretchen Wold, and Julia Meech. *Splendid Legacy: The Havemeyer Collection.* New York: Metropolitan Museum of Art, 1993.

French Painting and Ukiyo-e: The Eye of Tadamasa Hayashi, a Bridge Between the Eastern and Western Cultures/Furansu kaiga to ukiyo-e: Tōzai bunka no kakehashi, Hayashi Tadamasa no me ten. Edited by Hasegawa Hiroshi et al. Tokyo: Japan Association of Art Museums and the Yomiuri Shinbun, 1996.

Futagawa Yukio, ed. *Taliesin.* Vol. 2 of *Frank Lloyd Wright Selected Houses.* Tokyo: A. D. A. Edita, 1990.

"Gallery XI—The W. S. and J. T. Spaulding Collection of Surimono." In *Catalogue of the Inaugural Exhibition*, 143–44. Cleveland: Cleveland Museum of Art, 1916.

Gannett, William C. *The House Beautiful.* River Forest, Ill.: Auvergne Press, 1896–97.

Gentles, Margaret. "Clarence Buckingham, Collector of Japanese Prints." *Apollo* 84, no. 55 (1966): 208–15.

Gill, Brendan. *Many Masks: A Life of Frank Lloyd Wright.* New York: G. P. Putnam's Sons, 1987.

Glaser, Curt, and Fritz Rumpf. *Sammlung Tony Straus-Negbaur.* Berlin: Paul Cassirer, 1928.

Goc, Michael J. *Many a Fine Harvest: Sauk County 1840–1990.* Friendship, Wis.: Sauk County Historical Society and the New Past Press, 1990.

Gookin, Frederick W. *Catalogue of a Loan Exhibition of Ancient Chinese Paintings, Sculptures and Jade Objects from the Collection formed by Charles Lang Freer and given by him to the nation through the Smithsonian Institution.* Chicago: Art Institute of Chicago, 1917.

————. *Catalogue of a Loan Exhibition of Japanese Color Prints.* New York: Japan Society of New York, 1911.

————. *Catalogue of a Loan Exhibition of Japanese Colour Prints.* Chicago: Art Institute of Chicago, 1908.

————. *Catalogue of an Exhibition of Color Prints by Suzuki Harunobu.* Chicago: Caxton Club, 1905.

————. *The Chicago Literary Club: A history of its first fifty years.* Chicago: Privately printed, 1926.

————. *Japanese Colour-Prints and Their Designers.* New York: Japan Society, 1913.

————. "Japanese Paintings and Prints." *Bulletin of the Art Institute of Chicago* 17 (May 1923): 53–55.

————. "A Notable Addition to the Buckingham Collection." *Bulletin of the Art Institute of Chicago* 28 (November 1934): 78.

————. *Rare and Valuable Japanese Color Prints, the Noted Collection Formed by a Distinguished French Connoisseur of Paris.* New York: Walpole Galleries (sale 12), 20 January 1921.

————. *Rare and Valuable Japanese Color Prints, the Property of Messrs. William S. and John T. Spaulding of Boston, Mass.* New York: American Art Association, 16–18 November 1921.

————. *Ukiyo-e Paintings, Japanese and Chinese Color-Prints: The S. H. Mori Collection.* New York: American Art Association, 9–10 December 1926.

Gordon, Elizabeth. "Wright's Way with Little Things." *House Beautiful* (Oct. 1959): 232–33, 316–20.

Green, William. "A Chat on Arthur Davison Ficke (1883–1945)." *Andon* 11 (autumn 1983): 1–12.

————. "Dr. Arthur B. Duel (1870–1936)." *Andon* 13 (spring 1984): 1–10.

————. *Japanese Woodblock Prints: A bibliography of writings from 1822–1992 entirely or partly in English text.* Leiden: Ukiyo-e Books, 1993.

————. "Lost in Time: The Unpublished Masterpiece on Katsukawa Shunshō." *Andon* 16 (winter 1984): 1–6.

————. "Mary A. Ainsworth: Pioneer American Woman Collector of Japanese Prints." *Impressions* 12 (summer 1986): 1–9.

————. "A peerless pair: Frederick W. Gookin and Frank Lloyd Wright and the Art Institute of Chicago's 1908 exhibition of Japanese prints." *Andon* 14 (summer 1984): 14–19.

————. "Published writings on Japanese prints of Arthur Davison Ficke." *Andon* 7 (autumn 1982): 22–25.

Guerrero, Pedro E. *Picturing Wright: An Album from Frank Lloyd Wright's Photographer.* San Francisco: Pomegranate Artbooks, 1994.

"Gūkin shi no raiyū" (Gookin's visit). *Ukiyo-e no kenkyū* 13–14 (Nov. 1925):17–19.

Gunsaulus, Helen C. "The Clarence Buckingham Collection of Japanese Prints." *Bulletin of the Art Institute of Chicago* 33, no. 4 (1939): 56–58.

Gunsaulus, Helen C., and Charles Fabens Kelley. "Frederick W. Gookin (1853–1936)." *Bulletin of the Art Institute of Chicago* 30 (Feb. 1936): 19.

Guth, Christine M. E. *Art, Tea, and Industry: Masuda Takashi and the Mitsui Circle.* Princeton: Princeton University Press, 1993.

————. "The Exotic, the Aesthetic, the Spiritual: Japanese Art in the Eyes of Early American Collectors." In Amy G. Poster, *Crosscurrents: Masterpieces of East Asian Art from New York Private Collections,* 28–43. Exh. cat. New York: Japan Society and Brooklyn Museum of Art, 1999.

————. "The Cult of Kannon among Nineteenth Century American Japanophiles." *Orientations* 26 (Dec. 1995): 28–34.

Hamilton, Mary Jane. *Frank Lloyd Wright and the Book Arts.* Madison: Friends of the University of Wisconsin-Madison Libraries, 1993.

————. "Maginel Wright Barney: An Artist in Her Own Right." *Wisconsin Academy Review* (fall 1992): 4–11.

————. *The Meeting House: Heritage and Vision.* Madison: Friends of the Meeting House, 1991.

Handy, Moses P., ed. *The Official Directory of the World's Columbian Exposition.* Chicago: W. B. Conkey Co., 1893.

Hanks, David. *The Decorative Designs of Frank Lloyd Wright.* New York: Dutton, 1979.

Happer, John S. *Japanese Sketches and Japanese Prints.* Tokyo: Kairyudo, 1934.

Harvard College Class of 1888: Fiftieth Anniversary Report. Cambridge, Mass.: Printed for the class, 1938.

Harvard College Class of 1892, Report XII 1892–1932. Norwood, Mass.: Plimpton Press, 1932.

Harvard College Class of 1888: Secretary's Report No. VII, Twenty-fifth Anniversary. Cambridge, Mass.: Harvard College, 1913.

Hawkins, Lucy Rogers. "Local Merchant Collects Japanese Prints as Hobby." *Evanston News-Index,* 3 December 1932, 3.

————. "North Shore Personalities." *Winnetka Talk,* 28 November 1935, 28, 33.

Hayashi Minao. *Shunjū-sengoku jidai seidōki no kenkyū* (Study of ritual bronzes of the Warring States Spring and Autumn Period). Tokyo: Yoshikawa Kōbunkan, 1989.

Hearn, M. F. "A Japanese Inspiration for Frank Lloyd Wright's Rigid-Core High-Rise Structures." *Journal of the Society of Architectural Historians* 50 (Mar. 1991): 68–71.

Heckscher, Morrison, and Elizabeth G. Miller. *An Architect and His Client, Frank Lloyd Wright and Francis W. Little.* Exh. cat. New York: Metropolitan Museum of Art, 1973.

Henning, Randolph C., comp. *"At Taliesin": Newspaper Columns by Frank Lloyd Wright and the Taliesin Fellowship 1934–1937.* Carbondale and Edwardsville: Southern Illinois University Press, 1992.

Hess, Jeffrey A. *Their Splendid Legacy: The First 100 Years of the Minneapolis Society of Fine Arts.* Minneapolis: Minneapolis Society of Fine Arts, 1985.

Hickman, Money L. *Shoki hanga* (Early prints). *Bosuton bijutsukan 1/Museum of Fine Arts, Boston I* volume of Ukiyo-e shūka (Masterpieces of ukiyo-e). Tokyo: Shōgakukan, 1983.

————. *Kiyonaga. Bosuton bijutsukan 2/ Museum of Fine Arts, Boston II* volume of Ukiyo-e shūka (Masterpieces of ukiyo-e). Tokyo: Shōgakukan, 1985.

Hickman, Money L., and Elizabeth Swinton. *Utamaro. Bosuton bijutsukan 3/Museum of Fine Arts, Boston III* volume of Ukiyo-e shūka (Masterpieces of ukiyo-e). Tokyo: Shōgakukan, 1978.

Higuchi Hiroshi, ed. *Ukiyo-e no ryūtsū, shūshū, kenkyū, happyō no rekishi* (History of the circulation, collecting, study, and publication of ukiyo-e). Supplementary vol. of *Ukiyo-e bunken mokuroku* (Catalogue of ukiyo-e documents), edited by Harigaya Shōkichi et al. Tokyo: Mitō Shooku, 1972.

Hillier, Jack. *Japanese Prints and Drawings from the Vever Collection.* 3 vols. London: Sotheby's, 1979.

Hitchcock, Henry-Russell. *In the Nature of Materials: The Buildings of Frank Lloyd Wright, 1887–1941.* New York: Duell, Sloane and Pearce, 1942.

Hoffmann, Donald. *Frank Lloyd Wright's Dana House.* Mineola, N.Y.: Dover Publications, 1996.

————. *Frank Lloyd Wright's Hollyhock House.* New York: Dover Publications, 1992.

"Honkai no posuta" (Our society's poster). *Ukiyo-e no kenkyū* 1, no. 3 (Mar.1922 [date given in English is mistakenly printed as Oct. 1921]): 22–23.

"The Howard Mansfield Collection: Japanese Potteries, The gift of Mr. Mansfield." *Bulletin of the Metropolitan Museum of Art* 32 (May 1937): 115–26.

Hosley, William. *The Japan Idea: Art and Life in Victorian America.* Hartford: Wadsworth Atheneum, 1990.

The Imperial: The First 100 Years. Tokyo: Imperial Hotel, 1990.

"An important gift of Japanese color prints." *Bulletin of the Minneapolis Institute of the Arts* 6 (Nov. 1917): 65–68.

Ingraham, Mark H. "The Van Vlecks: A Family of Intellect and Taste." *The Wisconsin Alumnus* (Mar.–Apr. 1981): 16–19.

Jacobs, Herbert, and Katherine Jacobs. *Building with Frank Lloyd Wright.* Carbondale and Edwardsville: Southern Illinois University Press, 1978.

"Japanese Art at the Chicago Exhibition." *The Builder* 65 (11 Nov. 1893): 349–51.

Japanese Color Prints…Brought Together by the Well-Known Connoisseur Bunkio Matsuki. New York: Anderson Galleries (sale 1456), 19–20 January 1920.

"Japanese Color Prints Shown." *Chicago Daily Tribune,* 26 March 1914, 10.

Japanese Engravings: Old Prints in Color Collected by S. Bing, Paris. New York: American Art Galleries, 1894.

"Japanese Print Auctions are Novel." *New York Times,* 13 January 1921, section 2, p. 4.

The Japanese Print Collection of Arthur Davison Ficke. Foreword by Arthur Davison Ficke. New York: Anderson Galleries (sale 1915), 29–30 January [1925].

"The Japanese Print Exhibition." *Bulletin of the Art Institute of Chicago* 1 (Apr. 1908): 36–38.

"Japanese Print Sells for $1,025." *New York Times,* 21 January 1920, 6.

"Japanese Prints Background of Arts Club Opening Tea." *Chicago Daily Tribune,* 12 November 1917, 15.

"Japanese Prints Sold. A set of Tokaido Gojusan Tsugi Brings $195—211 Numbers, $2,694." *New York Times,* 20 January 1920, 6.

Johnson, Rossiter, ed. *A History of the World's Columbian Exposition.* New York: D. Appleton and Co., 1898.

Jones, Ellen Lloyd, and Jane Lloyd Jones. *The Hillside Home School.* Hillside, Wis.: unpag., 1902–3.

Jordy, William H. "The 'Little house' at the Metropolitan," *The New Criterion* 1 (Jan. 1983): 56–61.

Jōzuka Taketoshi. *Gashō Hayashi Tadamasa* (Art dealer Hayashi Tadamasa). Fukuyama: Kita Nihon Shuppansha, 1972.

————. *Umi o wataru ukiyo-e: Hayashi Tadamasa no shōgai* (Ukiyo-e that crossed the ocean: The life of Hayashi Tadamasa). Tokyo: Bijutsu Kōronsha, 1981.

Kano Hiroyuki. "Furanku Roido Raito to Nihon kaiga" (Frank Lloyd Wright and Japanese painting). In *Frank Lloyd Wright and Japan/Furanku Roido Raito to Nihon ten,* edited by Hata Shinji, 11–15. Tokyo: Stichting Siebold Council, 1997.

Kaufmann, Jr., Edgar. "Frank Lloyd Wright's Architecture Exhibited." *The Metropolitan Museum of Art Bulletin* (fall 1982): 4–46.

Keyes, Roger S. *Japanese Woodblock Prints: A Catalogue of the Mary A. Ainsworth Collection.* Oberlin: Allen Memorial Art Museum, 1984.

————. *Surimono: Privately Published Japanese Prints in the Spencer Museum of Art.* Tokyo: Kodansha International, 1984.

Kinch, Richard. *Wingspread—the Building.* Racine, Wis.: Johnson Wax Foundation, 1981.

Kingsbury, Pamela D. *Frank Lloyd Wright and Wichita: the first Usonian design.* Wichita, Kans.: Wichita-Sedgwick County Historical Museum, 1992.

Kirishiki Shinjiro. "The Story of the Imperial Hotel, Tokyo." *Japan Architect,* no. 138 (1968): 113–38.

Kobayashi Tadashi and Howard Link. *Prints by Utagawa Hiroshige in the James A. Michener Collection.* Vol. 1. Honolulu: Honolulu Academy of Arts, 1991.

Kōshū. "Shugio Hiromichi shi o tou" (A visit with Shugio Hiromichi). *Bijutsu shinpō* 10 (Sept. 1911): 18.

Kostka, Robert. "Frank Lloyd Wright in Japan." *The Prairie School Review* 3 (1966): 5–23.

Kusaba Nobuyoshi. "Furanku Roido Raito shi kessaku shū hakkan ni tsuite" (A publication of Frank Lloyd Wright's collected masterpieces). *Kenchiku gahō* 9 (Nov. 1917): loose, unnumbered page of text.

Lancaster, Clay. "Japanese Buildings in the United States before 1900: Their Influence upon American Domestic Architecture." *The Art Bulletin* 35, no. 3 (1955): 217–25.

———. *The Japanese Influence in America*. New York: Walton H. Rawls, 1963.

Lane, Richard. *Hokusai: Life and Work*. New York: E. P. Dutton, 1989.

Lawton, Thomas. "Yamanaka Sadajirō: Advocate for Asian Art." *Orientations* 26, no. 1 (1995): 80–93.

Lawton, Thomas, and Linda Merrill. *Freer: A Legacy of Art*. Washington, D.C., and New York: Freer Gallery of Art, Smithsonian Institution, and Harry N. Abrams, 1993.

"Lawyer Obtains Mrs. M. N. Wright's Japanese Prints." *Chicago Daily Tribune*, 29 February 1928, 7.

Ledderose, Lothar. "Some Observations on the Imperial Art Collection in China." *Transactions of the Oriental Ceramic Society* 43 (1978–79): 33–46.

Ledoux, Louis V. "The Utamaro Exhibition." *Ukiyo-e no kenkyū* 5, no. 2 (1926):1–3.

Leonard, Stephen J., and Thomas J. Noel. *Denver: Mining Camp to Metropolis*. Niwot, Colo.: University Press of Colorado, [1990].

Levine, Neil. "Hollyhock House and the Romance of Southern California." *Art in America* (Sept. 1983): 150–65.

———. *The Architecture of Frank Lloyd Wright*. Princeton: Princeton University Press, 1996.

Levy, Florence N., ed. *American Art Annual 1905–1906*. Vol. 5. New York: American Art Annual, 1905.

———. *American Art Annual 1907–1908*. Vol. 6. New York: American Art Annual, 1908.

———. *American Art Annual 1910–11*. Vol. 8. New York: American Art Annual, 1911.

———. *American Art Annual 1911*. Vol. 9. New York: American Art Annual, 1911.

———. *American Art Annual*. Vol. 14. Washington, D.C.: American Federation of Arts, 1917.

Lilien, Marya. "At Taliesin." *Capital Times*, 4 December 1936, 17.

Link, Howard. "James A. Michener: His Odyssey in Japanese Prints." In *Edo Beauties in Ukiyo-e/Bijinga*, edited by staff of Kokusai Art, 8–15. Tokyo: Kokusai Art, 1994.

Mansfield, Howard. "American Appreciation of Japanese Art." In *America to Japan*, edited by Lindsay Russell, 239–50. New York and London: G. P. Putnam's Sons, 1915.

———. "Japanese Prints: an address delivered by Howard Mansfield at The Grolier Club on Ladies' Day, April 10, 1896." *Transactions of the Grolier Club of the City of New York*. Part 3: Feb. 1894–July 1899, 111–30. New York: Grolier Club, 1899.

Manson, Grant C. *Frank Lloyd Wright to 1910: The First Golden Age*. New York: Reinhold Publishing Corporation, 1958.

Marcus, Stanley. *Minding the Store*. Boston: Little, Brown and Company, 1974.

Matsuki Bunkio. *Descriptive Catalogue of an Important Collection of Japanese and Chinese Pottery, Porcelain, Bronzes, Brocades, Prints, Embroideries, Kakemono, Screens, Ivories and Gold Lacquers Selected by Mr. Bunkio Matsuki*. Boston: Leonard and Company's Galleries, 1898.

Meech, Julia. "Frank Lloyd Wright and Japanese Art." In *International Symposium "Japonisme Comes to America,"* 32–35. Tokyo: Setagaya Art Museum, 1992.

———. "Frank Lloyd Wright and the Art Institute of Chicago." *Orientations* 23 (June 1992): 64–76.

———. "Frank Lloyd Wright, Collector." *Frank Lloyd Wright Quarterly* 6 (spring 1995) 8–11.

———. *Rain and Snow: The Umbrella in Japanese Art*. Exh. cat. New York: Japan Society Gallery, 1993.

———. "Shugio Hiromichi and the Grolier Club." *Gazette of the Grolier Club*, n.s., no. 49 (1998): 79–90.

———. "The Other Havemeyer Passion: Collecting Asian Art." In Alice Coonley Frelinghuysen et al., *Splendid Legacy: The Havemeyer Collection*, 129–50. New York: Metropolitan Museum of Art, 1993.

———. "The Spaulding Brothers and Frank Lloyd Wright: Opportunity of a Lifetime." *Orientations* 26 (Mar. 1995): 36–49.

Meech, Julia, and Christine Guth. *The Matsukata Collection of Ukiyo-e Prints: Masterpieces from the Tokyo National Museum*. Exh. cat. New Brunswick: Jane Voorhees Zimmerli Art Museum, Rutgers, The State University of New Jersey, 1988.

Meech, Julia, and Gabriel P. Weisberg. *Japonisme Comes to America: The Japanese Impact on the Graphic Arts 1876–1925*. New York: Harry N. Abrams, 1990.

Meech-Pekarik, Julia. "Early Collectors of Japanese Prints and the Metropolitan Museum of Art." *Metropolitan Museum Journal*, 17 (1984): 93–118.

———. "Frank Lloyd Wright and Japanese Prints." *The Metropolitan Museum of Art Bulletin*, 40 (fall 1982): 48–57.

———. *Frank Lloyd Wright and Japanese Prints: The Collection of Mrs. Avery Coonley*. Exh. brochure. Washington, D.C.: American Institute of Architects Foundation, 1983.

———. "Frank Lloyd Wright's Other Passion." In *The Nature of Frank Lloyd Wright*, edited by Carol R. Bolon, Robert S. Nelson, and Linda Seidel, 125–53. Chicago: The University of Chicago Press, 1988.

Menocal, Narciso G., ed. *Taliesin 1911–1914, Wright Studies*. Vol. I. Carbondale and Edwardsville: Southern Illinois University Press, 1992.

Metzgar, Judson D. *Adventures in Japanese Prints*. Los Angeles: Grabhorn Press for Dawson's Bookshop, [1944].

Michener, James A. *The Floating World*. New York: Random House, 1954.

———. *Japanese Prints from the Early Masters to the Modern*. Rutland, Vt., and Tokyo: Charles E. Tuttle Co., 1959.

Millet, J. B. "The Tile Club." In *Julian Alden Weir: An Appreciation of His Life and Works*, edited by The Phillips Publications. New York: E. P. Dutton and Co., 1922.

Milwaukee Art Museum. *The Domestic Scene (1897–1927): George M. Niedecken, Interior Architect*. Milwaukee: Milwaukee Art Museum, 1981.

Mirviss, Joan B., with John T. Carpenter. *The Frank Lloyd Wright Collection of Surimono*. New York and Phoenix: Weatherhill and Phoenix Art Museum, 1995.

Mme. X. "Wright Collection Joy to Connoisseur." *Chicago Sunday Tribune*, 18 November 1917, part 7, p. 4.

Morse, Edward S. *Japanese Homes and Their Surroundings*. Boston: Ticknor and Company, 1886.

"Mrs. William Spaulding." *New York Times*, 18 August 1950, 21.

Muschamp, Herbert. *Man About Town: Frank Lloyd Wright in New York City*. Cambridge, Mass., and London: MIT Press, 1983.

Nagai Kafū. *Nagai Kafū nikki* (Diary of Nagai Kafū). Vol. 2. Tokyo: Tōto Shobō, 1958–59.

Nagata Seiji. *Shiryō ni yoru kindai ukiyo-e jijō* (Data for the circumstances of ukiyo-e in recent times). Tokyo: Sansaisha, 1992.

Niimi Ryū. "Method and Ritual: A Special Interpretation of Wright's Space as Anti-modernist." In *Frank Lloyd Wright Retrospective/Furanku Roido Raito kaiko ten*, edited by Jonathan Lipman, 44–52. Exh. cat. Tokyo: Mainichi Shinbun, 1991.

1905–1915: The Progressive Era. Vol. 13 of *The Annals of America*. Chicago: Encyclopedia Britannica, 1976.

Noguchi Kōichi. *Ginza monogatari* (Tale of the Ginza). Tokyo: Chūkō Shinsho, 1997.

Norton, Margaret Williams. "Japanese Themes and the Early Work of Frank Lloyd Wright." *The Frank Lloyd Wright Newsletter* 4 (second quarter 1981): 1–5.

Norton, Thomas E. *100 Years of Collecting in America: The Story of Sotheby Parke Bernet*. New York: Harry N. Abrams, 1984.

Nute, Kevin. *Frank Lloyd Wright and Japan*. New York: Van Nostrand Reinhold, 1993.

———. "Wright the Architect." In *Frank Lloyd Wright's Fifty Views of Japan: The 1905 Photo Album*, edited by Melanie Birk, 89–101. San Francisco: Pomegranate Artbooks, 1996.

"155 Japanese Art Color Prints Are Sold for $23,295." *New York Herald*, 7 January 1927.

O'Hern, John D. "Frank Lloyd Wright's Darwin D. Martin House: Historical Report and Analysis of Original Conditions," August 1988. University Archives, State University of New York at Buffalo.

Oka Isaburō. "Hashiguchi Goyō." In *Taishō no yūshū to roman: Hashiguchi Goyō ten* (Taishō melancholy and romanticism: Exhibition of Hashiguchi Goyō). Exh. cat. Kyoto: Kyoto Shinbun, 1976.

———. *Taishō no onna: Hashiguchi Goyō ten* (Taishō women: exhibition of Hashiguchi Goyō). Exh. cat. Tokyo: Riccar Museum, 1976.

Oriental Art: Snuff bottles, bronzes, jades, pottery and porcelains, paintings, furniture and decorative objects. New York: Parke-Bernet Galleries (sale 2636), 14–15 December 1967.

Packard, Harry G. C. "Nihon bijutsu shūshūki" (Annals of a collection of Japanese art). *Geijutsu shinchō* 314 (Feb. 1976): 136–40.

Paul, Margot. "A Creative Connoisseur: Nomura Shōjirō." In Amanda Mayer Stinchecum et al., *Kosode: 16th–19th Century Textiles from the Nomura Collection*, 12–21. Exh cat. New York: Japan Society and Kodansha International, 1984.

Pearlstein, Elinor. "The Chinese Collections at The Art Institute of Chicago: Foundations of Scholarly Taste." *Orientations* 24 (June 1993): 36–47.

Peattie, Elia W. "The Fine Arts Building in Chicago." In *The Book of the Fine Arts Building*. Chicago: Privately printed, [1911].

Petteys, Chris. *Dictionary of Women Artists*. Boston: G. K. Hall Co., 1985.

Pfeiffer, Bruce Brooks. "Frank Lloyd Wright: Collecting Japanese Art." In Joan B. Mirviss with John T. Carpenter, *The Frank Lloyd Wright Collection of Surimono*, 3–9. New York and Phoenix: Weatherhill and Phoenix Art Museum, 1995.

Pfeiffer, Bruce Brooks, and Yukio Futagawa, eds. *Frank Lloyd Wright*. 12 vols. Tokyo: A. D. A. Edita, 1984–88. Vols. 1–8, *Monograph*; vols. 9–11, *Preliminary Studies*; vol. 12, *In His Renderings*.

Pins, Jacob. *The Japanese Pillar Print: Hashira-e*. London: Robert G. Sawers, 1982.

"A Pleasing Novelty": Bunkio Matsuki and The Japan Craze in Victorian Salem. Salem, Mass.: Peabody and Essex Museum, 1993.

Powell, Patricia. "Elvehjem Museum of Art: Three Collections and Their Donors." *Wisconsin Academy Review* (Sept. 1990): 24–25.

Quinan, Jack. *Frank Lloyd Wright's Larkin Building, Myth and Fact*. New York: Architectural History Foundation, 1987.

———. "Wright the Photographer." In *Frank Lloyd Wright's Fifty Views of Japan: The 1905 Photo Album*, edited by Melanie Birk, 73–87. San Francisco: Pomegranate Artbooks, 1996.

Raymond, Antonin. *An Autobiography*. Rutland, Vt., and Tokyo: Charles E. Tuttle Co., 1973.

Regnery, Henry. *The Cliff Dwellers: The History of a Chicago Cultural Institution*. Chicago: Chicago Historical Bookworks, 1990.

"Retain Auction Proceeds: Anderson Galleries Win Contest Over Wright Sale." *New York Times*, 20 February 1927, section 1, p. 6.

Rosenfield, John M. "Japanese Art Studies in America since 1945." In *The Postwar Developments of Japanese Studies in the United States*, edited by Helen Hardacre, 161–94. Leiden, Boston, and Köln: Brill, 1998.

Salmony, Alfred. "The Yamanaka Sale." *Art News* 43, no. 7 (1944): 14.

Sanders, Barry, ed. *The Craftsman, An Anthology*. Santa Barbara: Peregrine Smith, 1978.

Scully, Vincent, Jr. *Frank Lloyd Wright*. New York: George Braziller, 1960.

Secrest, Meryle. *Frank Lloyd Wright*. New York: Alfred A. Knopf, 1992.

Shand-Tucci, Douglass. *Boston Bohemia 1881–1900*. Vol. 1. Amherst: University of Massachusetts Press, 1995.

———. "First Impressions on the Rediscovery of Two New England Galleries by Ralph Adams Cram." *The Currier Gallery of Art Bulletin* (fall 1979): 2–15.

Shankel, Carol. *Sallie Casey Thayer and Her Collection*. Lawrence: University of Kansas Museum of Art, 1976.

Shishi Sai'an. "Hanga no hoshoku" (Revamping prints). *Bijutsu gahō* 10, no. 42 (1919): 13.

[Shugio Hiromichi]. *Catalogue of an Exhibition of Japanese Colored Prints and Illustrated Books*. New York: Grolier Club, 1889.

———. *Catalogue of an Exhibition of Japanese Prints*. New York: Grolier Club, 1896.

———. "Japanese Art and Artists Today II, Ceramic Artists." *The International Studio* 41 (Oct. 1910): 286–93.

———. "Odoroku bakari no kyōki" (A surprisingly strong memory). *Taikan* (Feb. 1922): 174–75.

Smith, Henry D., II. "Hiroshige in History." In Matthi Forrer, *Hiroshige*, 33–45. Munich and New York: Prestel, 1997.

Smith, Henry D., II, and Amy G. Poster. *Hiroshige: One Hundred Famous Views of Edo*. New York: George Braziller, 1986.

Smith, Kathryn. "Frank Lloyd Wright and the Imperial Hotel: A Postscript." *The Art Bulletin* 67 (June 1985): 296–310.

———. *Frank Lloyd Wright: Hollyhock House and Olive Hill*. New York: Rizzoli, 1992.

———. *Frank Lloyd Wright's Taliesin and Taliesin West*. New York: Harry N. Abrams, 1997.

———. "F. L. Raito no shirarezaru teikoku hoteru bekkan" (Frank Lloyd Wright's unknown Imperial Hotel annex). *Space Design/Supesu dezain* 286 (July 1988): 77–80.

"The Spaulding Collection." *Life* (1 Nov. 1948): 76.

Spencer, Robert C., Jr. "The Work of Frank Lloyd Wright." *The Architectural Review* 7 (June 1900): 61–73.

Statler, Oliver. *Modern Japanese Prints: An Art Reborn*. Rutland, Vt.: Charles E. Tuttle Co., 1959.

Stephens, Amy Reigle, ed. *The New Wave: Twentieth-century Japanese Prints from the Robert O. Muller Collection*. London and Leiden: Bamboo Publishing and Hotei–Japanese Prints, 1993.

Stinchecum, Amanda Meyer. *Kosode: 16th–19th Century Textiles from the Nomura Collection*. Edited by Naomi Noble Richard and Margot Paul. Exh. cat. New York: Japan Society and Kodansha International, 1984.

Stipe, Margo. "Wright and Japan." In *Frank Lloyd Wright: Europe and Beyond*, edited by Anthony Alofsin, 24–44. Berkeley: University of California Press, 1999.

———. "Wright's First Trip to Japan." *Frank Lloyd Wright Quarterly* 6 (spring 1995): 21–23.

Storrer, William Allin. *The Architecture of Frank Lloyd Wright: A Complete Catalogue*. Cambridge, Mass., and London: MIT Press, 1974.

———. *The Frank Lloyd Wright Companion*. Chicago and London: University of Chicago Press, 1993.

Suzuki Jūzō. *Hiroshige*. Tokyo: Nihon Keizai Shinbun, 1970.

Sweeney, Robert L. *Frank Lloyd Wright: An Annotated Bibliography*. Los Angeles: Hennessey and Ingalls, 1978.

———. *Wright in Hollywood: Visions of a New Architecture*. New York: The Architectural History Foundation, Inc.; Cambridge, Mass., and London: MIT Press, 1994.

Tafel, Edgar. *About Wright: An Album of Recollections by Those Who Knew Frank Lloyd Wright*. New York: John Wiley and Sons, 1993.

———. *Apprentice to Genius: Years with Frank Lloyd Wright*. New York: McGraw-Hill, 1979.

Takahashi Seiichiro. *Traditional Woodblock Prints of Japan*. Translated by Richard Stanley-Baker. The Heibonsha Survey of Japanese Art, vol. 22. New York and Tokyo: Weatherhill and Heibonsha, 1976.

Takamizawa Takako. *Aru ukiyo-eshi no isan: Takamizawa Enji oboegaki* (Legacy of a certain ukiyo-e artist: Notes about Takamizawa Enji). Tokyo: Tōsho Sensho, 1978.

Tanigawa Masami. "Iwayuru 'Raito jiken' ni tsuite" (Concerning the so-called Wright Incident), 125–28. In *Frank Lloyd Wright kenkyū* (Frank Lloyd Wright research). Tokyo: Privately published, 1990.

———. *Raito to Nihon* (Wright and Japan). Tokyo: Kajima Shuppankai, 1977.

———. "Wright's Achievement in Japan." In *Frank Lloyd Wright Retrospective/Furanku Roido Raito kaiko ten*, edited by Jonathan Lipman, 58–62. Exh. cat. Tokyo: Mainichi Shinbun, 1991.

———. "Wright the Tourist." In *Frank Lloyd Wright's Fifty Views of Japan: The 1905 Photo Album*, edited by Melanie Birk, 15–19. San Francisco: Pomegranate Artbooks, 1996.

———. *Zumen de miru F. L. Raito/Measured Drawings of Wright's Japanese Work*. Tokyo: Shokokusha, 1995.

Teall, Gardner. "The Water-colors of Hiroshige." *International Studio* 85 (Nov. 1926): 57–62.

"$36,975 for Wright Prints." *New York Times*, 8 January 1927, 12.

Thornburg, Barbara. "The Wright Stuff: A Painstaking Restoration of Hollyhock House." *Los Angeles Times Magazine*, 20 May 1990, 32.

Tomita Kojiro. "The William S. and John T. Spaulding Collection of Japanese Prints." *Museum of Fine Arts Bulletin* 20 (June 1922): 31–35.

———. "The William S. and John T. Spaulding Collection of Japanese Prints." *Bulletin of the Museum of Fine Arts* 39 (Oct. 1941): 73–78.

Twombly, Robert C. *Frank Lloyd Wright: His Life and His Architecture*. New York: John Wiley and Sons, 1979.

Ueno Naoteru. "Hashiguchi Goyō koden" (A brief biography of Hashiguchi Goyō). *Ukiyo-e no kenkyū* 1, no. 2 (1921): 2–5.

Umi o watatta Meiji no bijutsu (Japanese art that crossed the ocean)/*World's Columbian Exposition of 1893 Revisited*. Tokyo: Tokyo National Museum, 1997.

"Unity Club of Unity Church." *Oak Leaves*, 24 March 1906, 12.

Van Vleck Ledger Books. 13 vols. Elvehjem Museum of Art, University of Wisconsin-Madison.

Watanabe Shōzaburō, comp. *Catalogue of the Memorial Exhibition of Hiroshige's Works on the 60th Anniversary of His Death*. Tokyo: Watanabe Shōzaburō, 1918.

Watanabe Tadasu, ed. *Watanabe Shōzaburō*. Tokyo: Watanabe mokuhan bijutsu gaho, 1974.

Waterhouse, David B. *Images of Eighteenth-Century Japan: Ukiyo-e Prints from the Sir Edmund Walker Collection*. Toronto: Royal Ontario Museum, 1975.

Weisberg, Gabriel P. *Art Nouveau Bing: Paris Style 1900*. New York: Harry N. Abrams, 1986.

———. "L'Art Nouveau Bing." *Arts in Virginia* 20 (fall 1979): 2–15.

Wells, James M. *The Arts Club of Chicago: Seventy-fifth Anniversary Exhibition 1916–1991*. Chicago: Arts Club of Chicago, 1992.

Weston, Victoria. *East Meets West: Isabella Stewart Gardner and Okakura Kakuzō*. Boston: Isabella Stewart Gardner Museum, 1992.

White, Julia M. "Hokusai and Hiroshige Through the Collector's Eye." In *Hokusai and Hiroshige: Great Japanese Prints from the James A. Michener Collection, Honolulu Academy of Arts*, 11–17. Exh. cat. San Francisco: Asian Art Museum of San Francisco, 1998.

"Wife Fails to Halt Wright Art Sale." *New York Times*, 7 January 1927, 19.

Wight, Peter B. "Country House Architecture in the Middle West." *Architectural Record* 38 (Oct. 1915): 385–421.

Wijdeveld, H. Th., ed. *The Life-Work of the American Architect Frank Lloyd Wright*. Santpoort, Holland: C. A. Mees, 1925.

Wild, Payson Sibley. *The Chicago Literary Club: Its history from the season of 1924–1925 to the season of 1945–1946*. Chicago: Privately printed, 1947.

"William S. Spaulding." *New York Times*, 16 August 1937, 19.

"William Stuart Spaulding, 72, Refinery Head." *Boston Evening Transcript*, 16 August 1937, 11.

Woollcott, Alexander. "Profiles: The Prodigal Father." *The New Yorker* (19 July 1930): 22–25.

The Work of Frank Lloyd Wright: Work done since the Spring of 1911, only, is included in this exhibit. Exh. list. [Chicago: Art Institute of Chicago, 1914].

"Wright and Family Apart in One House to 'Save his Soul.'" *Chicago American*, 8 September 1911, afternoon edition, 2.

"Wright exhibit stirs Chicago architects." *Record Herald*. Undated newspaper clipping, [8 April 1914]. Frank Lloyd Wright Archives, 8009.115. (A handwritten inscription on the clipping says *Record Herald*. A search of the *Record Herald* from 4 April through 12 April 1914 did not turn up any trace of this article.)

Wright, Frank Lloyd. *An Autobiography*. London: Longmans, Green and Co., 1932.

———. *An Autobiography*. Rev. ed. New York: Duell, Sloan and Pearce, 1943; Barnes and Noble Books, 1998, reprint. Rev. ed. New York: Horizon Press, 1977.

———. *Antique Colour Prints from the Collection of Frank Lloyd Wright*. Chicago: Arts Club of Chicago, 1917.

———. *Ausgeführte Bauten und Entwürfe von Frank Lloyd Wright*. Two folios. Berlin: Ernst Wasmuth, 1910–[11].

———. "Frank Lloyd Wright." *Architectural Forum* 68 (Jan. 1938): 1–102.

———. *Frank Lloyd Wright, Collected Writings*. Edited by Bruce Brooks Pfeiffer. 5 vols. New York: Rizzoli, 1992–95.

———. *The Frank Lloyd Wright Collection of Japanese Antique Prints*. New York: The Anderson Galleries (sale 2120), 6–7 January 1927.

———. *Hiroshige: An Exhibition of Colour Prints from the Collection of Frank Lloyd Wright*. Chicago: Art Institute of Chicago, 1906.

———. *The Japanese Print: An Interpretation*. Chicago: Ralph Fletcher Seymour Co., 1912.

———. *The Natural House*. New York: Horizon Press, 1954.

———. "Nihon kenchiku ni taisuru shokan narabi ni teikoku hoteru no sekkei" (Views on Japanese architecture and also the construction of the Imperial Hotel). *Kenchiku sekai* (1917): 3–6.

———. "Taliesin: The Chronicle of a House with a Heart." *Liberty* (23 March 1929): 21–29.

———. *The Usonian House*. Souvenir of the exhibition "Sixty Years of Living Architecture, the Work of Frank Lloyd Wright." New York: Solomon R. Guggenheim Museum, 1953.

Wright, John Lloyd. *My Father, Frank Lloyd Wright*. New York: Dover Publications, Inc., 1992. A slightly altered version of the work originally published as *My Father Who Is on Earth*, New York: G.P. Putnam's Sons, 1946.

Wright, Miriam Noel. "The Romance of Miriam Wright." *Milwaukee Journal Sunday Magazine*, 8 May–5 June 1932.

Writings on Wright: Selected Comments on Frank Lloyd Wright. Edited by H. Allen Brooks. Cambridge, Mass., and London: MIT Press, 1985.

Yamaguchi Seiichi. *Fuenorosa: Nihon bunka no senyō ni sasageta isshō/Ernest Francisco Fenollosa: A Life Devoted to the Advocacy of Japanese Culture*. 2 vols. Tokyo: Sanseidō, 1982.

———. "Kobayashi Bunshichi jiseki" (Kobayashi Bunshichi and his achievements). *Saitama daigaku kiyō* 6 (Feb. 1988): 1–45.

Yoshida Teruji. *Ukiyo-e no chishiki* (Knowledge of ukiyo-e). Vol. 6 of *Yoshida Teruji chosakushū* (Collected writings of Yoshida Teruji). Tokyo: Ryokuen Shobō, 1963.

CREDITS

Numbers refer to illustrations.

3: Courtesy The Frank Lloyd Wright Archives, Scottsdale, Ariz. (1189.014); 4: Courtesy The Frank Lloyd Wright Archives, Scottsdale, Ariz. (6004.001); 5: Photo © 1938 Time Inc. Reprinted by permission; 6: Photo: James Roy Miller. Herbert and Katherine Jacobs Frank Lloyd Wright Collection, Courtesy The Art Institute of Chicago; 7: Photo: Pedro E. Guerrero © 1985 Pedro E. Guerrero; 9: Photo © Elvehjem Museum of Art; 11: Courtesy Museum of Fine Arts, Boston; 13: Courtesy Frank Lloyd Wright Preservation Trust, Oak Park, Ill.; 14: From *The Columbian Gallery: A Portfolio of Photographs from the World's Fair.* Chicago: The Werner Company, [1893]. Courtesy Frank Lloyd Wright Preservation Trust, Oak Park, Ill.; 15: Courtesy The Frank Lloyd Wright Archives, Scottsdale, Ariz. (0004.004); 16: Courtesy The Frank Lloyd Wright Archives, Scottsdale, Ariz. (9506.0014); 17: Photo: Henry Fuermann and Sons, Chicago. Courtesy The Metropolitan Museum of Art, New York, Purchase, Herman G. Pundt Gift and Edward Pearce Casey Fund, 1981 (1981.1005.17). All Rights Reserved; 20: Courtesy Kelmscott Gallery, Chicago, and Benton Harbor, Mich.; 23: Photo: Lori Van Houten; 24: Photo: Philip Mrozinski; 25: Courtesy The Frank Lloyd Wright Archives, Scottsdale, Ariz. (0600.0002); 28: Courtesy The Metropolitan Museum of Art, New York. Photo © 1994 The Metropolitan Museum of Art. All Rights Reserved; 30: Courtesy Kelmscott Gallery, Chicago, and Benton Harbor, Mich.; 31: Courtesy University Archives, State University of New York at Buffalo; 32: Photo: Henry Fuermann and Sons, Chicago. Courtesy Centre Canadien d'Architecture/Canadian Centre for Architecture, Montréal; 33: Courtesy The Art Institute of Chicago. Photo © 2000 The Art Institute of Chicago. All Rights Reserved; 34: Photo: Henry Fuermann and Sons, Chicago. Courtesy The Metropolitan Museum of Art, New York, Purchase, Hermann G. Pundt, Gift and Edward Pearce Casey Fund, 1981 (1981.1005.4). All Rights Reserved; 35: Photo: Henry Fuermann and Sons, Chicago. Courtesy The Metropolitan Museum of Art, New York, Purchase, Hermann G. Pundt Gift and Edward Pearce Casey Fund, 1981 (1981.1005.5). All Rights Reserved; 36: Photo: Muller, Buffalo. Courtesy University Archives, State University of New York at Buffalo; 37: From Gookin, *The Chicago Literary Club,* 1926. Photo: Matzene. Courtesy William Green; 38, 39: Courtesy The Art Institute of Chicago Archives; 40, 41: Photo: Frederick O. Bemm. Courtesy The Art Institute of Chicago Archives; 42: Photo: © 2000 Judith Bromley; 43: From Hess, *Their Splendid Legacy: The First 100 Years of the Minneapolis Society of Fine Arts,* 1985; 44: Courtesy Frank Lloyd Wright Preservation Trust, Oak Park, Gift of Llewellyn Wright; 45: Courtesy The Metropolitan Museum of Art, New York, Collection of Jean Stevenson Haverstock. All Rights Reserved; 46: From Lancaster, *The Japanese Influence in America,* 1963; 48, 49: Courtesy The Art Institute of Chicago. Photo © 2000 The Art Institute of Chicago, All Rights Reserved; 51: Courtesy The Metropolitan Museum of Art, New York. Photo © 1979 The Metropolitan Museum of Art, New York. All Rights Reserved; 52: Photo: Marceau, New York. Courtesy The Metropolitan Museum of Art, New York. All Rights Reserved; 53: From *Harvard College Class of 1888: Secretary's Report No. VII, Twenty-fifth Anniversary,* 1913. Courtesy Harvard University Archives; 54, 58: Courtesy William Stuart Spaulding Archives, Santa Barbara, Calif.; 59: Courtesy Museum of Fine Arts, Boston. Reproduced with permission. © 2000 Museum of Fine Arts, Boston. All Rights Reserved; 60: Courtesy Imperial Hotel, Tokyo; 61: Courtesy Ōkura Shūkokan Museum of Fine Arts, Tokyo; 62–67: Courtesy Museum of Fine Arts, Boston. Reproduced with permission. © 2000 Museum of Fine Arts, Boston. All Rights Reserved; 68: Photo: George Collins Cox (1851–1902). Courtesy Charles Lang Freer Papers, Freer Gallery of Art Archives, Smithsonian Institution, Washington, D.C.; 69: Photo: Ogawa Kazumasa. Courtesy Shugio Ippei; 70: Courtesy Shugio Ippei; 71: Courtesy William Green; 72: Courtesy The Art Institute of Chicago. Photo © 2000 The Art Institute of Chicago. All Rights Reserved; 73: Courtesy The Frank Lloyd Wright Archives, Scottsdale, Ariz. (6702.0007); 74: Designed by Miko McGinty; 75: Courtesy Phil H. Feddersen, Architect; 79: Courtesy The Frank Lloyd Wright Archives, Scottsdale, Ariz.; 80: Photo: Henry Fuermann and Sons, Chicago. Courtesy The Frank Lloyd Wright Archives, Scottsdale, Ariz. (1500.0012); 81: Photo: Henry Fuermann and Sons, Chicago. Courtesy The Frank Lloyd Wright Archives, Scottsdale, Ariz. (1403.0038); 82: Photo: Henry Fuermann and Sons, Chicago. Courtesy State Historical Society of Wisconsin, Madison (WHi [x3] 41629); 83: From *Bulletin of the Art Insti-*